Introduction to the Law of Argentina

General Editors of the Series: Prof. Tuğrul Ansay & Prof. Don Wallace, Jr.

List of the Introduction books already published are as follows:

Introduction to the Law of Israel (1995)
Introduction to Hungarian Law (1998)
Introduction to Belgian Law (2001)
Introduction to Italian Law (2002)
Introduction to the Law of the United States (second edition 2002)
Introduction to the Law of South Africa (2004)
Introduction to Swiss Law (third edition 2004)
Introduction to German Law (second edition 2005)
Introduction to Polish Law (2005)
Introduction to French Law (2008)
Introduction to Greek Law (third edition 2008)
Introduction to Turkish Law (sixth edition 2011)
Introduction to the Law of Kazakhstan (2012)
Introduction to the Law of Croatia (2014)
Introduction to the Law of Austria (2015)
Introduction to Brazilian Law (second edition 2017)
Introduction to the Law of Argentina (2018)

Introduction to the Law of Argentina

Edited by
Ursula Basset

Wolters Kluwer

Published by:
Kluwer Law International B.V.
PO Box 316
2400 AH Alphen aan den Rijn
The Netherlands
E-mail: international-sales@wolterskluwer.com
Website: lrus.wolterskluwer.com

Sold and distributed in North, Central and South America by:
Wolters Kluwer Legal & Regulatory U.S.
7201 McKinney Circle
Frederick, MD 21704
United States of America
Email: customer.service@wolterskluwer.com

Sold and distributed in all other countries by:
Air Business Subscriptions
Rockwood House
Haywards Heath
West Sussex
RH16 3DH
United Kingdom
Email: international-customerservice@wolterskluwer.com

Printed on acid-free paper.

ISBN 978-94-035-0365-3

e-Book: ISBN 978-94-035-0370-7
web-PDF: ISBN 978-94-035-0371-4

Printed in the United Kingdom.

Editor

Ursula C. Basset holds LLB from National University of Buenos Aires and PhD from Pontifical Catholic University of Buenos Aires. She is the Chair in Private Law and Family Law (Austral University), Chair in Family Law and Law of Successions (Pontifical Catholic University of Buenos Aires), Director of Research (Austral University) and member of the Drafting Commission for the Civil and Commercial Code of Argentina (2011–2014).

Contributors

Ignacio Ezequiel Alterini obtained his LLB from Pontifical Catholic University of Buenos Aires, LLM from Pontifical Catholic University of Buenos Aires and PhD from Austral University. He is Chair in Private Law, Obligations, Tort Law and Property Law (Austral University) and Director of the Department of Civil Law and Executive Director of the Master in Civil Law (Austral University).

Alejandro Dalmacio Andrada holds LLB (Pontifical Catholic University of Rosario) and PhD (Catholic University of Buenos Aires). He is Chair in Law of Obligations (Pontifical Catholic University of Rosario), Director of the Doctorate (Pontifical Catholic University of Rosario) and Judge of the Court of Appeal in Administrative Matters, Rosario.

Alejandro Borda, LLB, obtained his PhD from National University of Buenos Aires. He is the Chair in Contract Law (Pontifical Catholic University), Lecturer in Contract Law (National University of Buenos Aires) and a member of the Drafting Commission for the Civil and Commercial Code (2011–2014).

Andrea Mariel Brunetti obtained his LLB from National University of Rosario. She holds specialization degree in Criminal Investigations, Business Law and Justice (National University of Rosario). She obtained his master degree and is a PhD Candidate at National University of Rosario. She serves as a judge in Family Law.

Gisela Ferrari obtained her LLB from Pontifical Catholic University, Argentina, LLM from London School of Economics and Political Science and is a PhD Candidate at Pontifical Catholic University, Argentina and the National Council of Research – CONICET. She works as Lecturer in Constitutional Law and Human Rights Law (Pontifical Catholic University and Austral University).

Eliana M. González, LLB, is a PhD Candidate at Pontifical Catholic University of Rosario. She is a mediator, lecturer in charge of the Chair of Family Law and Successions at Pontifical Catholic University or Rosario.

Jorge Nicolás Lafferriere holds LLB from National University of Buenos Aires and PhD from Pontifical Catholic University of Argentina. He is Chair in Civil Law (Pontifical Catholic University of Argentina). He serves as Lecturer in Civil Law (University of Buenos Aires) and is Director of Legal Research (Pontifical Catholic University of Argentina).

Juan G. Navarro Floria completed LLB at Pontifical Catholic University of Buenos Aires and PhD at Complutense University, Madrid. He is Chair in Civil Law and Law and Religion (Pontifical Catholic University of Buenos Aires).

Agustín Parise, LLB, holds LLD (University of Buenos Aires), LLM (Louisiana State University) and PhD (Maastricht University). He is Assistant Professor of Law (Faculty of Law, Maastricht University).

Facundo Sarrabayrouse obtained LLB from Austral University, Argentina – Exchange Program, University of California Hastings College of the Law. He is a partner at Roca & Sarrabayrouse (Buenos Aires based white collar crime law firm). He also serves as Lecturer on Criminal Law and White Collar Crime at National University of Buenos Aires, Austral University, Torcuato Di Tella University and Pontifical Catholic University of Rosario.

Juan Manuel Sarrabayrouse completed his LLB at Austral University, Argentina - Exchange Program, Duke University School of Law, NC, USA. He holds specialization and master degrees on Criminal Law (Austral University, Argentina). He is a partner at Roca & Sarrabayrouse (Buenos Aires). He is Lecturer on Criminal Law and White Collar Crime at Austral University and Torcuato Di Tella University.

Summary of Contents

Table of Contents

Preface

This is the first edition of the Introduction to the Law of Argentina. Prof. Tugrul Ansay was convinced that it was worth to provide a glance to a very complex mixture of legal sources, with a relatively modern outcome. The law of Argentina is in many ways a tale thought for the present times.

What makes the law of Argentina interesting?

On the one side, it expresses a multicultural convergence: a mixture of Spanish law and aboriginal customs, that has a name of its own: "derecho indiano". *Derecho indiano* is the term most frequently used to denote the legal system in force in the Spanish colonies during the early modern period. *Derecho indiano* was a special collection of norms, adapting Castilian law to the customs and culture of the colonies overseas. It stemmed out of the study, observation and acceptance of local customs, that were taken into account to mold Castilian law in order to adapt it to the inhabitants of the colonies. It was an asystemic, casuistic, predominantly public, fluid and tolerant legal system. This peculiar side of Argentinian legal history entails a meaningful message to our current dilemmas on globalization and the preservation of diverse cultural identities. Not that there were not abuses and excesses, but there is undoubtedly something to learned from new legal system built upon a dialogue between cultures.

Argentina owes Spain its first legal system, that lasted until its first Civil Code in 1869. By that time, Argentina widened its scope and turned to new horizons. A clue to this new Civil Code is the astonishing mind of the author of this first Civil Code – Dalmacio Vélez Sársfield, whose library contained volumes as dissimilar as Greek tragedy, philosophy, Roman law, legal doctrine about the French Civil Code, the writings of American legal doctrine and the draft Civil Code of Spain and Brazil, among many other treasures of literature and science. He was a universal spirit. Velez Sarsfield was not a particularly religious person himself, but he understood that his country was deeply attached to Catholicism and respected the customs of the society he lived in when ruling for it. His sources, depending on the subject, were European, but he never neglected the sources of the local traditions, even if, in times in which Argentina had to show herself as an independent country, those sources could not be shown expressly. Argentina is a Latin American Nation, but its legal culture was forged taking into account the richness of the European codification without neglecting its own identity. This dogmatic approach to codification was built like a magnificent medieval cathedral: built to last. And, as a matter of fact it lasted almost 150 years.

Argentina has one of the oldest constitutions of the world. Concluded in 1853 and with some modifications in 1860, its sources come mainly from the American Constitution: it was a liberal Constitution favorable to abstract and flexible rules. This Constitution informed by its American liberal source had to live with a Civil Code (and later, a Commercial Code) inspired in the European codifications, bound to concrete regulations and to assume Argentina's cultural and religious identity. The Constitution and the Civil Code had to live side by side, and the jurisprudence and the doctrine built, out of such dissimilar universes, an integrated legal system. Later on, Argentina completed its codification process with a criminal code, several civil and commercial procedural codes, a code on criminal procedure, among others.

As in many other countries Argentina was also subject to the de-codification trends. Fragmented legal acts created new institutions that partially contradicted the existing ones. By 2010, the Government believed it to be the right time to change. The drafting of new Civil and Commercial Code (unifying Civil and Commercial Law, but recodification is only partial) was entrusted to a Commission composed by 99 jurists, divided into 33 sub-commissions and presided by the President of the Supreme Court of Justice and two other jurists. It took one year to draft the new Civil and Commercial Code (CCC), and three months to revise it and issue the final Draft. This process was understood to be too hasty by the many critics it had. The main idea was that to continue to introduce partial reforms to the old Civil Code, would only create more tensions between the norms and more difficulties to the interpreters. The result was a quite modern text based more upon general principles than on concrete rules, sometimes more oriented to provide directives to the judges and depending on (and confiding in) Judges than on the legislators. This new Code entered in vigor in 2015 only. It is fresh and it is still to be seen how it will apply, how its physiognomy will be like once it is fully embedded in Argentine legal culture and in its doctrine. Right now, it is still a time for transition. Even if the old Civil Code is no longer operative, it still pervades minds and thoughts, it is still, for many, a key to interpret the new Code.

It is not only the open format of the Code, but also its contents that surprise. Firstly, it has a preliminary title, dealing with great principles that work as directives to the Judge. The sources of Argentinian law might be understood as open now: Article 1 CCC establishes that the interpretation of the law must be according to the National Constitution and the Treaties to which Argentina is signatory party. However, in Article 2 CCC, the legislator asks the Judge to provide an interpretation based "on Human Rights treaties, legal principles and values" according to the whole legal system. This openness to abstract and eventually subjective sources like principles and values, and Human Rights treaties, without specifying if they are limited to those Argentina has signed is a unique feature. The legal system of Argentina has a complex texture that may be expanded by a vast universe of values, principles and treaties. For certain, the Civil and Commercial law is constitutionalized and "conventionalized": it will be always permeable to international law that will, ultimately provide an interpretation or eventually correct the already open rules of the CCC. Does the legality principle still stand or will the law be ultimately the interpretation provided by the concrete judge?

What are the main features of the new Code? The abuse of dominant position, the recognition of not only individual, but also collective rights, the protection of the environment, the rights of indigenous communities to possession and communitarian property rights, the sanctity of human persons (however contested these days in which Argentina is debating abortion), human the place given to the protection of human dignity and vulnerability, the very progressive legislation on family law (a very quick and easy divorce with no waiting periods, same sex marriage, same sex parenthood), medical law (medical consent, advanced directives, research in humans), the presumption of liability once the damage has been caused, the introduction of the final clause as a constitutive element of contracts (its frustration may mean the termination of the contract), the introduction of new contracts, consumer law, a single person shareholder company ... And this is the third feature that makes the law of Argentina interesting from a theoretical viewpoint: its freshness. It is a new approach, a very modern approach, whether one agrees to it or not.

About This Book

This book deals with many aspects of the legal system of Argentina. However, some of them have not been addressed. Maybe a further edition will provide an opportunity to complete what is lacking. Many chapters were written while Argentina was already debating significant legal reforms. For instance, a commission to revise the 2015 CCC was created as soon as in 2018. It is expected that the reforms will be restricted to the minimum. Moreover, another commission of jurists has been working on a new Criminal Code. However, since their work is ongoing, it is safe to presume that the current criminal code will be still be in vigor while this book is issued. The final draft of the new Criminal Code is not ready yet. The worst is probably the Criminal Law Procedure, which this book had to leave out. There is a whole Criminal Procedure Code that has been passed four years ago. However, because of disagreements concerning its content it has never been applied (its application has been suspended, even if a parliamentary commission is expected to decide its implementation any minute since 2016). It should be expected to be applied, but it is unclear what decision is to be taken on this matter, mostly if a new Criminal Code is been drafted simultaneously. Given that the situation is unclear, it was judged better not to provide a chapter on Criminal Procedure law. This will be hopefully made up for in a future edition.

This book illustrates the current state of art of the law as it is applied, providing here and there a contextual approach to the understanding of the legal acts. Even so, the Argentinian judges are competent to declare the unconstitutionality of any legal provision applicable to any particular case they have to decide upon, and they tend to do this more often than the legal doctrine and the legislators would wish them to. If someone plans to litigate in Argentina, it would be wise to check the latest jurisprudence, to better understand the frame of his or her claim. This can be easily done in the main search engines of legal doctrine or simply asking a local expert. In this respect, Argentina is very Latin.

It is also necessary to bear in mind that Argentina is a federal country. In this book, because of its nature, only national legislation is provided. And this is right, because Civil, Commercial and Criminal law is national (it is competence of the National Parliament to provide it). Nevertheless, procedural laws are local, and many administrative provisions are local as well. Normally, there are great similarities between local legislation and national rules. It is safe to check, though.

All the authors of this book are experts on their subjects. Many of them are judges themselves or important scholars in their domain. From the next page, they hope to provide the reader with a full immersion on the rich and vast world of the law of Argentina.

CHAPTER 1

Sources of Law and Legal History*

Agustín Parise

1 INTRODUCTION

A look into sources of law and legal history assists in unveiling the context within which law develops in a specific jurisdiction. This chapter aims to address a number of the substantive areas of law that will be further developed in this volume. Readers will be therefore presented in this chapter with an overview of the sources of law in Argentina, followed by brief elaborations on a selection of areas of substantive law: constitutional law, commercial and civil law, and criminal law. This chapter focusses almost exclusively on the period that Argentine legal historians refer to as national codified period. This period attends the law that developed and applied in Argentina since 1810 until the present, more specifically the adoption of national codes that took place mainly since the second half of the nineteenth century.[1]

* Parts of this chapter were extracted *verbatim* from earlier works, namely, from Julieta Marotta & Agustín Parise, *On Codes, Marriage, and Access to Justice: Recent Developments in the Law of Argentina*, 7 JCLS 237 (2014); Agustín Parise, "Judicial Decision-Making in Latin America: Unveiling the Dynamic Role of the Argentine Supreme Court", in *Legislators, Judges, and Professors* 151 (J. Basedow, H. Fleischer & R. Zimmermann eds., Mohr Siebeck 2016); Agustín Parise, *Ownership Paradigms in American Civil Law Jurisdictions: Manifestations of the Shifts in the Legislation of Louisiana, Chile, and Argentina (16th-20th Centuries)* (Brill Nijhoff 2017); and Agustín Parise, "Harmonization of Private Law in Latin America and the Emergence of Third-Generation Codes", in *The Future of Contract Law in Latin America: The Principles of Latin American Contract Law* 29 (S. Vogenauer & R. Momberg eds., Studies of the Oxford Institute of European and Comparative Law, Hart Publishing 2017). When available, references are provided also to electronic sources, where readers, beyond the borders of Argentina, can easily retrieve the official texts of the referred legislation.

1. Abelardo Levaggi, *Manual de Historia del Derecho Argentino (Castellano-Indiano/Nacional)* 223 (2d ed., Vol. I, Depalma 1996).

2 SOURCES OF LAW

Argentina is a federal republic, as stated in the Argentine Constitution,[2] being the second largest country in South America with a population of about 40 million inhabitants.[3] It is divided into 23 provinces and the Autonomous City of Buenos Aires. Argentina inherited the continental European system[4] of law from Spain. In public law, however, especially in constitutional law, it considered elements of the US model.[5] The Argentine Constitution adopted a federal system of government;[6] and implemented a tripartite division of powers, encompassing a legislature, a judicial branch, and an executive office led by a president.

The Argentine Supreme Court started to operate in 1863, and it is placed at the vertex of the federal judicial structure.[7] Courts are divided according to subject matter (i.a., social security, criminal, civil and commercial);[8] and at the federal level they are structured in three levels: Supreme Court, federal courts of appeal, and federal district courts.[9] The Argentine Supreme Court is a court of constitutional guarantees, as correctly pointed by Germán J. Bidart Campos.[10] That highest court secures the compliance with constitutional provisions, and it therefore offers justices a

2. Article 1, Constitución de la Nación Argentina, at http://servicios.infoleg.gob.ar/infolegInternet/anexos/0-4999/804/norma.htm (accessed March 6, 2017).
3. Germán C. Garavano, *Información & Justicia III* 15 (Konrad Adenauer Stiftung—Unidos por la Justicia 2011).
4. The terms Civil Law, Romano-Germanic, and Continental European can be used indistinctly in this chapter to refer to the prevailing system in Argentina.
5. Ricardo Zorraquín Becú, *La recepción de los derechos extranjeros en la Argentina durante el siglo XIX*, 4 Revista de Historia del Derecho 325, 357 (1976).
6. *See* the complete text of the Constitution of 1853, at "Constitución de la Confederación Argentina", in *Anales de Legislación Argentina: Complemento Años 1852-1880* 9-33 (La Ley 1954).
7. Jonathan M. Miller, *Courts and the Creation of a "Spirit of Moderation": Judicial Protection of Revolutionaries in Argentina, 1863–1929*, 20 Hastings Int'l & Comp. L. Rev. 231, 238 (1997); and Mario Masciotra, "El activismo de la Corte Suprema de Justicia (Argentina)", in *El Papel de los Tribunales Superiores* 73 (Roberto O. Berizonce, Juan C. Hitters & Eduardo D. Oteiza coord., Rubinzal-Culzoni 2006).
8. Alejandro M. Garro, *Judicial Review of Constitutionality in Argentina: Background Notes and Constitutional Provisions*, 45 Duq. L. Rev. 409, 411 (2007).
9. *See* the clear diagram of the federal structure in Garavano, *supra* n. 3, at 35. The organization of federal courts is established in Decree-Law 1285 of 1958. *See* Art. 1, Decreto-Ley 1285 of 1958, at http://servicios.infoleg.gob.ar/infolegInternet/anexos/35000-39999/37915/norma.htm (accessed March 6, 2017). The provincial structure of courts is also divided into three levels. *See* Garro, *supra* n. 8, at 411; Garavano, *supra* n. 3, at 36; and Gretchen Helmke, *Courts under Constraints: Judges, Generals, and Presidents in Argentina* 175 (Cambridge University Press 2005).
10. Germán J. Bidart Campos, *La Corte Suprema: El Tribunal de las Garantías Constitucionales* 14 (Ediar 1984), cited by Marcos A. Sequeira, *La causa "Candy" y el rol de la Corte Suprema de Justicia de la Nación: primero decido, luego razono*, La Ley Suplemento Especial Candy S.A. c. AFIP s/acción de amparo (July 2009) 45.

fundamental role in the dynamics of state government.[11] The Argentine Supreme Court is not a specialized constitutional court, and it is not divided into chambers.[12]

The National Congress has the power to enact substantive law (i.a., civil and commercial code, criminal code),[13] while provinces preserve the power to enact their procedural codes. Further, provinces enact their own constitutions in accordance with the Argentine Constitution, and ensure administration of justice and municipal regimes.[14] The Argentine Constitution is at the vertex of the hierarchy of the Argentine legal framework.[15] In 1994, however, the latest reform to the Argentine Constitution took place, and granted, by means of Article 75, paragraph 22, constitutional status to a selection of international treaties. In addition, it should be noted that federal legislation prevails over provincial legislation.[16]

Sources of law are a means of creation and formation of the mandatory norms of a state.[17] Sources refer to the origins of the law, the causes that create and shape it, together with the modes in which it is represented.[18] As mentioned by Claude du Pasquier, source of law points to the metaphor of tracing the sources of a river, seeking for its origins in the social life and its appearance in the surface of the law.[19] Yet, many understandings have been given to the term source.[20] Scholars in Argentina tend to subscribe to a widespread classification of sources, even when these can be divided according to several criteria. For example, sources of law can be divided into formal or direct and material or indirect.[21] Formal sources point to the principle of authority, while material sources point to the argument of reasonableness.[22] Attention must be devoted to both formal and material sources, since sociological and historical factors do

11. Roberto O. Berizonce, "Sobrecarga, misión institucional de los tribunales superiores y desahogo del sistema judicial", in *El Papel de los Tribunales Superiores* 433, 470 (Roberto O. Berizonce, Juan C. Hitters & Eduardo D. Oteiza coord., Rubinzal-Culzoni 2006).
12. Article 23, Decreto-Ley 1285 of 1958 states that the Supreme Court may be divided into chambers. *See also* Víctor Bazán, "Justicia constitucional y protección de los derechos fundamentales en Argentina", in *Justicia Constitucional y Derechos Fundamentales Aportes de Argentina, Bolivia, Brasil, Chile, Perú, Uruguay y Venezuela 2009* 15, 16 (Víctor Bazán & Claudio Nash eds., Konrad Adenauer Stiftung 2010).
13. Article 75(12), Constitución de la Nación Argentina, *supra* n. 2.
14. Articles 5, 28, and 123, Constitución de la Nación Argentina, *supra* n. 2. *See also* Julieta Marotta, *Access to Justice and Legal Empowerment of Victims of Domestic Violence through Legal Organizations in the City of Buenos Aires: A Qualitative Empirical Legal Study* 44–45 (UNU-MERIT MGSoG 186, Boekenplan 2017).
15. Article 31, Constitución de la Nación Argentina, *supra* n. 2; and María A. Gelli, *Constitución de la Nación Argentina: Comentada y Concordada* 284–295 (2d ed., La Ley 2004).
16. Articles 5 and 31, Constitución de la Nación Argentina, *supra* n. 2. *See also* Julio C. Rivera, *Instituciones de Derecho Civil—Parte General* 129 (3d ed., Vol. 1, LexisNexis—Abeledo Perrot 2004).
17. Rivera, *supra* n. 16, at 113.
18. Beatriz Escudero de Quintana, *La Parte General del Derecho Civil después de la Ley 26.994* 57 (Vol. 1, Eucasa 2016).
19. Claude Du Pasquier, *Introduction à la théorie générale et à la philosophie du droit* 36 (Delachaux & Niestlé 1942). *See also* José M. Díaz Couselo, *La historia jurídica y el problema de las fuentes del derecho*, 14 Revista de Historia del Derecho 95, 96 (1986).
20. For an overview of different approaches *see* Díaz Couselo, *supra* n. 19, at 97–102.
21. Díaz Couselo, *supra* n. 19, at 100–101.
22. *Código Civil y Comercial de la Nación Comentado* 28 (Vol. 1, Ricardo L. Lorenzetti dir., Rubinzal-Culzoni 2014).

play a role in the shaping of norms: these are not gestated in a vacuum.[23] *Formal sources* enjoy authority and are mandatory due to the prescription of the legal framework itself.[24] They have the ability to—by themselves—produce law.[25] Legislation is considered a primary formal source,[26] followed on some occasions by custom; while other authors also include jurisprudence, as long as it is mandatory for other courts.[27] *Material sources* do not have authority or are not mandatory due to the legal framework itself, yet they are factors or elements that contribute to establish the content of a norm, to its knowledge, and to its application.[28] Material sources do not possess the ability of producing law by themselves, though indirectly—by means of a formal or direct source—assist in creating law.[29] These second sources contribute to the creation of law by means of the persuasion power they emanate.[30] Doctrine of scholars and jurisprudence are typically considered material sources,[31] though a court decision will be a formal source in that particular case.[32]

A few lines can be devoted to preliminarily define sources of law in Argentina. *Legislation* is traditionally defined as the precept that is mandatory, common, just, stable, sufficient, and that has been promulgated.[33] *Custom*[34] is defined as the use that is implanted in a certain community and that is considered mandatory in that community.[35] Recognized by a social community,[36] custom has the power to establish, preserve, and extinguish juridical relations.[37] Custom operates in conjunction with other sources.[38] *Jurisprudence* refers to court decisions that set a creed when deciding matters subject to their ruling.[39] Most litigants currently do not hesitate in Argentina to mention in their petitions the judicial precedents they might know in a specific area.[40] Jurisprudence is also important for the evolution of doctrine as a source, since without jurisprudence the work of scholars would be abstract or partial.[41] Jurisprudence is an important material source, since it helps understand a system beyond the limitations of legislation, showing its real degree of implementation.[42] It should be finally noted that

23. Díaz Couselo, *supra* n. 19, at 120.
24. Rivera, *supra* n. 16, at 114.
25. Díaz Couselo, *supra* n. 19, at 100.
26. Escudero de Quintana, *supra* n. 18, at 58.
27. Rivera, *supra* n. 16, at 114.
28. *Ibid.*
29. Díaz Couselo, *supra* n. 19, at 100.
30. Escudero de Quintana, *supra* n. 18, at 57.
31. Rivera, *supra* n. 16, at 114.
32. Escudero de Quintana, *supra* n. 18, at 62.
33. Rivera, *supra* n. 16, at 117.
34. On custom in Argentina during the nineteenth century *see* Víctor Tau Anzoátegui, *La costumbre en el Derecho Argentino del siglo XIX. De la Revolución al Código Civil*, 4 Revista de Historia del Derecho 231 (1976).
35. Rivera, *supra* n. 16, at 139.
36. On custom in Spanish America *see* Víctor Tau Anzoátegui, *La costumbre jurídica en la América Española (siglos XVI-XVIII)*, 14 Revista de Historia del Derecho 355 (1986).
37. Escudero de Quintana, *supra* n. 18, at 62.
38. Tau Anzoátegui, *supra* n. 36, at 361.
39. Rivera, *supra* n. 16, at 159.
40. *Ibid.*
41. *Ibid.* 160.
42. *Código Civil y Comercial, supra* n. 22, at 31.

jurisprudence is also a formal source in case of plenary decisions (*fallos plenarios*).[43] *Doctrine* consists of monographs, law review articles, and critical comments on court decisions and legislation.[44] These elaborations assist in interpreting the current texts and invite proposals for improvement.[45] Doctrine therefore contributes to produce changes in legislation and jurisprudence.[46] Argentina offers a fertile ground for debate amongst scholars, by means of symposia and debates that take place across the country;[47] and Argentine legal doctrine has therefore achieved an extraordinary and early development,[48] especially when compared with the developments in other Latin American jurisdictions. The study of doctrine also requires a legal historical approach that looks beyond the text and places it within a context, looking also to the role of jurists as actors in shaping law and society.[49]

Legal dogmatism that followed the enactments of national codes (i.a., civil code) was with time surpassed by a more realistic conception that allowed the perception of the law in "action."[50] Some Argentine scholars include general principles of law amongst the sources, being these principles the main ideas that guide an existing or possible norm.[51] Scholars also tend to include equity, as a material source, being a mitigation of the rigor of the law and an adaptation of the law to the facts of a particular case, being hence more fair or just.[52] Comparative law is also included as a source of law by a number of scholars, since courts in Argentina might encounter an argument in the foreign law provision or scholarly writing.[53] It should be noted that the Argentine and foreign provision should be substantially analogue, naturally.[54] Comparative law, as a material source, assists in the axiological assessment of the current national norm.[55]

3 LEGAL HISTORY

The present-day territory of Argentina was formerly a possession of the Castilian Crown. Historically, it has been referred to as Río de la Plata, due to the name of the main fluvial artery that crosses through the territory. In 1516, Juan Díaz de Solís

43. *Ibid.*
44. Rivera, *supra* n. 16, at 168.
45. *Ibid.*
46. Escudero de Quintana, *supra* n. 18, at 57.
47. Rivera, *supra* n. 16, at 168.
48. *Ibid.* 169.
49. Víctor Tau Anzoátegui, *La doctrina de los autores como fuente del derecho castellano-indiano*, 17 Revista de Historia del Derecho 351, 354 (1989).
50. María R. Pugliese la Valle, *La "idea de jurisprudencia" a través de los primeros años de la "Revista de Jurisprudencia Argentina"*, 22 Revista de Historia del Derecho 241, 277 (1994).
51. Rivera, *supra* n. 16, at 150.
52. *Ibid.* 170–171. For example, equity is present in Art. 2 of the Argentine Civil and Commercial Code, with a complementary function to that of legislation. *See also* Escudero de Quintana, *supra* n. 18, at 64.
53. Rivera, *supra* n. 16, at 173–174.
54. *Ibid.* 174.
55. Escudero de Quintana, *supra* n. 18, at 58.

NG-PI-End led the first European expedition that arrived in the region.[56] In 1776, the territory mainly comprised the newly created Viceroyalty of Río de la Plata.[57] During the following century, inhabitants joined other movements towards independence that arose in South America.[58] In May 1810, a short but intense revolution overthrew the local Viceroy, who was then replaced by members of a first *junta*.[59] Independence would be finally declared on 9 July 1816.[60]

The historical accounts presented in this chapter, as already mentioned, attend the national codified period. Codification, as understood today, finds its origins in Europe, where it developed significantly during the eighteenth and nineteenth centuries. Codification advocated for a new presentation and form of laws which would replace existing provisions, while grouping different areas in an organic, systematic, clear, accurate, and complete way.[61] In addition, codification suggested the laying out of a plan with terminology and phraseology.[62] The Americas were no exception to the codification movement, since the phenomena took place across the continent in civil law jurisdictions and in a number of mixed jurisdictions.[63] Codification continued to evolve worldwide during the twentieth and twenty-first centuries. In Argentina, national codes were enacted mainly during the second half of the nineteenth century,[64] and the codes—as reflected in this chapter—continue to adapt to the needs of society.

3.1 Constitutional Law

A Constitutional Convention met in the city of Santa Fe in early 1853, summoned by Justo J. de Urquiza, and having representatives from the different Argentine provinces, excluding Buenos Aires, which had seceded from the rest of the provinces.[65] The Argentine Constitution was signed in 1853, and was based, amongst others, on Spanish antecedents and US constitutional principles.[66] The constitutional draft by Juan B.

56. David Rock, *Argentina, 1516–1987: From Spanish colonization to Alfonsín* 8 (Rev. ed., University of California Press 1987).
57. Daniel K. Lewis, *The History of Argentina* 31 (Palgrave Macmillan 2003).
58. William Warren Sweet, *A History of Latin America* 140–146 (Rev. ed., Abingdon Press 1929).
59. Amongst the copious bibliography on the periods covering the Argentine revolution and independence, *see* the early and widely circulated—though contested—account in Luis L. Domínguez, *Historia Argentina* 201–238 (Imprenta del Orden 1861).
60. *Ibid.* 398–411.
61. Luis Díez-Picazo & Antonio Gullón, *Sistema de Derecho Civil* 51 (4th ed., Vol. I, Tecnos 1982); Arturo Alessandri Rodríguez & Manuel Somarriva Undurraga, *Curso de derecho civil, basado en las explicaciones de los profesores de la Universidad de Chile* 49 (2d ed., Vol. I, Editorial Nascimento 1945); and Genaro R. Carrió, *Judge Made Law under a Civil Code*, 41 La. L. Rev. 993, 993 (1981).
62. Jean L. Bergel, *Principal Features and Methods of Codification*, 48 La. L. Rev. 1084 (1988).
63. *See* generally Olivier Moréteau & Agustín Parise, *Recodification in Louisiana and Latin America*, 83 Tul. L. Rev. 1103 (2009).
64. For an account of earlier efforts in Argentina *see*, amongst others, Ricardo Levene, *Notas sobre la codificación en la historia del derecho argentino*, 8 Revista del Instituto de Historia del Derecho 159 (1957).
65. Ricardo Zorraquín Becú, *Las fuentes de la Constitución de 1853*, 16 Revista de Historia del Derecho 209, 210 (1988).
66. Viviana Kluger, "Argentina", in *The Oxford International Encyclopedia of Legal History* 215–216 (Vol. 1, Stanley N. Katz ed., Oxford University Press 2009). On the foreign influences on the

Alberdi, which was made available in the second edition of his *Bases*,[67] was also of value for the drafters of the Argentine Constitution.[68] Precedents to the 1853 text are found in a number of earlier efforts. For example, constitution-like texts were drafted as early as 1811, 1813, 1815, and 1817;[69] though the first constitutional drafts for Argentina were completed in 1819 and 1826.[70] The province of Buenos Aires did not subscribe to the 1853 text, since it had seceded from the rest of Argentina in 1852. The reunion of the province of Buenos Aires and the rest of Argentina would be therefore reflected the following year through the constitutional reform of 1860.[71] The 1853 text had already invited directly for legislative reform and codification,[72] calling for the National Congress to legislate in civil, commercial, mineral, and criminal matters, prohibiting provinces to enact legislation in those areas after the national codes would be enacted.[73]

Argentina modified the text of its constitution on several occasions, since the enactment of a first federal constitution in 1853.[74] The twentieth century brought changes to constitutional law in Argentina.[75] In 1949, during the presidency of Juan D. Perón, a reform to the constitutional text was implemented, incorporating social-protection ideas that had developed during the first half of that century.[76] That reform was short-lived, being overruled in 1956,[77] when the constitutional text was traced back to the pre-1949 version. In 1957, however, a constitutional reform incorporated Article 14*bis*,[78] which still today encapsulates the main tenets of social rights. The 1957 constitutional reform therefore prevailed in reestablishing some elements of social

---

Argentine Constitution, stressing that the US model was not the only one followed in Argentina *see* Abelardo Levaggi, *Espíritu del constitucionalismo argentino de la primera mitad del siglo XIX*, 9 Revista de Historia del Derecho 239 (1981).

67. *See* Juan B. Alberdi, *Bases y Puntos de Partida para la Organización Política de la República Argentina* (Olsen A. Ghirardi intro., Advocatus 2002, originally published in 1852) at chapters XV, XVI, and XXXI.
68. Zorraquín Becú, *supra* n. 65, at 225; and Abelardo Levaggi, *Manual de Historia del Derecho Argentino (Castellano-Indiano/Nacional)* 60 (3d ed., Vol. III, Abeledo Perrot 2013).
69. On the early period (i.e., 1815–1819) *see* Ricardo Zorraquín Becú, *El proceso constitucional de 1815 a 1819*, 17 Revista del Instituto de Historia del Derecho Ricardo Levene 105 (1966).
70. Ricardo Levene, *Historia del Derecho Argentino* 446–447 (Vol. X, Kraft 1958).
71. Víctor Tau Anzoátegui, *La Codificación en la Argentina (1810-1870): Mentalidad Social e Ideas Jurídicas* 340 (Imprenta de la Universidad 1977). On the constitutional text of 1860 *see* Martiré, *supra* n. 73.
72. *See* Art. 24 of that constitutional text; and *see also* Tau Anzoátegui, *supra* n. 71, at 318–319.
73. *See* Arts. 64 (11) and 105 of that constitutional text; and *see also* Tau Anzoátegui, *supra* n. 71, at 319.
74. For the period before 1853, *see* generally Abelardo Levaggi, *Constitucionalismo Argentino 1810–1850*, 5:2 Iushistoria Revista Electrónica 1 (2005); and Isidoro J. Ruíz Moreno, *La Lucha por la Constitución (1820–1853)* (Astrea 1976).
75. *See* generally Agustín Parise, "La Carta Fundamental de los argentinos: Desde lo intrínseco, un siglo y medio después", in *Essays in Honor of Saúl Litvinoff* 659 (Olivier Moréteau, Alberto Zuppi & Julio Romañach eds., Claitor's Publishing Division 2008). n.b., there were also changes in the late nineteenth century.
76. Benjamín Burgos, *Curso de derecho constitucional* 72 et seq. (Virtudes Editorial Universitaria 2001).
77. *Ibid.*; and *see also* "Proclama del 27 de abril de 1956", in *Anales de Legislación Argentina* 1, 2 (Vol. XVI-A, La Ley 1956).
78. *See* the English translation of Art. 14*bis* of the *Argentine Constitution (1994)*, *supra* n. 75.

constitutionalism that had been eliminated when the 1949 constitutional reform of Perón was abrogated.[79] The century continued providing changes to the text of the Argentine Constitution. The de facto regimes introduced changes to the text in 1966, 1972, and 1976.[80] Finally, in 1994, during the democratic government of President Carlos S. Menem, the latest reform to the Argentine Constitution took place. That reform incorporated a number of changes. For example, it granted, by means of Article 75, paragraph 22, constitutional status to a selection of international treaties subscribed by Argentina.[81]

3.2 Commercial and Civil Law

Argentina adopted a civil and commercial code (*Código Civil y Comercial de la Nación*, hereinafter ACCC) in 2015. This code took effect on 1 August 2015,[82] and replaced two autonomous codes that had been enacted during the second half of the nineteenth century. An account of the codification path followed in these two areas of law will follow below, and will eventually lead to the adoption of that new and unified text.

3.2.1 Commercial

The adoption of a national commercial code was delayed in Argentina until 1862.[83] That substantive code, however, was adopted before the civil code, revealing hence a curious feature.[84] Eduardo Acevedo—from Uruguay—and Dalmacio Vélez Sarsfield—from Argentina—worked during ten months[85] in the drafting of a commercial code that was presented to the governor of the province of Buenos Aires in 1857.[86] The text encapsulated the commercial law of its time;[87] and as other nineteenth-century commercial codes, their text conceived that area of the law on a subjective

79. Daniel A. Sabsay, *Manual de Derecho Constitucional* 339 (La Ley 2011); and Gelli, *supra* n. 15, at 116.
80. Burgos, *supra* n. 76, at 72 et seq.
81. *See* the English translation of Art. 75(22) of the *Argentine Constitution (1994)*, *supra* n. 75.
82. Article 1, Ley 27.077 of 2014, at http://servicios.infoleg.gob.ar/infolegInternet/anexos/235000-239999/239773/norma.htm (accessed March 6, 2017).
83. On an earlier draft of a commercial code (1824) for Río de la Plata *see* Julio C. Guillamondegui, *Primer proyecto de Código de Comercio Rioplatense (1824)*, 16 Revista del Instituto de Historia del Derecho Ricardo Levene 204 (1965).
84. Graciela Medina, "Argentina on the Eve of a New Civil and Commercial Code", in *The Scope and Structure of Civil Codes* 43, 47 (Julio C. Rivera ed., Springer 2013).
85. Héctor Cámara, "Código de Comercio de la República Argentina y reformas o tentativas hasta la actualidad", in *Centenario del Código de Comercio* 109, 112 (UNAM 1991).
86. *Código de Comercio para la Nación Argentina. Sancionado por el Honorable Congreso Nacional. El 10 de Setiembre de 1862* v (El Nacional 1863); Levaggi, *supra* n. 68, at 183; and *Centenario del Código de Comercio de la Provincia de Buenos Aires*, 8 Revista del Instituto de Historia del Derecho 170 (1957).
87. Miguel C. Araya, *El contenido del derecho comercial a partir del Código Civil y Comercial*, Revista Jurídica Argentina La Ley, April 20, 2015, 1, 2 (2015). *See also* Tau Anzoátegui, *supra* n. 34, at 333–334.

basis.[88] The text, drafted mainly by Acevedo in consultation with Vélez Sarsfield,[89] was approved without parliamentary debate by the Buenos Aires Congress in 1859.[90] The National Congress extended the application of that code to all of Argentina in 10 September 1862,[91] taking effect as the *Código de Comercio para la Nación Argentina* (hereinafter, Argentine Commercial Code).[92] The Argentine Commercial Code had 1755 articles and was divided into four books: Book I of persons of commerce (*de las personas del comercio*), Book II of contracts (*de los contratos*), Book III of rights and obligations that derive from navigation (*de los derechos y obligaciones que resultan de la navegación*), and Book IV of insolvency of merchants (*de la insolvencia de los comerciantes*). Again, that was the first national code for Argentina, preceding other enactments in substantive areas of law, such as civil and criminal law.[93] The Argentine text spread across Latin America, influencing the likewise influential commercial code of Chile of 1865,[94] and being adopted by Uruguay (with minor changes) and by Paraguay.[95]

Acevedo and Vélez Sarsfield had an eclectic approach to sources when drafting the Argentine Commercial Code. Their sources have been deemed universal, aiming to adapt the law to the society of that time.[96] The drafters indicated, in the *exposé des motifs* submitted before the Buenos Aires administration in 1857, that:

> The first of all Codes, the French Code, source of all other, no longer reflecting the status of the law nor the requirements of trade, had been successively improved and reformed mainly by the Spanish Code, by the one of Portugal, by the one of the Netherlands, by the Code of Württemberg, and by the one for the Brazilian Empire. We have done what jurists from those nations did when elaborating their codes, [while having] the advantage that today the study of comparative legislation embraces a further extension since it can be done on [a larger number] of commercial laws on the same subject.[97]

Acevedo devoted special attention in his draft to the Spanish *Ordenanzas del Consulado de Bilbao* (1737) and to the five European texts mentioned in the excerpt above.[98] In addition, the manuscripts elaborated by Vélez Sarsfield indicate some

88. Julio C. Rivera, "The Scope and Structure of Civil Codes. Relations with Commercial Law, Family Law, Consumer Law and Private International Law. A Comparative Approach", in *The Scope and Structure of Civil Codes* 3, 21 (Julio C. Rivera ed., Springer 2013).
89. Cámara, *supra* n. 85, at 112. On the debate about the authorship *see* Abelardo Levaggi, *Dalmacio Vélez Sarsfield, Jurisconsulto* 132 et seq. (Ciencia, Derecho y Sociedad 2005).
90. Levaggi, *supra* n. 68, at 183.
91. Levaggi, *supra* n. 89, at 164.
92. *Código de Comercio para la Nación Argentina, supra* n. 86.
93. Levaggi, *supra* n. 68, at 185.
94. *Ibid.*
95. Cámara, *supra* n. 85, at 110.
96. Levaggi, *supra* n. 68, at 183.
97. *Código de Comercio para la Nación Argentina, supra* n. 86, at vi.
98. Cámara, *supra* n. 85, at 111.

doctrinal sources. For example, they refer to the writings by Gabriel Massé and Pierre-Sébastien Boulay-Paty.[99] German authors, such as Carl J. A. Mittermaier, were also examined by the drafters.[100]

De-codification had a significant impact on the Argentine Commercial Code,[101] a phenomenon that was experienced also by other commercial codes across the globe.[102] That process eroded most of the original text of 1862, as would be modified in 1889.[103] For example, bankruptcy provisions were soon removed from the code, together with the enactment of special legislation on, amongst other areas, bill of exchange, insurance, warrant, and agricultural pledge.[104]

A number of reforms were envisioned for the Argentine Commercial Code. An early reform was commissioned in 1870 because the subsequent enactment of the civil code demanded the elimination of interpolations that had originally aimed to cover *lacunae*.[105] Sixto Villegas and Vicente G. Quesada led that work, which ultimately did not prosper.[106] Lisandro Segovia was then commissioned to reform the code starting in 1886, yet his drafts including advanced doctrinal principles were not accepted by the legislature,[107] being considered too audacious.[108] The main reform to the Argentine Commercial Code was introduced after the work of a Codifying Commission of the House of Representatives in 1889.[109] The commission analyzed the work of Segovia and the earlier work of Villegas and Quesada.[110] Their reform, however, was deemed conservative. The members of the commission indicated that the advantages of the existing code would not survive if a completely new code would have been implemented.[111] Therefore, reforms were implemented mainly in corporations (*sociedades anónimas*) and by the inclusion of new titles (i.a., checks).[112] The reform was not welcomed free of criticism by jurists of the time, who deemed it perhaps too conservative or lacking of originality.[113] More attempts for partial or integral reform followed in Argentina, yet they failed. For example, attempts were taken in 1935, 1936, and 1959, led by amongst others, Carlos C. Malagarriga and Dimas González

99. Levaggi, *supra* n. 89, at 159.
100. *Código de Comercio para la Nación Argentina*, *supra* n. 86, at vii; and Levaggi, *supra* n. 89, at 160.
101. Araya, *supra* n. 87, at 3.
102. Rivera, *supra* n. 88, at 21.
103. Medina, *supra* n. 84, at 54. For more information on the 1889 reform, *see* Cámara, *supra* n. 85, at 116 et seq.
104. Medina, *supra* n. 84, at 54; and Rivera, *supra* n. 88, at 20.
105. Cámara, *supra* n. 85, at 114.
106. Levaggi, *supra* n. 89, at 164 and 168.
107. Cámara, *supra* n. 85, at 114 et seq.
108. Levaggi, *supra* n. 68, at 185.
109. Cámara, *supra* n. 85, at 116.
110. Juan C. Frontera, *La erosión del código de comercio de la república argentina a través del instituto de la quiebra -primer estudio sobre su descodificación*, 4 Iushistoria Revista Electrónica 1, 13 (2007).
111. Cámara, *supra* n. 85, at 116.
112. *Ibid.*
113. *Ibid.* 117. It should be noted, however, that some scholars deemed the 1889 reform as a new commercial code. *See* for example Levaggi, *supra* n. 68, at 185.

Gowland.[114] Efforts for revision and recodification were welcomed in Argentina during the second half of the twentieth century, and they paved the way for the adoption of the ACCC.

3.2.2 Civil

Vélez Sarsfield was appointed in 1864 to draft a civil code for Argentina.[115] His resulting work was approved without parliamentary debate[116] by the National Congress on 25 September 1869, taking effect as the *Código Civil de la República Argentina* (hereinafter, Argentine Civil Code) on 1 January 1871.[117] The Argentine Civil Code had 4051 articles and was divided into two preliminary titles and four books: Book I of persons (*de las personas*), Book II of personal rights in civil relations (*de los derechos personales en las relaciones civiles*), Book III of real rights (*de los derechos reales*), and Book IV of real and personal rights-dispositions in common (*de los derechos reales y personales—disposiciones communes*). The Argentine text spread across Latin America, influencing, for example, the drafters of the civil code of Uruguay of 1868[118] and being adopted *in totum* by Paraguay in 1877.[119]

The Argentine codifier had an eclectic approach to law,[120] and therefore identified materials from many sources. Vélez Sarsfield worked with legislative acts, drafts of codes, codes, and doctrine that served him as guides.[121] Similar to other drafters, he used the ideas and codes that existed at the time.[122] He was especially interested in the jurists and works that theorized on modern law while building from Roman law principles.[123] Finally, Vélez Sarsfield added to those materials the identification of local

114. Cámara, *supra* n. 85, at 118 et seq.
115. For previous efforts *see* Tau Anzoátegui, *supra* n. 34, at 125, 324–340; and Abelardo Levaggi, *Manual de Historia del Derecho Argentino (Castellano-Indiano/Nacional)* 265–266 (Vol. II, Depalma 1987).
116. Levaggi, *supra* n. 115, at 269. *See also* the complete study by Jorge Cabral Texo, *Historia del Código Civil argentino* 156 et seq. (Jesús Menéndez 1920).
117. *See* the text of the Argentine Civil Code at "Ley 340", in *Anales de Legislación Argentina: Complemento Años 1852-1880* 496 (La Ley 1954). *See* Moréteau & Parise, *supra* n. 63, at 1143; and Levaggi, *supra* n. 115, at 266.
118. Moréteau & Parise, *supra* n. 63, at 1147. A report of 1867 by a Codifying Commission in Uruguay mentioned amongst its sources the project of Vélez Sarsfield, which was not yet law in Argentina. *See* Agustín Parise, *The Place of the Louisiana Civil Code in the Hispanic Civil Codifications: Inclusion in the Comments to the Spanish Civil Code Project of 1851*, 68 La. L. Rev. 823, 850 (2008).
119. Raúl Sapena Pastor, *Fuentes Próximas del Código Civil* 1 (Editorial el Foro 1986); Levaggi, *supra* n. 1, at 241; and Moréteau & Parise, *supra* n. 63, at 1125.
120. Alejandro Guzmán Brito, *La codificación civil en Iberoamérica. Siglos XIX y XX* 453 (Editorial Jurídica de Chile 2000).
121. Agustín Parise, *Legal Transplants and Codification: Exploring the North American Sources of the Civil Code of Argentina (1871)*, 1:2 Isaidat L. Rev.1, 7 (2010); and Raymundo Salvat, *El Código Civil Argentino (Estudio General): Historia, Plan o Método y Fuentes*, 7 Revista Argentina de Ciencias Políticas 420, 436 (1913).
122. Levaggi, *supra* n. 89, at 180.
123. *Ibid.*

customs.[124] It can be claimed that the resulting text of the Argentine Civil Code was tinted with an individualistic and liberal conception, as most nineteenth-century civil codes that found a precedent in the *Code Napoléon*.

The text of the Argentine Civil Code was subject to many alterations that were introduced mainly through revisions.[125] For example, *secular laws* were enacted in the 1880s in Argentina. Accordingly, a law on civil marriage was adopted in 1888, together with laws on civil registry that were adopted in 1884 and 1898.[126] The first decades of the new century also brought new legislation that affected the civil code. For example, the National Congress adopted a law on agricultural leases in 1921 and a law on the rights of women in 1926.[127] Most partial reforms, however, dealt with specific areas of the civil code[128] and lacked a comprehensive approach. The Argentine Civil Code was also eroded by a continuous process of de-codification.[129]

Revision and recodification efforts of the civil code were undertaken in Argentina starting at the turn of the twentieth century. Three of those efforts were undertaken in 1936, 1954, and 1968; and assisted in leaving behind the liberal conception that had characterized the first-generation code. At the break of the twentieth century scholarly writings indicated a need to harmonize the civil code with the new context.[130] Accordingly, a first recodification effort was started in 1926 with the appointment of a Codifying Commission.[131] The latter delegated to one of its members—Juan A. Bibiloni—the drafting of a pre-project.[132] The pre-project was revised by the commission, and Héctor Lafaille and Gastón Tobal undertook the final drafting of a project that was completed in 1936,[133] was notably brief, and was ultimately never adopted by the legislature.[134] In the 1950s, scholars claimed that there was a need to change civil code provisions to make them reflect current standards.[135] Within that scenario, a second recodification effort was undertaken in 1950 by the Civil Law Institute of the Ministry

124. Raymundo M. Salvat, *Tratado de Derecho Civil Argentino: Parte General* 132 (9th ed., Vol. I, Tipográfica Ed. Argentina 1950).
125. Jorge J. Llambías, *Tratado de Derecho Civil, Parte General* 199 et seq. (6th ed., Vol. I, Editorial Perrot 1975).
126. Abel Cháneton, *Historia de Vélez Sársfield* 335 et seq. (Vol. II, Editorial "La Facultad" 1937).
127. *Ibid.*
128. Levaggi, *supra* n. 115, at 271.
129. Moréteau & Parise, *supra* n. 63, at 1145.
130. *See* generally Agustín Parise, *La comisión de reformas al Código Civil (1926). Aproximación histórico-jurídica a su proyección*, 3 Iushistoria Revista Electrónica 1 (2006).
131. Enrique R. Aftalión & Fernando García Olano, *Introducción al Derecho* 454 (4th ed., s.n. 1939); and Juan C. Rébora, *Nota e informe presentados por el profesor Dr. Juan Carlos Rébora al Honorable Consejo Académico de la Facultad de Ciencias Jurídicas y Sociales de la Universidad de La Plata, con motivo de su actuación dentro de la Comisión de Reformas del Código Civil*, 5 Revista Jurídica Argentina La Ley 66, 69 (1937).
132. Aftalión & García Olano, *supra* n. 131, at 454. *See* generally Juan A. Bibiloni, *Anteproyecto de reformas al código civil argentino: presentado a la comisión encargada de redactarlo* (Vol. I-VII, Valerio Abeledo 1929–1932).
133. *See* Guillermo A. Borda, *Tratado de Derecho Civil Parte General* 148 (9th ed., Vol. I, Editorial Perrot 1987); and Moréteau & Parise, *supra* n. 63, at 1145.
134. *See* Aftalión & García Olano, *supra* n. 131, at 454; and Levaggi, *supra* n. 115, at 272.
135. Susana T. Ramella, *Propiedad en función social en la constitución de 1949. Una "mentalidad" del Antiguo Régimen representada en el constitucionalismo social de la época*, 35 Revista de Historia del Derecho 297, 308 (2007).

of Justice, under the leadership of Jorge J. Llambías.[136] The work resulted in a pre-project that welcomed the developments of the national jurisprudence.[137] The pre-project was also brief, and was completed in 1954, though never adopted by the legislature.[138] A third major revision effort was completed in 1968. That effort, however, did not aim to achieve recodification, and was limited to achieve revision of 204 articles.[139] The new texts were adopted by Law 17.711 of 1968,[140] and drafted by José F. Bidau, Abel M. Fleitas, and Roberto Martínez Ruiz, with the decisive participation of Guillermo A. Borda.[141] Their revision work introduced principles of social solidarity in a code that had been known as individualistic.[142]

Recodification efforts were launched since the 1980s in Argentina, envisioning changes in both the civil and commercial codes. The first generation codes needed a refurbishment that could no longer be achieved by means of revision or decodification. Projects of unified civil and commercial codes were therefore completed in Argentina in the years 1987, 1992, 1993, and 1998, though never took force of law.[143] Those efforts indeed aimed towards the unification of civil and commercial provisions in a single text.[144] After all, as explained by Graciela Medina, Argentina offered a possibility to "observe a commercialization of civil law and a civilization of commercial law."[145] The 1987 draft was led by, amongst others, Héctor Alegría and Sergio Le Pera, and received approval from the National Congress, yet it was rejected by the Executive in 1991.[146] The 1992 draft was led by, amongst others, Alegría, Alberto Bueres, Jorge Mosset Iturraspe, and Ana I. Piaggi,[147] and ultimately only received approval of the House of Representatives the following year.[148] The 1993 draft was the result of the work of a commission appointed by a decree of the Executive, and led by, amongst

136. *Anteproyecto de Código Civil de 1954 para la República Argentina* 7 (Universidad Nacional de Tucumán 1968); and Levaggi, *supra* n. 115, at 272.
137. Levaggi, *supra* n. 115, at 272; and Moréteau & Parise, *supra* n. 63, at 1145.
138. Levaggi, *supra* n. 115, at 272.
139. Borda, *supra* n. 133, at 143. *See also* Luis M. Valiente Noailles, *Comentarios a las reformas al código civil (Ley 17.711): Legislación, doctrina, jurisprudencia* 7 et seq. (Ediciones Depalma 1968); and Guillermo A. Borda, *La reforma de 1968 al código civil* (Editorial Perrot 1971).
140. *See* the abstract of Ley 17.711 of 1968, at http://servicios.infoleg.gob.ar/infolegInternet/verNorma.do;jsessionid=2A64BFFD8831E8807AF68251CBB685E2?id=103603 (accessed March 6, 2017).
141. Levaggi, *supra* n. 115, at 271.
142. *Ibid.*; and Moréteau & Parise, *supra* n. 63, at 1145.
143. Medina, *supra* n. 84, at 58. About some of those drafts *see Estudios sobre el Proyecto de Código Unificado de 1998* (Roberto Brebbia dir., Zavalía 2001); Julio C, Rivera, *El Proyecto de Código Civil para la República Argentina,* 35 Revista Jurídica Universidad Interamericana de Puerto Rico 381 (2001); and Augusto C. Belluscio, *Le Code civil et commercial argentin de 2014: (aperçu général et droit des personnes et de la famille)*, 2015-3 Revue internationale de droit comparé 663, 664 et seq. (2015).
144. Lisandro Rienzi, *Unidad del derecho privado. El problema de la autonomía del derecho comercial y la unificación de la legislación Civil y Comercial,* Doctrina Judicial November 26, 2014, 6 (2014).
145. Medina, *supra* n. 84, at 59.
146. Rienzi, *supra* n. 144.
147. *El Proyecto de Unificación de Código Civil y su Historia, Cámara de Diputados de la Nación, Comisión de Legislación General,* at www1.hcdn.gov.ar/dependencias/clgeneral/historia.html (accessed March 6, 2017).
148. Rienzi, *supra* n. 144.

others, Augusto C. Belluscio, Aída R. Kemelmajer de Carlucci, Le Pera, Julio C. Rivera, and Eduardo A. Zannoni,[149] and was presented before the National Senate in 1993, yet it was not approved.[150] Finally, the 1998 draft was elaborated by a commission led by, amongst others, Alegría, Atilio A. Alterini, Jorge H. Alterini, and Rivera,[151] and following the fate of the previous drafts, was ultimately not adopted.[152] Some of those recent attempts valued a number of international and comparative law instruments. In the area of contract law, for example, the 1987 draft incorporated provisions on formation of contracts to be found in the UN Convention on Contracts for the International Sale of Goods (CISG).[153] The 1998 draft, likewise, incorporated modern principles of contact law, and aimed to internationalize contact law. Drafters looked also at European early harmonization efforts, especially the project of a European civil code of the Pavia Group, the McGregor code, and the first part of the Principles of European Contract Law (PECL).[154] That draft also looked at the Unidroit Principles for International Commercial Contracts[155] and CISG.[156] The 1998 draft, however, failed to clearly harmonize the Argentine provisions with those of other Latin American jurisdictions, notably Mercosur members.[157]

3.2.3 Unified Code

The most recent recodification attempt of the commercial and civil texts was presented before the Executive in March 2012.[158] A Codifying Commission started to work in early 2011,[159] and was led by Justice Elena Highton de Nolasco of the Argentine

149. *El Proyecto de Unificación de Código Civil, supra* n. 147.
150. Rienzi, *supra* n. 144.
151. Moréteau & Parise, *supra* n. 63, at 1146.
152. Rienzi, *supra* n. 144.
153. Alejandro M. Garro, *Unification and Harmonization of Private Law in Latin America*, 40 Am. J. Comp. L. 587, 607 (1992).
154. Claudia R. Brizzio, *Teoría general del contrato y contratos predispuestos en el anteproyecto de Código Europeo de Contratos y en el proyecto de Código Civil argentino de 1998*, 1999-1 Doctrina Judicial 839 (1999); and Claudia R. Brizzio, *Anteproyecto de Código Europeo de Contratos—Estudio Preliminar*, 1999-C Revista Jurídica Argentina La Ley 985 (1999).
155. Claudia R. Brizzio, *Códigos únicos y "restatements" para unificar la regulación internacional del contrato*, Revista de Responsabilidad Civil y Seguros 123 (2001).
156. Atilio A. Alterini, *Tendencias en la contratación moderna*, 1999-B Revista Jurídica Argentina La Ley 1229 (1999); Eduardo L. Gregorini Clusellas, *Proyección del contrato en el Siglo XXI*, 2004-A Revista Jurídica Argentina La Ley 847 (2004); and Lauro Da Gama e Souza, *The Unidroit Principles of International Commercial Contracts and their Applicability in the Mercosur Countries*, 36 Revue juridique Thémis 375, 416 (2002).
157. Brizzio, *supra* n. 155.
158. Esteban Louge Emiliozzi, *El proceso de recodificación y unificación del derecho privado en la Argentina*, 29 Cartapacio de Derecho, 1 (2016); and Aída Kemelmajer de Carlucci, *Las nuevas realidades familiares en el Código Civil y Comercial argentino de 2014*, Revista Jurídica Argentina La Ley, October 8, 2014, 1 (2014).
159. Decreto 191 of 2011, at http://servicios.infoleg.gob.ar/infolegInternet/anexos/175000-179999/179643/norma.htm (accessed March 6, 2017). The work started on March 2, 2011 (Kemelmajer de Carlucci, *supra* n. 158). *See also* Jonathan M. Brodsky & Enzo E. Donato Brun, *Aspectos generales de los contratos en el Proyecto de Código Civil y Comercial de la Nación*, I:1 Revista En Letra 79, 82 (2014); and Academia Nacional de Derecho y Ciencias Sociales de Buenos Aires, *La Academia Nacional de Derecho y Ciencias Sociales de Buenos Aires aprueba y*

Supreme Court and former Justice Kemelmajer de Carlucci of the Supreme Court of the province of Mendoza, operating under the presidency of Chief Justice Ricardo L. Lorenzetti of the Argentine Supreme Court.[160] Miguel F. De Lorenzo was appointed secretary for the Codifying Commission.[161] A number of working groups were created in order to enable an ample participation of specialists from Argentina and Latin America.[162] The team included more than one hundred experts in different fields, including law professors, practitioners, and judges.[163] The Codifying Commission created a website to offer constant information and updates on the fate and reception of the draft,[164] while they also operated an email account where citizens could send their proposals and concerns.[165] That recodification effort unified the civil and commercial codes into a single body, because on 1 October 2014, the National Congress adopted Law 26.994, which approved the text of the ACCC[166] without parliamentary debate.[167] The ACCC has 2671 articles and is divided into a Preliminary Title and six books: Book I of the general part (*parte general*), Book II of family relations (*relaciones de familia*), Book III of personal rights (*derechos personales*), Book IV of real rights (*derechos reales*), Book V of *mortis causa* transmission of rights (*transmisión de derechos por causa de muerte*), and Book VI of dispositions in common for real and personal rights (*disposiciones comunes a los derechos personales y reales*).[168] Previous attempts likewise included a *general part*, hence subscribing to the approach of the BGB.[169] The ACCC therefore includes a methodological tool that offers coherence to the entire framework, especially since it deals with both commercial and civil law provisions.[170] As previously mentioned, the ACCC took effect on August 1, 2015.[171]

hace propio el dictamen emitido por el Instituto de Derecho Constitucional "Segundo V. Linares Quintana", Revista Jurídica Argentina La Ley–Suplemento Academia Nacional de Derecho y Ciencias Sociales de Buenos Aires, December 18, 2014, 2 (2014).

160. Decreto 191, *supra* n. 159. *See also* José F. Márquez, *El fideicomiso en el Proyecto de Código*, Revista Jurídica Argentina La Ley, August 13, 2012, 1 (2012).
161. Ricardo L. Lorenzetti, *Presentación del Código Civil y Comercial de la Nación*, Revista Jurídica Argentina La Ley, October 6, 2014, 1 (2014).
162. *Ibid.*; and María C. Marsili, *El Código Civil y Comercial y la materia comercial*, Revista Jurídica Argentina La Ley, June 29, 2015, 1 (2015).
163. *Fundamentos del Anteproyecto de Código Civil y Comercial de la Nación* at http://www.nuevocodigocivil.com/wp-content/uploads/2015/02/5-Fundamentos-del-Proyecto.pdf, 7 (accessed March 6, 2017); Lorenzetti, *supra* n. 161; and Ernesto E. Martorell, *La inoponibilidad de la persona jurídica en el Código Civil y Comercial. Responsabilidad por uso disfuncional de la sociedad*, Revista Jurídica Argentina La Ley, November 26, 2014, 1 (2014).
164. *See* http://www.nuevocodigocivil.com (accessed March 6, 2017).
165. Lorenzetti, *supra* n. 161; and Kemelmajer de Carlucci, *supra* n. 158.
166. Ley 26.994 of 2014, at http://servicios.infoleg.gob.ar/infolegInternet/anexos/235000-239999/235975/norma.htm (accessed March 6, 2017).
167. Alejandro P. Monteleone Lanfranco, *Las asociaciones civiles en el Código Civil y Comercial*, Revista Jurídica Argentina La Ley, April 10, 2015, 1 (2015).
168. Ley 26.994, *supra* n. 166.
169. Esteban R. Hess, *Primeras aproximaciones a la parte general del nuevo Código Civil y Comercial de la Nación, aprobado por Ley 26994/2014*, 29 Cartapacio de Derecho 1, 6 (2016).
170. *Ibid.* 15.
171. According to Art. 7 of Law 26.994, the code was to take effect on January 1, 2016. However, Law 27.077 of 2014 accelerated the entering into effect of the ACCC, moving the date to August 1, 2015. Some scholars indicated that the acceleration aimed to turn a future derogation more cumbersome, in case a change of administration in December 2015 would have welcome a

The ACCC invites for a plurality of sources of law that aim to help solve conflicts.[172] It states that legislation is the main formal source of law,[173] followed by uses, practices, and custom when legislation or interested parties refer to them and when not contradicting the law.[174] Legislation and custom are therefore formal sources. In addition, this type of sources includes practices in situations that are not regulated by law, the Argentine Constitution, and the decisions by international courts and organizations created by means of the international treaties subscribed by Argentina and included in the already mentioned Article 75, paragraph 22 of the Argentine Constitution.[175] Jurisprudence, which was included in the original draft of the code, yet then removed, is not a principal source.[176] This is no impediment to appeal to jurisprudence as a source of inspiration for a solution, however.[177] Material sources are not binding, and include doctrine and nonbinding jurisprudence.[178] Finally, it should be noted that the ACCC invites for a "dialogue of sources" aiming to a systemic perspective.[179]

3.3 Criminal Law[180]

Codification of criminal law was delayed in Argentina until the late nineteenth century. The path to a first and then to a second (and current) code was signposted by a number of reforms and earlier drafts. As mentioned before, the Argentine Constitution demanded from the National Congress the enactment of a national criminal code, and also it triggered the need to enact federal laws on crimes that fell within federal

---

revision or derogation of Law 26.994 before January 1, 2016. *See*, Flavio Lowenrosen, *Hace poco más de un mes comenzó su vigencia el Código Civil y Comercial*, elDial.com-CC4009; Louge Emiliozzi, *supra* n. 158; and *Academia Nacional de Derecho y Ciencias Sociales, supra* n. 159.

172. *Código Civil y Comercial, supra* n. 22, at 26. On the sources of law in the ACCC *see also* Julio C. Rivera, "La constitucionalización del derecho privado en el proyecto de código civil y comercial", in *Comentarios al Proyecto de Código Civil y Comercial de la Nación* 1, 9 (Julio C. Rivera dir., Abeledo Perrot 2012); Renato Rabbi-Baldi Cabanillas, "Consideraciones filosófico -jurídicas en torno del Título Preliminar del proyecto de Código Civil y Comercial de 2012", in *Comentarios al Proyecto de Código Civil y Comercial de la Nación* 23, 26–27 (Julio C. Rivera dir., Abeledo Perrot 2012); and Renato Rabbi-Baldi Cabanillas, "Derecho", in *Código Civil y Comercial de la Nación Comentado* 56, 56 (Vol. 1, Julio C. Rivera & Graciela Medina dir., La Ley 2014).
173. Rabbi-Baldi Cabanillas, *supra* n. 172, at 59.
174. As stated in Art. 1. *See* Ley 26.994, *supra* n. 166.
175. *Código Civil y Comercial, supra* n. 22, at 28; and Rabbi-Baldi Cabanillas, *supra* n. 172, at 56–57.
176. Marisa Herrera & Gustavo Caramelo, "Título Preliminar", in *Código Civil y Comercial de la Nación Comentado* 5, 12 (Vol. 1, Marisa Herrera, Gustavo Caramelo & Sebastián Picasso dir., Infojus 2015); and Rabbi-Baldi Cabanillas, *supra* n. 172, at 60.
177. Herrera & Caramelo, *supra* n. 176, at 12.
178. *Código Civil y Comercial, supra* n. 22, at 28.
179. Herrera & Caramelo, *supra* n. 176, at 16.
180. For a complete overview of the codified period of criminal law in Argentina *see* Abelardo Levaggi, *Historia del Derecho Penal Argentino* (Abeledo Perrot 1978), especially Chapter 14; and the more recent Abelardo Levaggi, *El Derecho Penal argentino en la historia* (Eudeba 2012), especially Chapter 3. For a clear and brief historical account, in English, *see* Marcelo Ferrante, "Argentina" in *The Handbook of Comparative Criminal Law* 12, 13–14 (Kevin J. Heller & Markus D. Dubber eds., Stanford University Press 2011).

jurisdiction.[181] Before the enactment of the criminal code, important provisions were found in Law 49 of 1863, establishing the crimes that were subject to federal courts and their punishment.[182] That law welcomed the supplemental character of provincial law for crimes against the nation when facing a *lacuna*.

Carlos Tejedor[183] was appointed by the Executive to draft a criminal code in late 1864.[184] He presented the first part of his work (referred to as general part)[185] in late 1865 and the second part (referred to as special part)[186] in 1868.[187] The Tejedor Draft comprised 450 articles, and it was accompanied by valuable notes with references to doctrine and legislation.[188] Tejedor presented the concordances with precedents in Roman, Spanish, and early independent period texts.[189] As mentioned before, provinces could enact codes until the Federal government would fill that *lacuna*,[190] and therefore the work of Tejedor was adopted by a number of provinces.[191] The Tejedor Draft was highly regarded even beyond the Argentine borders, for example, being adopted by Paraguay.[192] Finally, it is worth noting that the Tejedor Draft preserved death penalty, though only in very limited cases.[193] Therefore, even when not abolitionist in nature, the Tejedor Draft paved the path in that direction due to the restrictions it imposed on death penalty.[194]

The notes that accompanied the articles of the Tejedor Draft point to numerous sources. Tejedor benefited significantly from the drafting of Paul van Feuerbach for

181. Francisco P. Laplaza, *El proceso histórico de la Codificación Penal Argentina (I)*, 24 Revista del Instituto de Historia del Derecho Ricardo Levene 59, 74 (1978).
182. Laplaza, *supra* n. 181, at 75.
183. On the ideas of Carlos Tejedor, *see* José M. Díaz Couselo, *Las ideas de Carlos Tejedor sobre los efectos de la ignorancia de la ley en el ámbito del derecho penal*, 22 Cuadernos de Historia 181 (2012); and Alberto D. Leiva, *La enseñanza penal de Carlos Tejedor*, 26 Revista de Historia del Derecho 195 (1998).
184. Moisés Nilve, *El proyecto Tejedor en la historia del Derecho Patrio*, 7 Revista del Instituto de Historia del Derecho 57, 58 (1955–1956).
185. For a description of that part *see* Levaggi, *supra* n. 115, at 347; and Laplaza, *supra* n. 181, at 76.
186. For a description of that part *see* Levaggi, *supra* n. 115, at 348.
187. The draft is dated 1867. Nilve, *supra* n. 184, at 61–62.
188. Carlos Tejedor, *Proyecto de Código Penal para la República Argentina trabajado por el encargo del gobierno nacional (Parte Primera)* (Imprenta del Comercio del Plata, 1866); and Carlos Tejedor, *Proyecto de Código Penal para la República Argentina trabajado por el encargo del gobierno nacional (Parte Segunda)* (Imprenta del Comercio del Plata, 1867). *See also* Nilve, *supra* n. 184, at 62.
189. Levaggi, *supra* n. 115, at 348.
190. *See* Art. 108 of the Constitution of 1853, *supra* n. 6. *See also* J. Carlos García Basalo, *La Codificación Penal Provincial Argentina (1876-1886)*, 34 Revista de Historia del Derecho "Ricardo Levene" 125, 128 (1998).
191. García Basalo, *supra* n. 190, at 125–224; Nilve, *supra* n. 184, at 62–64; Laplaza, *supra* n. 181, at 79–80; and José M. Díaz Couselo, *Delitos contra la religión y el culto en la codificación penal argentina (1853–1941)*, 48 Revista de Historia del Derecho 33, 49–59 (2014). Indeed, that silence of the federal government gave a window from 1853 to 1886 to the provinces to legislate. García Basalo, *supra* n. 190, at 128.
192. Nilve, *supra* n. 184, at 64.
193. Laplaza, *supra* n. 181, at 76. On death penalty in Argentina before the codification period, *see* Abelardo Levaggi, *La pena de muerte en el derecho argentino precodificado. Un capítulo de la historia de las ideas penales*, 23 Revista del Instituto de Historia del Derecho Ricardo Levene 17 (1972).
194. Levaggi, *supra* n. 1933, at 80.

Bavaria in 1813.[195] He also used the works of Edward Livingstone for Louisiana,[196] and, amongst others, the codes of Belgium, Bolivia, France, Netherlands, Peru, Prussia, and Spain.[197] Tejedor likewise benefited from doctrinal works in Spanish (i.a., Joaquín F. Pacheco)[198] and in French (i.a., Adolphe Chauveau[199]). The Tejedor Draft implied a break with the preterit system,[200] and reaffirmed that the period between 1810 and the enactment of the criminal code was one of transition between the old regime and the modern legal paradigm.[201] The Tejedor Draft was well circulated and was known and studied by almost all members of the Argentine legal discourse, having even been invoked before courts as a legal principle.[202]

The examination of the Tejedor Draft was subject to delay.[203] Some months after presenting the Tejedor Draft,[204] Villegas, Andrés Ugarriza, and Juan A. García were appointed to revise the Tejedor Draft;[205] yet they ultimately opted to present a draft of their own.[206] These three jurists worked for 12 years on their draft;[207] and, differently from the Tejedor Draft, their 1881 draft was only adopted by the province of Córdoba.[208] Two characteristics of this 1881 draft should be noted: it abolished the distinction of public and private crimes, and it established a maximum and a minimum

195. *See* Tejedor, *Proyecto de Código Penal (Parte Primera), supra* n. 188; and Tejedor, *Proyecto de Código Penal (Parte Segunda), supra* n. 188. *See also* Nilve, *supra* n. 184, at 62. On the use of the text from Bavaria *see* Thomas Duve, *¿Del Absolutismo Ilustrado al Liberalismo Reformista? La recepción del Código Penal bávaro de 1813 de P.J.A. von Feuerbach en Argentina y el debate sobre la reforma del derecho penal hasta 1921*, 27 Revista de Historia del Derecho 125 (1999).

196. *See* the reference to Eduard Livingstone and Louisiana in the note to Arts. 2 and 3, Title 6, Book 1, Part 1. Tejedor, *Proyecto de Código Penal (Parte Primera), supra* n. 188, at 62–63. *See also* Nilve, *supra* n. 184, at 62. On the efforts of Livingstone for Louisiana and on their influence beyond those borders *see* Agustín Parise, *Codification of the Law in Louisiana: Early Nineteenth -Century Oscillation Between Continental European and Common Law Systems*, 27 Tul. Eur. & Civ. L.F. 133, 141–146 (2012).

197. *See* the reference to those texts in the note to Art. 2 of the preliminary title. Tejedor, *Proyecto de Código Penal (Parte Primera), supra* n. 188, at 4. *See also* Díaz Couselo, *supra* n. 191, at 37; and Duve, *supra* n. 195, at 130.

198. *See* the reference to the work of Joaquín F. Pacheco in the note to Art. 2 of the preliminary title. Tejedor, *Proyecto de Código Penal (Parte Primera), supra* n. 188, at 4.

199. *See* the reference to the work of Adolphe Chauveau in the note to Art. 1, Section 2, Title 2, Book 2, Part 2. Tejedor, *Proyecto de Código Penal (Parte Segunda), supra* n. 188, at 480.

200. Díaz Couselo, *supra* n. 183, at 210–211.

201. Natalia Stringini, *La continuidad de la tradición jurídica indiana en el pensamiento de Carlos Tejedor. El caso del delito de cohecho*, 45 Revista de Historia del Derecho 43, 50 (2013).

202. Levaggi, *supra* n. 115, at 348; and Mario C. Vivas, *El proyecto nacional de 1881 como Código Penal de la provincia de Córdoba*, 4 Revista de Historia del Derecho 305, 309–310 (1976).

203. Tau Anzoátegui, *supra* n. 34, at 346.

204. Levaggi, *supra* n. 115, at 348.

205. Nilve, *supra* n. 184, at 62; and Laplaza, *supra* n. 181, at 79.

206. *Proyecto de Código penal: presentado al poder ejecutivo nacional por la comisión nombrada para examinar el proyecto redactado* (Imprenta de el Nacional 1881). *See also* Laplaza, *supra* n. 181, at 79.

207. The original appointees were replaced through the years. Díaz Couselo, *supra* n. 191, at 59.

208. Levaggi, *supra* n. 115, at 349; Laplaza, *supra* n. 181, at 85; and Vivas, *supra* n. 202, at 310.

for each punishment, within which a judge would be able to decide.[209] That 1881 draft was ultimately left aside mainly because many provinces had already adopted the Tejedor Draft.[210]

The *Código Penal de la República Argentina*[211] (hereinafter, First Argentine Criminal Code), being based on the Tejedor Draft, was adopted without parliamentary debate in 1886 and took effect on 1 March 1887.[212] This code allowed the persistence of Law 49, since federal crimes were still subject to that special enactment.[213] The First Argentine Criminal Code preserved death penalty for situations almost identical to those of the Tejedor Draft.[214] Nevertheless, the code reformed some aspects of the Tejedor Draft. For example, it eliminated the distinction between crimes, delicts, and contraventions; and eliminated the provisions on civil liability.[215] The First Argentine Criminal Code had 299 articles and was divided into two books: Book I of general dispositions (*disposiciones jenerales* [sic]) and Book II of crimes and punishments (*de los delitos y sus penas*).[216] At the time of enactment of the code, Argentina was the only civil law country in the continent that did not have a national criminal code adopted according to a constitutional command.[217]

The First Argentine Criminal Code was subject to criticism that triggered the immediate need for reform;[218] and, therefore, Norberto Piñero, Rodolfo Rivarola, and José N. Matienzo submitted a draft by 1891.[219] Their work included 352 articles, enriched with notes on Argentine and foreign sources explaining the motivation of the articles.[220] That draft went beyond being a mere reform proposal, since it aimed to put forward a new code.[221] The proposed text offered a more modern method when compared with the previous texts.[222] It further projected the derogation of Law 49, since it called for the unification of the federal jurisdiction.[223] The drafters of the new text were enrolled in the up-and-coming positivistic school,[224] being members of the Argentine Society for Legal Anthropology (*Sociedad de Antropología Jurídica*).[225] Their draft benefited from, amongst others, the Italian code of 1889, which was at that time

209. Levaggi, *supra* n. 115, at 349.
210. Laplaza, *supra* n. 181, at 83.
211. *Código Penal de la República Argentina* (Felix Lajouane 1887).
212. It was enacted by means of Law 1920 of 1886. *See* Levaggi, *supra* n. 115, at 350; and Laplaza, *supra* n. 181, at 83.
213. Enrique Álvarez Core, *La génesis de la penalística argentina* (1827–1868), 30 Revista de Historia del Derecho 13, 14–15 (2002).
214. Levaggi, *supra* n. 193, at 91.
215. Levaggi, *supra* n. 115, at 349.
216. *Código Penal, supra* n. 211.
217. Díaz Couselo, *supra* n. 191, at 62, reproducing a statement by Eugenio R. Zaffaroni.
218. Levaggi, *supra* n. 115, at 350.
219. Laplaza, *supra* n. 181, at 88.
220. *Ibid.* 89.
221. Levaggi, *supra* n. 115, at 351.
222. *Ibid.*
223. Laplaza, *supra* n. 181, at 89.
224. Levaggi, *supra* n. 115, at 351. On the place of the Positivistic School in Argentina *see* Abelardo Levaggi, *Esbozo de las ideas penales argentinas en la década de 1890*, 30 Revista de Historia del Derecho "Ricardo Levene" 233 (1995).
225. Laplaza, *supra* n. 181, at 88.

the most modern because of the ideas it encapsulated.[226] The 1891 draft ultimately did not succeed in being adopted, and was replaced by a partial revision instrumented by means of Law 4189 of 1903.[227] This partial revision turned out to be cumbersome, since it implemented an almost new general part within an old code.[228]

The path to adapt the text of the First Argentine Criminal Code to the local needs was pursued by means of partial revision efforts.[229] For example, an early effort can be noted in the work of Segovia. He elaborated on his own initiative a draft of a criminal code in 1895, and that effort was welcomed by a number of scholars and was presented in law reviews.[230] He also included notes to his articles, indicating the sources and references to, amongst others, the codes of Belgium, Brazil, Chile, France, Germany, Italy, Netherlands, a number of Swiss cantons, the Tejedor Draft, the 1891 text, and the First Argentine Criminal Code.[231] Segovia, who was indeed a learned scholar—also in civil and commercial law—included references to doctrinal writings by, amongst others, Francisco Carrara, Giulio Crivellari, Pietro Ellero, Raffaele Garofalo, Jacques-Joseph Haus, Joseph Ortolan, and Tejedor.[232] The work of Segovia was influential on the drafts that followed and in the second Argentine criminal code.[233] Another example can be found in the 1906[234] work of five jurists[235]and a medical doctor.[236] Their draft of a criminal code was very well received by different actors,[237] and was also deemed positivistic, yet it did not subscribe blindly to the *Scuola Italiana*.[238] Even when it did not succeed in being adopted, the 1906 text paved the way for a draft that would be completed in 1916.[239] A third and final example can be found in that resulting 1916 text.[240] Rodolfo Moreno advocated that year for the adoption of the 1906 draft, yet with some modifications.[241] His draft was subject to examination by a special commission that included, amongst others, Jerónimo del Barco and Julio Herrera.[242] The *exposé des motifs* of the new text—which would be ultimately adopted as the second Argentine

226. Levene, *supra* n. 70, at 642.
227. Not all scholars subscribed to that idea, however. Laplaza, *supra* n. 181, at 90.
228. Levaggi, *supra* n. 115, at 351.
229. Francisco Laplaza, *El proceso histórico de la Codificación Penal Argentina (II)*, 25 Revista del Instituto de Historia del Derecho Ricardo Levene 199, 202 (1979).
230. Laplaza, *supra* n. 181, at 90-91.
231. *Ibid.* 92.
232. *Ibid.*
233. *Ibid.*
234. *Proyecto de Código penal para la República Argentina, redactado por la Comisión de Reformas legislativas, constituida por decreto del Poder Ejecutivo de fecha 19 de diciembre de 1904* (Tipografía de la Cárcel de Encausados 1906).
235. That is., Rodolfo Rivarola, Diego Saavedra, Cornelio Moyano Gacitúa, Norberto Piñero, and Francisco Beazley. Levaggi, *supra* n. 115, at 351.
236. That is., José M. Ramos Mejía. Levaggi, *supra* n. 115, at 352.
237. *Ibid.*
238. José D. Cesano, *El pensamiento de Cornelio Moyano Gacitúa (1899-1905) en la tradición criminológica argentina*, 21 Cuadernos de Historia 111, 125-126 (2011). On the influence of the *Scuola Italiana* in Argentina *see ibid.* 118.
239. Laplaza, *supra* n. 229, at 203-205.
240. *Proyecto de Código penal para la República argentina, presentado por el señor diputado dr. Rodolfo Moreno (hijo)* (Talleres gráficos de L. J. Rosso y cía. 1916).
241. Levaggi, *supra* n. 115, at 352.
242. *Ibid.*; and Levaggi, *Historia del Derecho Penal, supra* n. 180, at 202.

criminal code—highlighted some relevant aspects of the text, i.a., that it was best to state elastic punishments and give judges the ability to apply these in an extensive manner.[243]

The above-mentioned final draft was approved without parliamentary debate by the House of Representatives, while the National Senate suggested some modifications (i.a., reestablishment of death penalty)[244] on 10 September 1921, taking effect as the *Código Penal de la Nación Argentina* (hereinafter, Second Argentine Criminal Code)[245] on 29 April 1922.[246] The Second Argentine Criminal Code had 306 articles and was divided into two books: Book I of general dispositions (*disposiciones generales*) and Book II of crimes (*de los delitos*).[247] Scholars have debated, without a clear conclusion, if the Second Argentine Criminal Code is to be considered: classical or neoclassical, fully or mildly positivist,[248] or eclectic.[249] It should be noted that the Second Argentine Criminal Code proscribed the death penalty from the Argentine criminal law system.[250] This is the current criminal code in Argentina, though it has naturally undergone numerous alterations in the wording of its provisions.

A number of recodification efforts were launched in Argentina as soon as the 1930s and 1940s by means of partial revision and special legislation, since normative dispersion reemerged soon after the enactment of the Second Argentine Criminal Code.[251] For example, Eusebio Gómez and Jorge E. Coll were appointed to elaborate a draft of a criminal code in 1936, though they proposed few changes in the special part of the existing code.[252] Their draft was not adopted, and was embedded in positivistic ideas that circulated within part of the legal discourse.[253] Later, in 1941, José Peco presented a draft of a criminal code that was regarded neo positivistic,[254] and the political events of the early 1940s restrained the needed study of that draft.[255] In 1943, the Federation of Argentine Bar Associations (*Federación Argentina de Colegios de Abogados*) presented, on its own initiative, a complementary law to the Second Argentine Criminal Code.[256]

Reform efforts alto took place in the 1950s, 1960s, and 1970s. A new drafting commission, this time led by Isidoro de Benedetti and Carlos Victorica Soneyra, was appointed in 1951.[257] The text they proposed was influenced by the positivistic ideas of

243. Levaggi, *supra* n. 115, at 353.
244. *Ibid.*
245. For additional information on the Second Argentine Criminal Code, *see* Levaggi, *Historia del Derecho Penal, supra* n. 180, at 200–204.
246. It was adopted by means of Law 11.179 of 1921. Laplaza, *supra* n. 229, at 210.
247. Ley 11.179 of 1921, at http://servicios.infoleg.gob.ar/infolegInternet/anexos/15000-19999/16546/norma.htm (accessed March 6, 2017).
248. Laplaza, *supra* n. 229, at 207.
249. Levene, *supra* n. 70, at 643.
250. Levaggi, *supra* n. 193, at 91.
251. Levaggi, *supra* n. 115, at 354.
252. Laplaza, *supra* n. 229, at 213.
253. Levene, *supra* n. 70, at 643.
254. *Ibid.* 644.
255. Laplaza, *supra* n. 229, at 214–215.
256. *Ibid.* 215.
257. *Ibid.* 216.

that time.[258] A period of de-codification developed at that time around the Second Argentine Criminal Code, by means of the enactment of special legislation.[259] Yet, integral reform was likewise pursued later during that decade, for example when Sebastián Soler[260] was appointed in 1958 to draft a new code.[261] Luis C. Cabral and Eduardo H. Marquardt were appointed to collaborate in that effort, and their work was completed in 1960.[262] Their effort benefited from a 1927 German draft[263] and from the 1950 code of Greece.[264] That 1960 draft was not adopted by the legislature, ultimately. Change was thought also by means of partial reforms, such as Law 17.567 of 1968, led by Soler, Carlos Fontán Balestra, and Eduardo Aguirre Obarrio.[265] Other examples of reform were the likewise important Law 20.509 of 1973[266] and Law 20.642 of 1974.[267] Changes took place, in a similar mode, during the de facto regimes.[268] During all these years the changes and alterations, in words of Francisco P. Laplaza, *exceed the imaginable*, inviting more to a compilation rather than to a codification of the law.[269] A draft was presented in 1974, and the drafting committee included, amongst others, Jesús E. Porto, Enrique R. Aftalión, Enrique Bacigalupo, and Ricardo Levene.[270] Even when it did not succeed, that draft showed that Argentina advocated during decades for a new code. It should be noted that most efforts had attended reform of the general part of the Second Argentine Criminal Code, hence being in line with, i.a., the work of Enrico Ferri in Italy or the later German reform of 1975.[271] However, Law 21.338 of 1976, during a de facto regime, introduced changes also in the special part of the Second Argentine Criminal Code, and likewise introduced changes by means of special legislation.[272] Finally, in 1979, a pre-project was presented by Soler, Cabral, and Aguirre Obarrio.[273] That work did not receive approval from the legislature, however.

The efforts for reform continued during recent decades. For example, Law 23.077 of 1984 reintroduced the previous wordings of a number of articles of the Second Argentine Criminal Code that had been reformed or abrogated during the de facto

258. *Ibid.*
259. Laplaza, *supra* n. 229, at 216.
260. On the ideas of Sebastián Soler, *see* José D. Cesano, *Sebastián Soler, La crítica al positivismo criminológico y el significado de su* Derecho Penal Argentino*: saberes jurídicos y contextos intelectuales. Una aproximación desde la historia de las ideas*, 20 Cuadernos de Historia 89 (2010).
261. Laplaza, *supra* n. 229, at 218–219.
262. *Ibid.* 219.
263. Their draft had neglected the most recent developments in German criminal law that had been presented in 1960 as the *Alternativ Entwurf*, since it was completed before the dissemination of the latter. Laplaza, *supra* n. 229, at 219.
264. *Ibid.* 220.
265. *Ibid.* 221.
266. *Ibid.* 222.
267. *Ibid.* 223.
268. *Ibid.* 224.
269. *Ibid.*
270. *Ibid.*
271. *Ibid.* 226.
272. *Ibid.*
273. *Ibid.* 227.

regimes.[274] Drafts were also projected, for example, in 1987, 1998, and 1999.[275] Efforts for reform were revamped during the twenty-first century, again. Accordingly, in 2004, a commission was appointed by the Ministry of Justice to elaborate an integral reform of the existing code.[276] That commission worked for two years, and gathered a number of leading scholars, i.a., David Baigún, Carlos Chiara Díaz, Daniel Erbetta, Raúl G. Ferreyra, and Edmundo S. Hendler,[277] yet their efforts did not prosper.[278] Another commission, established by the Executive in 2012,[279] and led by Eugenio R. Zaffaroni, with the participation of Federico Pinedo, Ricardo Gil Lavedra, María E. Barbagelata, and León C. Arslanián presented a pre-project of a criminal code.[280] That pre-project innovated, for example, by including environmental crimes.[281] That text was subject to heated debate and academic discussion, and aimed to solve the normative dispersion by encapsulating the provisions within 289 articles.[282] That effort also failed in being adopted. A very recent recodification effort was started in February 2017, when a commission was established by the Executive.[283] That effort is led by Mariano H. Borinsky, and benefits of the participation of, amongst others, Carlos M. González Guerra, Pablo N. Turano, Carlos A. Mahiques, Patricia M. Llerena, and Patricia S. Ziffer.[284] The task of this current commission will be to put forward a text that is able to overcome the effects and the needs that arose from the more than 1400 reforms that have affected the Second Argentine Criminal Code.[285] Similar to the path followed in civil a commercial law, the Argentine path in criminal law likewise reflects an almost uninterrupted streamline of codification efforts.

274. Ley 23.077 of 1984, at http://servicios.infoleg.gob.ar/infolegInternet/anexos/25000-29999/28066/norma.htm (accessed March 6, 2017).
275. *See* the references to the draft by Néstor Perl and Oscar Fappiano (1987), to the pre-project of 1998, and to the pre-project of 1999 in "Fundamentos del Anteproyecto de Reforma y Actualización Integral del Código Penal", in *Anteproyecto de Ley de Reforma y Actualización Integral del Código Penal de la Nación* 43, 43 (Ediar 2007).
276. Resolución 303 of 2004 of the Ministry of Justice and Human Rights, at http://servicios.infoleg.gob.ar/infolegInternet/anexos/100000-104999/102140/norma.htm (accessed March 6, 2017).
277. Daniel Erbetta, "Nota Introductoria", in *Anteproyecto de Ley de Reforma y Actualización Integral del Código Penal de la Nación* 21, 21 (Ediar 2007).
278. Decreto 103 of 2017, at http://servicios.infoleg.gob.ar/infolegInternet/anexos/270000-274999/271799/norma.htm (accessed March 6, 2017). *See also* Carlos A. Rodríguez, *Los delitos ambientales en el anteproyecto de Código Penal*, Revista Jurídica Argentina La Ley, July 22, 2014, 1, 2 (2014).
279. Decreto 678 of 2012, at http://servicios.infoleg.gob.ar/infolegInternet/anexos/195000-199999/196961/norma.htm (accessed March 6, 2017).
280. Rodríguez, *supra* n. 278, at 2. *See also* Daniel R. Pastor, *La recodificación penal en marcha Una iniciativa ideal para la racionalización legislativa*, Revista Pensar en Derecho 37 (2012).
281. Rodríguez, *supra* n. 278, at 2.
282. *See* for example *Publican oficialmente el texto del proyecto para reformar el Código Penal*, La Nación (April 24, 2014) at http://www.lanacion.com.ar/1684861-publican-oficialmente-el-texto-de-la-proyecto-para-reformar-el-codigo-penal (accessed March 6, 2017).
283. Decreto 103 of 2017, *supra* n. 278.
284. *Ibid.*
285. Resolución 303 of 2004, *supra* n. 276; Luigi Ferrajoli, "Presentación", in *Anteproyecto de Ley de Reforma y Actualización Integral del Código Penal de la Nación* 11, 12 (Ediar 2007); and *El nuevo Código Penal, o un contrato social moderno con delitos y penas coherentes*, La Nación (February 14, 2017) at http://www.lanacion.com.ar/1984477-nuevo-codigo-penal (accessed March 6, 2017).

4 CLOSING REMARKS

An approximation to sources of law and to legal history helps to fully understand a legal system and its potential needs for change. The scientific study of law becomes incomprehensible when lacking a historical perspective.[286] History is indeed one of the three pillars for the scientific study of law, the other two being the dogmatic study of current law and the philosophical study of what law ought to be (*de lege ferenda*).[287] History is intrinsic to law, and hence it is impossible to fully understand the law when neglecting history.[288] Neglecting history would result in a fragmentary and incomplete knowledge of law that attains only a superficial and external understanding.[289]

This chapter showed—by attending events that took place mainly since the second half of the nineteenth century—that the law in Argentina cannot be considered dormant. First, the chapter addressed the sources of law in Argentina. That first part helps understand the process of creation, formation, interpretation, and application of law. Second, the chapter offered a legal historical account of three main areas: constitutional law, civil and commercial law, and criminal law. The main actors and their main products were presented for each area, showing that the Argentine legal discourse advocated for changes in the law that would reflect the needs of the Argentine society. Changes considered local elaborations and took place almost uninterruptedly in the three areas during the period subject to study. Changes also welcomed doctrinal and normative elaborations that were gestated beyond Argentine borders. The result of that broad approach was enriching in Argentina, resulting in copious and leading doctrinal writings and resulting in a proliferation of law reform efforts, some still ongoing in this South American jurisdiction.

286. Víctor Tau Anzoátegui, *El Futuro de la Historia Jurídica en las Aulas* 86 (Advocatus 2010).
287. *Ibid.*
288. Levaggi, *supra* n. 1, at 4.
289. *Ibid.*

CHAPTER 2
Constitutional Law

Gisela A. Ferrari

The Argentine Constitution is one of the oldest constitutions still in force today. The original document, which blended American and European influences with local customs and institutions, has undergone several amendments since 1853.

Comprising 129 articles, plus a preamble and 17 temporary provisions, the Argentine Constitution is divided into two parts. The first one (Articles 1–43) consists of two chapters: "Declarations, Rights and Guarantees," which dates from 1853, and "New Rights and Guarantees," added by an amendment in 1994. This part is usually called the "dogmatic" part; it adopts the federal republican representative form of government (Article 1) and contains a bill of rights. The second one (Articles 44–129) is entitled "Authorities of the Nation." This part is commonly referred to as the "organic" part; it organizes and structures the Federal Government, which divides into three branches: the legislative, consisting of a bicameral Congress; the executive, consisting of the President; and the judicial, consisting of the Supreme Court and other federal courts. This part also regulates the relationship between the Provinces and the Federal Government.

The chapter will overview the key features of Argentine Constitutional Law. To this end, it will first briefly examine the Argentine constitutional history within the broader economic, social and political background; it will thus consider the sources of the original document, as well as the foreign influences and the evolution of the Argentine Constitution over time. Secondly, it will analyze the sources of Argentine Constitutional Law and the hierarchy of norms within the Argentine legal system. Thirdly, it will outline the main traits of the "organic" part: the structure and powers of the three branches of government and other institutions created by the Constitution. Finally, it will examine the "dogmatic" part: the fundamental rights and guarantees of the people of the Argentine Nation, and the major current judicial developments in this regard.

1 CONSTITUTIONAL HISTORY

1.1 From the Early Years after Independence to the Adoption of a Constitution

The years following independence in the nineteenth century were tumultuous for Spanish America: "[t]he wars of independence were longer and bloodier than the American Revolution, and civil wars between competing elites arrayed in liberal and conservative camps ensued following independence."[1] Argentina declared its independence from Spain in 1816; however, the country only adopted a constitution thirty five years later. Indeed, after two failed attempts to adopt a constitution in 1819 and 1826, order was first established by *caudillos*, men with military de facto power. The most powerful of them, Juan Manuel de Rosas, governed Argentina from 1829 to 1852, and strongly opposed the adoption of a constitution.

After his military defeat, on May 31, 1852 the member Provinces of the Argentine Confederation signed the San Nicolás Agreement, by which they agreed to call a Constitutional Convention. However, on September 11, the Province of Buenos Aires separated from the Confederation, and therefore did not participate in the Convention. The Argentine Constitution, approved on May 1, 1853, thus only ruled for the thirteen remaining Provinces.

The members of the Convention worked on the basis of three main sources: (a) the previous "failed" constitutions (of 1819 and 1826); (b) the work by Juan Bautista Alberdi, "Bases and starting points for the political organisation of the Argentine Republic;" (c) the Constitution of the United States.

In 1859, after the battle of Pavón and signing the Pact of San José de Flores, Buenos Aires was reincorporated to the Confederation. The Province suggested various reforms to the Constitution,[2] and a new Convention called in 1860 approved the suggested amendments, thus giving way to national reunification. Besides the 1860

1. Miguel Schor, "The Once and Future Democracy: Argentina at the Bar of Constitutionalism" Denis J. Galligan and Mila Versteeg (eds), *Social and Political Foundations of Constitutions* (Cambridge University Press 2013), 564.
2. The amendments ranged from terminological reforms (such as the replacement of the term "Confederation" with "Nation") to more substantial ones (such as the elimination of the requirement of approval by the Federal Congress for the entry into force of provincial constitutions).

amendment (which for some an exercise of original constituent power), reforms[3] to the constitution were made in 1866,[4] 1898,[5] 1949,[6] 1957,[7] 1972[8] and 1994.[9]

1.2 The American Influence

According to José Benjamín Gorostiaga, the most influential member of the 1853 Constitutional Convention, the Argentine constitution was "cast in the mold of the Constitution of the United States."[10] In effect, the fundamental principles of Argentine public law have their origin in the American constitutional system: Argentina has a republican, presidential and federal system, and a judiciary with the power to exercise judicial review in specific cases.

This characteristic does not differ much from the rest of the Latin American constitutions, which to a greater or lesser extent also copied the United States model. Nonetheless, the Argentine case is peculiar because the authority of American constitutional law and practice acquired, as Jonathan Miller argues, a "talismanic" proportion.[11]

The 1853–1860 constitution was the intellectual product of a generation of thinkers such as Juan Bautista Alberdi and Domingo Faustino Sarmiento, who were deeply convinced that the American model should be adopted to ensure political and economic development.[12] The Argentine Supreme Court, whose initial integration was

3. According to Art. 30 of the Argentine Constitution, which sets forth the amendment procedure, "[t]he Constitution may be totally or partially amended. The necessity of reform must be declared by Congress with the vote of at least two-thirds of the members; but it shall not be carried out except by an Assembly summoned to that effect". The Assembly, in practice, has been formed with representatives popularly elected to that effect.
4. In 1866, due to the marked increase in national expenditure generated by the Triple Alliance War, the Constitution was amended in order to ensure that import and export taxes were exclusively owned by the Federal Government.
5. This amendment changed the manner of election of the deputies, increased the number of ministers of the Executive and left the determination of their areas of specialty to the law.
6. Promoted by the government of Juan Domingo Perón, this amendment incorporated notions of state responsibility for the economic and social welfare of its citizens, recognised the legal equality of men and women, incorporated children's rights, and allowed for indefinite reelection of the president, among other reforms. It was in force until its suppression by the "Liberating Revolution" in 1956.
7. Due to internal conflicts, the Constitutional Convention disintegrated before concluding its work, and only managed to incorporate Art. 14*bis* to the Constitution, which protected labor and social security rights.
8. The reform of 1972 was transitory. It was enacted by a de facto power, which dictated a so-called Fundamental Statute that exhausted its maximum period of application without being ratified by a Constitutional Convention.
9. *See infra*, "1.3 The Twentieth Century and the 1994 Amendment".
10. Carlos F. Rosenkrantz, "Against Borrowings and Other Nonauthoritative Uses of Foreign Law" (2003) 1 [2] International Journal of Constitutional Law 270.
11. Jonathan Miller, "The Authority of a Foreign Talisman: A Study of U.S. Constitutional Practice as Authority in the Nineteenth Century Argentina and the Argentine Elite's Leap of Faith" (1997) 46 The American University Law Review 1483.
12. Alberdi, however, was not in favor of blindly following U.S. doctrine and practice, and called for original constitutional politics. *See*, e.g., Juan Bautista Alberdi, *Bases y puntos de partida para la organización política de la República Argentina* (La Cultura Argentina 1915) XVIII.

almost entirely constituted by former Constitutional Convention members,[13] adopted the imitative trend. During the first period of its history (1863–1903), the Court led by Gorostiaga based its decisions in the jurisprudence of American courts when the object of debate was the scope of constitutional provisions that had been taken from the text of the U.S. Constitution. The Court considered at this stage that American case law was binding.[14]

A constitutional model strongly influenced by the U.S. was thus implemented. Some scholars, such as Miller, find in the Argentine strategy the key to its economic success during the late nineteenth century and beginning of the twentieth century.[15] However, the view that U.S. jurisprudence was binding started diluting gradually from the early twentieth century. Nevertheless, U.S. constitutional standards remained relevant for Argentine judges.[16] Along the Argentine Supreme Court case law there are also countless references to decisions by the German Constitutional Court, the Spanish Constitutional Court, the United Kingdom House of Lords, the Supreme Court of Canada, the Constitutional Court of Italy, the French *Cour de cassation*, and more recently, the Inter-American Court of Human Rights and the European Court of Human Rights.

1.3 The Twentieth Century and the 1994 Amendment

The twentieth century saw Argentina failing to consolidate a democratic government and to sustain its economic success, as well as suffering from several *coups d'état* followed by military dictatorships: "[F]rom 1930 to 1983, Argentina was highly unstable due to a series of military coups. Successive governments drastically repressed political opponents and ignored legal limits on executive power. A fascist military junta eventually purged over 30,000 'subversives' between 1975 and 1981 ... [A]fter military rule ended in 1983, the return of democracy heralded the heyday of constitutionalism and the rule of law in Argentina. A consensus condemned the abuses of past authoritarian regimes and led moderate president Raul Alfonsín, other politicians, and the general public to focus on the importance of basic democratic principles and human rights."[17]

Other Argentine scholars have upheld the originality of the Argentine Constitution against the accusations of it being a mere copy of the U.S. document. *See* Martín Böhmer, "Borrowings and Acquisitions: The Use of Foreign Law as a Strategy to Build Constitutional Democratic Authority" (2007) *Seminario en Latinoamérica de Teoría Constitucional y Política (SELA)* 1.

13. Four out of five members had taken part in the adoption of the 1853–1860 constitution: Francisco de las Carreras, Salvador María del Carril, José Barros Pazos and José Benjamín Gorostiaga.
14. Julio C. Rivera (h), "El uso del derecho comparado en la interpretación constitucional" in Julio C. Rivera (h) et al (ed), *Tratado de los Derechos Constitucionales* (Abeledo Perrot 2014) 201–202.
15. Miller (n 11) 1485–1486.
16. Rivera (n 14) 203.
17. Mugambi Jouet, "The Failed Invigoration of Argentina's Constitution: Presidential Omnipotence, Repression, Instability, and Lawlessness in Argentine History" (2008) 39 [3] The University of Miami Inter-American Law Review 410–411.

A need to modernize the Constitution after various failed attempts to call for a Constitutional Convention, as well as the massive human rights violations committed by the military juntas that governed the country during the 1970s and early 1980s, led the country to amend its Constitution in 1994. The reform of 1994 was the most important modification ever made to the constitutional text. The changes were so substantial that many wondered whether it was an amended constitution or a new one, a point that the text approved in 1994 did not clarify.

As far as the bill of rights is concerned, a second chapter, entitled "New Rights and Guarantees," was added to the first part. This new chapter comprises the recognition of several political rights (the right to resist the oppression from de facto governments, real equality of opportunities for men and women in candidacies for elective office and political parties, the right to form political parties, the right of popular initiative in legislative matters, popular consultation, *inter alia*) (Articles 36–40), environmental and consumer protection rights (Articles 41 and 42), and constitutional guarantees (the writ of amparo, of habeas corpus and of habeas data) (Article 43). Other rights were acknowledged in the second part, such as the right to equal opportunities and treatment (especially for children, women, the elderly and the handicapped) (Article 75.23) and indigenous peoples' rights (Article 75.17).

Regarding the organization and division of powers, the section dealing with the legislative branch was added two chapters, one dedicated to the "Office of the Auditor General of the Nation" (Chapter VI, Article 85) and other to the "Defender of the People" (Chapter VII, Article 86). Another new section addresses the "Office of the Public Prosecutor" (Article 120), an autonomous organ. The structure of the three branches of the State was likewise amended: among other changes, within the executive, the manner of election and the duration of the term of the President and Vice President were modified, and the Chief of the Cabinet of Ministers was created; within the legislative, the period of ordinary sessions was extended, and a third senator for each Province was introduced; within the judiciary, the Judicial Council and a trial jury for the removal of federal judges were created. Lastly, the governmental autonomy of the City of Buenos Aires was acknowledged; the City was thus granted powers of legislation and jurisdiction (Article 129).

One of the most important and controversial changes has been the status of treaties within the Argentine legal system. The Constitution now accords constitutional hierarchy, under certain conditions, to certain human rights conventions[18] (Article 75.22). Thus, the 1994 constitutional amendment has had a strong impact in the field of human rights in Argentina.

2 SOURCES OF ARGENTINE CONSTITUTIONAL LAW

The first and most important source is, of course, the written constitution from 1853–1860, as reformed by the amendments made in 1866, 1898, 1957 and 1994.

18. *See infra*, "2. Sources."

The Constitution consists of a preamble,[19] 129 articles divided into two parts, and 17 temporary provisions. Although, as stated above, the first part primarily deals with constitutional rights, obligations and guarantees, and the second with the organization and structure of government, the 1994 reform added rules to the second part that incorporated a series of values, principles and rights that obligatorily refer back to the first part.[20] Moreover, the first part contains some provisions regarding, among others, the form of government and the relationship between the Federal Government and the Provinces.[21]

Besides the Constitution, other sources of Constitutional Law in Argentina are:[22]

(a) Laws passed by the Federal Congress that regulate constitutional matters, such as the Acephaly Act No. 20.972 (which determines who holds the Presidency of the Nation in case of absence of both the President and the Vice President), the Ministries Act No. 22.520 and the Political Parties Act No. 23.298. The 1994 reforms required the Congress to dictate several laws in order to complement, determine and regulate a large number of the new constitutional rules.

(b) Some international treaties, such as human rights treaties, treaties of integration into supranational organizations, and the Vienna Convention on the Law of Treaties. The constitutional reform of 1994 has introduced a major change in this area, as now the Constitution directly confers constitutional hierarchy to eleven international human rights instruments[23] and provides for a special procedure through which other human rights treaties can acquire that same hierarchy.[24] Therefore, since 1994, the Argentine constitutional rights system has a double source: a domestic source and an international source.

19. The preamble condenses the fundamental political decisions, the aims, the objectives, the values and the principles advocated by the constituents in 1853. The preamble provides a valuable element of interpretation; the Argentine Supreme Court has stated that some of its clauses (for instance, "guarantee justice") are operative, and has given them direct application in its sentences.
20. *See*, e.g., Art. 75.19, which contains principles on human development, economic progress, social justice, education, and the protection of the cultural identity and plurality; Art. 75.23, true equality of opportunity and treatment.
21. *See*, e.g., Arts. 1–6.
22. Germán J. Bidart Campos, *Manual de la Constitución Reformada* (Ediar 1998) ch 1 n 22.
23. The American Declaration of the Rights and Duties of Man; the Universal Declaration of Human Rights; the American Convention on Human Rights; the International Covenant on Economic, Social and Cultural Rights; the International Covenant on Civil and Political Rights and its Optional Protocol; the Convention on the Prevention and Punishment of Genocide; the International Convention on the Elimination of all Forms of Racial Discrimination; the Convention on the Elimination of all Forms of Discrimination against Woman; the Convention against Torture and other Cruel, Inhuman or Degrading Treatments or Punishments; the Convention on the Rights of the Child.
24. According to Art. 75.22, "[o]ther treaties and conventions on human rights, after being approved by Congress, shall require the vote of two-thirds of the totality of the members of each Chamber in order to enjoy standing on the same level as the Constitution." Through this procedure, the Inter-American Convention on Forced Disappearance of Persons and the Convention on the

3 HIERARCHY OF NORMS WITHIN THE ARGENTINE LEGAL SYSTEM

The hierarchy of norms was modified with the 1994 amendment. This change is reflected in two subsections of Article 75 (22 and 24), and has three implications:

(1) The general principle now is that treaties prevail over laws: "Treaties and concordats have higher standing than laws" (Article 75.22, paragraph 1). This new principle contrasted with the case law of the Supreme Court in force until 1992, which did not recognize the supralegal status of treaties.
(2) The same principle applies for "treaties of integration which delegate competence and jurisdiction to international organizations" and "[a]ny rules enacted pursuant thereto" (i.e., the community law emanating from the organs of the supranational organization) (Article 75.24). The approval and denouncement regime of this kind of treaties varies according to the Member States of the treaty: the required Congress majorities are decreased in the case of treaties signed with other Latin American states.
(3) Lastly, by virtue of Article 75.22, paragraphs 2 and 3, there are international human rights treaties that have constitutional hierarchy. Such treaties do not form part of the text of the Constitution, but have the same rank and share the supremacy of the Constitution.

A provision of Article 75.22 which has proven to be controversial is the following: after listing the human rights treaties that have constitutional hierarchy, the text goes on to state that "under the conditions under which they are in force, stand on the same level as the Constitution, *[but] do not repeal any article in the First Part of this Constitution, and must be understood as complementary of the rights and guarantees recognized therein.*" Some authors construe this provision to mean that the first part of the Constitution has priority over treaties with constitutional hierarchy, whereas the second part of the Constitution would be placed under such treaties. Other authors, on the contrary, consider that the whole text of the Constitution has the same standing, which is shared with the treaties with constitutional hierarchy.[25] If one were to accept this last thesis, then the Argentine legal pyramid would be composed as follows:

(a) the Constitution and international treaties with constitutional hierarchy (Article 75.22, paragraphs 2 and 3). Some authors consider that the interpretation made of Constitution by the Supreme Court in its judgments has the same standing as the Constitution;[26]

Non-Applicability of Statutory Limitations to War Crimes and Crimes against Humanity attained constitutional hierarchy in 1997 and in 2003, respectively.

25. For a thorough discussion of these two viewpoints, as well as constitutional supremacy in Argentina after the 1994 amendment, and the relationship between domestic Argentine law and international law in general, *see* Germán Bidart Campos (n 22) ch 5 n 19–25.
26. *See*, e.g., Bidart Campos (n 22).

(b) international treaties without constitutional rank (Article 75.22, paragraph 1), integration treaties and the community law derived therefrom (Article 75.24);
(c) laws enacted by the Federal Congress;
(d) all other norms enacted by the Federal Government (executive decrees, and all other norms and regulations);
(e) all norms enacted by provincial governments (Articles 5 and 31) (in hierarchical order: provincial constitutions, laws enacted by provincial legislatures, provincial executive decrees, and all other provincial norms and regulations).

The adequacy of norms of lower rank to norms of higher rank is monitored mainly by the judiciary through judicial review.

4 STRUCTURE, POWERS AND ORGANIZATION OF GOVERNMENT

This section will analyze the structure, powers and organization of government in Argentina. First, it will look into the federalist system of government, and thus it will examine: the key features of the Federal Government and the Provinces; the constitutional distribution of powers between these two levels of government; the main characteristics of municipalities; the status of the City of Buenos Aires; the supremacy of federal law over provincial law; and finally, it will overview how federalism works in practice. Second, it will survey the structure and organization of the Federal Government: the composition and powers of the executive, legislative and judicial branch, as well as of the Public Ministry. Lastly, it will consider two specific problems: the exercise of legislative powers by the executive, and the use of constitutional emergency powers.

The content of two constitutional provisions ought to be mentioned as part of the introduction to this section. One of them is Article 36, added by the 1994 amendment and dealing with the protection of the legal transmission of power and the defense of the Constitution. Indeed, it states that "[t]his Constitution shall remain in force even if its observance is interrupted by acts of force against the institutional order and the democratic system. Such acts shall be irrevocably void." Additionally, it establishes the punishment for the authors and for those who, as a consequence of those acts, usurp the functions reserved to the authorities of this Constitution or those of the Provinces. Finally, it adds that "[a]ll citizens have the right of resistance against those who execute the forcible acts stated in this article."

The second provision that should be mentioned at this stage is Article 29, which forbids the Congress from vesting on the Federal Executive Power extraordinary powers or total public authority and from granting "acts of submission or supremacy whereby the lives, the honor or the property of Argentines will be at the mercy of governments or any person whatsoever." The provision declares acts of this nature "utterly void," and sets out the punishment for those "who formulate, consent to or sign them." The provision lays down the same prohibition for provincial legislatures with regard to provincial governors.

4.1 Federalism

Article 1 proclaims that "[t]he Argentine Nation adopts the federal, republican, representative form for its government."

The Federal Government is divided into three branches: the legislative, consisting of a bicameral Congress; the executive, consisting of the President; and the judicial, consisting of the Supreme Court and other federal courts.

According to Article 3, "[t]he authorities that direct the Federal Government reside in the city which is to be declared the Capital of the Republic by a special law of Congress." The Capital of the Republic is the City of Buenos Aires.

The Member States of the federal state are known in Argentina throughout its constitutional history as "Provinces." The Provinces are not sovereign (Articles 5 and 31), but they are autonomous (Articles 5, 122 and 123).

The Constitution only sets out the organization and structure of the Federal Government. Provincial governments are organized by provincial constitutions, which must be in accordance with the prescriptions of federal law;[27] for instance, they must respect the distribution of powers between the federal and provincial governments made by the Constitution. Additionally, the Constitution contains some guidelines for the provincial organization of government:

(a) The structure of provincial governments must be consistent with that of the Federal Government, as prescribed in Article 5: "Each Province shall adopt for itself a constitution under the republican, representative system, in accordance with the principles, declarations, and guarantees of the National Constitution." The division of the structure of the Federal Government in three branches is thus reproduced in essence in provincial governments.

(b) Each Province must ensure its own administration of justice, municipal government, and elementary education (Article 5). As far as the municipal government is concerned, according to Article 123, provincial constitutions shall assure municipal autonomy.

The principles for the distribution of powers are mainly contained in Articles 121–128. The first of the aforementioned states that "[t]he Provinces retain all powers not delegated by this Constitution to the Federal Government, and those they have expressly reserved by special covenants at the time of their incorporation [into the Argentine Republic]."

In order to outline the distribution of powers, a distinction is usually made between:

---

27. *See*, e.g., Art. 31 (*see infra* "4.2 Supremacy of Federal Law over Provincial Law").

(a) *Exclusive powers of the Federal Government*: It conducts international relations (Articles 27, 75.22, 75.24, 99.11[28]); enacts *derecho común*[29] or substantive law (legislation on civil, commercial, criminal, labor, social security, and other matters) and other federal or special laws (laws of naturalisation and nationality, laws on bankruptcy, counterfeiting of currency and public documents of the State, etc.) (Article 75.12); declares a "federal intervention" (Article 6[30]); declares a state of siege (Article 23); *inter alia*. In general, and as a principle, almost all of the powers assigned to the Federal Government by the Constitution can be considered exclusive. Articles 126 and 127 list several powers which are forbidden to the Provinces.[31]

(b) *Exclusive powers of the Provinces*: They enact their local constitution; elect their governors, legislators, and other provincial officers; establish direct taxes; dictate their procedural laws; set out their municipal regime and their primary education, etc. These competences are derived from the reservation contained in Article 121, and from the autonomy established by Articles 122, 123 and 124.

(c) *Concurrent powers*: Both the Federal Government and the Provinces can establish indirect internal taxes (Article 75.2); exercise the powers arising from Articles 75.18 and 125, plus those arising from Articles 75.17 and 41.

(d) *Powers that can be exceptionally exercised by the Federal Government or by the Provinces*: There are exclusive powers of the Provinces that can be exceptionally exercised by the Federal Government. That is the case of the establishment of "direct taxes proportionately equal throughout the territory of the Nation, for a specified period of time, provided that the defense, common security and general welfare of the State require them" (Article 75.2). There also exclusive powers of the Federal Government that can exceptionally be exercised by the Provinces. That is the case of enacting Civil, Commercial, Criminal, or Mining Codes before the Federal Congress

28. It must be noticed, however, that Provinces may sign treaties under specific circumstances, pursuant to Art. 124: "With the knowledge of the National Congress, the Provinces (...) may enter international agreements as long as these are not incompatible with the foreign policy of the Nation and do not affect the powers delegated to the Federal Government or the public credit of the Nation."
29. The literal translation of this term is "common law"; however, in Argentine civil law jurisdiction, this term does not refer to the judge-made law of common law jurisdictions, but to statutory law on civil, commercial, criminal, and other matters.
30. According to Art. 6, "[t]he Federal Government may intervene in the territory of a Province in order to guarantee the republican form of government or to repel foreign invasions, and, at the request of the Province's appointed authorities, to support or reestablish them should they have been deposed by sedition or invasion from another Province." *See also* Arts. 75.31 and 99.20.
31. These include enacting laws dealing with commerce, or internal or foreign navigation; establishing provincial customhouses; coining money; establishing banks having note-issuing powers without the authorization of the Federal Congress; enacting Civil, Commercial, Penal, or Mining Codes after the Congress has enacted them; enacting special laws on citizenship and naturalization, bankruptcy, or counterfeiting of currency or State documents; imposing tonnage duties; arming ships of war or raise armies (except in the event of foreign invasion or of such imminent danger as not to admit delay, giving immediate notice to the Federal Government); appointing or receiving foreign representatives; declaring or waging war against another Province.

has done so, and arming ships of war or raise armies in the event of foreign invasion or of such imminent danger as not to admit delay, giving immediate notice to the Federal Government (Article 126).

(e) *Powers shared by the Federal Government and the Provinces*: These powers should not be confused with the "concurrent" ones. The shared powers need to be exercised *jointly* by the Federal Government and the Provinces (one or more than one Province). For example, the establishment of the Capital of the Republic (Article 3), the creation of new Provinces (Article 13), etc.

Although the text of the Constitution refers to "municipal government" in Article 5, and some authors have long regarded this expression as an indication of municipal autonomy, the Supreme Court held until 1989 that municipalities were simply entities with administrative decentralization, which gave them the status of "autarkic" but not "autonomous."

The 1994 amendment recognized municipal autonomy: Article 123 establishes that "[e]ach Province dictates its own Constitution, in conformity with what is established in Article 5, assuring municipal autonomy and regulating its scope and content in the institutional, political, administrative, economic, and financial structure." A minimum dose of autonomy is thus required by the Constitution in these five areas. Consequently, municipalities now integrate the federal structure, along with the Federal Government and the Provinces. However, municipalities are not a part of the "federal relationship" between the Federal government and the Provinces, since municipal powers are included within the area of each Province's powers.

The 1994 reform also recognized the autonomy of the City of Buenos Aires in Article 129. Indeed, according to this Article, the City "shall have an autonomous system of government, with its own legislative and jurisdictional powers, and a head of government who shall be elected directly by the people of the City. A law shall guarantee the interests of the National Government while the City of Buenos Aires is the capital of the Nation." The same provision envisages the enactment of an "organizational statute of the City's institutions."[32]

What is the status of the City of Buenos Aires since 1994, then? Is it a Province, a municipality, or a sui generis political unit? While these questions remain controversial, Article 129 has a clear axis: the City shall have an autonomous government regime with its own powers of legislation and jurisdiction. Therefore, it can be argued that since 1994 the two-pillar federal structure (Federal Government-Provinces, and arguably a third within the latter: municipalities) now incorporates a sui generis entity, the City of Buenos Aires. Although the City does not reach the status of Province, the system laid down by Article 129 allows for locating it somewhere between a Province and a municipality.

32. Despite this designation, the City called a constitutional convention, which adopted the "Constitution of the City of Buenos Aires" in October 1, 1996, raising more doubts about the City's status.

4.2 Supremacy of Federal Law over Provincial Law

Federal law broadly refers to the law that emanates from the Federal Government. In this sense, it comprises:

(a) *Federal law as a set of rules enacted by the organs of the Federal Government.* Article 31 refers especially to these rules when it states that the federal legal order prevails over the provincial order: "This Constitution, the laws of the Nation that as a result thereof may be enacted by the Congress, and treaties with foreign powers, are the supreme law of the Nation, and the authorities of every Province are bound to conform to it, notwithstanding any provision to the contrary which the Provincial laws or constitutions may contain." After the 1994 amendment, this Article has to be integrated with the provision contained in Article 75.22 on the constitutional hierarchy of several treaties.[33]

A very important distinction must be made within this broad concept of federal law: the so-called *derecho común* or substantive law (legislation on civil, commercial, criminal, labor, social security, and other matters), which differs from "strictly federal" laws. One the one hand, substantive law is federal because it is enacted by the Federal Government (and in this sense it prevails over provincial laws, according to Article 31), but on the other hand it is not, since it is applied and interpreted by provincial courts and does not count as "federal law" for the purposes of the federal extraordinary appeal.[34]

(b) *Federal law as "intrafederal law,"* which encompasses the relations of the Provinces with the Federal Government as well as interprovincial relations: "legal covenants" (agreements between the Federal Government and the Provinces), interprovincial treaties, etc.

In Argentine politics and constitutional practice, multiple factors suggest a rather weak federalism. Bidart Campos points out the following: central economic policies; a tax regime largely concentrated in the Federal Government; subsidies and contributions to the Provinces with funds from the "national treasure;" federal centralization of services that are susceptible of territorial division; the practice of federal interventions; the imposition by the Federal Government of an electoral system for the appointment of provincial authorities and the annulment by the Federal Government of provincial elections; the dispossession of portions of territory and natural resources of the Provinces by the Federal Government; among many others.[35]

The 1994 amendment has introduced several modifications in this regard. Some authors argue that these reforms have strengthened federalism, while others consider that it has been somewhat debilitated. The latter base their thesis, for example, on the now direct election of the President and Vice President, which unbalances the vote

33. *See supra*, "2.2 Hierarchy of Norms Within the Argentine Legal System."
34. *See infra*, "6.4 Kinds of Laws Passed by the Federal Congress."
35. Bidart Campos (n 22) ch VII n 62–63.

power and favors a few Provinces and the City of Buenos Aires with respect to the rest of the districts; they thus claim that the electoral college protected the interests of the less populated Provinces better than the new system. The former, for their part, hold that the new text positively contributes to federalism or, at least, provides an opportunity to invigorate it. In favor of this position, the following provisions can be cited:

(a) Certain bills related to federalism must now be discussed and voted on first at the Senate (Article 75.2 and 75.19).
(b) The old "progress clause" has been updated and it currently states that the Federal Congress must "provide for the harmonious growth of the Nation and for populating its territory" and "promote differentiated policies that lead to balancing the irregular development of Provinces and regions" (Article 75.19).
(c) Regarding the distribution of resources, Article 75.2 provides that "[a] legal covenant, based on agreements between the Nation and the Provinces, shall institute regulations for co-participation in these taxes, guaranteeing the automatic remittal of the funds. The distribution between and among the Nation, the Provinces and the City of Buenos Aires, shall be effectuated in direct relation to the competencies, services and functions of each one of them, observing objective criteria for distribution; said distribution shall be equitable, show solidarity, and shall give priority to achieving an equivalent level of development, quality of life and equality of opportunity throughout the entire National territory."
(d) With respect to education, attention must now be paid to provincial and local particularities: thus, the Federal Congress must "pass laws on the organization of and basis for education which consolidate National unity, paying respect to Provincial and local particularities" (Article 75.19).
(e) The Constitution now explicitly recognizes that "[t]he original ownership over natural resources existing in their territory belongs to the Provinces" (Article 124).
(f) Provinces are also empowered to "create regions for economic and social development and establish bodies with power to achieve their goals" and to "enter international agreements as long as these are not incompatible with the foreign policy of the Nation and do not affect the powers delegated to the Federal Government or the public credit of the Nation" (Article 124), etc.

5 STRUCTURE AND ORGANIZATION OF THE FEDERAL GOVERNMENT

The 1994 constitutional reform modified substantially the structure of the Federal Government when compared with the one of the 1853–1860 Constitution. These changes with be dealt with later when analyzing the various governmental organs.

As stated above, the Federal Government is divided into three branches: the legislative branch, consisting of a bicameral Congress; the executive branch, consisting of the President, plus the Vice President (who is, simultaneously, President of the Senate), the Chief of the Cabinet of Ministers and the Ministers; and the judicial branch, consisting of the Supreme Court and other federal courts, plus the Judicial Council and the trial jury for the removal of lower federal court judges. Other bodies created by the 1994 amendment are the Office of the Auditor General of the Nation, the Defender of the People, and the Office of the Public Prosecutor. The latter, a kind of "fourth power" according to certain scholarship, will be dealt with after examining the three classic branches of government; the rest will be considered when analyzing the legislative branch, as the provisions that create them were written in the chapter dedicated to the Federal Congress.

6 LEGISLATIVE BRANCH

The second part of the Constitution, entitled "Authorities of the Nation" begins with the dispositions that set out the structure, composition and powers of the Federal Congress.

The Federal Congress is bicameral because the state is federal: taking the Constitution of the United States as a model, Argentine constituents adopted the theory that the House of Deputies represents the "people," whereas the Senate represents the Member States or Provinces.

6.1 House of Deputies

According to Article 45, the Chamber of Deputies is composed of representatives elected directly, by a simple majority of votes, by the people of the Provinces and of the City of Buenos Aires, which for this purpose are considered for as individual states making up their own electoral districts. The mentioned Article fixes the number of representatives at one for every 33,000 inhabitants or fraction thereof that is not smaller than 16,500. The Congress may establish the number of Deputies in accordance with a census that can only be renewed every ten years, being empowered to increase but not to decrease the base indicated for each Deputy.

In order to become a Deputy, it is necessary to be at least 25 years old, have four years of holding citizenship, and be a native of the Province that elects him or been in residence in the Province during the previous two years (Article 48).

The Deputies hold office for a term of four years, and may be reelected (Article 50). However, the House must be renewed by halves every two years (for which purpose, those appointed for the first legislature had to draw lots to determine, after they met, those that would have to leave in the first period; the first draw took place on July 13, 1855, and several have taken place since) (Article 50).

Although the lawmaking process is not a separate or exclusive power of each Chamber but of the Congress as a whole, there are "exclusive powers" of the Chamber of Deputies: bills on raising revenue and on recruitment of troops must be debated and voted on first at this Chamber (Article 52); bills proposed by the electoral body in exercise of the right of popular initiative must be submitted to this Chamber (Article 39); and lastly, the initiative to submit a bill to a popular referendum must come from this Chamber as well (Article 49).

6.2 Senate

The Senate is composed of three Senators from each Province, and three from the City of Buenos Aires: "Two seats [correspond] to the political party obtaining the greatest number of votes, and the remaining one to the political party receiving the next largest number of votes" (Article 54). Although the three Senators represent the same entity, their representation is not unified: each Senator has one vote.

Since 1994, the Senators are no longer elected by provincial legislatures (as directed by former Article 46), but by the electoral body; the election now is direct (Article 54).

In order to be elected Senator, the candidate must be at least thirty years old, have been a citizen for a minimum of six years, enjoy an annual income of two thousand "strong pesos" or its equivalent,[36] and to be a native of the Province that elects him or been in residence in the Province during the previous two years (Article 55).

Senators hold office for a term of six years, and may be reelected *indefinitely*; however, the Senate must renew itself by one-third of the electoral districts every two years (Article 56).

The Vice President is the President of the Senate, but he or she has no vote, except in the case of a tie in the voting (Article 57).

The Senate also has "exclusive powers." Indeed, the bill for the federal tax co-participation legal covenant must be first debated and voted on in the Senate (Article 75.2); the same applies to bills that aim to provide for the harmonious growth of the Nation, the promotion of differentiated policies that lead to balancing the irregular development of Provinces and regions, etc. (Article 75.19). Moreover, in case of foreign invasion, the Senate authorizes the President to declare in state of siege one or several places of the Republic (Article 61). Finally, the Senate consents the following appointments made by the President: judges of the Supreme Court (Article 99.4); superior officers of the Armed Forces (Article 99.13); of ambassadors, ministers plenipotentiary and charge d'affaires (Article 99.7, in this case the Senate's consent is also required for their removal).

6.3 Powers of Congress

Most of the powers of Congress are laid out by Article 75. According to this provision, among other faculties, the Congress is empowered:

36. Some authors argue that this requirement had its origin in the old belief that only those who enjoyed a high income could access the education and the training necessary to be a suitable candidate for the Senate. In any case, nowadays it can be argued that this condition no longer equates suitability, and it is therefore no longer enforceable.

(a) to "legislate in customs matters," and "establish import and export duties" (Article 75.1);
(b) to "impose indirect taxes,"[37] and to "impose direct taxes proportionately equal throughout the territory of the Nation, for a specified period of time;" as these taxes are subject to co-participation (except for those which have a total or partial specific allocation), the Congress is empowered to institute regulations for co-participation in these taxes through a legal covenant based on agreements between the Federal Government and the Provinces (Article 75.2);
(c) to "grant subsidies from the National Treasury to those Provinces whose revenues, according to their budgets, are insufficient to meet their ordinary expenses" (Article 75.9);
(d) to fix annually "the general budget of expenditures and the calculation of resources of the National administration," and to "approve or reject the spending account" (Article 75.8);[38]
(e) to regulate exterior and interprovincial trade and commerce (Article 75.13);
(f) to "establish and regulate a Federal bank with the power to issue money, as well as other National banks" (Article 75.6); to "coin money, to regulate its value and that of foreign currency" (Article 75.11); and to "borrow money on the credit of the Nation" (Article 75.4);
(g) to "approve or reject treaties entered with other nations and with international organizations, and concordats with the Holy See" (Article 75.22); to grant constitutional hierarchy to approved treaties (Article 75.22); to "approve treaties of integration which delegate competence and jurisdiction to international organizations" (Article 75.24);
(h) to establish federal courts inferior to the Supreme Court (Article 75.20, also 108);[39]
(i) to "declare a state of siege in one or several parts of the Nation in case of internal disturbance" (Article 75.29) and to order the federal intervention of a Province or of the City of Buenos Aires (Article 75.31); to approve, revoke or suspend the intervention or the state of siege decreed by the President during a recess of Congress (Article 75.29 and 75.31);
(j) to legislate on diverse matters related to equality, growth, development, technology and education (Articles 75.17, 75.18, 75.19, 75.23, *inter alia*);

37. This is a power also held by Provinces, and therefore one of the "concurrent powers" described in "4.1 Federalism."
38. The 1994 amendment institutionalized the constitutional practice which consisted of the Executive sending the general budget bill to Congress; accordingly, Art. 100.6 states that the Chief of Cabinet must submit it to Congress with the prior consent of the Cabinet and the approval of the President.
39. This power implies establishing the organs of administration of justice and their jurisdiction, as well as enacting the rules of procedure.

(k) to regulate the exercise of personal rights contained in the Constitution (Article 14[40]);

(l) finally, "enact all laws and regulations that may be necessary to carry out the foregoing powers, and all others granted by the present Constitution to the Government of the Argentine Nation" (Article 75.32)—this clause is known as the "implicit powers" clause.

6.4 Kinds of Laws Passed by the Federal Congress

Among the laws passed by the Federal Congress, Argentine constitutional law distinguishes different categories, whose designation has been mostly coined in practice by doctrine and jurisprudence. These denominations are used for the sake of convenience, although sometimes they are not technically or scientifically justified. The Congress passes three kinds of laws: (a) federal laws; (b) *derecho común* or substantive laws; (c) local laws. However, the terminology used to refer to these types of laws is varied and intricate. For example, some authors refer to these three kinds of as "national" laws; federal laws are occasionally referred to as "special" laws of the Congress, and as "general" laws by Article 75.12; finally, substantive laws are usually called "ordinary" laws.

Federal and substantive laws are applied throughout the territory of the Republic, whereas local laws are only intended to be applied in the capital and in federal territories (at present there are no longer fully federalized territories). The following are the main characteristics of each type:

(a) *Federal laws*: This kind of law is quite difficult to conceptualize. A law can be federal because of its subject matter (e.g., legislation on citizenship, political parties, national elections), because of the persons to which it is directed (e.g., ambassadors, plenipotentiary ministers), and exceptionally because of the place where it is intended to be applied (e.g., borders). As a principle, federal laws contain rules of institutional or public law; however, the possibility of federal laws on private law cannot be excluded. An exemplary enumeration might clarify the panorama. The following have been considered federal laws by the Supreme Court: laws on the organization of federal courts, intellectual property, expropriation, citizenship, immigration, postal service, provincial boundaries, national railways, customs, organization of national ports, lawsuits against the Federal Government, counterfeit currency, national elections, income tax, amnesty, etc.

Federal laws are enforced throughout the country by federal courts.

40. In this sense was construed the following provision contained in Art. 14: "All the inhabitants of the Nation are entitled to the following rights, in accordance with the laws that regulate their exercise... ."

(b) *Derecho común or substantive laws*: These laws comprise legislation on civil, commercial, criminal, labor, social security, and other matters, and are governed by Article 75.12.

According to this provision, substantive laws are enforced, in principle, by provincial courts, and exceptionally by federal courts. In order to make such enforcement possible, each provincial legislature must dictate procedural codes; in Argentina, therefore, while substantive laws are homogenous throughout the state, procedural laws differ from Province to Province.

(c) *Local laws*: Before the 1994 amendment, since the capital had no power of legislation, the Federal Congress enacted so-called local laws that were applied in the City of Buenos Aires. After the reforms, the City continues being the federal capital, but the Constitution has granted it an autonomous system of government, with its own legislative and jurisdictional powers (Article 129). Therefore, the legislation that may now dictate the Federal Congress for the City is restricted to what is reasonably necessary in order to guarantee the interests of the Federal Government.

6.5 Lawmaking Process

Article 63 sets out the length of legislative sessions: "[b]oth Chambers shall assemble by themselves in regular sessions every year from March 1 to November 30." This Article also provides for extraordinary legislative sessions, convened by the President of the Nation, or by initiative of the Congress itself.

The quorum for legislative sessions is the absolute majority of the members of each Chamber; however, "a lesser number may compel the absent members to attend the sessions, under such terms and penalties as each Chamber shall establish" (Article 64).

Bills on certain matters need a special quorum to be approved. For example, bills that modify the electoral system and the system of political parties need to be approved by an absolute majority of the totality of the members of the Chambers (Article 77), whereas treaties and conventions on human rights require, after being approved by Congress, the vote of two-thirds of the totality of the members of each Chamber in order to enjoy standing on the same level as the Constitution (Article 75.22).

The lawmaking process in Argentina (Articles 77–84) consists of three stages:

(1) *The initiative stage*: Bills can be introduced by either Chamber of Congress or by the Executive (Article 77); after the 1994 reform, citizens have the right of initiative in presenting bills in the Chamber of Deputies (Article 39).

(2) *The debate and voting stage*: Except for the aforementioned specific cases of special quorum, bills are passed by an absolute majority of the members present at the session. When a bill is passed by the Chamber in which it originated, it is forwarded for debate to the other Chamber. If approved by both, it is presented to the Executive for its review (Article 78).

Article 79 provides for the possibility of each Chamber, after approving a bill of law generally, to delegate to its committees the approval of specific parts of a bill, with the vote of an absolute majority of the totality of its members. Once the bill is approved by the committee, the regular procedures shall be followed.

Other rules relevant for this stage are contained in Article 81; e.g., no bill that has been wholly rejected by one of the Chambers may be reintroduced during that year's sessions.

Finally, according to Article 40, at the initiative of the Chamber of Deputies, Congress may submit a bill to a popular referendum. In that case, "[t]he affirmative vote on the bill by the people of the Nation shall make it law and its enactment shall be automatic."

Lastly, Article 82 forbids the tacit or implied approval of bills: "The will of each Chamber must be manifested expressly (...) in all cases."

(3) *The enactment stage*: After approval by Congress, the bill is sent to the President (Article 78). The President has ten days to sign or veto the bill; however, the President's silence during this time frame is considered as approval (Article 80). Bills that are partially rejected may not be approved as to their remaining parts, with some exceptions (Article 80).[41]

Article 83 sets out the veto override procedure. Thus, a bill wholly or partially rejected by the Executive shall be returned with its objections to the originating Chamber. If both Chambers pass it by a two-thirds majority, the bill becomes law. On the contrary, if the Chambers disagree with each other regarding the Executive's objections, the bill may not be reintroduced in the sessions of that year.

It must be noted that in some cases in Constitution provides that the approval by the Executive is automatic, or that the passed bill cannot be vetoed (e.g., Articles 40 and 83).

6.6 Impeachment Proceedings

The *juicio político* or impeachment is the process by which the Congress formally levels charges against a high official of government, and if successful, it entails the removal of the accused person from office. The process does not seek criminal punishment, although once convicted through this procedure, the person could be subject to indictment, trial, and punishment according to law before the ordinary courts (Article 60).

According to Article 53, the Congress may impeach: (a) the President; (b) the Vice President; (c) the Chief of the Cabinet of Ministers; (d) the Ministers; and (e) the members of the Supreme Court.

41. *See infra*, "9 Specific Problems."

The grounds for impeachment are: (a) poor performance; (b) committing an offense when carrying out duties; and (c) common crimes (Article 53).

The Chamber of Deputies may bring charges before the Senate after being apprised of the charges and having declared by a two-thirds majority of the members present that there is cause for bringing an action (Article 53).

The Senate is then charged with trying in public trial the persons impeached by the Chamber of Deputies. When the accused person is the President of the Nation, the Senate is presided over by the President of the Supreme Court. A two-thirds majority of the members present is needed to declare the accused guilty (Article 59).

The main purpose of the impeachment procedure is to remove the accused person from office; additionally, him or her may be declared incapable of holding any employment of honor, trust, or pay of the Nation (Article 60).

6.7 Standing Bicameral Committee

The Standing Bicameral Committee is a body composed of Deputies and Senators, and whose membership must reflect the proportion of the political (party) representation of each Chamber.[42]

The Committee has three functions: (a) examine decrees of necessity and urgency issued by the President and forward its report within ten days to a plenary session of each Chamber of Congress for its express treatment (Article 99.3); (b) review decrees issued by the Executive that exercise powers delegated by Congress (Articles 76 and 100.12); (c) examine decrees that partially promulgate laws (Article 100.13).

6.8 Office of the Auditor General of the Nation

The 1994 reform incorporated two new bodies in the chapter that contains the rules governing the legislative branch: the Office of the Auditor General of the Nation and the Defender of the People.[43]

The former plays an advisory role to the Congress; indeed, according to Article 85, "[e]xternal review of the wealth, economic aspects, finances and operations of the national public sector shall be an attribute of the Legislative Power. The review and the opinion of the Legislative Power on the performance and general state of public administration shall be supported by reports from the Office of the Auditor General of the Nation."

42. Law No. 26.122 regulates the composition, quorum and functioning of the Committee.

43. However, before the amendment, Law No. 24.156 had already created the Office of the Auditor General, and Law No. 24.284 the Defender of the People. It must be noted that Arts. 85 and 86 state that these bodies have functional autonomy (in the case of the Defender, it is also added that he or she will act "without taking orders from any authority"). In addition, neither of the two exercise functions related to the legislative function. Therefore, in spite of having been incorporated in the chapter corresponding to the Legislative Power, some authors consider that they do not fit institutionally inside the spectrum of either of the three traditional branches of government. *See* Bidart Campos (n 22) ch XXXI n 15–16.

This "body of technical assistance of the Congress, with functional autonomy" has two main functions:

(1) review the legality, manage, and audit all activities of centralized and decentralized public administration;
(2) intervene in the procedures of approval or rejection of the accounting of collection and investment of public funds.

Finally, the law that regulates the operation and composition of the body must be approved by the absolute majority of the members of each House, taking into account that "[t]he president of the body shall be appointed upon the proposal of the opposition political party having the greatest number of legislators in the Congress."

6.9 The Defender of the People

Although with a particular style, the 1994 amendment has incorporated the traditional Ombudsman to the Constitution. Thus, Article 86 states that the Defender's "mission is the defense and protection of human rights and other rights, guarantees and interests protected by this Constitution and by the law, against deeds, acts, and omissions of the Administration, and the review of the exercise of public administrative functions." To this end, the Defender "has standing to litigate."

The Defender is an independent body and operates with full functional autonomy, without taking orders from any authority. He or she is appointed and removed by Congress by a vote of two-thirds of the members present in each one of the Chambers, remains in office for five years, and may be reappointed only once (Article 86).

The organization and operation of this body is be ruled by a special law.[44]

7 EXECUTIVE BRANCH

Article 87 states that "The Executive Power of the Nation shall be discharged by a citizen with the title of 'President of the Argentine Nation.'" However, within the chapter that regulates the organization and powers of the Executive, there are also provisions that refer to the Vice President, to the Chief of the Cabinet of Ministers, and to other Ministers of the Executive.

7.1 Presidentialism in Argentina

The new constitutional provisions, as amended in 1994, brought change to the presidential system. The question is whether presidentialism has been attenuated or, on the contrary, has been strengthened compared to the one designed by the

44. Law No. 24.284.

1853–1860 Constitution. By interpreting the rules independently of their practical application, authors have replied to this question very differently: whereas some hold that the new rules have moderated presidentialism, others state that presidential power has been increased.

On the one hand, the presidential mandate was reduced from six to four years, and the possibility of one immediate reelection was admitted. On the other hand, several measures were introduced that "have the potential to reduce the extraordinary premium placed on winning the presidency, improve the role of the opposition and create a system in the whole more adaptable to changing political circumstances."[45] Indeed, there are now express prohibitions aimed at the President regarding the exercise of legislative powers delegated by Congress (with the exceptions laid down by Article 76) and regarding the issuance of decrees of necessity and urgency (again with some exceptions laid down in Article 99.3). Moreover, the Congress may remove the Chief of Cabinet under the circumstances described in Article 101. Finally, other measures seek to reduce presidential power, such as "greater guarantees for the impartial selection and nomination of judges, the creation of organs for congressional control of the administration, or the introduction of a mechanism of referenda that provides congress with the capacity to bypass the presidential veto."[46]

However, if one turns to constitutional practice and political reality, the question surely becomes more complex. The political style of the Executive since the 1994 reform indicates that there is still a very strong concentration of presidential power. It can be argued that although the many institutions introduced by the reform have the potential to moderate presidentialism, in practice the reform has not been effective, and that reforms such as the possibility of reelection of the president have prevailed over the changes introduced to attenuate presidential power.

7.2 President and Vice President of the Republic

The eligibility requirements in order to be elected President or Vice President of the Nation are: (a) to have been born in Argentine territory, or if born in a foreign country, to be the child of a native citizen; (b) to possess the other qualifications required to be elected Senator (Article 89).[47] Of these qualifications, besides the annual income, only the age requirement can be applied to the case of the election of the President and Vice President (he or she has to be a minimum of thirty years old, according to Article 55).[48]

45. Gabriel Negretto, "Constitution-Making and Institutional Design: The Transformations of Presidentialism in Argentina" (1999) 40 [2] European Journal of Sociology 229.
46. *Ibid.*
47. The condition of member of the Roman Catholic Church, contained in former Art. 76, was eliminated by the 1994 amendment.
48. Indeed, the other two requirements are: (a) to have been a citizen of the Nation for six years, which does not apply since if the President was born in Argentina then he or she must be an Argentine citizen since birth, and if born in a foreign country to a native citizen, then the citizenship requirement would (arguably) directly not apply; (b) to be a native of the Province that elects him or been in residence in the Province during the previous two years, which does not apply either, as the President is not elected by one Province but by all.

The manner and time of the election of the President and Vice President, laid out in Articles 94–98,[49] changed substantially in 1994. Indeed, the traditional indirect election by electoral colleges was replaced with direct election in two rounds (second ballot, or ballotage). To that end, the national territory comprises a single district (Article 94). The election has to be held within the two months prior to the conclusion of the mandate of the President in office (Article 95).

According to the second ballot system designed by the Constitution, the candidates of the ticket that received the most votes in the first round shall be proclaimed President and Vice President of the Nation if the ticket has obtained: (a) more than 45% of the validly cast affirmative votes (Article 97); or (b) at least 40% of the validly cast affirmative votes and, in addition, there exists a difference greater than ten percentage points over the ticket that follows it in number of votes (Article 98). Otherwise, a second electoral round is required, and it shall be held between the two tickets of candidates receiving the most votes, within thirty days after the first electoral round (Article 96).

With regard to the term length and the possibility of reelection, Article 90 states that he President and Vice President remain in office for a term of four years[50] and may be reelected or succeed each other for only one consecutive term. If they have been reelected or succeeded each other, they may not be elected to either office, except after the interval of a term.

Article 88 deals with "acephaly" (i.e., cases in which the head of state needs to be replaced) and identifies two sets of cases:

(1) A set of cases in which the cause of acephaly affects only the President, thus the Executive Power is exercised by the Vice President: according to Article 88, "[i]n case of illness, absence from the Capital, death, resignation, or removal of the President, the Executive Power shall be exercised by the Vice President of the Nation." In some of these cases (e.g., absence from the Capital), the President only needs to be replaced temporarily, therefore the Vice President's exercise of the Executive Power is a sort of substitution until the President resumes his or her functions. In other cases (e.g., death, resignation), the President needs to be replaced permanently, thus the vacancy must be permanently covered: the Vice President becomes President and exercises the Executive Power for the remainder of the presidential term.
(2) A set of cases in which both the President and the Vice President are affected by a cause of acephaly: according to Article 88, "[i]n the event of removal, death, resignation, or incapacity of the President and the Vice President of the Nation, the Congress shall determine which public official shall fill the Presidency until the cause for the disability ceases or a new President is

49. *See also* Arts. 148–155 of the Electoral Code.
50. Article 91 adds that "[th]e President of the Nation leaves office the day that his four-year term expires; without any event that may have interrupted his term being considered as a reason for completing it later."

elected." This determination was made by the Congress in an anticipated and general way by means of a law (Acephaly Laws Nos. 252 and 20.972).

7.3 Powers of the President of the Republic

Most of the powers of the President are laid out by Article 99. The President has, among others, the following powers:

(a) The President is the head of state and head of government of Argentina, and directs the executive branch of the Federal Government: "He is the supreme chief of the Nation, chief of the government, and the politician responsible for the general administration of the country" (Article 99.1).[51] The President is also the commander-in-chief of all Armed Forces of the Nation (Article 99.12).[52]

(b) The President has regulatory powers, and may issue four different types of regulations:[53] (i) implementation regulations, which according to Article 99.2 are "the instructions and regulations that may be necessary for the execution of the laws of the Nation;" when issuing them, the President must be "careful not to alter their spirit through regulatory exceptions;" (ii) autonomous regulations, which are not provided for expressly in the Constitution but are based on the need of the Executive to develop the principles of its own organization and functioning; (iii) delegated regulations and (iv) necessity and urgency regulations, both of which are in principle prohibited by Article 76 and Article 99.3, with the exceptions laid out by both provisions.[54]

(c) The President participates in the lawmaking process. Indeed, according to Article 99.3, he or she "participates in the enactment of the laws according to

51. In this sense, Art. 99.17 states that the President "may request any information he considers appropriate from the Chief of the Cabinet of Ministers and from the heads of all branches and departments of the administration, and, through them, from all other employees, and they are required to provide it," whereas Art. 99.10 adds that the he or she "supervises the exercise of authority by the Chief of the Cabinet of Ministers regarding the collection of the Nation's revenues and their investment, in accordance with the law or the budget of National expenditures."

52. In this regard, Art. 99.14 holds that the President "has the Armed Forces at his disposal, and takes charge of their organization and deployment, according to the needs of the Nation," and Art. 99.15 adds that the he or she "declares war and orders reprisals with the authorization and approval of Congress."

53. "Usually, the different types of Executive regulations are classified into implementation regulations, delegated regulations, necessity and urgency regulations, and autonomous regulations, although it has to be noted that in practice the boundaries between them are often blurred. Any example from the Official Gazette is sufficient to verify this. Therefore, any generalization regarding regulations must be taken as a mere hypothesis of analysis (...). The practice, in these times of perpetual emergency, is chaotic: Many are issued, and on prohibited subject matters" (Agustín Gordillo, *Tratado de Derecho Administrativo y Obras Selectas* (Fundación de Derecho Administrativo 2013) vol. I, 19–20).

54. *See infra*, "9 Specific Problems."

the Constitution, promulgates them, and has them published;" the President is thus allowed to: (i) present bills to the Congress for their discussion, with some exceptions (Article 77); (ii) examine the bill the Congress has passed, and approve the bill either by promulgating it expressly or letting the ten day time frame go by for it to be "tacitly promulgated;" (iii) have laws published; (iv) veto wholly or partially a bill (Article 83). If a bill is partially vetoed, "those parts that are not rejected may be promulgated if they have normative autonomy and their partial approval does not alter the spirit or the unity of the bill as passed by Congress" (Article 80).[55] Additionally, the President opens the sessions of Congress each year (Article 99.8), and extends the regular sessions of Congress, or convokes it for extraordinary sessions when an important interest in order or progress requires it (Article 99.9).

(d) The President appoints and removes: (i) the Chief of the Cabinet of Ministers and the other Ministers of the Cabinet, the officials of his office, consular agents, and employees whose appointment is not otherwise regulated by the Constitution, all of this on his own (Article 99.7); (ii) ambassadors, ministers plenipotentiary, and charge d'affaires, with the consent of the Senate (Article 99.7); (iii) the superior officers of the Armed Forces, with the consent of the Senate (and on his own on the battlefield) (Article 99.13). Moreover, the President appoints: (i) the judges of the Supreme Court, with the consent of the Senate by two-thirds of its members present, in a public session convened for that purpose (Article 99.4); (ii) the judges of lower federal courts, taking into account the qualifications of the candidates, based on a binding list of three candidates nominated by the Judicial Council, with the subsequent consent of the Senate, also convened in public session (Article 99.4).

(e) The President, as head of state, conducts foreign relations and assumes the international representation of the state. Thus, the President recognizes foreign states and governments, "receives their Ministers and admits their consuls" (Article 99.11). Regarding international treaties, the President "concludes and signs treaties, concordats, and other negotiations required for the maintenance of good relations with international organizations and foreign nations" (Article 99.11). The Congress may approve or reject the treaties signed by the Executive (Article 75.22); if approved, the President may then ratify them.

(f) Finally, the President may "grant pardons or commute punishment for crimes subject to federal jurisdiction, after a report by the appropriate court, except in cases of impeachment by the Chamber of Deputies" (Article 99.5).

55. *Ibid.*

7.4 Chief of the Cabinet of Ministers

The 1994 amendment has incorporated the Chief of the Cabinet of Ministers who, without being a prime minister, was given special and different powers to the generic ministerial ones.

Since the Chief of the Cabinet is neither a prime minister nor a minister, and the Constitution has accorded him or her powers in a quite unique way, different from other presidentialist systems and also from parliamentary systems, it is relevant to first examine the Chief's position within the Executive. There is a hierarchical relationship between the President and the Chief of the Cabinet, who the former and removes on his or her own (Article 99.7). In addition, as stated, the President is the head of state and head of government of Argentina (Article 99.1); however, as regards the headship of administration, whereas the President is "the politician *responsible* for the general administration of the country" (Article 99.1), the Chief of the Cabinet of Ministers "*exercise[s]* the general administration of the country" (Article 100.1). This has been construed as meaning that the President could exercise that headship concurrently with the Chief of the Cabinet of Ministers, except in cases where the latter has exclusive power. With respect to the Chief of the Cabinet's relationship with the ministers, while some authors consider that the Chief of the Cabinet is hierarchically superior to them, others regard all of them as equals.

The Constitution also provides for a censure motion and for the removal of the Chief of Cabinet by the Congress in Article 101: indeed, the Chief of the Cabinet "may be cross-examined for the purposes of considering a censure motion, by an absolute majority vote of the totality of the members of either of the Chambers, and he may be removed by an absolute majority vote of the members of each of the Chambers." The Constitution has not provided for the so-called constructive censure motion, which generally allows Congress to withdraw confidence from a head of government only if there is a positive majority for a prospective successor. The Constitution has neither incorporated a usual counterweight for censorship, namely, the power of the President to dissolve Congress.

The powers of the Chief of the Cabinet are mainly spelled out in Article 100. Two subsections of this article contain generic powers, such as the power to issue the acts and regulations that may be necessary to exercise the functions that the Constitution grants to him or her, and those that the President of the Nation delegates to him or her (Article 100.2, *see also* 100.4). In addition, the Chief of Cabinet is empowered:

(a) with regard to the administration, to make the appointments of employees, except for those appointments which fall to the President (Article 100.3); to see to the collection of the revenues of the Nation and to execute the National Budget law (Article 100.7);
(b) with respect to the sessions of the Cabinet of Ministers, the Chief coordinates, prepares for and convenes them, and also presides over them in the event of the President's absence (Article 100.5);
(c) regarding the relationship with the legislative branch, to attend sessions of Congress and participate in its debates, but without voting (Article 100.9); to

produce reports and explanations that any of the Chambers may request from the Executive Power (Article 100.11); once ordinary sessions of Congress have begun, to present together with the other Ministers a detailed account of the state of the Nation concerning the affairs of the respective departments (Article 100.10); to attend Congress at least once a month, attending each Chamber alternately, to inform them of the government's progress (Article 101); to send to Congress the bills concerning the Ministries and the National Budget (Article 100.6);

(d) in respect of the President's legislative powers, to approve (jointly with the other Ministers) decrees of necessity and urgency, and decrees that partially promulgate laws, and to personally submit these decrees for consideration by the Standing Bicameral Committee within ten days of their enactment (Article 100.13, also 99.3 and 80); to approve decrees that exercise powers delegated by Congress, which are also subject to the review of the Standing Bicameral Committee (Article 100.12, also 76);

(e) finally, to approve decrees establishing implementing regulations for laws, decrees that provide for the extension of ordinary sessions of Congress or the convening of extraordinary sessions, and the messages of the President promoting a legislative initiative (Article 100.8).

7.5 Ministers

The Ministers, whose number and competence is established by a special law,[56] make and implement decisions on policies in conjunction with the other Ministers that are part of the government's cabinet. They "have under their responsibility the handling of the Nation's business," and "endorse and legalize the acts of the President through their signatures, without which the [President's] acts have no effect" (Article 100). The Ministers have the leadership, direction and control of their respective offices; they issue instructions and manage the economic-financial regime of their departments. "Ministers may not, in any case, issue resolutions on their own, except for those concerning the economic and administrative system of their respective departments" (Article 103).

Ministers are both appointed and removed by the President (Article 99.7). They can also be subject to impeachment by Congress (Article 53).

56. The 1853 Constitution established five ministries and fixed their respective competences. The 1898 reform only set out the number of ministries, and left the determination of their competences to a special law to be passed by Congress. The 1994 reform prescribed that the number and competence of ministers would be established by a special law. Accordingly, Law No. 22.520, with several amendments, currently states that the number of ministries is twenty-one, and fixes their competences as follows: Ministry of the Interior; of Public Works and Housing; of Foreign Affairs; of Defense; of Finance; of Production; of Agroindustry; of Tourism; of Transport; of Justice and Human Rights; of Security; of Labor; Employment and Social Security; of Social Development; of Health; of Education and Sports; of Science, Technology and Productive Innovation; of Culture; of Environment and Sustainable Development; of Modernization; of Energy and Mining; of Communications.

7.6 Attorney of the National Treasury

The Attorney of the National Treasury is not provided for by the Constitution but by a special law,[57] and is in charge of the legal advice of the President. The Attorney reports directly to the President, and has a hierarchy equivalent to that of the Ministers.

8 JUDICIAL BRANCH

The Constitution has few rules on the judicial branch; indeed, only eleven make up the chapter on the judicial power, as compared to the forty-two articles for the legislative power, and the twenty articles for the executive power. According to Article 108, "[t]he Judicial Power of the Nation shall be vested in a Supreme Court and in such lower courts as Congress may constitute in the territory of the Nation." The Constitution as amended in 1994 also provides for a Judicial Council (Article 114), as well as a trial jury for the removal of judges of federal lower courts (Article 115).

The head of the judiciary is the Supreme Court. The Constitution directly establishes only the Supreme Court and "lower courts," whose organization and competence is left to the Congress to determine by means of a law.[58]

8.1 Appointment, Removal and Security of Tenure of Federal Judges

The judges of the Supreme Court are appointed by the President, with the consent of the Senate by two-thirds of its members present. The judges of lower federal tribunals are likewise appointed by the Executive, taking into account the qualifications of the candidates, based on a binding list of three candidates nominated by the Judicial Council, and the appointment also has to be consented by the Senate (Article 99.4).

The protection of judges from arbitrary removal, as well as other guarantees of judicial independence, have been recognized in the Constitution, mainly through Article 110.[59] Indeed, as stated in the mentioned article, "judges, both of the Supreme Court and of the inferior courts of the Nation, shall hold their offices during their good behavior;" the salaries of members of the judiary are fixed by law, and shall not be diminished in any way while holding office (Article 110). Moreover, no judge may be deprived of his office or suspended except by a judgment, and the transfer of a judge shall not take place except by a new appointment and with his consent.

57. It was originally created in 1863 by Law No. 74, and it is currently regulated by Laws No. 24.667 and 22.520, as well as several decrees.
58. The federal justice is currently regulated by Decree-Law No. 1285/1958.
59. Other measures to strengthen judicial independence, such as the creation of the Judicial Council and the trial jury in 1994, etc., have not quite had the intended effect in practice. *See*, e.g., the 2015-2016 Global Competitiveness Rankings elaborated by the World Economic Forum, which ranked Argentina 129th of 140 countries in judicial independence (available at http://repo rts.weforum.org/global-competitiveness-report-2015-2016/competitiveness-rankings/rticle 75. paragraph Art. 129). laid down in the Constitution, the latter by provincial rules set out by each of the province).

Before the 1994 reform, the tenure during "good behavior" implied that a judge, once appointed, should continue in office for life unless removed for misbehavior. However, a controversial reform in 1994 established an age limit for judicial tenure; indeed, Article 99.4 holds that "[a] new appointment, preceded by the same consent, shall be necessary in order to maintain in office any of these magistrates once they attain the age of seventy-five. All appointments of magistrates whose age is that indicated or greater shall be made for five years and may be repeated indefinitely following the same procedure." This amendment was ruled unconstitutional by the Supreme Court in 1999, in the *Fayt* case.[60]

Judges of the Supreme Court can be subject to impeachment by Congress (Article 53), whereas judges of lower federal courts can be removed by the trial jury created for this purpose (Article 115).

8.2 Organization and Powers of Federal Judges

The traditional division of the judicial structure in Argentina has been the distinction between federal courts and provincial courts—the former governed by the rules laid down in the Constitution and by the Federal Congress, the latter by rules set out by each Province. After the 1994 reform, this structure is integrated with a third kind of administration of justice, which is that of the City of Buenos Aires (Article 129).[61]

The jurisdiction of federal courts is determined by Articles 116 and 117 of the Constitution, and regulated in various laws. It has the following characteristics: (a) it is limited and exceptional, which means that it is only exercised in the specific cases that the Constitution and the federal laws indicate; (b) it is exclusive, which means that, in principle, provincial courts cannot hear federal jurisdiction cases.

Article 116 sets out in general terms the cases of federal jurisdiction without distinguishing the particular court that should hear each type of case; indeed: "[t]he Supreme Court of Justice and the lower courts of the Nation have jurisdiction over and decide all cases that ... [follows an enumeration of the cases of federal jurisdiction]." The only specific rule is found Article 117, which indicates the cases in which the Supreme Court exercises original and exclusive jurisdiction. According to Article 116, federal courts hear cases that involve certain matters, parties or places.

First, there are two cases of "subject matter jurisdiction:"

(1) Cases involving matters related to the Constitution, other federal laws, and international treaties: "cases that deal with matters governed by the Constitution and the laws of the Nation, except as provided in clause 12 of Article 75,[62] and over treaties with foreign nations" (Article 116). However, a case is

60. *Fayt Carlos Santiago c Estado Nacional* 322 Fallos 1408. *See* Ileana Gomez, "Declaring Unconstitutional a Constitutional Amendment: The Argentine Judiciary Forges Ahead" (2000) 31 The University of Miami Inter-American Law Review 93.
61. *See infra* "8.3 Judiciary of the City of Buenos Aires: Controversy over Its Powers."
62. As mentioned above, the Congress passes three kinds of laws: (a) federal laws; (b) *derecho común* or substantive laws; (c) local laws (*see supra* "6.4 Kinds of Laws Passed by the Federal

only required to be filed before a federal court when it is "directly" and "immediately" related to federal law. When the case is mainly related to substantive law and only indirectly related to federal law, the case must be filed before a provincial court; nonetheless, there must be a possibility of reaching a federal court by way of appeal at some point.

(2) Cases related to admiralty and maritime jurisdiction: within the causes of admiralty and maritime jurisdiction, not only those relating to maritime activity, but also to aeronautics, according to the aeronautical code, are included.

Second, federal courts hear cases that involve certain parties, regardless of the kind of law that must be applied to the case (i.e., even when the case is directly related to substantive law):

(a) cases (suits) in which the Nation is a party;[63]
(b) cases concerning ambassadors, public ministers and foreign consuls;
(c) other cases that involve certain parties: "in cases arising between two or more Provinces, between one Province and the citizens of another, between citizens of different Provinces, and between a Province or its citizens against a foreign State or citizen."

Finally, although Article 116 does not contain any explicit reference to cases that involve certain places, such federal jurisdiction exists, for example, when a criminal case must be heard by a federal court because of aspects related to the place of commission of the crime. Federal jurisdiction in criminal matters can also arise in certain cases regardless of the place of commission of the crime; for instance, because of the nature of the crime and of the person suspected to have committed it (e.g., bribery when the suspected perpetrator is an official of the Federal Government).

8.3 Judiciary of the City of Buenos Aires: Controversy over Its Powers

Before the 1994, because the City of Buenos Aires had no autonomous system of government, all courts in charge of the administration of justice in the City were federal courts. There was a just a terminological distinction between them: there were courts that heard substantive law cases who were named "national" courts (these were the equivalent of provincial courts), and courts that heard federal law cases who were named federal courts. The 1994 amendment granted the City of Buenos Aires an

Congress"). This provision seeks to exclude cases involving matters related to substantive laws from the federal jurisdiction, in accordance with the provision contained in Art. 75.12. Those cases are heard, in principle, by provincial courts.

63. The term "Nation" is equivalent to Federal Government, and in this case also includes certain entities and state-owned companies which could compromise the eventual responsibility of the State. *See* Law No. 3952 (regarding lawsuits against the Nation) and Law No. 19.549 (regarding administrative procedure, and which regulates the administrative claim that is needed before filing the lawsuit).

"autonomous system of government, with its own legislative and jurisdictional powers" (Article 129). This could be construed as meaning that, similarly to the Provinces, the City should have its own local courts.

However, Article 75.12, when stating that substantive law must be applied by provincial courts, does not refer explicitly to the City of Buenos Aires. The law that guarantees the interests of the Federal Government in the capital (Law No. 24.588), enacted after the reform, asserts in Article 8 that the "national" courts of the City of Buenos Aires "shall maintain its present jurisdiction" and that the City of Buenos Aires shall have its own powers of jurisdiction in matters related to neighborhood, misdemeanors and infractions, as well as local contentious administrative and tax matters. Consequently, the City of Buenos Aires has very limited local jurisdictional powers, as "national" courts continue to hear statutory law cases.

However, if, as a matter of principle, substantive law cases evade the jurisdiction of federal courts, and there is no federal interest that is compromised if such cases are heard by local courts in the City of Buenos Aires, there is no reason why federal courts should continue to hear such cases in the City, as they did before the reform. Accordingly, there should only be federal courts that exercise federal jurisdiction (the one that arises from Article 116), while the so-called national courts should make way for local courts which, like provincial courts, apply substantive law and local law.[64]

8.4 Supreme Court of Justice

The Supreme Court is the highest court of the Argentine judiciary, as well as the final interpreter of the Constitution.

Article 111 sets out the qualifications to be a Supreme Court judge; thus, it is necessary to be a lawyer of the Nation, with eight years of practice, and have the same qualifications required to be a senator.[65] The Constitution does not determine the composition of the Court; instead, it is determined by the Federal Congress by means of a law. Accordingly, Decree-Law No. 1285/1958 fixes the number of judges at five since its reform in 2013.

The jurisdiction of the Supreme Court can be derived from Articles 116 and 117. Indeed, the Court may exercise original and exclusive jurisdiction in "all matters concerning foreign ambassadors, ministers and consuls, and in those in which a Province shall be a party," and shall have appellate jurisdiction in all other cases mentioned by Article 116 (which, as stated above, outlines the jurisdiction of federal courts in general terms) according to the rules and exceptions that Congress may prescribe. It follows that the Court exercises two types of jurisdiction: (a) an original and exclusive jurisdiction, in the cases specified by Article 117; (b) an appellate jurisdiction, in the cases established by Congress, as stated in the same provision. In

64. Various agreements have been signed in this regard, such as the Agreement on the Progressive Transfer of Jurisdiction over Criminal Matters from the National Justice to the Judicial Branch of the City of Buenos Aires (signed on December 7, 2000, and approved by Law No. 25.752).
65. *See supra*, "6.2 Senate."

turn, according to the law that has regulated it,[66] the appellate jurisdiction of the Court is exercised through: (a) ordinary appeal, in cases: (i) where the Federal Government is a party, depending on the amount in controversy; (ii) of extradition of criminals; (iii) of maritime jurisdiction; (b) extraordinary appeal, in cases where an "extraordinary federal appeal" (*recurso extraordinario federal*) is filed pursuant to Article 14 of Law No. 48.

Nevertheless, the Court has lately sought to gradually reduce the scope of its jurisdiction, with the intention of concentrating its efforts on its role as final interpreter of the Constitution and guarantor of constitutional rights. Indeed, the Court has issued various judgments during the last decade with the aim of redesigning its institutional role; for example, the *Itzcovich* case,[67] regarding the Court's ordinary appeal jurisdiction in certain social security cases, and the *Barreto*[68] and *Mendoza*[69] cases, related to the material scope of the Court's original jurisdiction. In the 2015 *Anadon* case,[70] the Court stated that as a result of diverse factors—mainly the increased workload of the tribunal that followed the constitutionalisation of human rights—it was necessary to limit the jurisdiction of the Court according to significance criteria: "There are important reasons for preserving and strengthening the institutional role of the Court which justify the use of a rigorous hermeneutical criterion to interpret the cases that give rise to its appellate jurisdiction, in order to deepen the exercise of its most eminent constitutional jurisdiction."[71] The Court thus ruled unconstitutional the provision that establishes the ordinary appeal in cases where the Federal Government is a party depending on the amount in controversy.

The role of the Court as the final interpreter of the Constitution is primarily played through the "extraordinary federal appeal" provided for in Article 14 of Law No. 48. This appeal allows for a kind of constitutional or federal *cassation* that seeks to maintain the supremacy of the Constitution and of federal law, as well as to achieve a uniform application of federal constitutional law. In order to file an extraordinary appeal, certain requirements must be met; the most relevant are:

(a) The case must involve a constitutional question directly related to the judgment under appeal; i.e., a matter of law in which, directly or indirectly, the Constitution is compromised (either its interpretation or its supremacy). The constitutional question can be "simple" (i.e., about the pure and simple interpretation of federal norms or acts) or "complex" (i.e., when it refers to a conflict between the Constitution and infraconstitutional norms or acts).

66. *See* Art. 24 of Decree-Law No. 1285/58 for a complete list of the cases over which the Court has jurisdiction.
67. 328 Fallos 566.
68. 329 Fallos 759.
69. 329 Fallos 2316.
70. 338 Fallos 724.
71. *Ibid.*

(b) The appeal must be filed against a final judgment delivered by the superior competent court for the case.[72]

The extraordinary appeal must be filed before the court that issues the judgment. Should the lower court not grant it, a complaint (*recurso de queja*) can be filed directly before the Supreme Court.

The extraordinary appellate jurisdiction is largely discretionary. Law No. 23.774, enacted in 1990, incorporated the *certiorari* to the Civil and Commercial Procedural Code (Article 280). Accordingly, at its sole discretion and merely invoking Article 280, the Court may reject the extraordinary appeal (or the complaint filed against the refusal of the appeal) in cases where: (a) there is no sufficient affront to federal norms; or (b) the issues in question are insubstantial or irrelevant.

8.5 Judicial Council and Trial Jury

Two new bodies were incorporated by the 1994 reform within the judiciary's orbit: first, the Judicial Council, a body which exercises (nonjudicial) powers proper to the judicial branch (Article 114); second, the trial jury established by Article 115, which is in charge of removing federal lower court judges accused by the Judicial Council, a procedure that replaced impeachment of these judges by Congress.

According to Article 114, the Judicial Council is in charge of the selection of judges and the administration of the Judiciary. The Council's powers can be classified as follows:

(a) powers related to the appointment of lower court judges: the Council selects candidates for inferior courts through public competitions, and issues binding lists of three candidates for appointment of judges of the lower courts (a decision made by the President, with the subsequent consent of the Senate, according to Article 99.4);
(b) administrative powers: the Council is in charge of administering revenues and executing the budget that the law assigns for the administration of justice;
(c) disciplinary powers: the Council exercises disciplinary powers over judges, and determines the commencement of removal proceedings against them, and in such case, orders their suspension and formulates the corresponding charges (so that the trial jury can then trial and eventually remove them);[73]

72. The superior court varies according to the nature of the case and the instances provided for it by the applicable procedural laws. In provincial jurisdiction, the state court must have intervened before an extraordinary appeal can be filed. Law No. 26.790 has incorporated to the procedural laws the "per saltum" or "by pass" that allows to reach the Supreme Court through an extraordinary appeal disregarding this requirement, in exceptional cases of notorious institutional gravity that need a definitive and expeditious solution.
73. The procedure is thus similar to impeachment, as the Judicial Council, like the House of Deputies, is in charge of accusation, whereas the trial jury, like the Senate, is in charge of trial and eventual removal of the judge.

(d) regulatory powers: the Council establishes the regulations regarding judicial organization and all regulations necessary to assure the independence of judges and the effective rendering of judicial services.

The Constitution sets out guidelines for the composition of the Council in Article 114: it "shall be reconstituted periodically so that an equilibrium is achieved among the representation of popularly elected political organs, judges of all instances, and federally licensed attorneys. It shall also include persons from the academic and scientific fields, of a number and manner of appointment the law shall indicate" (Article 114). Consequently, the composition of the Council in concrete terms, as well as the procedure for the selection of candidates and for the removal of judges, is left to the Congress to determine by a special law enacted by the absolute majority of all the members of each House.[74]

In turn, Article 115 provides that federal lower court judges may be removed by a trial jury on the grounds laid down for impeachment in Article 53. Both the composition and the procedures of the jury shall be specified in the special law mentioned in Article 114. The law must be in accordance with certain rules that the Constitution lays down:

(a) regarding the composition of the jury, it must be integrated with legislators, judges, and federally licensed attorneys;
(b) as for the procedure: (i) the decision of the jury is final and cannot be appealed, and may not have other effect than the removal of the accused (in the sense that the condemned party may be later subject to accusation, trial, and punishment according to law, but before the ordinary courts); (ii) if no decision was taken after one hundred and eighty days since the opening of the proceedings for removal, the proceedings are to be filed and, in that event, the suspended judge shall be reinstated.

8.6 Constitutional Review in Argentina

The Constitution, unlike some provincial constitutions in Argentina, does not provide for constitutional review of legislation. The doctrine of constitutional review has been elaborated by the jurisprudence of the Supreme Court of Justice.

74. The composition and procedures of the Judicial Council and the trial jury in concrete terms have been regulated by Laws Nos. 24.937, 24.939, 26.080 and 26.855. These laws were controversial because of the delicate balance that had to be struck in the representation of the different sectors mentioned in Arts. 114 and 115 (i.e., popularly elected political organs, judges of all instances, federally licensed attorneys, etc.), as well as in the form of election of members, in order to protect, *inter alia*, the independence of the judiciary. Because of this, Law No. 26.855 was ruled unconstitutional by the Supreme Court of Justice in the *Rizzo* case (*see Rizzo Jorge Gabriel c. Poder Ejecutivo Nacional*, 336 Fallos 760; Alberto B. Bianchi, "Crónica de una inconstitucionalidad manifiesta" (2013) 2013-D La Ley 26). For a detailed account of the regulatory background, *see* Sabsay, Daniel Alberto, y Sabsay, Kevin, "Sobre el Consejo de la Magistratura de la Nación y su reforma" (2009) 2009-F La Ley 896.

In effect, as early as 1886, the Court (following the US Supreme Court *Marbury v. Madison* case) ruled a law of Congress unconstitutional in the *Municipalidad de la Capital c. Elortondo* case, stating that "[t]he power and the duty of courts to examine the laws in the concrete cases brought to their decision, comparing the laws with the text of the Constitution in order to determine whether or not they comply with it, and to refrain from applying them if found that they do not, are essential for Argentine constitutional organization. This moderating power constitutes one of the fundamental purposes of the federal judiciary, as well as one of the greatest guarantees to assure the rights enshrined in the Constitution against possible and involuntary abuses by public authorities."[75]

At federal level, constitutional review has the following characteristics:

(a) The review system is diffuse: all judges at all levels can carry it out, like in the US system. The utmost means of obtaining an unconstitutionality ruling within the federal judicial system is the federal extraordinary appeal filed before the Supreme Court, without prejudice to the possibility of lower federal court judges of exercising constitutional review.[76]

(b) Regarding the procedural aspects of constitutional review, courts may declare legislation unconstitutional when hearing a case whose main purpose is other than obtaining this ruling (the "indirect, incidental or exceptional" way). The Court stated until 1985 that there were no "direct" ways to promote judicial review of legislation (i.e., bring a case before a court whose main purpose is to obtain a ruling declaring unconstitutional a piece of legislation, also known as "action of unconstitutionality"). However, Court has progressively accepted this possibility, which can be exercised mainly through the writ of amparo, the writ of habeas corpus, and the declaratory judgment provided in Article 322 of the Civil and Commercial Procedural Code, among others.[77]

(c) The persons that may request the review are: (i) the holder of a right or legitimate interest that has been harmed or affected; (ii) when the action of amparo[78] "complains of any form of discrimination, or regards the rights that protect the environment, competition, the user, the consumer, or rights of a

75. 33 Fallos 162.

76. Argentina is "the only Latin American country that has kept the diffuse method of judicial review as the only one applicable in order to control the constitutionality of legislation," while in other Latin American countries the method is still applied but jointly with the concentrated method (i.e., mixed system of judicial review) (Allan R. Brewer-Carías, *Constitutional Protection of Human Rights in Latin America: A Comparative Study of Amparo Proceedings* (Cambridge University Press 2009) 101).

77. However, these are not "pure" actions of unconstitutionality, in the sense that they always have a purpose other than obtaining the unconstitutionality ruling. However, these actions do exist at provincial level, as they are provided for in various provincial constitutions.

78. *See infra*, "10.5 Amparo, Habeas Data and Habeas Corpus."

collective nature in general," it may be brought "by the affected party, the Defender of the People, and the associations that support these ends."[79]

(d) Traditionally, constitutional review could only be exercised when one of the affected parties requested it; however, the Supreme Court has recently admitted the possibility for judges to carry out judicial review ex officio in certain cases.[80]

(e) The effect of the eventual declaration of unconstitutionality is limited to the case in whose context the review is carried out: the legislation is struck down and its application ruled out only for the parties involved, whereas its validity outside the case is left intact. However, the Court has asserted that some declarations of unconstitutionality can have erga omnes effects.[81]

(f) The following may be subject to judicial review: provincial constitutions, laws, international treaties without constitutional hierarchy, decrees, regulations and administrative acts, judicial sentences (which can be reviewed in order to determine if they are arbitrary and thus unconstitutional), among others. A special case is the constitutional reform process, which was reviewed by the Supreme Court in the *Fayt* case.[82] Moreover, while it is accepted that domestic private international law is subject to judicial review, it has been argued that such control may not be carried out over foreign law applied by domestic courts in accordance with private international rules; other authors hold, contrarily, that these rules should also be subject to constitutional review and eventually struck down.[83]

Laws and governmental acts are presumed to be valid and, therefore, constitutional. Thus, the declaration of unconstitutionality should only be issued when the incompatibility with the Constitution is absolute and evident. The Supreme Court has coined this principle, and held that legislation may be struck down only when a strict necessity requires it.

Following the US Supreme Court, the Argentine Supreme Court has developed the political question doctrine. According to this doctrine, only legal questions may be judiciable; political questions, on the contrary, are nonjusticiable. The rule for what is considered a political question is quite imprecise and has varied over time. In general terms, a political question can be regarded as the result of the exercise of an exclusive

79. This last provision allows for the "collective" amparo, similar to the class actions of other jurisdictions. *See* Mairal H, "Argentina" (2009) 622 The Annals of the American Academy of Political and Social Science 54; Rivera (h) J C, "La noción de derechos de incidencia colectiva en la jurisprudencia de la Corte Suprema de Justicia de la Nación y de los tribunales inferiores" (2008) II Jurisprudencia Argentina 1141. *See infra* "10.6 Collective Rights and Actions."
80. *See Mill de Pereyra* and *Banco Comercial de Finanzas* cases, between 2001 and 2004: *Mill de Pereyra c Provincia de Corrientes* 324 Fallos 3219, *Banco Comercial de Finanzas SA* 327 Fallos 3117.
81. *See*, e.g., the 2009 *Halabi* case: *Halabi Ernesto c PEN* 332 Fallos 111.
82. *See* n 60.
83. *See*, e.g., Sara Lidia Feldstein de Cárdenas, "El control de constitucionalidad del derecho extranjero" (2008) II [3] Revista Electrónica del Instituto de Investigaciones "Ambrosio L Gioja" 32.

power by a governmental body; as a result, the political question is best resolved through the political process, and the issue cannot be heard in a court of law. The main consequence of this approach is that these questions are exempted from judicial review. The Court has considered as political questions the declaration of the state of siege, of federal intervention, and of war, *inter alia*. However, a progressive reduction of the catalog of political questions can be appreciated over time in the case law of the Court.

Finally, there are also provincial judicial review systems for the protection of local constitutions. Their rules and requirements at times differ from the analyzed guidelines for judicial review at federal level. For example, in some cases provincial constitutions set out that the declaration of unconstitutionality within their jurisdictions may have erga omnes effects (e.g., Article 175 of the Constitution of Chubut and Article 208 of the Constitution of Río Negro).

8.7 Binding Force of Case Law in Argentina

Argentina is a civil law jurisdiction. The Constitution "does not mandate the decisions of the courts of the Argentine judicial system stare decisis."[84] However, without a formally institutionalised system of binding precedent or of stare decisis, jurisprudence can act spontaneously as a source of law; indeed, at times, because of the prestige of the court, or because of the nature of the matter that was decided, a judgment may become exemplary and capable of provoking imitation, serving as a model for analogous cases in the future.

In the case of the jurisprudence of the Supreme Court of Justice, although no written rule enshrines the formal obligation of the lower courts to follow the Court's judgments, the Court has reiterated over time that lower court decisions may not deviate from its "precedents" without bringing forth new arguments that justify departing from them: "Although the Argentine Supreme Court has repeatedly asserted that there is no obligation for lower courts to follow its jurisprudence, the assertion always comes accompanied with a warning: lower courts must not rebel against the authority of Supreme Court precedents; otherwise their decisions shall be struck down."[85]

8.8 Exercise of Judicial Functions by Administrative Agencies

The Constitution prohibits the President from exercising judicial functions, assuming jurisdiction over pending cases, or reopening those already decided (Article 109). This constitutional provision does not forbid, however, the exercise of judicial functions by administrative bodies. According to the case law of the Supreme Court, quasi-judicial proceedings by administrative agencies, in which these bodies exercise discretion of a judicial nature, are admitted; nevertheless, these judicial functions in charge of the

84. Santiago Legarre, "Precedent in Argentine Law" (2011) 57 Loyola Law Review 782–783.
85. *Ibid.*, 786.

administration are constitutional only on the condition that there is a possibility of recourse before the judiciary. This is named "sufficient judicial control," and implies: (a) the possibility of lodging an appeal against the administrative body's decision before a judge; (b) the impossibility for an administrative quasi-judicial decision to be final and definitive.

8.9 The Public Ministry

The Public Ministry is defined by Article 120 as "an independent body with functional autonomy and financial self-sufficiency," whose function is to "promote the intervention of the judicial [system] in defense of lawfulness and of the general interests of society, in coordination with the other authorities of the Republic."

The Public Ministry is the only body that is not included within the sections dedicated to the executive, legislative or judicial branch. Instead, a special section incorporated by the 1994 reform—the fourth section of the second part of the constitutional text—regulates the Office's composition and powers. Hence there are authors who, after the reform, speak of a "fourth power" outside the three classic branches of government, while others argue that although it is not part of the judicial branch, it is an auxiliary body attached to the judiciary as an "extra-power" body.

Regarding its composition, Article 120 mentions only two of its officials: the Chief Prosecutor of the Nation and the Chief Public Defender of the Nation. The provision adds that the Office's members shall enjoy functional immunities and noninterference with their remuneration. Everything else must be established by Congress.[86]

The Public Ministry is composed by two different bodies:

(1) *The Office of the Public Prosecutor, led by the Chief Prosecutor of the Nation*: This body has powers: (i) regarding the defense of the Constitution and the general interests of society, for example, to issue opinions on cases before the Supreme Court of Justice of the Nation whenever the interpretation of a provision of the Constitution or human rights treaties is contested; (ii) regarding criminal matters, to establish the criminal prosecution policy, to prosecute all federal crimes, to manage extradition requests, among others.

(2) *The Office of the Public Defender, led by the Chief Public Defender of the Nation*: This body guarantees access to justice and comprehensive legal assistance in both individual and collective claims, and promotes policies aimed at protecting fundamental rights, especially of those who are vulnerable. For example, Official Public Defenders provide legal assistance or representation to those who do not have enough economic resources to face the costs of a judicial process, or are in a vulnerable situation; and provide

86. These laws are: No. 24.946 (Organic Law of the Public Ministry), No. 27.148 (Organic Law of the Public Prosecutor's Office), and No. 27.149 (Organic Law of the Public Defender's Office).

judicial (and on occasions extrajudicial) assistance to minors, as well as to persons whose exercise of legal capacity has been restricted as a consequence of intellectual disabilities.

9 SPECIFIC PROBLEMS

In this section, two specific issues regarding the way in which the Argentine Constitution works in practice will be analyzed. Both of them have led to an accumulation of power in the Executive branch and an impact on constitutional rights.

First, several factors have been identified as contributors to the "deformation of the original structure of separation of powers of the 1853 Constitution of Argentina,"[87] giving way to a substantial accumulation of power in the Executive. "Today, the original conception of separation of powers (three branches of co-equal importance, with checks and balances in a horizontal relationship) has shifted to a vertical relationship with the executive branch at the top. Checks and balances have disappeared and, in fact, presidents exercise the lawmaking power through executive orders issued on grounds of necessity and urgency."[88] Among the factors that have undermined the separation of powers in Argentina, the exercise of legislative powers by the Executive is often cited. The first part of this section will examine, thus: (a) the delegation of legislative power to the Executive by the Congress (Article 76); (b) the issuance of dispositions of a legislative nature by the Executive (Article 99.3); (c) the partial promulgation of laws by the Executive (Article 80).

Second, the institutionalisation of emergency powers—mainly through tolerance of abuses regarding declarations of state of siege, increases in the power of Congress, and emergency decrees—has also led to a deviation of constitutional practice from the constitutional design of government, as well as to an impact on fundamental rights. The second part of this section will analyze, then, this phenomenon.

9.1 The Exercise of Legislative Powers by the Executive

The 1994 reform incorporated three prohibitions with regard to lawmaking power that did not exist before the amendment; however, immediately after formulating them, the constitutional text introduces exceptions to each of the prohibitions. The three prohibitions are: (a) the delegation of legislative power to the Executive by the Congress (Article 76); (b) the issuance of dispositions of a legislative nature by the Executive (the possibility of issuing decrees of necessity and urgency) (Article 99.3); (c) the partial promulgation of laws by the Executive (Article 80). Some of these institutions, like the decrees of necessity and urgency and the delegation of legislative power to the Executive, existed before the amendment in the constitutional practice,

87. Manuel José García-Mansilla, "Separation of Powers Crisis: The Case of Argentina" (2004) 32 Georgia Journal of International & Comparative Law 319.
88. *Ibid.*, 309.

and their abuse led to the incorporation of their prohibition with certain exceptions. Nevertheless, the practice since 1994 has also shown an abuse of the authorized exceptions.[89]

The first prohibition is related to the delegation of legislative power to the Executive. Article 76, after establishing the prohibition, goes on to state "except in specified matters concerning administration or public emergency, with a fixed period of time for exercise of the delegated authority, which may only be exercised within the terms established by Congress." The expressions "specified matters concerning administration or public emergency" are quite vague, which can lead to abuses.[90] The decrees that exercise powers delegated by Congress must be approved by the Chief of the Cabinet of Ministers, and then subject to the review of the Standing Bicameral Committee (Article 100.12).

The second prohibition relates to the issuance of dispositions of a legislative nature by the Executive "in any case whatsoever, under penalty of their absolute and incurable nullity" (Article 99.3). By way of exception, however, the President may dictate decrees of necessity and urgency when: (a) "exceptional circumstances make it impossible to follow the regular procedures provided by [the] Constitution for the passing of laws;" *and* (b) "the situation does not involve rules that regulate criminal, tax, or electoral matters or the regime governing political parties" (Article 99.3). The decision to issue this kind of decree must be taken "at a general meeting of Ministers," and the Ministers, together with the Chief of the Cabinet, must endorse the decree.

After the decree is issued, the Chief of the Cabinet must submit it within ten days for the consideration of the Standing Bicameral Committee, which must in turn forward a report within ten days to a plenary session of each Chamber of Congress for its immediate and express treatment (Article 99.3).[91]

The purpose of these decrees is that the exceptional severity of the emergency requires an immediate measure, which makes it impossible (or highly inconvenient) to follow the ordinary lawmaking process, since it does not provide an urgent solution. Nonetheless, since 1989, the concepts of emergency and necessity have been broadly construed, and a large number of these decrees have been issued. This phenomenon

89. Some authors uphold the 1994 reforms arguing that the now express constitutional limitations to the exercise of these powers may be more effective in reducing abuses than the weak control by the judiciary and the legislative branch before the amendment. Negretto states, for example, that "[a]s a matter of historical practice, (...) the president has de facto exercised these powers before the reform, but also the courts legitimated them with fewer limitations than in the present constitution. In this sense, while in the past the president used emergency decrees and the partial promulgation of laws without legislative intervention, now, the validity of these powers requires their explicit treatment by a congressional bicameral commission with plural representation. This may very well raise the costs of unilateral action by the executive. Something similar could be said of the delegation of legislative powers, which in the immediate past has been used with very few constraints in terms of content or time limits" (Negretto (n 45), 228).

90. Law No. 26.122, which establishes the legal regime for decrees of necessity and urgency, decrees that exercise delegated legislative powers and decrees that partially promulgate laws, has not laid down further rules specifying the occasions in which delegation of legislative powers is permitted.

91. Article 99.3 further states that "[a] special law approved by an absolute majority of the totality of the members of each Chamber shall regulate the procedure and the scope of the intervention of Congress." This law was enacted in 2006 (Law No. 26.122).

was partly boosted by the recognition that the Supreme Court granted to these rules in the *Peralta* case (1990).[92] In practice, thus, the raison d'être of these decrees has been somewhat distorted. Even after the express incorporation of the Article 99.3 prohibition in the Constitution, decrees of necessity and urgency have continued to be issued prolifically, partly because neither the constitutional text or the special law dictated by Congress to regulate these decrees provide concrete guidelines on what constitutes a serious emergency or an exceptional circumstance that requires their issuance.

The third and last prohibition refers to the partial promulgation of laws by the Executive. Pursuant to Article 80, "[b]ills that are partially rejected may not be approved as to their remaining parts." Nevertheless, the constitutional text immediately goes on to set out the exception to that rule, by stating that the parts that are not rejected may be promulgated if: (a) "they have normative autonomy;" *and* "their partial approval does not alter the spirit or the unity of the bill as passed by Congress." The decrees that partially promulgate laws, like the decrees of necessity and urgency, must be approved by the Chief of the Cabinet, jointly with the other Ministers, and submitted for consideration by the Standing Bicameral Committee within ten days of their enactment (Article 100.13).

These three prohibitions and their exceptions have proven to be quite ineffective in practice, to the point that it is possible to assert that "today the most important legislator in Argentina is the executive branch."[93]

9.2 Constitutional Emergency Powers

The second phenomenon that presents specific problems is the institutionalisation of emergency powers, which has led to restriction of personal constitutional rights and guarantees, circumvention of constitutional procedures, and power concentration. This result was attained mainly through long-term tolerance of abuses regarding declarations of state of siege, increases in the power of Congress, and emergency decrees.[94]

First, as regards the state of siege, the power of the government to suspend individual rights and liberties is explicitly provided for in the event of "internal disorder or foreign attack that endangers the exercise of this Constitution and of the authorities created thereby." In such case, "the Province or territory in which the disturbance of order exists shall be declared in a state of siege and the constitutional guarantees shall be suspended therein" (Article 23). The institution was repeatedly used in Argentine history: from 1854 to 2001, "the state of siege was declared fifty-seven times."[95] The degree of adequate judicial control over the governmental restriction of constitutional rights and guarantees during states of siege has changed over time.

92. *Peralta, Luis Arcenio c Estado Nacional* 313 Fallos 1513.
93. García-Mansilla (n 87), 319.
94. *See* Carlos Rosenkrantz, "Constitutional Emergencies in Argentina: The Romans (not the Judges) Have the Solution" (2011) 89 Texas Law Review 1557.
95. *Ibid.*, 1558.

Second, "[p]arallel to the augmentation of the power of the president during the state of siege—notwithstanding the progressively stronger opposition of the supreme court, especially in cases where personal liberty was involved—the supreme court incrementally expanded the ability of congress to infringe economic rights during constitutional emergencies even without declaring a state of siege."[96]

Finally, constitutional emergencies have also had an impact on the power of the Executive to issue dispositions of a legislative nature. "For some time, courts were strong defenders of the principle of division of powers. During the following years, the supreme court transitioned away from the requirements imposed by the division-of-powers model to a rather lax authorization to the president to surpass congress in cases of emergency."[97] Like in the previous cases, the degree of judicial monitor has been fairly inconsistent.

10 FUNDAMENTAL RIGHTS, LIBERTIES AND GUARANTEES

The 1853–1860 Constitution included a bill of rights, recognizing several civil and political rights, in regard to both nationals and foreigners. The 1957 reform added one article to the original text (Article 14*bis*), which incorporated various socio-economic rights.

The broader 1994 reform had a powerful impact on constitutional rights. A whole new chapter was added to the first part of the Constitution. While the previous chapter remains intact, now as the first chapter of the first part (entitled, like before, "Declarations, Rights and Guarantees"), the new chapter, named "New Rights and Guarantees," incorporates numerous rights (consumer and environmental rights, right of legislative initiative, etc.) as well as guarantees (the writ of amparo, of habeas corpus and of habeas data). Fundamental rights were also incorporated in the second part of the Constitution; a noteworthy example is the right to true equality of opportunity and treatment (Article 75.23). Finally, since 1994, the Argentine constitutional rights system has a double source: a domestic source and an international source, for the amendment granted constitutional hierarchy to several human rights treaties, and provided for the possibility of other human rights instruments to enjoy that same standing (Article 75.22). The repertoire of fundamental rights and liberties has thus been significantly increased. Additionally, the Supreme Court has made important advances in the field of economic, social and cultural rights;[98] environmental rights;[99] nondiscrimination and equality;[100] and collective actions;[101] among many others.

96. *Ibid.*, 1560.
97. *Ibid.*, 1563.
98. *See*, e.g., *Asociación Benghalensis*, 323 Fallos 1339; *Campodónico de Beviacqua*, 323 Fallos 3229.
99. *See*, e.g., *Mendoza*, 331 Fallos 1622.
100. *See*, e.g., *González de Delgado*, 323 Fallos 2659; *Hooft, Pedro Cornelio*, 327 Fallos 5118; *Reyes Aguilera*, 330 Fallos 3853.
101. *See infra* "10.6 Collective Rights and Actions."

Finally, a process that boosted the Supreme Court's willingness to conform its judgments to international norms and decisions started in 1992 with the *Ekmekdjian* case, grew steadily and was consolidated with the partial renewal of the composition of the tribunal that took place between 2002 and 2004. When dealing with cases, the Court regularly takes into consideration decisions and recommendations issued by human rights bodies such as the UN Human Rights Committee, the UN Committee on the Rights of the Child, and the UN Committee on Economic, Social and Cultural Rights. The jurisprudence of the Inter-American Court of Human Rights plays a particularly relevant role in the judicial application of human rights by the Argentine judiciary. The Inter-American Court's influence has been reinforced by the doctrine of conventionality control.[102] This doctrine creates the obligation for all state parties to the American Convention on Human Rights (ACHR) to interpret any national legal instruments (from the Constitution to administrative regulations) in accordance with the ACHR—and with the Inter-American *corpus juris* more generally, including the interpretation of the Convention by the Inter-American Court.[103] The doctrine has consequently altered the traditional underlying conception of the Inter-American human rights system as subsidiary and complementary to the domestic legal order. Instead, it "places the American Convention and its Inter-American judicial interpreter, the Court, at the top of the legal order."[104] The Supreme Court has endorsed the doctrine, *inter alia*, in the *Mazzeo* (2007) and *Videla* (2010) cases.[105]

10.1 Fundamental Rights and Liberties

This section will outline the rights and liberties protected by the Argentine Constitution, diving them—although the constitutional text does not make such

102. Leonardo Franco, "Recepción de la jurisprudencia interamericana en el ordenamiento jurídico argentino" in Sergio García Ramírez and Mireya Castañeda Hernández (eds), *Recepción nacional del derecho internacional de los derechos humanos y admisión de la competencia contenciosa de la Corte Interamericana* (Universidad Nacional Autónoma de México 2009) 157–158. García-Mansilla (n 88d to the fuction to Argentine Constitutional Law, tguage, often more restricted in scope than more thorough.
103. The Inter-American Court first introduced the doctrine in 2006, in the *Almonacid Arellano et al v. Chile* case. The Court has been thenceforth developing and broadening the doctrine, mainly through the cases *La Cantuta v. Peru* (2006), *Dismissed Congressional Employees v. Peru* (2006), *Boyce et al v. Barbados* (2007), and *Radilla Pacheco* (2009), *inter alia*. *See*, e.g., Ariel E. Dulitzky, "An Inter-American Constitutional Court? The Invention of the Conventionality Control by the Inter-American Court of Human Rights" (2015) 50 Texas International Law Journal 46.
104. Dulitzky (n 103), 47.
105. María Sofía Sagüés, "La proyección de la jurisprudencia y resoluciones de los órganos de aplicación de derechos económicos, sociales y culturales en el plano interamericano por los Tribunales Constitucionales. Perspectiva argentina", in Armin von Bogdandy et al. (eds), *Construcción y papel de los derechos sociales fundamentales: Hacia un Ius Constitutionale Commune en América Latina* (Universidad Autónoma de México, 2011) 45.

distinction—into civil rights and liberties; economic, social and cultural rights; environmental rights; consumer rights; and indigenous peoples rights.

10.2 Rights and Liberties Protected by the Constitution

Before listing the rights and liberties protected by the Constitution, three matters need to be preliminarily examined. First, rights are not absolute but enjoyed "in accordance with the laws that regulate their exercise" (Article 14). These laws, in turn, have their own limit, as the restrictions that may be placed on the exercise of rights must be reasonable, pursuant to Article 28.[106] International human rights treaties that enjoy the same standing as the Constitution also refer to limitations in this regard.[107]

Second, the rights listed below are rights expressly recognized in the Constitution; however, Article 33 contains the so-called implicit rights clause: "The declarations, rights and guarantees that the Constitution enumerates shall not be construed as a denial of other rights and guarantees not enumerated therein, but which issue from the principle of the sovereignty of the people and from the republican form of government." On the basis of this clause, courts have been able to invoke the existence of certain rights that were not recognized in the constitutional text. Thus, for example, in 1986 the Supreme Court recognized the right to marry of divorced persons, arguing that marriage and constituting a family were basic human needs, comprised in the right to human dignity that, according to the Court, was protected by Article 31.[108]

Finally, the Constitution implements a broad and humanistic immigration policy, in line with the principles set out in the Preamble and Alberdi's thoughts on the subject.[109] For this reason, nationals and foreigners enjoy the same civil rights: while Article 14 recognizes those rights to all inhabitants of the Nation (i.e., without distinguishing between nationals and foreigners), Article 20 expressly adds that "[f]oreigners enjoy in the territory of the Nation all the civil rights of a citizen." In addition to this general principle, Article 20 then specifies several civil rights that

106. Article 28 contains the following rule, known as the principle of reasonableness: "The principles, guarantees and rights recognized in the foregoing articles may not be altered by the laws that regulate their exercise."

107. For example, Art. 30 of the American Convention on Human Rights sets out that "[t]he restrictions that, pursuant to this Convention, may be placed on the enjoyment or exercise of the rights or freedoms recognized herein may not be applied except in accordance with laws enacted for reasons of general interest and in accordance with the purpose for which such restrictions have been established."

108. *Sejean c Zacks de Sejean* 308 Fallos 2268. It could seem that after the 1994 reform, which incorporated several human rights treaties that explicitly recognize a great number of rights and freedoms, Art. 31 has lost most of its appeal. However, the Supreme Court has continued to invoke it in various cases; for example, to recognize the right to a trial before an impartial court (*see Llerena, Horacio* 328 Fallos 1491).

109. Article 25 states that "[t]he Federal Government shall encourage European immigration." This clause dates from 1853–1860, and needs to be interpreted dynamically as an obligation of the Federal Government to encourage immigration without distinction of nationality or origin.

foreigners may enjoy,[110] and sets out rules for their naturalization.[111] Articles 21 and 25 also contain provisions on civil rights of foreigners, such as their tax free entry into the country.

The following rights and liberties are explicitly recognized in the Constitution:

(a) *Civil rights and liberties*: freedom of thought, freedom of expression, freedom of press, right to academic freedom, freedom of association, freedom of movement, freedom of religion, right to choose an occupation, right to establish a business, right to work, right of petition (Article 14); prohibition of slavery (Article 15); right to equality[112] (equality as the basis of taxation and public burdens) (Article 16);[113] movement of goods free from duties in the interior of the Republic (Articles 9–12); free navigation of inland rivers (Article 26); right to own property, protection from expropriation, abolition of confiscation, provisions for intellectual property (Article 17); equal rights of the citizens of each Province (Article 8); right to privacy (with regard to home and correspondence) (Article 18); right to privacy,[114] principle of legality[115] (Article 19); right of citizens to oppose resistance to those committing the acts of force against the institutional order and the democratic system (Article 36).

110. "[T]hey may engage in their industry, trade or profession, own, purchase or transfer real property, navigate the rivers and coasts, freely practice their religion, [and] make wills and marry in accordance with the laws. They are not obligated to assume citizenship, or to pay extraordinary compulsory taxes."
111. "They may obtain naturalization by residing two continuous years in the Nation, but the authorities may shorten this term in favor of anyone so requesting, upon their asserting and proving services to the Republic."
112. "All [inhabitants of the Argentine Nation] are equal before the law."
113. With regard to the right to equality, the 1994 amendment has incorporated various provisions that express the need to complement formal equality (enshrined in Art. 16) with substantive equality. Indeed, several new provisions deal with nondiscrimination, affirmative action, and equality of opportunity and treatment. As stated in Art. 75.23, Congress must "legislate and promote proactive measures that guarantee true equality of opportunity and treatment," "in particular with respect to children, women, the elderly and people with disabilities." Pursuant to Art. 37, "[t]rue equality of opportunity between men and women in running for elected and party offices shall be guaranteed through affirmative actions in the regulation of political parties and in the electoral system." This resulted in Law No. 24.012, which requires that a minimum of 30% of the candidates for elected offices must be women. Moreover, without mentioning positive action, Art. 75.19 states that Congress shall "pass laws on the organization of and basis for education which (...) assure (...) the equality of opportunities and means without any discrimination whatsoever." Other constitutional provisions—such as Art. 75.17 on indigenous peoples rights—relate to minority rights and the right to equal treatment and opportunities. Finally, several human rights treaties that stand on the same level as the Constitution (Art. 75.22) contain clauses on equality, minorities and nondiscrimination. *See* Guillermo F. Treacy, "Categorías sospechosas y control de constitucionalidad" (2011) 89 Lecciones y Ensayos 181.
114. "The private actions of men that in no way offend public order or morality, nor injure a third party, are reserved only to God, and are exempt from the authority of the magistrates."
115. "No inhabitant of the Nation shall be compelled to do what the law does not order, or be deprived of what it does not forbid."

(b) *Political rights*: right to vote,[116] true equality of opportunity between men and women in running for elected and party offices (Article 37); right to form political parties, free exercise of activities by political parties (access to public information and communication of their ideas, economic support of their activities and the training of their leaders) (Article 38); right to legislative initiative (Article 39) and popular referendum (Article 40).

(c) *Economic, social and cultural rights*: in Article 14*bis*: (i) right to equal pay for work, right to safe work environment and right to rest and leisure;[117] (ii) right to join trade unions and right to strike;[118] (iii) right to social security, right to shelter and right to reasonable standard of living.[119] According to Article 75.19 and 75.23, Congress shall provide for: (i) human development and economic progress with social justice; (ii) research and scientific and technological development, the professional development of workers, participation of the family and society in educational matters, equal educational opportunities and means, free and equitable State public education, autonomy and self-sufficiency of the national universities, protection of cultural identity and pluralism, unrestrained creation and circulation of the works of authors, the artistic heritage, and cultural and audiovisual spaces; (iii) harmonious growth of the Nation and differentiated policies that lead to balancing the irregular development of Provinces and regions; (iv) special and integral social security system that protects needy children, from gestation through the end of elementary schooling, and that protects the mother during pregnancy and nursing.

(d) *Environmental rights*: right to a healthful and balanced environment fit for human development, duty to preserve the environment, rational use of natural resources, preservation of the natural and cultural patrimony and of biological diversity, right to environmental information and education (Article 41).

(e) *Consumer rights*: right of consumers and users of goods and services to the protection of their health, safety and economic interests, to adequate and

116. "Suffrage is universal, equal, secret and mandatory."

117. "Labor in its diverse forms shall enjoy the protection of the law, which shall ensure to workers: dignified and equitable working conditions; a limited working day; paid days of rest and vacation; fair remuneration; adjustable minimum living wages; equal pay for equal work; a share in the earnings of enterprises, with control over production and collaboration in management; protection against arbitrary discharge; permanence of public employment ...".

118. "... Free and democratic organization of labor unions, recognized simply by inscription in a special register. Trade unions are hereby guaranteed: [the right] to conclude collective bargaining agreements; [the right] to resort to conciliation and arbitration; the right to strike. Union representatives shall enjoy the guarantees necessary for the performance of their union tasks and those relating to the permanence of their employment."

119. "The State shall grant the benefits of social security, which shall be comprehensive and unwaivable. In particular, the law shall establish: compulsory social security, which shall be under the charge of national or provincial entities having financial and economic autonomy, administered by the interested parties with State participation, but without the existence of overlapping contributions; adjustable retirement pay and pensions; full protection of the family; protection of the welfare of the family; economic compensation to families and access to decent housing."

truthful information, to freedom of choice, and to conditions of equitable and dignified treatment; right to a competitive marketplace and establishment of consumer and user associations (Article 42).

(f) *Indigenous peoples rights*: recognition of ethnic and cultural preexistence of indigenous peoples, recognition of possession and community property over lands they have traditionally occupied (and transfer of other lands fit and sufficient for human development), recognition of the legal standing of their communities, right to bilingual and intercultural education, right to participate in the related administration of their natural resources and of other interests affecting them (Article 75.17).

10.3 Guarantees

This section will briefly analyze the due process guarantees contained in Article 18; the three constitutional remedies designed to provide emergency judicial relief against fundamental rights violations (amparo, habeas data and habeas corpus); and finally, the evolution and current state of affairs with regard to collective rights and actions.

10.4 Due Process Guarantees

Article 18 contains various due process guarantees, such as the right to counsel, rules for evidence collection, protection from ex post facto laws and from self-incrimination, and the principle of no punishment without law.[120] The same provision also prohibits capital punishment for political offenses, cruel treatment and torture. Finally, it adds that "[t]he prisons of the Nation shall be healthful and clean, for the custody and not for the punishment of prisoners confined therein; and any measure that under the pretext of precaution leads to mortifying them beyond what their custody demands, shall render liable the judge who authorizes it."

10.5 Amparo, Habeas Data and Habeas Corpus

Article 43 deals with three constitutional remedies designed to provide emergency judicial relief against fundamental rights violations: the writ of amparo, of habeas data and of habeas corpus.

The writ of amparo was originally developed in Mexico, and then extended through the rest of Latin America with local adaptations.[121] The amparo is a procedure intended to provide fast and simple judicial protection from violations of rights

120. "No inhabitant of the Nation may be punished without prior trial based on a law in force prior to the offense, or tried by special commissions, or removed from the jurisdiction of the judges designated by the law in force prior to the offense. No one can be compelled to testify against himself, or be arrested except by virtue of a written order from a competent authority. The right to due process in the defense of the person and of rights is inviolable."

121. *See* Brewer-Carías (n 76).

protected by the Constitution, an international treaty or a law. In 1957, the Supreme Court rendered a landmark decision in the *Angel Siri* case,[122] when despite the absence of constitutional and legal provisions on the subject, granted an order directing the police to cease the closure of a newspaper. This case laid the foundation of the amparo in Argentina. A year later, in the *Samuel Kot* case,[123] the Court extended the scope of the writ of amparo to cover the infringement on constitutional rights stemming from acts of individuals. After years of judicial development, the Federal Congress enacted statutes to regulate the amparo.[124] Later, in 1994, it was introduced in the text of the Constitution in Article 43. Pursuant to this provision, any person can file an amparo "against any act or omission by public authorities or by private individuals, that presently or imminently harms, restricts, alters or threatens, in an arbitrary or manifestly illegal manner, the rights and guarantees recognized by this Constitution, by a treaty, or by a law." An amparo can only be filed "whenever no other more appropriate judicial means exists." Article 43 explicitly allows the judge, if appropriate, to "declare the norm upon which the harmful act or omission is founded unconstitutional." The second paragraph of Article 43 admits various forms of the collective amparo, which will be analyzed below.[125]

The writ of habeas data is regulated in third paragraph of Article 43, and can be filed by any person who wishes to "find out and to learn the purpose of data about him which is on record in public registries or data banks, or in any private [registers or data banks] whose purpose is to provide information." Additionally, "in case of falsity or discrimination," the person can also "demand the suppression, rectification, confidentiality, or updating" of the data. Finally, the provision adds that "[t]he secrecy of journalistic information sources shall not be affected."

The fourth and last paragraph of Article 43 regulates the writ of habeas corpus, which may be filed "by the affected person or by anyone else on his behalf" in cases: (a) where "the harmed, restricted, altered, or threatened right is that of physical liberty;" (b) of "illegal worsening in the manner or conditions of detention;" or (c) of "forced disappearance of persons." The judge shall immediately resolve the writ, "even while a state of siege is in effect."

10.6 Collective Rights and Actions[126]

Collective entities can also be fundamental rights holders. Before the 1994 reform, the Constitution did not refer to collective entities when establishing rights, except for the recognition of trade unions in Article 14*bis*. Nonetheless, in the aforementioned *Samuel Kot* case, the Court conceded that the writ of amparo could proceed to remedy

122. 239 Fallos 459.
123. 241 Fallos 291.
124. The most relevant of these statutes are Law No. 16.986 (1966) on amparo against acts of a public authority, and Law No. 17.454 (1967) on amparo against acts of private individuals.
125. *See* "10.6 Collective Rights and Actions."
126. *See*, e.g., Hector A. Mairal, "Collective and Class Actions in Argentina" (*Stanford Global Class Actions Exchange*, 2007) <http://globalclassactions.stanford.edu/sites/default/files/ documents/Argentina_National_Report.pdf> accessed January 16, 2017.

a violation of rights whose holder was a limited liability company. After the amendment, the Constitution refers to collective entities in many of its provisions: Article 38 refers to political parties, Article 42 to consumer and user associations, Article 43 to associations that support the ends protected by the collective amparo, etc. The Constitution thus recognizes certain rights of these entities, and affords the same protection to foreign collective entities, in the same way it acknowledges civil rights of foreign individuals in Article 20.

In addition, the second paragraph of Article 43 regulates the collective amparo, which can be filed whenever the action is intended to complain of "any form of discrimination," or refers to "the rights that protect the environment, competition, the user, the consumer, *or rights of a collective nature in general.*" In such cases, the action "may be brought by the affected party, the Defender of the People, and the associations that support these ends." This "collective" amparo is thus similar to the class actions of other jurisdictions.

Despite their recognition by the Constitution and by courts, a comprehensive regulatory framework applicable to collective actions has not been enacted yet. Currently, they are partially regulated by specific laws, such as Law No. 24.240, which deals with consumer protection. The new Civil and Commercial Code, which came into force in August 2015, recognizes the existence of collective rights. Indeed, Article 14 recognizes both individual and collective rights, and states that the law does not allow the exercise of individual rights in a way that can negatively affect the environment and collective rights in general.

The Supreme Court has played an important role in the development of these actions, while stressing the need for a law regulating them. In the absence of such a law, the Court laid down rules for collective claims in the 2009 *Halabi* case.[127] The existence of three categories of actions or claims was acknowledged:

(a) *Individual claims*: They are channelled through ordinary actions as well as the classic individual amparo (Article 43, paragraph 1), and intended to protect divisible, nonhomogeneous rights—i.e., repair an essentially individual damage.
(b) *Collective claims intended to safeguard collective goods*: They can be exercised through the collective amparo of Article 43, paragraph 2. These claims aim to protect interests that belong to the whole community, and are thus indivisible (e.g., environmental claims).
(c) *Collective claims concerning "individual homogeneous interests:"* They can also be exercised through the collective amparo provided for in Article 43, paragraph 2. In these kind of claims, a group of individuals seek to protect their "individual homogeneous interests"—i.e., their common interest in connection with individual rights, such as in the case of personal patrimonial

127. 332 Fallos 111. *See also PADEC c Swiss Medical* 336 Fallos 1236. In addition, the Supreme Court created in 2014 the "Public Registry of Collective Actions" to give publicity to collective claims filed before federal (including "national") courts. (For the distinction between federal and national courts, *see* "8.3 Judiciary of the City of Buenos Aires: Controversy over its Powers").

damages that derive from environmental damage, or when a group of consumers request judicial relief for burdensome obligations imposed by a service supplier in consumer contracts. As stated by the Court, in these cases: (i) there is a single fact or piece of legislation that causes injury to a plurality of individual rights; (ii) the claim is concerned with the common effects that the single fact or norm has on all subjects involved. Consequently, it is more reasonable that all the claims are dealt with jointly (except for the proof of the damage, which must be carried out individually, although within the same process).

Suggested Reading

The English version of the Argentine Constitution used to elaborate this chapter is the one published by Constitute Project and Oxford University Press: https://www.constituteproject.org/constitution/Argentina_1994.pdf.

Given the purpose of this introduction to Argentine Constitutional Law, the bibliography suggested below prioritizes books and articles written in the English language, even if they are often more restricted in scope than the works available in Spanish.

Further Reading

Bidart Campos G J, *Manual de la Constitución Reformada* (Ediar 1998).

Hernández A M, *Constitutional Law in Argentina* (2nd edn, Wolters Kluwer Law & Bussiness 2014).

Sagüés N P, *Manual de derecho constitucional* (Astrea 2016).

Sagüés N P, *La interpretación judicial de la Constitución* (Depalma 2006).

Gelli A, *Constitución de la Nación Argentina Comentada y Concordada* (La Ley 2014).

CHAPTER 3
Administrative Law

Alejandro Dalmacio Andrada

1 BRIEF HISTORICAL BACKGROUND

The scientific doctrine usually attributes the foundational moment of Administrative Law to the French Revolution.

Looking back to French law becomes a necessity even for certain legal systems such as Argentina, which adopted—as shall be seen shortly—a mixed model, but which has inherited significant elements from France, still persisting until the present time.

It has been rightly pointed out that: "After the French Revolution, when Administrative Law was born, and during the first half of the last century, Public Administration has been identified with the executive office, under the constitutional framework of the principle of division of powers. Administrative Law, thus, could be considered the special legal system of the Executive Power."[1]

As regards Argentine Administrative Law, it is derived from two diverse historical sources: it is a legacy of the French legal system and, at least in part, of the legal system of the United States of America.

There was a discussion in Argentina regarding the body which should exercise contentious administrative jurisdiction.

In fact, the followers of the French model thought that the administration itself should exercise jurisdictional functions of a contentious administrative nature. And, on the other hand, the followers of the American trend considered that the contentious administrative jurisdiction was a power which should be exercised by judicial bodies.

1. Garcia de Enterria, Eduardo & Fernandez, Tomás Ramón, Curso de Derecho Administrativo, Vol. I, p. 26, Civitas, 1999.

The Argentine Constitution of 1853 followed the Anglo-Saxon model. In fact, the Supreme Court of Justice and other lower courts were attributed the exercise of the judiciary office, which was prohibited to the President (Sections 91 and 92).[2]

Long after that, Act 12.967 instituted a Contentious Administrative court within the core of the Federal Chamber of the City of Buenos Aires, capital of the country. Sometime later, Act 13.278 established two new federal courts with exclusive jurisdiction over administrative matters.

The Provinces felt compelled to follow the model and created Contentious Administrative courts within their jurisdiction.. However, several turned to the European model, by granting jurisdiction over the matter to state courts and establishing the reviewing character of contentious administrative jurisdiction.[3]

Having stated the above, it is necessary to linger for a minute on the letter and spirit of Argentine Administrative Law so as to better comprehend Argentine's institutions.

2 CONCEPT OF ADMINISTRATIVE LAW

There are different definitions of Administrative Law in Argentinian legal doctrine:

- It is said to be a "set of positive public law rules and principles which are effectively applied to the institution and operation of public services and the consequent Public Administration jurisdictional controller."[4]
- Or the "set of internal public law rules and principles aimed at the organization and operation of the public administration, as well as the regulation of inter-organic, inter-administrative relations, and those of the administrative bodies with the parties they manage."[5]
- Or the study of the "the legal system of the State's administrative functions; that is, the set of rules and principles integrating the legal system and regulating the role of the Executive Office, and two other relevant and complementary aspects … This is, the mode of organization of the State to exercise these roles and the connection between the State, in the exercise of these roles, with the individuals."[6]

2. The adoption of this model is reinforced by Acts 27 and 48, which attribute competent jurisdiction to federal judges over contentious administrative affairs.
3. Domingo, Hugo L. *supra*, p. 176, the author explains that the 1873 Constitution of the Province of Buenos Aires was taken as a model by several Argentine provinces. We recommend reading Domingo's work dedicated to the origins of the Province of Santa Fe and, especially, the Constitutional reform of 1890.
4. Bielsa, Rafael, Derecho Administrativo, Vol. I, pp. 5 and et seq.
5. Marienhoff, *supra*, p. 160, para. 32. He adopts the objective or material criteria, which means that when he talks about public administration, he is referring to the activity of any of the state bodies if the juridical nature of the activity developed is administrative.
6. Balbín, *supra*, points out, in fact, that "Administrative Law is technically a set of principles and rules over the Executive Office, by virtue of its structure and its own public purposes and, basically, of the connections of individuals to it" (p. 171).

The most prominent characteristic of Administrative Law is that of being a local, that is, provincial law.[7]

3 DIVISION OF POWERS AND ADMINISTRATIVE LAW

Division of powers is understood by legal doctrine as "a guarantee to freedom," so that "power contains power." However, even if Argentina might be said to undergo a crisis in its Parliament, there are several reasons to remain hopeful, both concerning the judicial control of the laws as for the judicial control of State acts.

In terms of the first of said controls, there is however a trend of the National Supreme Court of Justice to allow magistrates to ex officio declare the unconstitutionality of laws and regulations.[8]

As regards the second of these controls, it should be noted that, in the field of administrative law, the evolution of case law in the National Supreme Court of Justice in terms of political issues warns of a clear progress in the consolidation of the rule of law which does not contemplate the existence of thematic blocks or sets exempt from judicial control.

Thus, it rightly stated many years ago that it is an attribution of the Judiciary Office to judge "the existence and limits of the exclusive powers of the other offices" (Judgments 210:1095) and the "excess of the attributions in which these may incur" (Judgments 254:43).

It should be noted that this trend is verified in topics as diverse as the review of minimum and indispensable requirements which condition the creation of the laws in the sphere of Congress (Judgments 256:556); the nullity of certain rulings by the Executive Office (Judgments 323:2256); the scope of the privileges agreed for the members of Congress pursuant to Sections 60 and 61 of the National Constitution—68 and 69 after the reform of 1994—(Judgments 135:250); the control of democratic procedures in the electoral sphere ("Ponce versus San Luis," dated February 24, 2005).

So, although there have been—and still are—judges in Argentina who have not exercised the essential control as they should have, there are still some noteworthy precedents in the Court case law from which its adequate exercise can be derived, especially after the return of democracy, in 1983.

---

7. This explains why much of the case law quoted in this chapter on the subject comes from provincial courts.
8. In fact, the requirement that that control be executed at the request of the interested party happened to be a Praetorian addition established by the Court in 1941 with reference to *Ganadera Los Lagos* (Judgments: 190:142). As explained by the high Court in the recent case *Rodríguez Pereyra*, dated November 27, 2012 (Judgments: 335:2333): "... Such requirement was based on the warning that the constitutionality check without the party's request would imply that the judges can supervise the legislative acts or administration decrees of their own initiative, and that such activity would affect the balance of powers. However, faced with this argument, it was later proposed that, if the judicial attribution of the constitutional control is accepted, it is not consistent to affirm that the two democratic powers of the Constitution are not tampered with when there is a request by the interested party, but that they are so when there is no such request (Judgments 306:303)."

The Supreme Court of the Autonomous City of Buenos Aires stated that: "we cannot properly refer to the supremacy of the Constitution, if the one in charge of controlling the constitutional legitimacy of the acts is the same power which issues them. The division of powers means, in the political philosophy of El Federalista, which has inspired our Republican model, a separation of offices and reciprocal control of the exercise of their duties."[9]

4 SOURCES OF ADMINISTRATIVE LAW

The primary source of the law, or all legal systems and, therefore, of Administrative Law, is the National Constitution, which is the leading source.

The fundamental law supersedes all the set of rules (Section 31 of the National Constitution). If this was always the case, it is even more so now following the contributions of Neo-Constitutionalism, which has pointed the Constitution as an operational and binding set of rules.

Below the Constitution are the laws, a qualitatively more important source, and regulations, a quantitatively more important source.[10]

Other sources of Administrative Law are instructions and official communications; administrative acts and contracts "direct and immediate sources of Administrative Law, as well as decrees, resolutions and municipal ordinances."[11]

As regards the latter, it should be noted that in most provinces, municipal ordinances constitute acts which can be contested through the contentious administrative recourse.

Another important source is international Human Rights treaties, mostly those which have a supranational application judicial entity, such as the Pact of San José, Costa Rica (Inter-American Court of Human Rights), and those which are incorporated into the Constitution but which do not have an international court, such as the integration treaties authorized pursuant to Subsection 24 of Section 75 of the National Constitution, which are not governed by a supranational court.[12]

5 CONNECTIONS OF ADMINISTRATIVE LAW WITH OTHER BRANCHES OF LAW

The connections of Administrative Law with other branches of the law may present points of conflict, others which are subject to discussion, not all of them definitely overcome since there are conflicting positions which are difficult to bridge. This is the case of Criminal Law, Labor Law and even Civil Law.

9. Dated 14.7.1999 "Partido Justicialista y otros c/Gobierno de la Ciudad de Buenos Aires (Legislatura)", file 50/99-F-326.
10. Marienhoff, *supra*, pp. 219 and 250.
11. Marienhoff, *supra*, pp. 323, 325/326, 328, 330/331.
12. Gordillo, *supra*, VI-12 and 13. This work features a full development of the supranational sources of Administrative Law. The significance of the Inter-American Convention against Corruption and the International Convention against Trans-National Bribery (Act 25.319) should be noted.

Administrative law bears an intimate relationship with Constitutional Law, since Administrative Law is nothing but a continuity of Constitutional Law, with no continuity solution.

As regards Provincial and Municipal Public Law, it is not entirely appropriate to talk about relationships since it is a part of Administrative Law, integrating it.

Although some undergraduate law programs include it as an autonomous course of study, what is truly decisive is that the discussions over municipal contentious law are substantiated in administrative contentious venues through strictly administrative categories: administrative acts, public contracting, responsibility of the State, etc.

In the last decades, Environmental Law has been placed at the core of the national legal scene.[13] From there, the relationships with Administrative Law become increasingly apparent.

In the contentious administrative sphere, it is common to challenge acts of undoubted environmental content.[14] Thus, for instance, several claims—usually denied—have been initiated, contesting acts ordering to suspend the operation of telephone antennae or directly prohibiting the installation of antennae; other acts have ordered the relocation of establishments dedicated to intensive cattle fattening;[15] the Federal Court has explained that the application of the precautionary principle forced to suspend land clearing authorizations and their execution in the four departments of the Province of Salta until the performance of an accumulative impact study;[16] and, as regards the distribution of competencies—nation, provinces and communities—, the petition for annulment of a Communal Ordinance which would have prohibited the use of certain phyto-sanitary products has been denied since it was considered that there can be no constitutional grievance when the lower rule protects more than the higher one.[17]

There are important connections between Administrative Law and Tax Law.

13. There are several reasons which have led to position Environmental Law in Argentina: the provision of Section 41 of the National Constitutional, which places the law in a healthy and balanced environment and distributes the competencies among Nation and Provinces; the passing of the new General Environmental Act 25.675; and, especially, the decisions of the Federal Court in its last case law cycle, which has prioritized the environmental issue. In other aspects, Environmental Law has gained full autonomy in graduate and undergraduate law programs and has generated great interest from students and graduate students in the specialization and masters degree programs.
14. In France, it is worth mentioning the decision of the State Council of February 25, 1998, which admitted Greenpeace's claim to suspend the authorization for the cultivation of three transgenic corn species, based on the principle of precaution.
15. Acts which are generally not illegitimate, notwithstanding the responsibility of the State for any lawful acts which may apply.
16. This can be seen in further detail in the comment, Andrada, Alejandro D. and Hernández, Carlos A. Soja, precautionary principle and agro-chemicals, in Revista de Derecho de Daños, 2011-1, Daño ambiental, pp. 437 and et seq., especially, p. 447, Rubinzal Culzoni, Santa Fe, 2011.
17. Chamber of Contentious Administrative Affairs No. 2 of Rosario, "Speedagro S.R.L. versus Arequito Community", decision dated October 3, 2011, A. y S. T. 45, p. 30. This ruling analyzes the meaning of the term "complement" in Section 41 of the National Constitution.

Beyond the scientific autonomy of Tax Law, the doctrine states that the bodies and the form of application of financial standards are administrative in nature, as are the recourses against the acts ruled by the tax administration.[18]

It should be added that tax law currently shows an increasing complexity and litigious nature, with several claims initiated against provincial and municipal acts[19] determining obligations.

Administrative Law has no close relationships with Criminal Law. These two branches have some points of proximity but cannot mix.

An "administrative criminal law" has been established, independently from substantive criminal law. The Federal Court has declared that: "The acquittal of the defendants in the criminal venue does not entail an obstacle for determining their disciplinary assessment, since the administrative ruling is independent from the judicial one by virtue of the different purposes they pursue and the legal property protected by each, as well as the principles which apply in one and the other sphere, and the fundamentally diverse values at stake."[20]

What needs to be respected, of course, is the right to a defense of public agents, even when facing the possibility of minor penalties, such as a warning. And they should be able to exercise said defense before issuance of the final act. It is obviously not enough with the defense that the agents may state upon contesting or appealing the punitive measure.

There are close connections between Administrative Law and Labor Law.

Although Section 2 of the Labor Contract Law states that: "... The provisions of this law shall not apply to: a) those reporting to the national, provincial or municipal administration, except if expressly included thereunder or under the collective bargaining work conventions ... ." It is also true that the relationship between the public agent with the State does not differ substantially from the one established in the private sector.

This explains why, for instance, the standards of the labor contract law have been proposed to consider the term of the termination prescription of actions initiated by public officials on salary matters;[21] or that, *verbi gratia*, the guardianship aspect of labor law has been considered to provide protection to the public worker hired for an extensive period of time and later terminated.[22] In several cases, the Court has understood that the administration resorted to legally authorized juridical figures, with an obvious deviation of power aimed at covering permanent appointments under the appearance of definite time contracts, incurring in an illegitimate behavior which results in liability.

18. Marienhoff, *supra*, p. 178.
19. In the author's province, for example, several contentious administrative recourses have been interposed against acts which set an adjustment for right of registration or inspection, to which the rules of the "tariffs" apply. Well, in these cases, the administrations sued must prove the effective provision of the service, which certainly cannot be fulfilled with the mere registration of the activity.
20. Judgments: 305:102, cons. 6.
21. A two-year term applied, for instance, by the case law in the Province of Santa Fe.
22. Protection spirit which can be found in several judgments of the Federal Court, such as *Ramos*, dated April 6, 2010 and *Cerigliano*, dated April 19, 2011.

Administrative Law and Civil Law differ because the former is made up of coordination standards, while the latter is made up of subordination standards.[23]

The connections between both types of law currently exhibits diverging positions in terms of two relevant topics: the responsibility of the State and the statute of limitations.

The very recent National Civil and Commercial Code (CCC) of Argentina establishes that its provisions do not apply to the responsibility of the State (Section 1764) and that such responsibility is governed by the standards and principles of Administrative Law (Section 1765).

On the other hand, in August 2014, the new Law of Responsibility of the State (hereinafter LRE, as per the Spanish acronym) became effective. It is a federal law. It has a national scope, and applies to the National Government. It is effective in the provinces which adhere to said law, pursuant to Section 11 of the Law.

A part of the case law considers that the text of the CCC is unconstitutional because, to the best of their knowledge, the responsibility of the State is a matter of General Law which should be included in the CCC. Another part of the case law does not share this alleged unconstitutionality.[24]

Another point of conflict related to jurisdiction is that of the statute of limitations.

One sector thinks that its regulation, as every matter pertaining to the relationship between creditor and debtor, is attributable to General Law, and should be regulated by the Civil and Commercial Code. However, the new National CCC establishes that: "... Local legislation shall regulate the latter regarding the term of obligations" (Section 2532 in fine). In the defense of the lawmaker's criteria, it might be argued that if the provinces are able to create their own obligations, with good reason, they are more than entitled to establish the corresponding terms.

The relationship of Administrative Law—or rather, Administrative Procedural Law—with Civil Procedural Law is one of complementarity. In fact, several provincial contentious Administrative Codes set forth that, when an issue is not regulated by the Code, the Civil Code should be resorted to as a complement. This happens often in several areas, such as the evidentiary stage (regulation of evidence, etc.), which is of no surprise, given that the Codes or regulatory laws of the contentious administrative procedure are brief or succinct when compared to the prolific and wordy regulations contained in the Civil and Commercial Procedural Codes.

6 ADMINISTRATIVE ACT AND DEFECTS OF ILLEGITIMACY OF THE ADMINISTRATIVE ACT

It could be argued that the administrative act is that ruled in relation to the administrative function.[25]

23. Marienhoff, *supra*, pp. 181 and 182.
24. This issue is later examined when dealing with the responsibility of the State.
25. Gordillo, Agustín, Tratado de Derecho Administrativo, 5th Edition, Vol. 3, El acto administrativo, I-10, Fundación de Derecho Administrativo, Buenos Aires, 2000.

In the national sphere, Act 19.549 sets forth the essential requirements of the administrative act: (a) Being ruled by a competent authority. (b) Being based on the facts and background which have caused it and on the applicable law. (c) The object must be certain and physically and juridically possible. It should decide over all petitions made but may not involve others which have not been proposed with a previous hearing by the interested party, provided it does not affect acquired rights. (d) Before its issuance, the essential and substantial procedures should be fulfilled, as well as those implicit in the legal system. (e) It shall have a motivation, and the reasons leading the Administration to rule the Act shall be specifically expressed. (f) It shall meet the purpose resulting from the standards which grant the corresponding powers to the issuing body, without having other purposes, whether public or private, that those justifying the act, its cause and object. The measures involved by the act shall be proportionately adequate to said purpose. (g) In terms of form, it is established that the Act shall be indicated expressly and in writing, indicating the time and place of issuance, and containing the signature of the issuing authority; only as an exception and if so allowed by the circumstances may a different form be used.[26]

As regards the defects of the Administrative Act, competence will be addressed in the first place.[27,28]

Well, the defect of lack of competence is often mentioned by appellants in the contentious administrative venue. Thus, for instance, in the Province of Santa Fe, a defect is constituted when the act is ruled by the signature of the communal President alone and not by the communal Commission, as required by the standard;[29] in another case, it was determined that the Chief of Police acted without having due competence given that the issuance of the execution and autonomous rulings, as well as internal order standards, are an attribution of the Governor of the Province.[30]

The defect of breach of substantial forms is often invoked in the public employment disciplinary contentious sphere, and it is considered applicable in those cases in which the agent is penalized without a preliminary report.

The deviation of power is also a frequently alleged defect in the contentious administrative recourses. It applies when a public official acts for a personal benefit, when he acts to benefit a third party or group of third parties, or when he acts in order to benefit the administration, which is quite frequent a case, such as the case law has noted.[31]

The defect of unequal treatment is invoked in innumerable cases, being perhaps the most widely used in contentious administrative claims. But for this to proceed, the identity of subjective and objective situations should concur perfectly.

26. Diez, Manuel M., with the collaboration of Hutchinson, Tomás, Manual de Derecho Administrativo, Vol. 1, p. 192, 8th Edition, Editorial Plus Ultra, Buenos Aires, 1996.
27. Lisa, Federico & Weder, Rubén, El proceso contencioso administrativo en la Provincia de Santa Fe, Vol. 1, pp. 92 and et seq., Juris, Rosario, 1998.
28. Gordillo, *supra* and Vol. VIII-25.
29. Case *Malagueño*, of the Supreme Court of the Province of Santa Fe, T. 98, p. 152, quoted by Lisa and Weder, quoted, p. 95.
30. Case *Mendoza*, of the Santa Fe Court dated December 30, 1991, quoted by Lisa and Weder, *supra*, pp. 93 and 94.
31. Gordillo, *supra* and Vol. IX-25 and 26.

It is known that, with respect to propositions based on the guarantee of equality that inequality should result from the text itself of the law applied and not from the interpretation given to it by the competent authority.[32]

Other defects are those of lack of grounds and false grounds.

In relation to the above, the Court of Santa Fe has stated that: "... given that the act is not contemplated in none of the *de facto* alternatives pursuant to which it was understood that the personnel covered by decree 2112 should be transferred, the corresponding act seems to be ... devoid of grounds ... ."[33]

The motivation of the act imposes a minimum explanation. Lisa and Weder say that, in the same way as the element which constitutes grounds for the act is present if sufficient background exists to justify its ruling, motivation is only fulfilled if said background is adequately expressed in the corresponding act.[34]

The Court of Santa Fe has stated that motivation "should indicate the rationale on which the Public Administration, in consideration of the assumptions in fact and law, and applying the good administration rules, has based the determination of the act and has provided it with content. In other words, the administrative authority must necessarily justify the act by means of the exposure of the *de facto and de jure* assumptions which serve as a basis or rationale."

And it required that: "motivation has to be enough for its scope to allow to reconstruct in each specific case the logical process through which administrative will has been created and to be able to evidence the concatenation relating the different propositions."[35]

Specifically, this High Court approved a recourse which contested an act revoking the appointment of a plaintiff as a public official in the understanding that the mere mention in the act of the provisions set forth by Acts 7519 and 8621, Statute and Classification of Commune Personnel was insufficient;[36] in another case, a recourse was also accepted in which an agent had been terminated due to an act that only stated that he "had not fulfilled the minimum indispensable requirements to continue a stable relationship."[37]

And the courts have been strict in relation to the motivation of discretionary acts. Thus, the Supreme Court of Justice has expressed that: "The exercise of discretionary powers does not exempt the administrative body from checking the precautions required by Act 19.549 for all administrative acts, but rather compels to a stricter compliance with the due motivation of the act...,"[38] and the Court of Santa Fe, quoting Tomás R. Fernández, demanded that: "discretionary decisions should be supported and justified by the objective data over which they operate ... ."[39]

The defects of consent account for several cases of "error" and "violence."

32. Judgments 320:228.
33. CSSFe, case *Lallana*, A y S. T. 132, p. 176.
34. Lisa & Weder, *supra*, p. 105.
35. CSSFe, case *Villar* A. y S. T. 84, p. 362.
36. CSSFe, case *Flores*, A. y S. T. 76, p. 442.
37. CSSFe, case *Abramor*, A. y S. T. 115, p. 334.
38. CSJN, 2011/12/27, *Silva Tamayo*.
39. CSSFe, case *San Martín*, A. y S. T. 97, p. 263.

The case law illustrates this with cases of essential error: "a pardon referring to a person other than the one intended by the Executive Office; a declaration of martial law which, due to a material error in the preparation of the decree, refers to a place other than the one intended; veto on a law different than the one considered due to an error in the number; the appointment to a public office of a person other than the one intended, due to having a similar name … ."[40]

The violence over the official deems the act null and void, as well as when the administrator forces an express or implicit consent to the act, in those cases in which such consent is a condition for its validity.[41]

The excess of penalty constitutes a defect classified in an area difficult to access by the court which faces the risk of substituting the administrative assessment for his own. However, recourses have been admitted which, for instance, warned of the unreasonableness of a penalty in relation to the accusation and the special circumstances of the case.[42]

7 ADMINISTRATIVE CONTRACTS

Within the acts performed during the exercise of the administrative role, in some cases there are unilateral manifestations of the administration it conducts on its own and, in other cases, there are concurrent acts performed jointly in agreement between the administration and other parties.[43]

The general interest may be fulfilled by the State directly or indirectly. In fact, the administration may in itself build a way and leave it to the public criteria, or may do so indirectly by contracting with private parties.[44]

In the contractual sphere, it is not easy to establish a difference (within the range of administration contracts) between the two species of "ordinary contracts" and "public contracts."

Diverse parameters have been used to distinguish the nature of the relationship. In the Federal Court case law, it is warned that, for determining the nature of the agreement, several criteria have been adopted. In several precedents which go beyond the higher court, such as in *Albano* (1968), *Ingeniero Livio Dante Porta* (1973), *Intecar* (1979), there was an oscillation between the idea of the legal system and the public purpose. Also, that as from 1984, as happened in the cases *EFA* and *La Buenos Aires*, the Court considered the purpose of the contract and the presence of extraordinary clauses[45]

40. Gordillo, *Agustín, supra*, IX-46.
41. Gordillo, *Agustín, supra*, IX-51.
42. CSSFe, A. y S. T. 102, p. 116; T. 111, p. 132, quoted by Lisa & Weder, *supra*, p. 111.
43. Gordillo, Agustín, Tratado, Vol. 1, 10th Edition, X-7, Fundación de Derecho Administrativo, Buenos Aires, 2009.
44. Diez, Manuel M. in collaboration with Hutchinson, Tomás, *supra*, p. 281.
45. Coviello, Pedro J. Los contratos de derecho privado de la Administración, pp. 225 and s.s., in *Cuestiones de Contratos Administrativos* (in honor of professor Comadira), Ediciones RAP, Buenos Aires, 2007.

It is interesting to briefly point out the interpretation criteria in administrative contracts.[46]

Undoubtedly, the good faith principle is fully applicable to administrative contracts.[47]

Another generally admitted rule is the inadmissibility of contractor's claims against the State if the contracts have been pronounced void. Administrative contracts are only valid if they are preceded by a public bid.[48]

Another principle may be summarized as follows: the doubt is fatal for the concessionaire of the contract.[49]

It is difficult to summarize the effects of the administrative contract. In general, one could begin by remembering the four rules of Jèze regarding the execution of administrative contracts. For the first rule, this renowned writer established the firm principle of fulfillment which is lightened in the subsequent rules. The second rule refers to force majeure, while the third one refers to the responsibility derived from nonfulfillment, and the latter to the theory of unforeseeability.[50]

One of the most invoked rights of the contractor is the right to maintain the economic-financial equation. Even when the court practice shows that, on occasion, there is confusion regarding the reasons which alter the economic-financial balance of the contract, and sometimes concomitant arguments are proposed, a systematization effort from a rational perspective allows to dissociate several causes which alter or modify the essential balance.

It is therefore possible to visualize an assumption of contractual responsibility of the State when it fails to fulfill the agreed obligations or introduces changes to an agreement; an assumption of attributable cause to the administration, which configures the "Acts of the State;" an assumption of cause which cannot be claimed against the State, which features the theory of unforeseeability.[51]

---

46. It can be seen in the work by Comadira, Julio R., *Elementos de Derecho Administrativo*, La Ley, Buenos Aires, 2005, particularly pp. 877 and et seq.
47. CSN, 1988/06/09 *Juan María de Vido e Hijos S.C.A.*
48. CSN, 1987/11/17, *Stamei S.R.L. versus National University of Buenos Aires*. The High Court here explained that the award of an administrative contract which was performed omitting a public bid, despite it being requested by law, is null of absolute nullity. Also, it ruled that: "The indemnity recourse claimed by the winner of a public work should be rejected ... if the company, upon omission of a public bid during contracting, knowingly assumed the risk of a subsequent declaration of nullity thereof ... ".
49. Comadira, *supra*, p. 878, quoting case of the Supreme Court *Hotel Internacional Iguazú, S.A.*, 1986/04/22, in which the following was expressed: "That, on the other hand, the silence by the Administration is not an acceptable behavior to be considered a positive statement of will, since except as otherwise expressly stated in the rules, silence must be interpreted in a negative sense (Sections 913, 918, 919, 1145, 1146 of Civil Code and Section 10 of Act 19.549). Nothing should be considered as granted except if provided in unequivocal terms or through an equally clear implication. The affirmative statement needs to be proved; silence implies denial, and doubt is fatal for the concessionaire's right (Judgment case law: 149:218—last whereas clause—)" (cons. 8).
50. Jèze, Gastón. Principios generales del Derecho Administrativo, T. V, pp. 16 and et seq.
51. Each of these figures generates its own effects, its statute of limitations, etc., which, due to their extent, cannot be developed here.

An issue which warrants great importance is to determine whether the *exceptio non adimpleti contractus*, as set forth in Section 1201 of the Civil Code and now in Section 1031 of the very recent CCC, is applicable in the sphere of Administrative Law.

The clause is applicable when, as a consequence of the administration fact, there is a "reasonable impossibility" for the contracting party to meet its obligations.[52] Different authors have drawn attention to certain nuances to be taken into account when applying the clause:

- They point out the importance of the distinction based on whether administrative contracts entail or not a monopoly or exclusivity.[53]
- They also have signaled that it is unfair that for the administration to demand compliance from the contractor when it itself fails to meet its obligations.[54]
- Moreover, it has been stated that: "the higher the public interest commitment in the execution of the contract, the more requirements there will be for the fulfillment exception to proceed, but in no case shall it entail the extreme of denying the right to invoke said exception to the contractor."
- On the contrary, when the public purpose the administrative contract is intended to meet is less relevant, the requirements for contractual breach exception shall be less."[55]

8 THE PUBLIC EMPLOYMENT CONTRACT

A detailed consideration should be made for the relationship of public employment which constitutes the main material area of competence in the contentious administrative jurisdictional bodies.[56]

The first question to be asked is: What is the purpose of this relationship? The Court of Santa Fe answers this question by explaining that the relationship is established between the "administration and a private party for the execution of certain works whose performance responds—eventually—to a public and general interest purpose, whose fulfillment constitutes an essential role of public entities."[57]

The said juridical relationship is of a contractual nature.[58]

The appointment to public employment positions warrants some specific comments.

52. Marienhoff, Tratado, Vol. III-A, pp. 380 and et seq.
53. Gordillo, Agustín, Tratado, Vol. 1, XI-43, 5th Edition, Fundación de Derecho Administrativo, Buenos Aires, 1998.
54. Cassagne, Juan C. El contrato administrativo, p. 205, Abeledo Perrot, Buenos Aires, 1999.
55. Comadira, Julio P. La excepción de incumplimiento contractual en el Derecho Administrativo, pp. 695 and et seq., in the collective work "Cuestiones de contratos administrativos" (*supra*).
56. This issue is considered by: Lisa, Federico J. Los elementos de la relación de empleo público en la jurisprudencia (Sujetos, objeto y contenido), Revista de Derecho Público 2007-2, Contratos administrativos II, Rubinzal Culzoni, Santa Fe, pp. 171 and et seq.; and, in the same publication, Andrada, Alejandro D., El empleo público en la Provincia de Santa Fe, 2012-1, Empleo público I, pp. 287 and et seq.
57. Case *Bongiovanni*, A. y S. T. 135–343.
58. CSN, Judgments: 210:85; 266:19; 311:216, among others.

As is well known, "qualification" is the requirement set forth by the Constitution "to be appointed to public office" (Section 16 of the National Constitution). The Court of Santa Fe has considered that qualifications, as a constitutional requirement to be appointed to public office "cannot stem from any *iuris et de iure* assumption, and should be proved pursuant to the legal standards."[59]

A recent issue which has received interest from the case law and some judicial questioning is related to the behavior of the Magistrates Council regarding the contestability of their acts.

The Court of the Province of Buenos Aires has stated that "challenging the decisions made within the framework of selection procedures for personnel to fill positions in the provincial judiciary by individuals dismissed from said positions constitutes the subject matter of the contentious administrative jurisdiction, but has warned that the Judiciary Office should not substitute the Council in its exclusive and proprietary roles."[60] The Second Chamber in Contentious Administrative Affairs of Rosario, explained that: "... Whenever there is a standard and a defect of illegitimacy is invoked, the control required from this Chamber is compelled in order to check the acts and statements issued with the constitutional and administrative legal system, to conclude in a conformity or non-conformity judgment with it, and without that entailing—of course—an invasion of the internal discretionary core of the respective decisions."[61]

The right to receive a salary or compensation stands out among employees' rights.

In several claims, its rationale is based on challenging a new salary policy, generally invoking the right to a fair compensation.

It should be noted that it is difficult for the court to have access to certain aspects, since it cannot invade those related to opportunity, merit or convenience considered at the time of issuing the new salary scheme.[62]

Salary reduction, in normal times, cannot be considered legitimate.[63]

Another interesting subtopic is that of unpaid salaries and the right to strike.

In the case *Aguirre*[64] the Second Chamber in Contentious Administrative Affairs of Rosario analyzed the sensitive issue of the strike in public employment and, more precisely, the right of agents to receive a salary for days off during the strike is not considered illegal.

59. A. y S. T. 204-254; T. 207-334.
60. SCJBA, 28/9/99, case *Guridi*, El Derecho, Administrative Law Supplement dated August 29, 2000.
61. CCA 2 of Rosario, case *Borgarello*. It can be seen in Andrada, *supra*, p. 298.
62. The Court of Santa Fe in *García Leiva* (A. y S. T. 112-143) has ruled that: "...the compensation for state employees is generally determined based on essentially discretionary powers of the competent authorities, closely related to the weighing of political, economic, social or other circumstances, but all of them always independent from the judges' appraisal."
63. The Second Chamber of Contentious Administrative Affairs of Rosario, in the case entitled *Urquiza* (A. y S. T. 26-58), concluded that "in the special circumstances of the case, having applied to the agent the provisions of order 3707, a salary reduction such as the one verified in the case proceedings could not be deemed legitimate, since the agent had been working for the municipality for over twenty five years, and his work hours had not been cut down."
64. A. y S. T. 24-145.

Since in that case the strike had not been deemed illegal, it was appropriate to remember that absence due to strike does not entail a liable noncompliance with the obligation to work, but does not entitle the worker, per se, to be paid for the time off during the strike. In order to receive payment for said time off, an additional requirement applies: that the employer's liability be founded in a law which reasonably imposes it, or in a convention, or that the employer incur in a simultaneous liability. This was precisely what happened in this case.[65]

Of a different order but sharing similarities is the issue of the personnel hired for an extended period of time and then terminated by the administration.

The National Court, on April 6, 2010, pronounced the sentence on the case proceedings *Ramos*, which achieved leading case hierarchy in the case law of the Higher Court. It admitted an extraordinary recourse placed by a worker hired for twenty-one years, in violation of the maximum term contemplated by the law, considering that the duties performed by the plaintiff were not transitory in nature. Also, the Court noted that the employee "was scored and assessed annually ... his seniority on the job was acknowledged ... and he received social benefits from his employer."

It also deemed that the defendant resorted to figures legally authorized for exceptional cases, with an obvious deviation of power aimed at covering up a permanent appointment under the appearance of a finite time contract, incurring in an illegitimate conduct resulting in liability and justifying the admissibility of compensation.

As was to be expected, the Argentine courts followed this guideline from the Federal Court regarding hired public personnel.

Finally a few words concerning the duties towards the plaintiffs. The duties or obligations of the employees towards plaintiffs are set forth by the general and sectorial set of rules for the different positions and titles.

The fulfillment of the appointed duty constitutes an obligation which is considerably wide in scope.[66]

65. After contrasting the essential judicial doctrine with the situation of the case, the court checked that there were unpaid salaries for the workers. The noncompliance by the administration was thus proved with respect to salaries owed to its employees. Under these circumstances, the court argued as follows: "... the contract theory, which is an integral part of the general theory of Law, teaches us that in the sphere of contractual liability, the liability of the debtor upon non-compliance with the obligation is presumed and does not require evidence. Its liability is implied in this non-compliance." The court also set forth that: "The essential presumption is based and explained by what generally happens (*ex eo quod plerumque fit*, LLambías, Tratado, Vol. I, p. 191), because when debtors fail to meet their obligations, whether private or public subjects, it is usually because they have not taken the precautions warranted by the case ... ." The court considered that in the case, the liability of the accused Municipality was presumed, which had not affected the corresponding presumption.

66. Therefore, as stated by the Court of Santa Fe: "the diversity of continuous and changing administrative tasks explains this characteristic inaccuracy in terms of the activities to be developed, which means that a single category may entail the performance of several roles, and some of them even impose higher requirements than others. This, however, does not necessarily mean that they correspond to a superior category, except, of course, if these roles exceed those reasonably contemplated within the typical duties of the position held by the plaintiff ..." (A. y S. T. 151-293).

The duty of obedience constitutes another duty expressly imposed by the different set of rules.

There are other obligations which have been studied by the case law: the plaintiff must behave appropriately, has the obligation to initiate a criminal report and claim, and the duty to communicate incompatible situations, etc.[67]

9 RESPONSIBILITY OF THE STATE IN ARGENTINA

Before the new Act 26.944 was passed, the responsibility of the State had achieved considerable development in the case law: the public subject was fully liable for his actions or omissions, for his lawful and unlawful actions, for the actions of its three powers, and the case law or Court Concepts were well grounded or consolidated, which means that the future case law was to a great extent predictable.

So, the issue is not that a law on the subject is inadequate or untimely, but rather that the new standard provide adequate protection for the rights of the affected private parties.

In fact, the Official Bulletin made the publication on August 8, 2014, and Act 26.944 became effective as from August 17, 2014. It is a federal law. It has a national scope and applies to the National Government. It is effective in the provinces which adhere to said law, pursuant to Section 11 of the Law.

From the area of private law, a reforming trend emerged in the last thirty years, which has recently seen fruits.

The Commission Draft for the new CCC established that the State is objectively liable for any damages caused by the irregular exercise of its duties, and that "the nature of the activity, the means available to the service, the relationship of the victim to the service and the degree of foreseeability of the damage" should be appraised. Section 1765 regulated the responsibility of the public official, while Section 1766 governed the liability for lawful activity, setting forth the scope of the indemnification.

However, these texts of the Commission Draft Project were substituted by the Executive Office. Section 1764 was rephrased to state that the provisions of this title of the CCC are not applicable to the responsibility of the State, whether directly or severally. And Section 1765 was rephrased to state that the responsibility of the State is governed by the standards and principles of national or local Administrative Law, as applicable.

These last texts became effective on August 1, 2015.

This state of affairs has resulted in two conflicting positions: that of those who consider that the regulation of the responsibility of the State should necessarily be found in the Civil Code, and another sector which, to varying degrees, understands that it is not a matter which of the provinces necessarily have to delegate on the national Government.

The first position alleges that the new law establishes a juridical inequality for anyone requiring reparation for damages, that it fosters a true regulatory mosaic which

67. Marienhoff, Tratado, Vol. III-B, pp. 222 and et seq.

threatens stability and juridical security. It is said that relationships between creditor and debtor pertain to the general law. The other position stated that, in terms of reparation for damages, relationships among private parties are governed by the principles of commutative justice, while in the area of Public Law, the principles of distributive justice prevail.

The LRE is assigned its precise and limited scope, restricting it in substance to the responsibility for failure to provide service, the constitutionality of the new law can generally be maintained, given that the new LRE has mainly ruled over a local matter which does not necessarily belong to the Civil Code.

In summary, if one is to interpret that Sections 1764–1766 of the CCC refer to limited scope local standards, particularly in the matter of lack of service, the constitutionality of such devices may be maintained.

The Federal Court confirmed in the cases *Vadell* and *Barreto*, amongst others, this interpretation.[68]

Turning to the LRE, it should be highlighted that this is a rather restrictive law. [69]

Some believe that the regulation of the reparation in the case of responsibility for lawful acts might be unconstitutional. For instance, in Section 4, when it requires an exclusive causality relationship. If the State were not liable if it were the source of a concomitant cause, this would equate to an exception to the general principle that all subjects are liable for the damage they have caused according to the exact extent of their participation in it.

The brevity and conciseness observed in other sections calls for a hermeneutic task which, without forcing the interpretation of the texts, can make the law more compatible with constitutional and conventional requirements.

As is to be expected, the purposes expressed by the authors of the LRE, who explained that they aimed at reflecting the Court case law, become relevant for the interpretation task.

Initially, it should be noted that the new LRE constitutes a set of regulations devised from the perspective of Administrative Law, from Public Law. It has not been intended to apprehend assumptions such as the owner or guardian State. Such assumptions are in fact governed by the standards and principles of Constitutional Civil Law, the Constitution, the Treaties and the Court case law which is its natural interpreter, guardianship of ownership law, equality before the law and full reparation.[70]

68. The first of the aforementioned judgments, Judgments: 306: 2030; and the second, dated March 21, 2006, La Ley, 2006-C, 172.
69. This can be clearly noted at the beginning of the law itself, when, with a flawed technique, before indicating the responsibility requirements (Section 3), the text hurriedly details the exclusions (Section 2); that is, the waivers or grounds for release of responsibility. Then, the rigorous requirements set forth to configure liability, the limited regulation of omissions, the scope of reparation in the field of the lawful activity, etc. clearly substantiate this.
70. Galdós, Jorge M. "La responsabilidad del Estado en la Ley 26.944 por el daño causado por las cosas de su propiedad", La Ley RCyS, Year XVI, Issue 12, p. 20.

Also, the new system of Responsibility of the State is not applicable to consumption relationships.[71]

On the other hand, it should be mentioned that the new LRE, in its Section 1, prohibited the dissuasive monetary penalty, not the periodic penalty payment (astreinte, per its Spanish term).

The LRE regulates the responsibility derived from the lack of service.

The Court explained that the responsibility for lack of service generates objective liability. Now, the objective character of liability for lack of service is expressly derived from the terms of the LRE. Section 1 sets forth that "The responsibility of the State is objective and direct" and Section 3, upon listing the requirements of responsibility, includes among them a "Lack of service which consists of an irregular action or omission by the State."

Of course, anyone suffering damages as a result of a failure to provide state services is entitled to full reparation, emerging damages and loss of profits, physical and moral damage, to the full extent recognized by the case law of the Court which the LRE aimed at regulating.

The new LRE briefly regulates the responsibility for omission pursuant to the following terms: Section 3 in fine: "... omission only generates liability when the breach of an express and definite action regulatory obligation is verified."

As a matter of fact the law has leaned towards the restrictive case law option. This can be inferred not only from the initial words of the text, which states that "omission only generates liability" but also from the requirement of the "express and finite" regulatory obligation.

The text should be translated into a "limitation of liability."[72] All in all, the lawmaker did not require that the regulatory obligation "be imposed by a formal law, which means that we can infer that it is sufficient for the Administration to irregularly breach its duties or obligations imposed by the Constitution, the law or the set of rules to make it liable."[73]

In summary, the law which has been passed looks more towards the State—and the states—than to the victims.

---

71. Chamatropulos, Demetrio A. La responsabilidad del Estado y el derecho del consumidor, in Revista de Derecho de Daños, 2015-1, Responsabilidad del Estado-II, pp. 143 and et seq., Rubinzal Culzoni, Santa Fe, 2015.
72. Mosset Iturraspe, Jorge, Criterios acerca de la responsabilidad del Estado, in "Ley 26.944 de Responsabilidad del Estado", -Rosatti (Director)- pp. 207 and et seq., especially, p. 247, Rubinzal Culzoni, Santa Fe, 2014. In turn, Cafferatta, Néstor A. is concerned about the regulation of omission in the new LRE from the environmental perspective, as expressed in his work "Responsabilidad del Estado por omisión ilegítima ambiental", in Revista de Derecho de Daños 2015-I, Responsabilidad del Estado II, pp. 209 and et seq., Rubinzal Culzoni, Santa Fe, 2015.
73. Rosatti, Horacio. Análisis exegético de la ley 26.944, in "Ley 26.944 de Responsabilidad del Estado", p. 545.

10 ADMINISTRATIVE PROCEDURE

The final section will provide an overview on Argentine Administrative Law without first providing a brief summary of some trends in contentious administrative procedures, that is, the essential procedural rules effective in the Argentine provinces and in the Autonomous City of Buenos Aires.

In contrast to what happens in the Nation, the provinces have their own system, that is, their own Codes of Contentious Administrative Affairs or laws regulating the contentious administrative process.

Towards the end of the nineteenth Century, some provinces had established the jurisdictional powers of the Higher Court through action in the contentious administrative sphere. However, the codification process proper starts with the Varela Code of 1905 in the Province of Buenos Aires—much later substituted by Act 12.008—which was taken as a model by several provinces; it was followed by the Salta Regulations in 1908, and many others.[74] In the Province of Santa Fe, it is worth mentioning that Act 4106 was passed in 1951, which was in effect until it was superseded by Act 11.330. In the Autonomous City of Buenos Aires, after the reform of the National Constitution of 1994, in 1996, pursuant to a new status recognized to the city, a local Constitution was approved and then the Contentious Administrative and Tax Code, by means of Act 189.

First of all, a brief reference to the process of exhausting the administrative recourse which precedes the initiation of recourses at the judicial level. Then, the most significant rules of the judiciary processes on the matter are addresses; that is, the Court, the parties and the object of the challenge.

10.1 Exhausting the Administrative Recourse: Governing Principles

The prior transit and exhausting of the administrative recourse is a rule in the provincial systems.

As regards the purpose and rationale of the recourse, it has been stated that it tends to produce a stage of conciliation prior to the litigation, since it gives the Public Administration the possibility of reviewing the case, preventing any mistakes and promoting the control of legitimacy, as well as allowing the necessary review by the hierarchical authority; that "there are reasonable grounds to be cautious which advise not to initiate legal actions on the tax administration without previously being aware of the extremes on which the private party bases its claim, and assessing them to determine the applicability thereof."[75]

The principles governing the exhaustion of the administrative recourse are the following: good administration, impartiality, search for the actual truth, attenuation of the formal requirements and *in dubio pro actione*.

After the latter, the effective judiciary guardianship which arises at different stages of the process between them, in the access to jurisdiction, and that concretely

74. Lisa & Weder, *supra*, p. 78.
75. CSN, 314:725, and more recently, in "EDEMSA", dated August 4, 2009.

operates by attenuating the requirement of exhaustion of the administrative recourse is highlighted; for instance, in cases of "useless ritualism;" mitigating the reviewing spirit; and, for instance, sugar coating the severity of the tax requirement of the *solve et repete* and allowing, *verbi gratia*, the payment of the obligation in installments, as admitted in certain cases by the case law of the Province of Santa Fe.[76]

In some systems, such as the one of the Province of Santa Fe, the law does not establish exceptions for the exhaustion of the administrative recourse. In other spheres, the regulatory system itself sets forth the exceptions.

10.2 Subjects of the Process

This section will briefly examine the Court and the parts of the contentious administrative process.

The Constitution demands that the Courts be judicial and not administrative.[77] This has already seen that originally the contentious administrative affairs were dealt with in the Higher Courts of several Argentine provinces.

However, then, in the last decades a clear trend of displacement of this competence from the Courts or State Higher Courts to other Courts has been witnessed.

Thus, Córdoba instituted two Chambers in 1984; Santa Fe, established two Chambers in 1996 (one based in Santa Fe and the other in Rosario); Salta created two Chambers pursuant to the Constitution of 1998; Buenos Aires created an entire venue based on the provisions of the Constitutional reform of 1994; in the Autonomous City of Buenos Aires, a venue similar to the federal venue has been designed, with single person First Instance Courts and Collegiate Courts of Appeal; in the Province of Entre Ríos, Chambers on this subject matter have been established.

There are two governing principles regarding the attribution of competence. One deals with the subject under discussion, as is the case in the federal venue, where the Chambers have interpreted that the competence attributed to that venue is established based on the subject matter. Another organic or subjective criteria establishes the competence of the Court based on who plays the role of the defendant. The latter criteria is the one adopted, for instance, by the Code of Contentious Administrative and Tax Affairs of the Autonomous City of Buenos Aires, and which has been quite effective because litigants are well aware of which jurisdictional venue to resort to, and it is the belief that this is what is most important.[78]

The claimant or plaintiff, naturally, is the individual or private entity which challenges the legitimacy of an administrative act. There is no controversy over this.

76. Andrada, Alejandro D. Tutela judicial efectiva: elementos y condiciones, pp. 229–237, Revista Argentina del Régimen de la Administración Pública, 2010, Year XXXII-381.
77. Lisa & Weder explain that Argentine do not have nor could there be among them an entity with an institutional insertion similar to that of the Council of the French State (*supra*, p. 79).
78. This prevents several conflicts of competence that arise in other venues.

Instead, there are several criteria established around the possibility that public subjects be a claimant. Several provinces allow the Administration to sue the annulment of an act.[79] The Autonomous City of Buenos Aires, on the other hand, contemplates the possibility of the Administrative Authority being the claimant (Section 10). The province of Santa Fe, provided it is not contemplated within the restricted assumption of Section 35 which allows municipalities to litigate against the Province, this is contemplated only for private parties as claimants or plaintiffs, and the detrimental action is expressly excluded.

As regards the defendant, two criteria should be observed: one establishes that the defendant can only be a public entity, such as the case of the Santa Fe system; another one apprehends those conflicts arising between public service providers or public works concessionaires and users, provided that they are governed by the administrative juridical system. Such is the case of the Province of Buenos Aires.

10.3 Purpose

Essentially, administrative acts are challenged in the contentious administrative venue. The different systems are framed in this sphere.

Instead, there are different regulations regarding facts or de facto proceedings used by some provinces to apprehend them; others are excluded in one way or another.

Exceptions to the recourse or exclusions are varied, based on the province analyzed: conflicts which must be resolved applying the Labor Law standards, discretionary acts with their different variants and hues, political acts, etc.

There are some legal systems, such as the one in the Autonomous City of Buenos Aires, in which the purpose is quite wide in scope. In fact, Section 2 sets forth: "For the purposes of this Code, contentious administrative affairs are any cases in which an administrative authority legitimately authorized to litigate, is a party, whichever its grounds or origin, both in the sphere of public and private law … ."

Further Reading

Aberastury, Pedro & Blanke, Hermann-Josef (coords.), *Tendencias actuales del procedimiento administrativo enLatinoamérica y Europa*, Eudeba y Fundación Konrad Adenauer, Buenos Aires, 2012.

Balbín, Carlos F., *Curso de Derecho Administrativo*, ts. I y II, La Ley, Buenos Aires, 2007.

Barraza, Javier I., *Manual de Derecho Administrativo*, La Ley, Buenos Aires, 2005.

Cassagne, Juan Carlos & Perrino, Pablo E., *El nuevo proceso contencioso administrativo de la provincia de Buenos Aires*, 1ª ed., LexisNexis, Buenos Aires, 2006.

Cassagne, Juan Carlos, *Curso de derecho administrative*, Buenos Aires, La Ley, 2016, 2 volumes

79. Lisa & Weder, *supra*, p. 84.

Comadira, Julio Rodolfo (coord.), Escola, Héctor Jorge (colab.) & Comadira, Juan Pablo (act.), *Curso de Derecho Administrativo*, ts. I y II, Abeledo-Perrot, Buenos Aires, 2012.

Tawil, Guido S. (dir.), *El procedimiento administrativo*, Abeledo Perrot, Buenos Aires, 2009.

CHAPTER 4

Law of Persons

Jorge Nicolás Lafferriere

1 INTRODUCTION

The human person (*persona humana*, as it appears in the wording of the new Civil and Commercial Code (CCC) of Argentina) is at the center of social and legal life. Roman law recognized and acknowledged this truth with the adage *hominum causa omne jus constitutum est.*[1] The Argentinian law of persons is quite peculiar: more than other legal systems, the centrality accorded to the human person, its rights and its dignity from conception and until death is great.

This chapter deals with the statute of the human person (lit. *persona humana*) in the Argentinian CCC (Law 26.994) which was passed in 2014 and came into force in August 2015. Since Argentinian legal system is "horizontal" (meaning that the Constitution and the International treaties forming part of it, are direct sources of our private law), the National Constitution and International Human Rights Treaties that relate to persons will be forcedly taken into account.

Briefly, first, the legal sources and contents relating to the human person are introduced. Afterwards, the diverse classes of persons as regulated by the CCC, the beginning of the existence of a human being, which is a characteristical note of Argentinian Private law, and will also imply the presentation of the status of the unborn child, are presented. Section 6 describes the general rules of legal capacity. Sections 7, 8 and 9 will expound personality rights, the name and the domicile of the human person. Finally, Sections 12 and 13 will explain the end of the existence of the human person. A coda (Section 13) concerns the rules to proof marital status and legal capacity.

1. *Digesto*, L. 2, De statu hominu. 1,5.

2 THE HUMAN PERSON IN THE CONSTITUTION AND HUMAN RIGHTS TREATIES

The centrality of the human person can be seen in the Constitution of Argentina which recognizes both freedom and equality as fundamental rights. Article 15 refers to freedom, while states that "In Argentina there shall be no slaves... Any contract for buying and selling people is a crime that will held responsible those who took counsel, and the clerk or the authorizing official. And slaves who by any means enter the territory of the Republic are free." Article 16 provides that "Argentina does not support prerogatives of blood or birth: no personal privileges or titles of nobility. All its inhabitants are equal before the law, and admissible to employment without any condition other than ability. Equality is the basis of taxation and public burdens." This view of freedom is complemented by Article 19 which states: "Private actions of men which in no way offend public order or morality or injure a third party, are only reserved to God and are exempted from the authority of magistrates. No inhabitant of the Nation shall be obliged to do what the law does not demand nor deprived of what it does not prohibit."

For its part, Article 75, paragraph 22 of the Constitution gives constitutional status to some international human rights treaties. Thus there is a constitutional concept of "person" because these treaties say that every human being is a person under the law:

(a) Article 6 of the Universal Declaration of Human Rights (1948) states that "Everyone has the right to recognition everywhere as a person before the law."
(b) Article 17 of the American Declaration of the Rights and Duties of Man (1948): "Every person has the right to be recognized everywhere as a person having rights and obligations, and to enjoy the basic civil rights."
(c) Article 16 of the International Covenant on Civil and Political Rights (1996) states: "Everyone shall have the right to recognition everywhere as a person before the law."
(d) The Article 1.2 of the American Convention on Human Rights (Pact of San José de Costa Rica, 1969) recognizes that "person means every human being" and Article 3 reads: "Every person has the right to recognition as a person before the law."

Thus, the notion of "human person" regulated in the CCC projects effects on the entire legal system.[2] But that regulation must be considered in light of these clear provisions that have constitutional status and that recognize that every human being has the right to recognition as a person before the law. The law does not concede personality to human beings, but "recognize" it as a natural condition. Therefore, it follows that the legal concept of person relates primarily to human beings and cannot

2. *See* Limodio, Gabriel Fernando, "Introducción al Código unificado" [Introduction to the Unified Code], El Derecho, Volume 263, 10/08/2015, nro 13.787, p. 1.

be manipulated to exclude some human beings from such legal guarantee. Such a manipulation of the notion of personhood would wipe out all the legal protection it deserves the human person and that is guaranteed by international human rights treaties.

3 THE HUMAN PERSON IN THE NEW CCC (LAW 26.994)

Book I of the CCC refers to the "General Part" and Title I deals with the issue of the "human person." This title does not contain a definition of human person. It has been said that "the person is presented as a core principle for the irradiation of rights."[3] The new CCC adopts the term "human person." Title I of Book I, dedicated to the human person, is divided into 10 chapters, namely:

- Chapter 1: Beginning of the existence of the human person.
- Chapter 2: Capacity, which is divided into three sections: Section 1 (General Principles); Section 2 (Minority) and Section 3 (Lack of Capacity). This Section 3 is subdivided into five paragraphs: 1st Common principles; 2nd Support systems and the exercise of capacity; 3rd Acts done by persons with restricted capacity; 4th Termination of capacity restrictions; 5th Prodigality.
- Chapter 3: Rights of personality.
- Chapter 4: Name.
- Chapter 5: Domicile.
- Chapter 6: Absence.
- Chapter 7: Presumption of death.
- Chapter 8: End of existence of the person.
- Chapter 9: Proof of birth, death and age.
- Chapter 10: Representation and assistance. Guardianship and custody, which is divided into three sections: 1st Representation and assistance; 2nd Guardianship and 3rd Conservatorship.

In this context, some articles are key to understanding the notion of human person assumed by the new CCC. First of all, the final writing of Article 19 states:

> Article 19. Beginning of existence. The existence of the human person begins at conception.

For the Code, the legal notion of "human person" fully identifies with the human being. The reference to conception dissipates any discussion about a prenatal stage in which the human being would not be a person. Article 19 is grounded in constitutional provisions and international human rights treaties and is complemented by Article 51

3. Lorenzetti, Ricardo Luis, "El derecho privado como protección del individuo particular" [Private Law as Protection of the Individual], RDPyC, nro 7, p. 77, quoted by Rivera, Julio César, "Codificación, Descodificación y Recodificación" [Codification, Decodification, Recodification], *Código Civil y Comercial Comentado*, Julio César Rivera and Graciela Medina (Eds), Thomson Reuters La Ley, Buenos Aires, 2014, Volume I, p. 39.

that refers to the inviolability of the human person by reason of his dignity. Thus, it is not acceptable any position that seeks to deny dignity to a human being, or exclude him from the legal protection of personality.

Equally important are the articles related to capacity, because they recognize that "every human being has the ability to have rights and legal duties" (Article 22).

Thus, it can be concluded that the CCC in its version finally enacted and promulgated is part of the humanist tradition of Argentina and the International Treaties on Human Rights, which recognizes:

- that every human being is a person from conception;
- that personality is not an artificial creation of the legislator but a fact of nature that the positive law recognizes; and
- that all human beings are human persons under the law.

4 THE CLASSIFICATION OF PERSONS IN THE CCC

The new CCC distinguishes between "human persons" and "juridical or legal persons." Regarding human persons there is no definition in the text of the Code and every human being is a human person under the law, without distinction. For its part, Article 141 defines legal persons:

> Article 141. Definition. Legal persons are all entities to which the law gives them ability to acquire rights and obligations for the fulfillment of its object and purpose of creation.

Legal entities are distinguished between public and private corporations. Under Article 146, "are public legal persons: a) the national government, the provinces, the Autonomous City of Buenos Aires, municipalities, autonomous agencies and other organizations incorporated in the Republic to which the law attributed that character; b) foreign states, organizations to which public international law recognizes legal personality and any other legal entity incorporated abroad whose public character results from its applicable law; c) the Catholic Church."

Meanwhile, according to Article 148, "are private legal persons: a) companies; b) civil associations; c) simple associations; d) foundations; e) churches, denominations, religious communities or entities; f) mutual benefit; g) cooperatives; h) the consortium of condominiums; i) any other referred to in this Code or other laws and its status as such is established or results from its purpose and performance norms."

5 THE BEGINNING OF THE EXISTENCE OF THE HUMAN PERSON IN THE ARGENTINE POSITIVE LAW

To consider the beginning of the existence of human persons in Argentina's positive law a plurality of sources should be taken into account, not only the provisions of the CCC. So, we present the issue in the Constitution and the international human rights treaties that have constitutional status under the conditions of its validity. Then we analyze the Penal Code and other national laws and provincial constitutions texts that include explicit rules on the protection of unborn life.[4]

Article 75, paragraph 23 of the Constitution provides a definition of the term *child*, which states that the National Congress will be empowered to issue a special and integral child protection social security system "from pregnancy until the end of breastfeeding." Under Article 75, paragraph 22 international human rights treaties have received constitutional status. Some of these treaties recognize the legal personality of every human being from conception. Indeed, by ratifying the Convention on the Rights of the Child by Law 23.849, Argentina made a number of interpretative declarations, including a declaration referring to what is meant by the term *child*. By Law 23.849 Article 2, in ratifying the Convention on the Rights of the Child, for Argentina, a *child* means "every human being from the moment of conception until age eighteen." When in 1994 constitutional status was granted to this international treaty under the conditions of its validity, the interpretative statement made by Argentina acquired constitutional hierarchy. Thus, according to the Constitution of Argentina, the child is a child subjected to legal protection and legal rights.

The Argentine Penal Code, Book II, Title I, regulates crimes against persons. Chapter I (crimes against life) of that Title contains regulations that deal with abortion as a crime (even when currently many legal drafts propose to legalize abortion). According to this, human life before birth is considered a legally protected interest, even if the protection is to a lesser extent than for adults. Thus, according to this, human life before birth is considered a legally protected interest, even if to a lesser extent that after birth occurs (Articles 85–88, Penal Code).

Some of the other national laws recognizing the beginning of the existence of the person at conception are:

(a) Law 24.901 (1997), which establishes the system of benefits for people with disabilities, in its Article 14 states: "The mother and the child will be guaranteed from the moment of conception, controls, adequate care and prevention for optimal physical, mental and social development."
(b) Article 9 of Law 24.714 (1996) about Family Allowances provides: "Prenatal allowance entail payment of a sum equivalent to the child allowance, to be paid from the moment of conception until childbirth."
(c) For Law 25.543 (2002) makes it obligatory to offer an HIV test to all pregnant women as part of normal prenatal care, to give possibility of treatment to the mother and her "unborn son" (Article 3).

The CCC approved by the Law 26.994 (BO 10/08/2014) refers to the unborn person in Chapter 1 of Title I, Book I, devoted to the beginning of the existence of the person. It consists of 3 Articles: 19 (beginning of the existence of the person), 20 (duration of pregnancy) and 21 (live birth).
Article 19 of finally sanctioned CCC provides:

4. *See* Herrera, Daniel A., *La persona y el fundamento de los derechos humanos [The Human Person and the Foundation of Human Rights]*, Buenos Aires, EDUCA, 2012.

> Article 19. Beginning of existence. The existence of the human person begins at conception.

Finally, Art. 19 CCC states that "[t]he existence of the human person begins at conception." The article was the axis of one of the major controversies throughout the drafting of the CCC. However, the wide recognition of personhood to the unborn person, prevailed.

Since Artificial Reproductive Techniques are expressly regulated in the CCC as a form of filiation (*see* Family Law, *infra*) and there are special laws, dealing with this practice, there is however an ongoing discussion among scholars over the extent of the meaning of the word "conception" (*see infra*). However, taking all sources and the context of the drafting into account, nevertheless the disadjustments of the different sources, it appears to be no doubt that Art. 19 makes no difference whether the conception occurs inside or outside the womb.

5.1 The Time of Conception

About the time of conception, the new CCC provides:

> Article 20. Duration of pregnancy. Time of conception. Time of conception is the time between the maximum and minimum fixed for the duration of pregnancy. It is presumed, unless proven otherwise, the maximum time that pregnancy lasts is three hundred (300) days and the minimum is one hundred eighty (180), excluding the day of birth.

Article 20 has almost no difference with the wording of Articles 76 and 77 of the previous Civil Code (Act 340). The text still has application in situations that may relate to the presumption of wedlock and extramarital affiliation.

The new Code abrogates Articles 65, 66, 67, 68 and 78 of the previous Civil Code that referred to the postponement of disputes during pregnancy and other forms of protection of the mother.

5.2 The Birth Alive Condition

Article 21 of the CCC provides:

> Article 21.- Birth alive. The rights and obligations of the unborn or implanted in women are irrevocably acquired if born alive. If not born alive, it is considered that the person never existed. The live birth is presumed.

The provisions of Articles 71, 72, 73, 74 and 75 of the previous Civil Code are subsumed in this Article 21. The new code considers that if a person is born dead he never existed. These provisions should not be understood as denying legal personality to the unborn child, because they were meant to deal with the problem of a fraud in hereditary rights. Authors agree that this provision relates to property rights.

5.3 Capacity of the Unborn Person

Under the CCC the unborn person enjoys the legal capacity accorded by Articles 22 and 23. On the other hand, concerning the exercise of capacity, Article 24 provides that the unborn person is "unable to exercise his capacity" and Article 101 states that "parents" are the representatives of the unborn person.

From the above provisions it can be concluded that the unborn person has legal capacity. Like all people, that capacity may be limited in some cases, but under no circumstances it can be interpreted as an alleged denial of personality.

5.4 Other Rules Concerning the Unborn Person

Article 574 of the CCC provides that "it is possible for a parent to recognize his unborn child, being subject to birth alive." It is a logical consequence of the rule in Article 19 and the condition of live birth has the same explanation that Article 21.

Article 592 also allows preventive contesting filiation presumed by law to the case of marital children: "Article 592.- Preventive Contesting Filiation presumed by law. Even before the birth of the child, the spouse can preventively challenge the filiation presumed by law of the person to be born … ." It should be clarified that both the unborn person and his mother may claim sustenance under the law (Articles 664 and 665 CCC).

5.5 The Unborn Person as an Heir

Among the rules relating to the unborn persons are considered heirs in the CCC:

> Article 2279.- Persons who can inherit. Those who can inherit the deceased are:
>
> a) existing persons at the time of his death;
> b) those conceived at the time of his death who are born alive;
> c) those born after his death conceived through human assisted reproductive techniques, with the requirements of Article 561;
> d) legal persons existing at the time of his death and the foundations created by his will.

The conceived persons may inherit if born alive and a special rule it has been set for those conceived by artificial reproductive techniques (ART).[5]

5.6 The Prohibition of Genetic Manipulation of the Human Embryo

Among the rules relating to the unborn person, there is also Article 57 CCC, which provides:

5. *See* Ferrer, Francisco A.M. "Personas que pueden suceder al causante" [Persons Who Can Be Heirs], La Ley 13/03/2015, 13/03/2015, 1—La Ley2015-B, 0—DFyP 2015 (abril), 06/04/2015, 91, AR/DOC/685/2015.

> Article 57. Prohibited practices. It is prohibited any practice designed to produce a genetic modification of the embryo to be transmitted to his offspring.

Article 57 forbids germ-line modifications and it is a very important provision to defend human values and the inviolability of the human person. This article is consistent with the interpretation of Article 19 that states that the existence of the human person begins at fertilization. When Article 57 speaks of the "offspring" of the embryo, recognizes that any human embryo is a "human person."

5.7 The Discussion About the Term "Conception"

The existence of human beings begins with its conception. However, controversies have been stirred to determine the meaning of the term. There are two positions on the matter: the first, maintains that conception occurs at fertilization; the second believes that conception occurs at implantation. The first position is more consistent with a rational interpretation of existing law and the fundamental principles arising from the international law of human rights.

In the jurisprudential level, the Federal Court of Salta and the Supreme Court of Mendoza have passed sentences in favor of the position that argues that conception must be understood as fertilization.[6] Similarly, there are also many authors who are in favor of the same position.[7]

The controversy has revolved around the interpretation of the judgment "Artavia Murillo" of the Inter-American Court of Human Rights of November 28, 2012, which condemned the State of Costa Rica because it did not allow in vitro fertilization techniques. Costa Rica's Constitution (like the Argentine Constitution) understand that life begins with the conception of the child. Thus, Costa Rica held that allowing in vitro fertilization harmed unborn persons whose life was protected by its Constitution (and by the Interamerican Convention on Human Rights, Art. 4) ... The Interamerican Court of Human Rights found that, given that the human embryo should not be considered a person under the American Convention, the restriction generated in access to IVF involved a trespass in the above rights. For the Court, when Article 4.1. of the Convention speaks of "conception" must be interpreted to refer to the "implantation."

The doctrine of the "Artavia" case law meant a heated debate to determine whether this judgement is applicable to Argentina or not, given that Argentina was not

6. (a) First Chamber of the Supreme Court of Mendoza Province, 30 de julio de 2014 in re n° 110.803, "L., E.H. C/ O.S.E.P. P/ ACCIÓN DE AMPARO P/ APELACIÓN s/ INC."; (b) Federal Court of Salta, in re "L.O., A. y otros c. Swiss Medical s/Amparo", 8 de julio de 2013; (c) Federal Court of Salta, "M., I. N. c/ OSDE s/AMPARO LEY 16.986", 19/07/2014, FSA 000135/2014.; (d) Dissenting opinion of judge Hugo O.H. Llobera, in re "C.K.J. y o c/ M.S.A.S/AMPARO", 1st. Chamber of the Civil and Commercial Court of Appeals, San Isidro, Buenos Aires, 12/11/2013.
7. Reviriego, Nicolás, in *Código Civil y Comercial de la Nación comentado [Civil and Commercial Code Commented]*, Julio C. Rivera and Graciela Medina (Directors), La Ley, Buenos Aires, 2014, Volume I, p. 125; Tobías, José W., *Código Civil y Comercial Comentado. Tratado Exegético [Civil and Commercial Code Commented. Exegetical Treaty]*, Jorge H. Alterini (Director), La Ley, Buenos Aires, 2015, Volume I, p. 147.

a party to it.[8] In the end, if the "Artavia" case were applicable, human life, and thus personhood, would begin in the womb of the mother in natural conception, and by the time of the transfer of the embryos, if the child was conceived by in vitro fertilization. Cutting a long story short, the implications could be enormous: if "Artavia" were not applicable to Argentina, personhood would begin with fertilization both in natural and artificial conception, thus frozen embryos should be considered as human persons and sons and daughters to those who gave legal consentment to their creation (*see* the Family law chapter on this matter). The fact is there is already regulation granting ART be covered by the health system, the CCC regulates the determination of kinship in ART and there are a number of administrative regulations concerning frozen eggs, embryos, consentment, among other issues. Even so, the CCC states that personhood starts with conception wherever conception is produced, and this changed deliberately to equalize the rights to recognition of legal personhood in children conceived by ART or naturally.[9]

6 LEGAL CAPACITY

The human person, for the mere fact of being such, is able to create or enter into legal relations and should be recognized in his legal capacity. In this sense, capacity is regulated in Chapter 2 of Title I of Book I of the CCC. This chapter begins with a section on General Principles, which in Articles 22 and 23 of the CCC provides:

> Article 22. Legal Capacity. Every human person is enabled to be a rightholder and a duty-bearer. The law may deprive or limit this capacity concerning facts, simple acts or certain legal acts.
> Article 23. Capacity to exert legal rights. Every human person can exercise his rights by himself, except as expressly provided in this Code and limitations set in a court judgment.

These two articles distinguish between "de jure legal capacity," which is the ability to be entitled to bear duties and rights, on the one hand; and the ability to exert those rights by himself or not. Every person is a rightsholder and dutybearer, unless the law, for certain purposes restrains this capacity specifically. However, not everybody is able to exert those duties and rights him or herself. They might need the assistance or representation of other persons to that end.

8. Lafferriere, Jorge Nicolás, Tello Alonso, Juan, "El diagnóstico genético preimplantatorio: de nuevo sobre los límites de 'Artavia Murillo' [Preimplantation Genetic Diagnosis: Again on the Limits of the Judgement 'Artavia Murillo'", La Ley Constitutional Supplement, 2014; De Jesús, Ligia M., Oviedo Álvarez, Jorge Andrés, Piero A. Tozzi, "El caso Artavia Murillo y otros vs. Costa Rica (Fecundación in vitro): la redefinición del derecho a la vida desde la concepcion, reconocido en la Convencion Americana" [The "Artavia Murillo and Others v. Costa Rica" Case (In Vitro Fertilization): The Redefinition of the Right to Life from Conception Recognized by the American Convention on Human Rights], Prudentia Iuris, n. 75, June 2013, pp. 135–164.
9. The contradiction between legal textes remains. The position of the author of this chapter, and also of a good part of Argentine legal doctrine is that "Artavia Murillo" does not apply to Argentina, and that "conception" as in the Art. 19 CCC implies fertilization in both natural and artificial conception.

Everybody has de jure capacity. Therefore, any restriction should be established by law. Those restrictions should be exceptional and are set to protect the moral and the common good.[10] In case of infringement of those restrictions, the civil sanction is absolute nullity. An example to those specific restrictions provided by law is set out in Articles 1001 and 1002 of the CCC. Under Article 1002, these incapacities include: "a) civil servants, for goods whose administration or disposal are or have been entrusted; b) judges, officials and court officers, arbitrators and mediators, in respect of goods related to the processes in which they are involved or have been involved; c) barristers and solicitors in respect of disputed property in processes in which they are involved or have been involved; d) spouses with each other, under the regime of community. The executors who are not heirs cannot hold sales contract on the property of testamentary."

On the other hand, the incapacity and restrictions in the exercise of rights are set to benefit the person concerned and can be supplied by a representative. The penalty when an incapacity in the exercise of rights is infringed is a relative nullity, which can be confirmed.

Incapacities on exercising legal capacity is set out in Article 24 of the CCC, which states:

> Article 24. Persons unable to exercise legal capacity. They are unable to exercise their legal capacity:
>
> a) the unborn person;
> b) the person who does not have the age and degree of maturity, to the extent provided in Section 2 of this Chapter;
> c) the person who was declared incapable by a court decision, to the extent provided in that decisión.

In terms of exercising legal capacity, the CCC distinguishes between representation and assistance. Article 100 establishes that "an incapacitated person by sentence can exercise his rights through his representatives." And Article 101 lists the "representatives:" parents, or guardians.

Instead, for people with restrictions to his capacity to exercise his rights, the Code provides for the concept of "assistance," which involves the support measures ("apoyos") designated in the respective sentence (Article 102).

Article 103 states that minors, incapable and persons with restricted capacity have the assistance of the Public Prosecutors and Defendants Office.[11] The Public Defendants performance may be judicial or extrajudicial. The judicial performance can be complementary or principal, as stated by Article 103:

10. Llambías, Jorge Joaquín, *Tratado de Derecho Civil. Parte General, [Treaty on Civil Law. General Section]* Volume I, Editorial Perrot, Buenos Aires, 13ra. edition, 1989, p. 396.
11. Polverini, Verónica, "El Ministerio Público en el Proyecto de Código Civil" [Public Prosecutor and Defendant Office in the Draft Civil Code], La Ley DFyP 2014 (october), 01/10/2014, p. 144, AR/DOC/4113/2013.

Article 103:...

a) it is complementary in all the processes that involve interests of minors, incapable persons and persons with restricted capacity; the failure to intervene of the Public Defendants Office causes the relative nullity of the act.
b) It is primary: i) when the rights of those represented are compromised, and there is inaction of their representatives; ii) when the object of the process is to enforce the duties of the representatives; iii) where there is no legal representative and it is necessary to provide representation.

For its stand, the Public Prosecutors and Defendants Office extrajudicial performance applies "in the absence, lack or inaction of the legal representatives, when social, economic and cultural rights are endangered" (Article 103).

We have already referred to the unborn person. The following paragraphs will deal with the general provisions on the ability of minors and on the restrictions on exercising legal capacity because of addictions and mental health.

6.1 Minority

The 2nd section of Chapter 2 of Title 1 of Book I of the CCC is dedicated to the "minor persons." Under Article 25, "a minor is a person who has not attained eighteen years." In addition, the Code calls "adolescent" the person who is older than thirteen (Article 25).

As a rule, the minor cannot perform juridical acts by himself. He is incapable to exercise its rights by himself and "exercises his rights through his legal representatives" (Article 26). The representatives are his "parents" or a "guardian" (Article 101 paragraph b). Considering the minor person to be incapable of exercising its rights was a decision taken to protect him from abuses.[12]

The same Article 26, however, establishes a rule that has been called "progressive capacity." Thus, it provides that the minor "which features age and degree of maturity can exercise by himself the acts that are permitted by law." This provision is complemented by the provisions about parental responsibility, which involve "the set of duties and rights that correspond to the parents over the person and property of the child, for protection, development and comprehensive training as long as he is a minor and he has not been emancipated" (Article 638). Article 639 sets out the general principles governing the institute of "parental responsibility," including "a) the best interest of the child; b) the progressive autonomy of the child according to his psychophysical characteristics, skills and development. A greater autonomy reduces the representation of parents in the exercise of the rights of children; c) the child's right to be heard and his views taken into account according to his age and maturity."

This progressive capacity should be understood as an application of the provisions of the Convention on the Rights of the Child, approved by Argentina by Law

12. Borda, Guillermo A., *Tratado de Derecho Civil, Parte General,* [*Treaty on Civil Law. General Section*], Volume I, 13ª edition, La Ley, Buenos Aires, 2008, nº 479, p. 451.

23.849. As the child develops physically and mentally, according to his biological development, will steadily gain greater understanding of his environment and life circumstances.[13]

Minors may perform the following acts by their self or with assistance:

- *Access to legal aid*: Article 26 also establishes the right of the minor to have the assistance of a counselor in case of conflict of interest with his representatives (Article 26). This provision is complementary to Article 27, Subsection c of the Law 26.061 of Rights of Children and Adolescents, which led to the concept of "child advocate."[14]
- *Exercise of the right to be heard*: Article 26 also states that "the minor is entitled to be heard in any judicial proceeding concerning him and to participate in decisions about his person." This provision is complemented by the mentioned provision of Article 639 paragraph c relating to parental responsibility and Article 24 of Law 26.061. Law 26.061, taking into account Article 12 of the Convention on the Rights of the Child, affirms that: "Article 12. 1. States Parties shall assure to the child who is capable of forming his or her own views the right to express those views freely in all matters affecting the child, the views of the child being given due weight in accordance with the age and maturity of the child. 2. For this purpose, the child shall in particular be provided the opportunity to be heard in any judicial and administrative proceedings affecting the child, either directly, or through a representative or an appropriate body, in a manner consistent with the procedural rules of national law."
- *Decision-making about their own bodies*: The CCC regulates differentially the ability of adolescents to make decisions regarding their own bodies. Decision-making about their own bodies: The CCC establishes two stages (a) Adolescence between 13-16 years; and, (b) Adolescence between 16-18 ages. In the first stage, we must distinguish between invasive or dangerous acts and those which are not.[15]

  Thus, according to Article 26, "it is assumed that the adolescent between thirteen and sixteen has ability to decide for himself regarding those treatments that are not invasive and do not compromise his health or cause a serious risk to his life or physical integrity … ."

  However, "if the decision involves invasive treatments that compromise his health or his physical integrity or life, the adolescent must give his consent with the assistance of his parents; the conflict between them is solved taking

13. Tobías, José W., in *Código Civil y Comercial Comentado. Tratado Exegético, [Civil and Commercial Code Commented. Exegetical Treaty]* Jorge H. Alterini (Director), La Ley, Buenos Aires, 2015, Volume I, p. 211.
14. *See* Basset, Ursula C. "El abogado del niño: Un estado de la cuestión sobre su designación" [The Child's Counselor: The State of Affairs over His Appointment], El Derecho Familia, 2014, Volume 54, p. 3.
15. *See* Basset, Ursula C, "El consentimiento informado de menores a tratamientos médicos en el código civil y comercial argentino" [Informed Consent of Minors to Medical Treatments in the Argentine Civil and Commercial Code], El Derecho Familia, 2014, Volume 57, p. 3.

into account his best interest, on the basis of medical opinion about the consequences of performing or not the medical act" (Article 26 CCC).

The same Article 26 establishes that "from sixteen years old, the adolescent is considered as an adult for decisions pertaining to the care of his own body."

- *Other acts that can be performed by minors:* From thirteen, adolescents have the capacity to defend themselves in a criminal trial without requiring permission from their parents (Article 680), the may recognize wedlock (art. 680). From thirteen, they may exercise parental responsibility for their children. However, the parents of the minor may object to the performance of acts that are harmful to the grandson, and can intervene when the minor parent fails to take action for the grandson proper development (Article 644). Also, Article 644 requires the consent of the minor's parents exercising parental responsibility for those acts of great relevance to the child's life, such as free and informed decision for his adoption, surgery that endangers his life, or other acts that can seriously injure his rights (Article 644). Minors can claim support from their parents, requiring the assistance of a special guardian, relative or any officer of the Public Ministry of Children (art. 679).

There are other rules on the exercise of legal capacity by a minor person along the entire CCC. A special case governed by Article 30 refers to the minor with qualifying professional diploma. In this case, he can exercise his profession on his own without prior authorization and the minor has the administration and disposition of property acquired with his profession and can be on civil or criminal trial linked to it (Article 30).

Another exception to the rule of incapacity of the minor may be found in Article 684 of the CCC which states that "the contracts involving small amounts of money held by the son, are presumed to be conducted with the consent of his parents." As for the ability to make a will, the CCC Article 2464 provides that only adult persons can make a will.

6.2 Majority and Emancipation

The incapacity of minors ends with majority. The person that has attained 18 years old is entitled to full civic rights and considered legally capable of handling his own affairs. However, it is possible to anticipate full capacity by emancipation, which is limited to the case of marriage. Thus, "marriage before eighteen years old emancipates the minor" (Article 27 CCC).

In this regard, it should be noted that the minimum age for marriage is 18 years (Article 403 paragraph f CCC), but this requirement can be dispensed in two ways. If the child is 16, he can marry with parental consent (Article 404). If his parents do not authorize his marriage, he can ask for judicial dispensation. If the minor has not reached the age of 16, he can marry prior judicial dispensation (Article 404).[16]

16. "The judge must have a personal interview with the future spouses and their legal representatives. The judicial decision must take into account the age and degree of maturity reached by the person, especially related to the understanding of the legal consequences of marriage act. The

According to Article 27, "the emancipated person has full capacity to exercise his rights by himself with the limitations set forth in the Code." Among the acts that the emancipated person is not legally able to do, not even with judicial authorization, there are: "a) approval of the accounts of his guardians; b) donation of goods that he had received free of charge; c) guarantee obligations" (Article 28). Meanwhile, according to Article 29, "the emancipated person requires judicial authorization to dispose of the property received free of charge. The authorization must be granted when the act is of any need or obvious advantage."

Emancipation is irrevocable (Article 27). In case of annulment of marriage, emancipation remains, "except with respect to the spouse in bad faith to who emancipation ceases from the date on which the judgment passed on res judicata" (Article 27).

6.3 Restrictions on Exercising Legal Capacity Because of Mental Health Reasons

In the 3rd Section (Restrictions on capacity) of Chapter 2 of Title I of Book I (General Part) of the CCC restrictions on legal capacity for reasons of mental health are regulated. In case of minor persons, the rule is incapacity. In the case of restrictions on capacity, the rule is that the person can exercise his legal capacity and that any limitations on capacity are the exception, established by ruling that requires to precise the acts and functions that are limited (arts. 32, 37 and 38 CCC).

The CCC regulates three types of capacity restrictions:[17]

(1) *Persons with restricted capacity*: Article 32 states: "The judge may restrict the capacity for certain acts of a person over thirteen years old who has an addiction or a permanent or prolonged mental impairment, of sufficient severity, whenever it deems that the exercise of his full capacity can result in damage to his person or property." In this case, the rule is the capacity, and the judicial decision sets the functions and actions that are limited, based on the opinion issued by an interdisciplinary committee. The judgment should set one or more supports to exercise legal capacity and define the modalities of action of the persons designated as supports, either with assistance functions (Article 102) or exceptionally with functions to represent the person (Section 101 Subsection c).

judge must also assess the opinion of the representatives, if it had been expressed. The dispensation for marriage between the minor and his guardian can only be granted if, in addition to the safeguards provided in the preceding paragraph, the accounts have been approved by the administration. Similarly if the marriage takes place, the guardian loses the allocation that corresponds to the income of the ward in accordance with Article 129 paragraph d)." (Art. 404).

17. Martínez Alcorta, Julio A. "El nuevo régimen de restricciónal ejercicio de la capacidad jurídica" [The New Regulation of the Capacity Restrictions], El Derecho Familia, 2014, nro 55, p. 9; Muñiz, Carlos M., "Personas con incapacidad y con capacidad restringida por razón de discapacidad mental en el Proyecto de Código Civil y Comercial" [Persons with Legal Incapacity and Restricted Capacity Because of Mental Health Disorders in the Draft Civil Code], La Ley DFyP 2012 (septiembre), 01/09/2012, 158, AR/DOC/4460/2012.

(2) *Incapacitated person*: This is a case of exception under the last paragraph of Article 32: "Exceptionally, when a person is absolutely unable to interact with his environment and express his will by any means, medium or appropriate format and the support system is ineffective, the judge may declare his incapacity and appoint a guardian." In this case, the person is incapable of exercising his legal capacity, even though the judgment should set the functions and acts that should be limited. He should be given a guardian who acts as his representative (Articles 100 and 101).

(3) Disabilitated persons (*personas con inhabilitación*): if a person shows prodigality in the management of his assets and he exposes his spouse, partner or minor children or disabled children to loss of heritage, he can be declared unable under Article 48. The prodigal person cannot dispose of his property by himself. In this case, the rule is capacity of the unable persons and the judicial decision must designate a support to assist the unable person in granting disposition inter vivos acts and other acts that the judge sets in his sentence (Article 49).

Those restrictions to the capacity to exert their rights by their own call for a support system, which is provided by the legal system as follows:

- According to Article 43, a support is any judicial or extrajudicial measure taken to facilitate the person in need to make decisions about himself, to manage his property and to perform legal acts in general.
- The support functions will be defined by the judge (Articles 32 and 38).
- The person who should be designated as a support can be proposed by the applicant (Article 43), although his proposal should be assessed by the judge to "strive for the protection of the person against possible conflicts of interest or undue influence" (Article 43).
- The task of the support is to promote autonomy and facilitate communication, understanding and expression of will of the person to exercise his rights (Article 43).
- The resolution must establish the conditions and effects of support measures and, if necessary, should be registered in the Registry of Civil Status and Capacity of Persons (Article 43).

In cases of incapable people, a guardian with representation functions (cfr. Arts. 100 and 101 inc. C) is designated.

For its part, as have already explained, Article 103 declares the role of Public Prosecutor and Defendant Office, which may be judicial (complementary or principal) or extrajudicial.

6.4 The Convention on the Rights of Persons with Disabilities and the Legal Capacity

The Convention on the Rights of Persons with Disabilities (hereinafter CRPD) adopted by Law 26.378 (BO 9/6/2008), since December 2014 has constitutional status in Argentina by Law 27.044 (BO 12/22/2014). This Convention is an undeniable pattern of interpretation[18] for the analysis of the legal capacity regime established by the CCC in relation to mental health. The Convention criteria in relation to the legal capacity of persons with disabilities is set out in Article 12 of the CRPD:

> Article 12—Equal recognition before the law
> 1. States Parties reaffirm that persons with disabilities have the right to recognition everywhere as persons before the law.
> 2. States Parties shall recognize that persons with disabilities enjoy legal capacity on an equal basis with others in all aspects of life.
> 3. States Parties shall take appropriate measures to provide access by persons with disabilities to the support they may require in exercising their legal capacity.
> 4. States Parties shall ensure that all measures that relate to the exercise of legal capacity provide for appropriate and effective safeguards to prevent abuse in accordance with international human rights law. Such safeguards shall ensure that measures relating to the exercise of legal capacity respect the rights, will and preferences of the person, are free of conflict of interest and undue influence, are proportional and tailored to the person's circumstances, apply for the shortest time possible and are subject to regular review by a competent, independent and impartial authority or judicial body. The safeguards shall be proportional to the degree to which such measures affect the person's rights and interests.
> 5. Subject to the provisions of this article, States Parties shall take all appropriate and effective measures to ensure the equal right of persons with disabilities to own or inherit property, to control their own financial affairs and to have equal access to bank loans, mortgages and other forms of financial credit, and shall ensure that persons with disabilities are not arbitrarily deprived of their property.

In this regard, it should be taken into account the General Comment no. 1 of the Committee on the Rights of Disabled Persons created by the CRPD, which noted the importance of the provisions of Article 12 and considered imperative to offer additional guidance on a general observation (Note no. 1 CRPD / C / GC / 1, 19.05.2014). In brief summary, this General Comment points out the importance of an appropriate balance between autonomy and protection and suggests that the provisions that are substitutes for the will of persons with disabilities should be removed. For the Committee, the person with mental disabilities should exercise by himself his rights, with safeguards and support measures, and without supplanting his own will.

18. Cf.: Argentina, Supreme Court, in re "Horacio Giroldi y otro". April 07, 1995, para. 11; in re "Simón, Julio Héctor y otros s/ privación ilegítima de la libertad", June 14, 2005, para. 17; in re "Mazzeo, Julio Lilo y otros s/ Rec. De casación e inconstitucionalidad", July 13, 2007, para. 20.

The CCC regulating the exercise of legal capacity tried to adapt its provisions to the Convention.[19]

6.5 Procedural Rules of the CCC

In relation to the process of capacity, the CCC incorporates some procedural rules, which can be summarized as follows:[20]

(1) There is a broad recognition of the right of the persons involved to participate in the process and to be heard (arts. 31, 33, 35, 36, 43 and concordant CCC).
(2) The court may order interim measures including restriction of capacity through support or representatives (Article 34 CCC).
(3) The Code incorporates criteria for accessibility and reasonable accommodation of the process according to the situation of the person involved (Article 35 CCC).
(4) The Code confirms and enhances the criterion of interdisciplinary intervention prior to the judicial decision and indicating what are the contents of the opinion of the interdisciplinary committee (arts. 31, 37, 40 CCC).[21]
(5) The Code sets the principle of immediacy and the judge's obligation to hold a personal interview with the person before taking any decision (Article 35 CCC).
(6) The person should have access to free legal assistance (Article 31 CCC).
(7) The persons designated as support of the person with restrictions to his capacity must promote his autonomy (Article 32 and 43 CCC), encouraging decisions that meet the preferences of the protected person (Article 32 CCC), and facilitating communication, understanding and expression of will of the person to exercise his rights (Article 43 CCC).

19. *See* Martínez Alcorta, Julio A. "El nuevo régimen de restricción al ejercicio de la capacidad jurídica" [The New Regime of Restrictions of Legal Capacity], El Derecho Familia, 2014, 55/-9; Peyrano, Guillermo F., "La capacidad de hecho y la capacidad de ejercicio en el nuevo Código Civil y Comercial de la Nación. Personas que pueden ser sometidas a restricciones de su capacidad de ejercicio" [Exercising Legal Capacity and the new Civil and Commercial Code. Persons Who Can Be Subject of Restrictions in Their Capacity], El Derecho, Volume 262, 27/04/2015, nro 13.715.
20. Peyrano, Guillermo F. "Declaración judicial de incapacidad o de restricciones a la capacidad de ejercicio. La sentencia (exigencias del Article 37 del nuevo Código Civil y Comercial) y el alcance temporal de sus efectos" [Judicial Declaration of Incapacity or Restrictions on Capacity. The Judgement (Requirements of Art. 37 of the New Civil and Commercial Code) and the Validity of Its Effects], El Derecho, Tomo 263, 15/06/2015, nro 13.748, p. 1; Peyrano, Guillermo F., "Algunos aspectos de los procesos por incapacidad en el nuevo Código Civil y Comercial de la Nación (la legitimación activa, las partes intervinientes, el juez competente y el estatus de la persona durante el trámite)" [Some Aspects of the Procedures Relating Incapacity in the New Civil and Commercial Code], El Derecho, Tomo 262, 11/05/2015, nro 13.724, p. 1.
21. Muñiz, Carlos M., "El abordaje interdisciplinario de la Salud Mental. Situación actual a partir de la ley 26.657 y el Decreto 603/2013" [Interdisciplinary Approach of Mental Health. The Situation after Law 26.657 and Decree 603/2013], La Ley DFyP 2014 (march), 03/03/2014, 162, AR/DOC/4184/2013.

(8) The Code states the criteria for the judge to discern the designation of supports, to "ensure the protection of persons with respect to possible conflicts of interest or undue influence" (Article 43 CCC).
(9) The Code says that the sentence must be registered in the Registry of Civil Status and Capacity of Persons (Article 39) and establishes that the sentence must be reviewed every three years (Article 40 CCC).
(10) The Code ratifies the criteria of the Law 26.657 on Mental Health concerning involuntary hospitalization (arts. 31 and 41 CCC).
(11) The Code regulates advanced directives concerning medical decisions and capacity (arts. 43 and 139 CCC).[22]

6.6 Acts Performed by the Incapacitated Person or the Person with Restricted Capacity

CCC distinguishes between the performance of acts before and after the registration of the judicial decision concerning the restriction of capacity.

Regarding acts after the registration of the sentence, Article 44 provides that "are invalid the acts performed in contrary to the provisions of the ruling and after the registration of the judicial sentence in the Registry of Civil Status and Capacity of Persons by the incapacitated person or the person with restricted capacity."

With respect to acts prior to the registration, they "may be declared invalid if they hurt the person with restricted capacity or incapacity, and on of the following conditions is met: a) mental illness was obvious at the time of the performance of the act; b) who performed the act was in bad faith; c) the act is free of charge" (Article 45). Finally, Article 46 regulates the special case of death of a person, stating that "the acts performed before the registration of the sentence can not be challenged, except that mental illness results from the act itself, that death has occurred after the action for declaration of incapacity or restricted capacity was promoted, the act is free of charge, or it is proved that who made the contract acted in bad faith."

6.7 Termination of Incapacity and Capacity Restrictions

According to Article 47 CCC, the termination of the incapacity or the capacity restrictions occurs after a new court ruling, which must have prior review by an interdisciplinary committee. If the restoration of the person is not total, the same article provides that the judge can extend the list of acts that the person can do alone or with the assistance of his guardian or support.

22. Lafferriere, Jorge Nicolás, Muñiz, Carlos, "Directivas anticipadas en materia de capacidad en el nuevo Código Civil y Comercial Unificado" [Advanced Directives in Capacity in the New Civil and Commercial Code], *Revista de Derecho de Familia y las Personas*, La Ley, 2015, p. 147, AR/DOC/1411/2015.

7 RIGHTS OF PERSONALITY

The notion of human person connects with the notion of human dignity. Human dignity is a perfection in being that implies respecting each person's inherent, inviolable and inalienable value. Dignity is the cornerstone of the Universal Declaration of Human Rights, whose preamble begins with a very strong statement: "Whereas recognition of the inherent dignity and of the equal and inalienable rights of all members of the human family is the foundation of freedom, justice and peace in the world." Similarly the first article of the Declaration provides: "All human beings are born free and equal in dignity and rights. They are endowed with reason and conscience and should act towards one another in a spirit of brotherhood." (Article 1). The link between human dignity and human rights appears in several provisions of other international human rights treaties.[23]

In the new CCC the dignity of the human person is a key principle. Article 51 recognizes: "The human person is inviolable and under all circumstances is entitled to recognition and respect for his dignity." This article opens the chapter on rights of personality and is presented as one of the cornerstones for the interpretation of the entire code. In addition, dignity is a fundamental principle of the human rights system and is consistent with Article 1 of the CCC which states that "the cases that this Code applies must be resolved according to the laws that are applicable, in accordance with the Constitution and human rights treaties on which the Republic is a party" and with Article 2 that provides that "the law should be interpreted taking into account his words, his purposes, similar laws, the provisions arising from human rights treaties, principles and legal values, consistently with the whole system."

Chapter 4 of Title I of Book I of the CCC presents different dimensions of human dignity involved today in civilian life. Article 52 sets the general rule of protection of rights of personality: "The person injured in his private life or family life, honor or reputation, image or identity, or impaired in his personal dignity in any way, can claim prevention and compensation for the damage suffered, as provided in Book III, Title V, Chapter 1." Thus, the dignity of the human person is one of the core principles of the entire legal system and in this way it has been recognized by the new CCC.[24]

---

23. For example, "No one shall be subjected to torture or to cruel, inhuman, or degrading punishment or treatment. All persons deprived of their liberty shall be treated with respect for the inherent dignity of the human person" (Art. 5, American Convention on Human Rights; *see also* Art. 10 of the International Covenant on Civil and Political Rights), "Forced labor shall not adversely affect the dignity or the physical or intellectual capacity of the prisoner." (Art. 6, American Convention on Human Rights), "everyone has the right to have his honor respected and his dignity recognized" (Art. 11, American Convention on Human Rights), "Everyone, as a member of society, has the right to social security and is entitled to realization, through national effort and international co-operation and in accordance with the organization and resources of each State, of the economic, social and cultural rights indispensable for his dignity and the free development of his personality." (Art. 22, Universal Declaration of Human Rights), "Everyone who works has the right to just and favourable remuneration ensuring for himself and his family an existence worthy of human dignity, and supplemented, if necessary, by other means of social protection" (Art. 23, Universal Declaration of Human Rights), among many others.
24. Dignity is also a limit to legal autonomy in the regulation of contracts and juridical acts (Arts. 279 and 1004 CCC).

Completing the general rules on rights of personality in the Code, Article 55 refers to the ability to provide consent to acts related with "rights of personality." It states that the consent for the provision of personal rights is admitted if not contrary to law, morals or good customs. This consent is not presumed and should be strictly interpreted and freely revocable.

The provisions of the CCC concerning the rights attached to physical integrity and spiritual integrity should be addressed next.[25]

7.1 Physical Integrity

Among personal rights related to physical integrity there is the right to life and the right to health. There are numerous provisions of international treaties on Human Rights concerning the right to life. This right includes two dimensions: first, a prohibitive dimension which is expressed in the commandment "not to kill." On the other hand, a "positive" dimension which is expressed as "promoting life." In the new CCC there is no explicit mention of the right to life, but its protection may be embodied in various provisions, which are also related to the right to health.

First, Article 54 lays down the general principle that "it is not required to fulfill the contract that aims at carrying out acts dangerous to life or integrity of a person, except that correspond to his normal activities and that are adopted measures appropriate to the circumstances and safety prevention." For its part, Article 56 prohibits "acts of disposal of the body that cause a permanent reduction of its integrity or are contrary to law, morals or good customs, except as may be required for improving the health of the person, and exceptionally of another person, in accordance with the provisions of the law."

The general rule in this issue is the need for informed consent, because "no one shall be subjected to tests or clinical or surgical treatment without their free and informed consent, except otherwise provided by law" (Article 59). This article follows almost verbatim the provisions of the Law 26.529 on patients' rights, which was amended in 2012 by Law 26.742. Article 59 defines informed consent for medical and health acts as "the declaration of will expressed by the patient, issued after receiving clear, accurate and appropriate information regarding: a) his health status; b) the proposed procedure, specifying the objectives; c) the expected benefits of the procedure; d) the risks, discomfort and foreseeable adverse effects; e) specification of alternative procedures and their risks, benefits and damages in connection with the proposed procedure; f) the likely consequences of not performing the proposed procedure or specified alternative; g) in case of suffering an irreversible, incurable

25. *See* Andruet, Armando S. (h) "Derechos y actos personalísimos. Comentarios al Código Civil y Comercial de la Nación" [Rights of Personality. Comments on the Civil and Commercial Code], La Ley DFyP 2014 (november), 03/11/2014, 153, AR/DOC/3894/2014; Rivera, Julio César, "Derechos y actos personalísimos en el proyecto de Código Civil y Comercial" [Rights of Personality in the Draft Civil and Commercial Code], *Pensar en Derecho*, Facultad de Derecho UBA, n° 0, 2012, pág. 161; Navarro Floria, Juan G., "Los derechos personalísimos en el nuevo Código Civil y Comercial" [Rights of Personality in the New Civil and Commercial Code], *El Derecho*, Tomo 262, 18/05/2015, nro 13.729, p. 1.

disease, or when the person is terminally ill or has suffered injuries that put him in the same situation, the right to refuse surgical procedures, hydration, nutrition, artificial resuscitation or withdrawal of life support, in case they are extraordinary or disproportionate to the prospects for improvement, or produce excessive suffering, or have the sole effect of extending the time of that irreversible and incurable terminal stage; h) the right to receive comprehensive hospice care in the process of his disease or condition."

In case that the person is absolutely unable to express his will at the time of care, the Code refers to the person who has been designated in advance (Articles 59 and 60). If no one has been designated, the consent "can be granted by the legal representative, support, spouse, partner, relative or close friend who accompanies the patient, provided that an emergency situation with a certain and imminent risk of harm severe to life or health" (Article 59). The same article provides that "in the absence of these, the doctor can dispense with the consent if his performance is urgent and aims to prevent serious harm to the patient."

In this regard, the removal of organs to be implanted in other people is governed by special legislation, which is the Law 24.193.

A special provision referred to eugenics can be found in Article 57, which prohibits "any practice designed to produce a genetic alteration of the embryo to be transmitted to his offspring."

The CCC also includes a basic rule relating to medical research on human beings "through interventions such as treatment, prevention methods, diagnostic or predictive tests, whose efficacy and safety are scientifically unproven" (Article 58 CCC). This article provides that research can only be done if it meets requirements linked to the existence of a research protocol, the qualification of the professionals, the approval of an ethics committee, the authorization of the appropriate public body, comparing risks and charges in relation to the expected benefits, consent, the absence of risk and discomfort to the patient disproportionate in relation to the benefits expected from the research, safeguarding the privacy and confidentiality of information, appropriate medical care and reassuring research participants the availability and accessibility to treatments that research has shown beneficial (Article 58).

Article 59 also states that "a person with disabilities may never be subject to health research without his free and informed consent, to which he should be granted access to the supports needed."

For its part, Article 60 provides for the possibility of a patient of giving advance directives regarding his own health and in anticipation of a situation of disability, including the possibility of designating the person or persons to express consent for medical procedures and to exercise his guardianship. This article prohibits euthanasia practices, as provided in Article 11 of Law 26.529. Finally, Article 61 provides for advance directives concerning their own exequies and burial, as for the donation of the whole or a part of his cadaver for therapeutic ends, scientific ends or similar.

As of 4 July 2018, a bill was passed ruling on organ donation. This law needs yet to be enacted by the Presidency. In its relevant parts, it establishes a presumption of consent for deceased organ donors. This presumed consent may not be overruled by the family. Since it partly contradicts the CCC, as the latter grants the right to decide by advanced directives on the dead body parts of the defunct, it could become an exception to the advanced directives system.

7.2 Spiritual Integrity

Spiritual integrity is understood as referring to rights of the new CCC that refer to rights of personality associated with spiritual integrity, which involve the protection of image, honor and privacy.

In this regard, Article 53 of the Code updated the provisions of Law 11.723 of Intellectual Property and regulates matters relating to image rights. Thus, Article 53 provides:

> Article 53. Right to the image. To capture or reproduce the image or voice of a person, in any manner that is done, you need his consent, except in the following cases: a) that the person is participating in public events; b) there is a scientific, cultural or educational priority interest, and sufficient precautions are taken to avoid unnecessary damage; c) it is a regular exercise of the right to report on events of general interest. In case of dead people, the consent can be given by their heirs or by the person designated by the deceased in a living will. If there is disagreement between heirs of the same degree, the judge would decide. Twenty years on from the death, the not-offensive reproduction of the image is free.

Regarding the protection of honor, Article 1740 states the scope of a full reparation. This article provides: "Article 1740.- Full Reparation. The reparation must be full. It consists in restoring the situation of the victim to the state before the harmful event, whether by payment in cash or in kind. The victim can choose the specific reimbursement, except as partially or totally impossible, unreasonably burdensome or abusive, in which case it should be set in money. In the case of damages resulting from injury of honor, privacy or personal identity, the judge may, at the request of a party, order the publication of the judgment or its relevant parts, at the expense of person who caused the damage."

Finally, the civil protection of privacy can be found in Article 1770 which includes virtually verbatim the provisions of the previous Article 1071*bis* of the Civil Code (Act 340). The new Article 1770 states: "Article 1770.- Protection of privacy. Whoever arbitrarily intrudes on a person's private life, publishing portraits, disseminating his correspondence, mortifying his habits or feelings, or disturbing in any way his privacy, should be condemn to cease such activities, in case before did not ceased, and to pay a compensation to be fixed by the judge, according to the circumstances. In addition, at the request of the victim, the judge may ordered to publish the judgment in a journal or newspaper, if this measure is appropriate for adequate compensation."

8 THE NAME OF THE HUMAN PERSON

The name is the exclusive designation of each human person. In Argentina the regulation by law to the name of the people took shape through Law 18.248 (published in 24/06/1969). Prior to that date, the regime was customary law.[26] With the enactment of the new CCC (Law 26.994), Law 18.248 was abrogated and new rules were established in relation to the name, in Chapter 4 of Title I of Book I of the CCC.

8.1 Right and Duty

As a general principle, Article 62 states that "the human person has the right and duty to use the name corresponding to him." There is a continuity between this provision and Article 1 of Law 18.248. The name of the person consists of a "first name" and "surname."

8.2 The First Name

The new CCC uses the term "prenombre" in Spanish, to refer to the "first name," and it designates the single element of the name used to identify the person within his family. Article 63 regulates the rules concerning the election of the first name.

The choice of the first name corresponds to the parents or the persons to whom they give their consent for such purpose; in the absence or disability of a parent, the election goes to the other; in the absence of both of them, the election must be made by the guardians, the public prosecutor or the officer of the Registry of Civil Status and Capacity of Persons (Article 63 paragraph a).

The principle for the election of the first name is freedom of choice. However, there are some constraints in Article 63 paragraph b: there is a limit of three "first names;" surnames cannot be elected as "first names;" the "first name" should not be identical to the "first name" of living siblings; Nor can be elected extravagant "first names." The wording of this paragraph of Article 63 has received some criticism for having oversimplified rules, putting at risk the child's interest. It has been criticized the elimination of the requirement that the "first name" should not be misleading as to the sex of the person.[27]

Subsection c clarifies that aboriginal names or derivatives of indigenous and Latin American aboriginal voices first names can be elected.

26. Llambías, Jorge Joaquín, *Tratado de Derecho Civil. Parte General, [Treaty on Civil Law. General Section]* Volume I, Editorial Perrot, Buenos Aires, 13ra. edition, 1989, p. 296.
27. Tobías, José W., in *Código Civil y Comercial Comentado. Tratado Exegético, [Civil and Commercial Code Commented. Exegetical Treaty]* Jorge H. Alterini (Director), La Ley, Buenos Aires, 2015, Volume I, p. 664. Tobías understands that many of the requirements of the old system will now be covered under the ban to choose "extravagant" names. The "best interests of the child" (Art. 3rd, Convention on the Rights of the Child), also constitutes "a constitutional limit to the rule of freedom of choice the first name" (p. 665).

8.3 The Surname

The surname is the common name for members of a family. CCC introduced at this point significant changes in relation to the rule of Law 18.248. In this regard, three different types of affiliation should be distinguished:

In the case of the marital affiliation, the spouses choose the surname of their child and if there is no agreement between them, the surname will be determined by lot at the Registry of Civil Status and Capacity of Persons (Article 64). The new CCC breaks with the criterion of the primacy of the paternal surname governing in Argentina. In any case, the same Article 64 states that "at the request of the parents or the person concerned with sufficient age and maturity, it can be added the surname of another." The choice of the order of the surname made for the first child of the marriage should be maintained for all children of the same marriage.

If the nonmarital child is recognized by only one parent, then it bears the name of that parent (Article 64). If the nonmarital filiation of both parents is determined at the same time, the rule indicated for marriage and children applied. In case the child is recognized subsequently by his parents, they should agree on the surname of the child. If there is no agreement, the judge will decide the order of surnames according to the best interest of the child (Article 64).

In the case of a minor without any affiliation, Article 65 states that it must be entered by the official of the Registry of Civil Status and Capacity of Persons with the surname he is using, or failing that, with a common surname. Meanwhile, if the person has sufficient age and degree of maturity and he has no surname inscribed, he may request the inclusion of the surname he is using (Article 66).

In the case of adoption,[28] the Code distinguishes between a full adoption or a simple adoption. In the case of full adoption, if it is a full adoption by one person, the adopted child takes the surname of the adopter; if the adopter has double surname, it can be requested that it be maintained (Article 626 paragraph a). If it is a full adoption by a married couple, the general rules on the surname of children born in wedlock are applied. However, paragraph c stipulates that exceptionally, and based on the right to identity, at the request of an interested party it can requested to add the surname of origin of the adopted child to the surname of the adopter. Finally, paragraph d sets a general principle that in all cases, if the adoptee has the age and degree of maturity, the judge must especially value his opinion.

Meanwhile, paragraph d of Article 627 states that at the request of the adoptee who has the age and degree of maturity or the adopters in case of a simple adoption, they can request to add the surname of origin of the adopted child to the surname of the adopter or adopters. In the absence of express request, the simple adoption is governed by the same rules of full adoption.

Finally, the surname of married persons is governed by Article 67. It has a rule that either spouse may opt to use the surname of the other, with the preposition "from" ("de" in Spanish) or not. In case of divorce or annulment, the person cannot use

28. Concerning the principles of adoption, *see* Arias de Ronchietto, Catalina E., *La adopción* [The Adoption], prologue by Guillermo A. Borda, Buenos Aires, Abeledo-Perrot, 1997.

anymore the surname of the other spouse, except that, on reasonable grounds, the judge authorizes it (Article 67). Finally, in the case of widowhood, the surviving spouse can still use the surname of the deceased spouse while not remarried, or as long as he has not constituted a convivial union (Article 67).

8.4 Name Change

As a rule, the name cannot be changed. However, the possibility of requesting a change of the "first name" or the "surname" because of a "just cause" is regulated in Articles 69 and 70.[29] There are two possible proceedings in order to change a name: an administrative one and a judicial one.

The administrative procedure is exclusively reserved for cases provided for in the final part of Article 69, namely: first name change because of gender identity; or for having suffered enforced disappearance or misappropriation, alteration or suppression of civil status or identity. The change of the first name because of gender identity is regulated by Law 26.743 that allows the change of the first name because of the self-perceived gender identity.[30] For the Code, such cases are just causes, and do not require judicial intervention (Article 69 CCC).

For its part, the name change procedure through the courts only applies if there are just causes (Article 69). The same article regulates some "just causes," namely: (a) the pseudonym, when it had acquired notoriety; (b) cultural, ethnic or religious roots of the name; (c) the accredited effect of the name on the development of the personality of the person concerned, whatever the cause.

In the case of the name change procedure through the courts, Article 70 declares that the request for a name change must be processed by the more abbreviated procedure provided by local law, with the intervention of the Public Prosecutor and Defendant Office. The Code also sets rules on the publication of notices once a month for two months, about the possibility of making opposition within fifteen working days from the last publication and the obligation of requiring information concerning the existence of precautionary measures (Article 70). The sentence must be registered in the Registry of Civil Status and Capacity of Persons and from that moment is effective against third parties (Article 70).

29. Muñiz, Carlos, "El nombre como proyección jurídica de la identidad y los 'justos motivos' para su cambio" [The Name as a Juridical Projection of Identity and the "Just Cause" for Change], RCCyC 2015 (september), p. 74, AR/DOC/2628/2015; Pagano, Luz María, "El cambio de nombre y los justos motivos en el Código Civil y Comercial" [Changing the Name and Just Causes in the Civil and Commercial Code], http://www.nuevocodigocivil.com/wp-content/uploads/2015/06/El-cambio-de-nombre-y-los-justos-motivos-...-por-Luz-Mar%C3%ADa-Pagano.pdf.
30. *See* Sambrizzi, Eduardo, "La ley 26.743 de identidad de género" [Law 26.743 on Gender Identity], El Derecho, Volume 248, 2012, p. 822.

8.5 Actions to Protect the Name

As a result of recognizing that the name is a right and a duty, Article 71 governs the "protective actions" of the name, which are:

- Action for name recognition: in cases where a person is denied in the use of his name, he can file a sue in order to be recognized in the use of his name. The judge may also order the publication of the judgment at the expense of the defendant (Article 71 paragraph a).
- Action to obtain the cessation of use of the name, when it is unduly used by another (Article 71 paragraph b). In this case, paragraph c) provides for the special case of a name used to designate things or fantasy characters. In this case, if that use causes material or moral damages to the person, the action may claim to cease in the use.

Article 71 says that in every case the person can sue to repair the damage and the judge may order the publication of the judgment. These actions can be exercised exclusively by the interested party; if deceased, by his descendants, spouse or partner, and failing that, by parents or siblings (Article 71).

8.6 Pseudonym

Pseudonym is the name a person voluntarily assigns to himself in order to be identified with it in certain life activities (artistic, literary, scientific, sports, etc.). In this regard, Article 72 of the CCC states that the notorious pseudonym enjoys the protection of the name.[31] Thus, the person can access the means of protection against ignorance in the use or usurpation of the pseudonym to the extent that the notoriety of the pseudonym is public and known tested.

9 THE DOMICILE OF THE PERSONS

The domicile is the residence of a person for legal purposes.[32] In its civil aspects, it is regulated in Chapter 5 of Title I of Book I of the CCC. There are two classes of domicile. The general domicile, which becomes effective for the majority of legal relations, and special domicile, that applies to one or more specific legal relationships.

The general domicile is classified, in turn, between real domicile and legal domicile. The real domicile is the place that the human person chooses as his habitual residence (Article 73). This residence consists of two elements: one objective, which is the actual residence in one place; one subjective, which is the desire to make this place the legal domicile of the person. While this subjective element is not mentioned in

31. Tobías, José W., in *Código Civil y Comercial Comentado. Tratado Exegético, [Civil and Commercial Code Commented. Exegetical Treaty]* Jorge H. Alterini (Director), La Ley, Buenos Aires, 2015, Volume I, p. 705.
32. Black's Law Dictionary, 9th ed. 2009.

Article 73, it appears in Article 77 when it refers to the change of domicile. In this regard, Article 77 states that "the domicile can be changed from one place to another. This power cannot be constrained by contract or by testamentary provision. The change of domicile is instantly verified by the fact of transferring residence from one place to another with the intention of remaining in it."

The other type of general domicile is legal domicile. It is an address compulsory, not voluntary, imposed by law and interpreted restrictively. In Article 74 it is defined as "the place where the law presumes, without admitting proof to the contrary, that a person resides permanently to exercise his rights and fulfill his obligations." Article 74 continues stating the cases of legal domicile, namely: (a) civil servants are domiciled in the place where they should perform their duties, if these are not temporary, periodic or single committee; (b) military on active duty are domiciled in the place where they are serving; (c) the homeless and those who have unknown address, have it in place of their current residence; (d) incapable persons have it in the house of their representatives.

Meanwhile, special domicile is one that has application in one or more specific legal relationships. One of these special domiciles is that agreed in a contract for the exercise of the rights and obligations emanating from it (Article 75).

A case of special domicile is the professional or commercial domicile, which in the new CCC is governed by Article 74 which states that if the person holds professional or economic activity is domiciled in the place where he fulfills the obligations arising from such activity (Article 74).

As for the effects of domicile Article 78 states that domicile determines the competence of the authorities in legal relations and that the choice of domicile produces the prorogation of jurisdiction. However, there is broad agreement in pointing out that the purpose of domicile exceeds that statement and is relevant to determining the applicable law, jurisdiction, the validity of notifications, the fulfillment of obligations, among other effects.[33]

Finally, Article 76 refers to the case of a person whose domicile is not known and establishes that his domicile is the place where he is in that moment; and if it is ignored, the last known address should be taken into account as the domicile.

10 ABSENCE

Regarding the administration of the property of a person, the CCC regulates the special case in which someone disappears from his home, with no news of him, and without leaving proxy (Article 79 CCC). In the event of absence, also known as "simple absence" to differentiate it from the presumption of death. The absence may create a situation of prejudice to the absentee property. The Code aims at appointing a guardian to his property. The Code allows the person to designate a "guardian" to property if

33. Tobías, José W., in *Código Civil y Comercial Comentado. Tratado Exegético, [Civil and Commercial Code Commented. Exegetical Treaty]* Jorge H. Alterini (Director), La Ley, Buenos Aires, 2015, Volume I, p. 715.

they required special care (Article 79). This same rule should be applied if there is a proxy, but his powers are inadequate or not properly plays the mandate (Article 79).

The legitimacy to request a declaration of absence applies to the Public Ministry and to any person having a legitimate interest in the absentee property (Article 80). Intervenes the judge of the domicile of the absent person (Article 81) and the procedure should include the citation of the absent person by edicts and the intervention of a public defender (Article 82). The judge passes sentence after having heard the defense, and if the legal ends are met, he must declare the absence and appoint a guardian (Article 83).

The powers of the guardian involve only those to perform acts of ordinary administration and conservation of goods (Article 83) and any act exceeding ordinary administration he must be authorized by the judge. The authorization shall be granted only in case of obvious and urgent need (Article 83). As for the fruits of managed assets, Article 83 provides that should be used for the support of the descendants, spouse, partner and ascendants of the absent.

The designation of the guardian ends by: (a) the presentation of the missing person or by proxy; (b) his death; (c) judicially declaration of his presumed death (Article 84).

11 PRESUMPTION OF DEATH

The CCC governs cases where a judge declares the presumption of death of a person because he has been away from home, with no news of him for a long period of time. In this regard, Chapter 7 of Title I of Book I of the CCC deals with the "presumption of death."

The legal system is structured around three cases:

(1) *Ordinary case*: it is governed by Article 85 and includes the absence of a person from his home without news of him for a period of three years. This period should be counted from the date of the last news of the absent (Article 85).
(2) *Generic extraordinary case*: according to Article 86, the death of an absent person is also presumed if the last time he was found at the scene of a fire, earthquake, act of war or similar event, likely to cause death or participated in an activity involving the same risk, and there is no news of him for a period of two years from the day the event occurred or may have occurred (Article 86 paragraph a).
(3) *Specific extraordinary case*: according to Article 86, the death of an absent person should be presumed if he was in a ship or aircraft wrecked or lost, and there are no news of his existence within six months from the day that the event occurred or may have occurred (Article 86 paragraph b).

The Code contains rules about the procedure and about the scope of the judgment of presumption of death. Regarding the procedure, those who have a subordinate right to the death of the person concerned are entitled to initiate the action (Article 87). The competent judge is the one of the domicile of the absent person (Article 87).

According to Article 88, the judge must appoint a counselor to the absent or the public defendant should intervene. The judge must summoned him through edicts once a month for six months. The judge must also appoint a guardian to the property of the absent person, if there is no agent with sufficient powers, or if for any reason it does not play the mandate properly. Article 88 also clarifies that it is not required to have previously declared the simple absence of the person.

When the six months period is finished and after hearing the defense, the judge must declare the legal presumption of death if the legal ends are accredited, set the presumptive date of death and order the registration of the judgment (Article 89).

As for the effects of the declaration of presumed death, the declared goods of the presumed death person should be given to his heirs and legatees (Article 91). However, the Code provides for three guarantees for the case the absentee reappears: (a) the need for an inventory; (b) the registration of the case in the appropriate register; (c) the obligation not to sell or encumber property without a judicial authorization (Article 91). The effect of the registration runs out after five years from the presumptive date of death or eighty years since the birth of the person (Article 92). After the registration period, the successors may dispose of the goods.

In case of recurrence of the absent, the declaration of death has no effect, and the person can claim the return of his goods (Article 91). Under Article 92, if the absent reappears after the registration period, he can claim: (a) the delivery of goods that exist in the state in which they are; (b) those goods acquired with the value of the missing; (c) the price due to pay; (d) fruits not consumed.

12 END OF EXISTENCE OF THE PERSON

Death puts an end to the existence of the human person.[34] This basic truth is recognized by Article 93 of the CCC that sets the general principle that the existence of the human person ends with death.

Death, from the perspective of law, is a legal fact, that is, an event that has legal consequences involved but does not depend on the will of the person. For civil law, the question is presented as a problem linked to the verification that death has already occurred. Indeed, while death is a mystery, because it is the separation of body and soul, the discussion has centered around the mechanisms to verify death. To verify the decease of a person the concerned professional must act with moral certainty, with the means usually available by medicine. In this regard, Article 94 provides that "the verification of death is subject to accepted medical standards, applying special legislation in the case of removal of organs from the corpse." According to this, four principles should be taken into account:

34. Tobías, José W. *Fin de la existencia de las personas físicas*, [The End of the Existence of Persons] Buenos Aires, Astrea, 1988; Muñiz, Carlos M., "Fin de la existencia de las personas físicas" [The End of the Existence of Persons], in *Principios de Derecho Privado*, [Private Law Principles] Limodio, Gabriel (Director), EDUCA, Buenos Aires, 2009, pp. 359–424.

1) The phenomenon of death and its concept is unique. In this regard, it is forbidden the possibility of considering a person alive for some effects and dead for others.
2) It should be considered contrary to the principle laid down in Article 51 a "medical-utilitarian" conception that defines death with an efficiency criterion in order to "maximize" the number of organ transplants. That criterion should be forbidden because it converts the person into an instrument rather than an end in himself, affecting his dignity and integrity.
3) The methods to be established for the verification of death must, within due limits to human knowledge, provide moral certainty about the fact of death and not merely a calculation of probability on it, without it being important how high this probability is.
4) A person should be considered death only if the cessation of vital functions can be understood by science as irreversible, taking into account the existing modern resuscitation techniques.[35]

Article 94 of the CCC refers therefore to the Law 24.193 which, for its part, in Article 23 states when should the person be considered death: "A person shall be considered dead when verifying cumulatively the following signs, which must persist uninterruptedly six (6) hours after their joint statement: a) irreversible absence of brain response, with complete loss of consciousness; b) absence of spontaneous breathing; c) Lack of cephalic reflexes and finding of non-reactive pinpoint pupils; d) brain inactivity supported by appropriate technical and / or instrumental means to various clinical situations ... Verification of the signs referred to in subsection d) is not required in case of total and irreversible cardiopulmonary arrest."

A special course is given for the case that the body of a person is not found or cannot be identified (Article 98 CCC). In this case, if there is certainty that the death actually occurred, the spouse or a relative can initiate the legal proceedings to declare the death and order its registration. It is worth mentioning that this is not a case of presumed death, but a case of a dead person. Article 98 provides that in these cases, the judge may have the death proven if the disappearance occurred in circumstances that death must be taken as true without any doubt.

Finally, in the case of the death of several people in a common disaster or in any other circumstances, Article 95 presumes that they all died at the same time, if it cannot be determined otherwise.

13 PROOF OF MARITAL STATUS AND CAPACITY OF PEOPLE

In Argentina, the function of recording the facts of the marital status of people corresponds to the provinces. However, there are common provisions throughout the country arising from the CCC and Law 26.413.

The basic rule is contained in Article 96 which states: "The birth occurred in the Republic, circumstances of time and place, gender, the name and affiliation of those

35. Muñiz, Carlos, "Comentario al art. 94 del Código Civil y Comercial de la Nación" [Commentary on Art. 9 of the Civil and Commercial Code], *Código Civil y Comercial Comentado [Civil and Commercial Code Commented]*, Alberto Bueres (Director), Editorial Hammurabi, Buenos Aires, 2015.

born, should be proofed by the records of the Registry of Civil Status and Capacity of Persons. Similarly, the death of the deceased in the Republic should be proofed by the same records. Rectifying records should be done according to the provisions of special legislation."

The special legislation is Law 26.413. Under this law, all acts or events that give rise to, alter or modify the civil status and capacity of persons, must be registered in the corresponding records of the provinces of Argentina and Buenos Aires (Article 1). This law also regulates what are the "records:" "The register shall be made by an entry in a book that can be made with numbered single folios that safeguard the safety requirements, a copy of which will be taken either manually, micro- film, computer file or other similar system. This copy shall be signed by the public official. The original and the copy so obtained shall be treated as public documents, as well as photocopies of items that are issued on the basis of these original records or their copies. The items must be authenticated by a competent authority. Births, marriages, deaths or disabilities are recorded in separate books ..." (Article 5).

In the case of birth or death occurring abroad, the CCC provides that they "are proofed by instruments granted under the laws of the place where they are produced, legalized or authenticated in the manner required by international conventions, and in the absence of conventions, by the consular provisions of the Republic" (Article 97). For its part, "certificates of entries made in Argentine consular records are sufficient to prove the birth of the children of Argentines and to prove the death of Argentine citizens" (Article 97).

Article 98 states that if there is no public registry or the records are missing or null, the birth and death of a person can be proved by other evidence. For its part, Article 99 provides that if it is not possible to establish the age of a person by the means indicated in this Chapter, the court must determine the age after consulting experts.

Further Reading

Limodio, Gabriel, Lafferriere, Nicolás, Muñiz, Carlos, Alioto, Daniel, *Derecho y persona humana en el Código Civil y Comercial,* Educa, Buenos Aires, 2016.

Navarro Floria, Juan G., *Los Derechos Personalìsimos*, Educa, Buenos Aires, 2016.

Peyrano, Guillermo, Lafferriere, Nicolás. *Restricciones a la capacidad civil,* Educa, Buenos Aires, 2016.

Rivera, Julio César, CROVI, Daniel, *Derecho Civil. Parte General,* Buenos Aires, Abeledo Perrot, 2016.

Saux, Edgardo, "Derechos y Actos personalísimos" [Rights of personality], in Lorenzetti, Ricardo (Ed.), *Código Civil y Comercial Comentado* [Civil and Commercial Code Commented], Rubinzal-Culzoni Editores, Santa Fe, 2014, Volume 1, p. 275.

Tobìas, Josè W., in Alterini, Jorge H. (Ed.) *Còdigo Civil y Comercial. Tratado Exegètico,* Buenos Aires, La Ley, 2016, *2da. Ed.* Volumes 1 and 2.

CHAPTER 5
Legal Persons

Juan Navarro Floria

The Argentine legislation provides for two types of persons. On the one hand, there are "human persons" (*personas humanas*); the quality as person is recognized to all human beings from the moment of their conception (Article 19, Argentine Civil and Commercial Code—*CCC*, after its acronym in Spanish), who are therefore vested with every right arising from their intrinsic dignity (Article 51, *CCC*). On the other hands, there are "legal persons" (*personas jurídicas*), to whom the law grants capacity as such.

The *CCC* in force since 2015 contains certain general rules, allegedly applicable to all legal persons. The specific rules for each type of legal persons are written under specific laws, except for a few cases ruled under the *CCC*. The interpretation of some of those general rules is still uncertain, because they have been recently enacted, and there is still no jurisprudence in their regard.

By virtue of the federal system of government in the Argentine Republic, legal entities' control, their authorization to function and registration if required fall within the jurisdiction of each of the provinces before the agency determined by each of them. In the Autonomous City of Buenos Aires, the pertinent agency is the *Inspección General de Justicia* (Superintendence of Corporations—*IGJ*, after its acronym in Spanish), reporting to the Federal Ministry of Justice. However, it is worth mentioning that national (federal) agencies have been established for certain legal persons, vested with authorization, registration and control powers. Diverse legal rules (the latest being National Law 26.047 of 2005) have provided for the existence of unified national registries for business companies (*Sociedades comerciales*), civil associations (*asociaciones civiles*), foundations (*fundaciones*) and foreign companies operating in the Argentine Republic. However, these registries have never come into effect due to absence of regulatory framework as well as the necessary adhesion of each province to the system.

1 LEGAL PERSONS IN GENERAL

The "capacity to hold rights and assume obligations," that is to say, legal capacity, is bestowed by the legal system. To a certain extent then, the Argentine law adheres to the theory of legal fiction: the juridical person does not exist per se, but rather as an instrument used by the Law to create what appears to be a person, equivalent or analogous to a human person, by the mere act of the law.

Still, it is worth reminding that the Argentine Constitution (Article 14), as well as international treaties on human rights having constitutional status expressly guarantee all inhabitants the right of association for useful purposes. Therefrom stems the right to establish legal persons. An arbitrary or whimsical denial by the authority to recognize legal persons created as a result from the right of association would thus be inadmissible.

As a general rule, the existence of legal persons start at the very time of their creation. An express authorization the State is not necessary (Article 142 *CCC*). This rule applies unless specific provisions for a given type of legal entity require such authorization. Also, as a general rule no registration of legal persons with a state authority is required, unless it is specified by the rules governing each particular type of person.

Once incorporated, legal entities have a distinct personality from their individual members. As a rule, individual members have a distinct personality from the legal person created or formed by them, and the former are, in principle, not liable for the acts of the latter (Article 143, *CCC*).

This rule is not absolute, though. The *CCC* expressly abides by the doctrine of disregard enabling to pierce the corporate veil and hold all natural persons concealed behind it liable for their actions. Article 144 reads: "acts towards the persecution of purposes other than those of the legal entity, or to breach the law, the public order or good faith, or to frustrate the rights of any person, such acts shall be attributed to whom as partners, associates, members, or controllers (direct or indirect) have made them possible, who shall be severally and unlimitedly liable for the damages caused by the entity."[1] This rule should be exceptionally and judiciously applied.

The ability or capacity of legal persons is restricted to their purpose; this is known as "principle of specialty," which needs to be broadly interpreted. Legal persons may perform all legal acts directly or indirectly oriented towards fulfillment of the purpose for which they have been created. In some cases, law restricts their engaging in certain acts (such as some rights in rem, which cannot be vested in legal persons, or may only be granted for a limited time as in the case of beneficial ownership). On the other hand, there are restrictions arising from their very nature (for instance, legal persons cannot perform family acts nor hold family rights).

The *CCC* classifies legal persons in public and private.

1. Quotes have been translated by the author of this chapter.

2 PUBLIC LEGAL PERSONS

"Public legal persons are governed by the laws and regulations of their incorporation insofar as concerns their recognition, beginning, capacity, operation, organization and purpose" (Article 147 CCC). Among them, the following are worth mentioning:

(a) *The State.* The Argentine Republic is a federal country. The Federal state, each of the provinces, the Autonomous City of Buenos Aires, as well as each municipal district are public legal persons. So are a large number of public agencies, to which the law ruling their creation has granted specific legal capacity (such as national universities).

(b) *Foreign states, such organizations to which public international law bestows legal character, and any other juridical person established abroad whose public nature arises from their applicable law* (Article 146, Section b, *CCC*). This paragraph not only embraces the states, but also international bodies such as the United Nations, the Organization of American States and several others.

(c) *The Catholic Church.* Although the Argentine Republic is not strictly speaking a denominational state, the Constitution grants special recognition to the Roman Apostolic Catholic Church, the majority religion preexisting the state itself. Further to the universal church and the Holy See (which is also a subject of international law), public legal persons are each of the dioceses and parishes under which the Roman Catholic Church is organized as well as each of the legal persons to which Canon Law (i.e., the Catholic Church's internal law) acknowledges capacity as such. And so are the Institutes of Consecrated Life and Societies of Apostolic Life (Catholic religious orders and congregations), which in Argentina own a special recognition and arrangement under Law 24.483, which renders Canon Law applicable to them even in the civil sphere.

(d) *The indigenous peoples.* The National Constitution acknowledges them as subjects of law preexistent to the national state. Still pending is the congressional passing of a specific law ruling their legal character, and their right to the lands historically inhabited by them.

(e) *Other nonstate public legal persons*, admitted as such by special laws, such as political parties, professional associations, trade unions (Law 23.551), and some social security health care funds (*obras sociales*, Law 23.660).

The condition of public juridical person is relevant because, for example, only private legal persons (not public ones) may appear in insolvency proceedings or go bankrupt (Law 24.522, Section 2).

3 PRIVATE LEGAL PERSONS

The *CCC* contains some general rules applicable to all private legal persons (*personas jurídicas privadas*), which are completed by rules specific to each of them, naturally prevailing over the former.

The entity's name (Article 151, *CCC*) must be sufficiently identifying and distinctive, and must include the type of person involved. It cannot include the name of individuals, unless express consent is granted by them.

The by-laws or the articles of incorporation must state the domicile, understood as the location or jurisdiction where the person will operate. The domicile determines the applicable law and the judges having jurisdiction thereon. The head office (*sede social*), instead, is the precise place where the juridical person's administration is run. The head office may be defined and amended by the entity's governing bodies, and it is the place where all notices addressed to such person will be held valid.

Legal persons are required to own assets and a "precise and determined" purpose, identified with the aim for which the person has been created, thus justifying its existence. Legal persons may last indefinitely, unless the law or statute stipulates otherwise.

Administrators of a juridical person are bound to act in good faith and avoid any conflict of interests with it. Should a conflict of interests arise, it should be immediately disclosed. If their guilty action (obviously, all the more so if malice is involved) should cause damage to the legal person, they are unlimitedly liable for any such damage (Article 166, *CCC*), either before the juridical person and its members or before third parties.

Legal persons are liable before third parties for the consequences of legal acts performed on their behalf by their administrators, and even by whom, though not strictly their administrators, act as such in a way that may lead a good-faith third party to deception. They also respond for damages caused by directors and managers acting in their capacity as such or fulfilling their functions; for damages caused by their dependent workers (not only employees, but any person acting to the benefit of the juridical person, even if no labor relationship exists), and for the consequences of the risk or vice of the property owned or used by the entity. In all such cases (actions by executives, dependent workers and facts of things) civil liability is objective, and therefore the juridical person may only be exempted from it by proofing act of God or guilt of the victim or of a third party regarding whom the person is not liable.

In principle, legal persons cannot be held criminally liable, except in cases stipulated under special laws (such as those related to drug trafficking or money laundering), wherein penalties are imposed for commission of certain crimes, such as dissolution or property seizure.

Legal persons may turn into another type of person, merge or split into two or more persons with the unanimous agreement of their members (or a majority as required by the special rules governing each type of person).

Legal persons dissolve (extinguish) by decision of their members made unanimously or by the majority required in each case by law or statute, or when their purpose has come to an end or becomes impossible to achieve, or upon expiration of their term (except when an extension is resolved by their members), bankruptcy, withdrawal of state's authorization to operate (when such authorization is required), exhaustion of their equity capital, or for such other causes as are set forth under the special law.

State's authorization may not be arbitrarily withdrawn; indeed, such withdrawal must be grounded on serious acts in violation of a statute or law, be preceded by a process guaranteeing the right to defense, and always be subject to subsequent judicial oversight (Article 164, *CCC*).

Once dissolution is effective and final, the liquidation process is initiated, wherein debts are paid, goods are liquidated, and the remaining property is handed over to any pertinent party pursuant to the applicable statute or legal rules.

3.1 Civil Associations

Civil associations ("asociaciones civiles," a sort of "civil -not commercial- society" typical of the Argentine law) are the basic type of legal persons, and are primarily used to establish nonprofit organizations, or entities pursuing common good as their purpose. They are pivotal to the social fabric. Rules applicable thereto are contained in the *CCC*, which provides for a much more detailed and demanding set of regulations than the one existing prior to enactment of the *CCC*.

The notion of "common good as corporate purpose" must be amply construed. Basically, it means that the purpose is not against the law. Civil associations pursue the most varied purposes: sporting, cultural, educational, gathering and recreational, social work and promotion, provision of health services or certain needs of their members or of the general population, environmental care—or its elements—, and an extensive series of countless possible purposes.

Given their very nature, associations require a plurality of members. There is not a statutory minimum number, although they must necessarily be at least five members to reach the statutory minimum for governing bodies. Neither is there a maximum number; some associations may have a few dozens of members, while others (for instance, major sports clubs) have thousands, even millions of them.

Civil associations require an authorization to operate issued by the state, granted by the jurisdictional competent authority (either a province or the city of Buenos Aires) of their head office. Their constitution must be written into a public instrument (usually, a public deed) which, upon receiving the state's authorization, must be registered in a public registry, as are any subsequent amendments. There are thus two successive steps, although they may occur simultaneously: authorization to operate and registration in a public registry—both steps obviously preceded by the articles of incorporation or charter.

At incorporation, attended by all founding members, further to expressing the will to create the association, a governing charter must be approved, listing the name, subject matter or purpose, domicile, if constituted indefinitely or for a certain period of time, equity composition and contributions to be made by the associates, classes or categories of members, with rights and obligations vested in each class or category, causes and procedures for which members' may be expelled or sanctioned, set of rules governing the administration and operation of the association's bodies, grounds for dissolution, and liquidation rules and assignment of any remaining property.

An association's supreme governing body is the General Assembly, made up by the associates or, if they are too many, by representatives elected by them. The by-laws determine when the Assembly will meet, the conditions to attend it, its powers and functioning rules (summons, quorum, required majorities and so forth). A minute book must be kept, recording the Assembly's discussions and resolutions.

The association's administration is vested in an Executive Board made up of associates, with a President (usually the one representing the association), the Secretary, the Treasurer and other members of the Executive Board (*vocales*). There may be other members as set forth under the by-laws. Administrators are liable to the association for their performance, and their management must be approved by the General Assembly.

Associations are subject to a twofold control process: an internal or private oversight by one or more account auditors (who may or may not be associates), and an external one, by the state authority.

Associates are not directly or subsidiarily liable for the association's debts. Their only obligation is to pay their member dues as set forth under the by-laws.

The association has disciplinary powers on its members. It is worth recalling that members hold the rights granted by the by-laws (usually, among others, to take part in the meetings and life of the association, to choose the members of the executive board, to benefit from the activity run by the association, to leave the association whenever they wish), but they also have duties and obligations imposed by law or the by-laws (usually, to behave dutifully towards the association, to pay their pertinent dues, to take part at the meetings, to respect the authorities).

If they do not fulfill the obligations imposed in the by-laws, they may be sanctioned: the association's sanctioning power is inherent to its nature and is usually written into the by-laws. However, any sanction must be preceded by the associate's chance to exercise the right of defense. Different kinds of sanctions may be applied: a warning, suspension of benefits enjoyed as an associate, even dismissal in the most serious cases. If the sanction is imposed by a body set forth under the by-laws (the executive board, a court of honor or a disciplinary court), associates may always resort to the Assembly. Upon exhaustion of internal resources, the sanction may be appealed before the Judiciary.

In principle, associations are made up of individuals. But there are "second-degree" entities, that is to say, associations whose members are other legal entities (civil associations, foundations, and others). These second-degree associations are usually called "federations" or "confederations" if they are third-degree associations (i.e., whose members are themselves federations).

In case of dissolution of a civil association, the remaining property cannot be distributed among its partners. It must be assigned, pursuant to its by-laws, to another legal entity with a common-good purpose domiciled in Argentina.

Under the *CCC*, on a supplementary basis, the provisions of the *Ley General de Sociedades* (the Companies' Act, *LGS* after its acronym in Spanish) apply to associations (Section 186). An arguable solution indeed, because there are substantial differences between an association for a common-good purpose (nonprofit organization), and a company for profit.

3.2 Simple Associations

The Argentine *CCC* also distinguishes private entities called "simple associations" (*simples asociaciones*), incorporated either by public instrument, or by private instrument provided that signature is certified before a notary public. These associations do not require state authorization to operate, and are not registered in a public registry. Therefore, they exist as from their incorporation. Civil associations, until obtaining authorization to function, are also deemed simple associations.

Simple associations are additionally ruled by the provisions governing civil associations, and must keep accounting records.

Their primary difference with regular civil associations is that in case of insolvency or insufficient assets, the administrators of a "simple association" are severally liable for debts originated during their tenure.

Now, what happens with the many spontaneous grass root associations or groupings formed in neighborhoods and towns for the most dissimilar common-good purposes, which fail to fulfill the *CCC*'s requisites in form for either civil associations (i.e., incorporation by public instrument, state authorization to operate, and registration) or simple associations? The question does not find a clear answer, due to a legal void. However, there is a common interpretation that leads to the conclusion that these groupings are an expression of the right to freedom of association guaranteed by the national Constitution, but not acknowledged as legal persons or legal entities. Their directors and members will therefore be personally and severally liable for the grouping's debts.

3.3 Foundations

Foundations (*fundaciones*) are legal persons pursuing a common good, nonprofit subject-matter, incorporated through the contribution of property that builds the equity destined for such purpose. Their distinctive feature is that they do not have any members, but only administrators of that property.

They are ruled under the *CCC*. Foundations need state authorization to function. Their incorporation is formal, for it must be executed through a public instrument (normally, a public deed) authorized by a public notary.

They may have one or several founders, who may be individuals or legal entities. If individuals, they may incorporate foundations *inter vivos* or by will, assigning all or part of their assets to the future foundation. In this case, the heirs and executors (if any) are duty-bound to execute the foundation's charter under the supervision of the estate's judge and the Public Prosecutors Office.

As an essential requisite, the foundation's initial equity must reasonably enable fulfillment of its purpose. Equity estimates must also bear in mind the goods of the founder and of such other persons as have undertaken to contribute property in the future. In order to obtain state approval, founders must submit a feasible action plan for the first three years.

The charter must define name, domicile and purpose (precise and determined), equity, duration, and the governing by-laws must be approved. The by-laws must establish, among other things, the rules governing the administrative body, the way in which members of this administrative body are to be renewed, and the assignment of property in case of dissolution (usually, to a nonprofit public-good entity domiciled in Argentina).

The foundation's government is in charge of an Administration Council composed of at least three individuals. The founder is entitled to make reservation of the right to make up the Council and to appoint the rest of the councilors, or else delegate this right onto a nonprofit public or private institution. The function of a councilor is *ad honorem*. If the Council has several members and by-laws provide this, an executive committee may be formed to fulfill the daily administration.

Foundations must assign most of their income to the fulfillment of their purposes, avoiding accumulation of income, and being banned from assigning any income to founder, officers or third parties.

They are bound to periodically inform the state authority about their performance, and are subject to permanent state oversight. The state authority acts in case the foundation may not function by itself, or if its purpose becomes impossible or exhausted. In this case, it may set a purpose akin to the former one, or arrange the foundation's merger with another foundation of a similar purpose. Against the decisions of the state authority, it is always possible to appeal before the Judiciary.

Foundations enjoy a privileged tax arrangement, being exempted from paying certain taxes. These benefits vary according to the foundation's purpose.

3.4 Civil and Commercial Companies

The new CCC should have included a chapter on Civil and Commercial Companies. However, to simplify the process of drafting, commercial companies were left out of the CCC, and are still regulated by the *LGS* (the 1972 companies' act, Law 19.550, with multiple amendments, the last being Law 26.994 approving the *CCC*). Pursuant to the definition therein, "there is a company whenever one or more persons, organized under one of the types provided for in this law, undertake to make contributions to be applied to the production of goods or services, sharing the benefits and bearing the losses" (Section 1).

This legal definition reveals the fundamental elements of the companies, namely:

(a) an entrepreneurial organization aimed at producing goods or services, where partners share a common profit or loss risk;
(b) profit as a purpose (i.e., to obtain a benefit for the partners), which distinguishes companies from civil associations, simple associations and foundations;

(c) submission to one of the statutory types for this sort of agreements. However, there are companies which do not fit into any of the statutory types and have their own governing rules.

Up to the 2015 amendment, an Argentinean company necessarily had to be composed of more than one partner. This reform enabled the incorporation of single partner companies, but in a more restrictive manner: they can only be stock corporations (*sociedades anónimas*) subject to strict state control and to certain formal requirements which in practice preclude or render inadequate their use by individuals or for small businesses.

The *LGS* contains rules applicable to all corporate types, and rules specific to each type.

Companies do not require prior authorization by the state to function, but they must register their charter and by-laws in the Public Registry of the jurisdiction (each province or Buenos Aires City) where they are incorporated. Incorporation may be executed by either public or private instrument depending of their type. Both stock companies and limited liability companies must publish their registration in the pertinent official gazette.

Companies may be composed of individuals or of legal entities, but stock companies can only make up other stock companies or limited liabilities companies. The law restricts the possibility of cross shareholding between companies (Section 32, *LGS*).

Companies may be dissolved due to partners' decision, expiration of the term for which they were established (except if extended, Section 95, *LGS*), fulfillment of the condition on which their existence was contingent, fulfillment of their purpose or supervening impossibility of its fulfillment, exhaustion of corporate capital, bankruptcy, withdrawal of authorization to function whenever necessary given the company's activity (for instance, financial entities) (Section 94, *LGS*). Up to 2015, partners' reduction to one was a ground for dissolution, but since then, unipersonal companies are permitted, provided they become stock companies (*sociedades anónimas*) and fulfill the statutory requisites thereof. A dissolved company retains its capacity only for liquidation purposes (Sections 101 through 112, *LGS*).

The intent of the law is for companies to adjust to one of the types set forth under it. Up to 2015, the lack of adjustment to any one of the types (or the conformation of a "*de facto* company" failing to fulfill legal formalities) was sanctioned in different ways. However, a relevant amendment of the *LGS* effective in 2015 has been to no longer sanction corporate irregularity and instead permit—though with some disadvantageous consequences for the partners—a sort of extensive contractual freedom in this respect.

Notwithstanding the aforesaid, the *LGS* presents types of companies into which newly incorporated companies should fit, namely:

3.5 Business Partnerships (*Sociedad colectiva*, Sections 125 Through 133, *LGS*)

The simplest type of company, made up of individuals who are subsidiarily, unlimitedly and severally liable for the company's liabilities. The full extent of such liability results in this type being of little use, except for small personal or family ventures.

3.6 Limited Partnerships (*Sociedad en comandita simple*, Sections 134 Through 140, *LGS*)

In this type of company, two classes of partners coexist: the active partners or *comanditados* (who are liable for partnership debts to the full extent, as do partners in a partnership), and the silent partners or *comanditarios* (who are only liable to the extent of their contributed capital). The partnership's management is exclusively vested in the former, the latter having only supervisory and advisory powers. It is also a type rarely used, except for some very specific activities. The sense of this company type is to allow what would be a general partnership to have access to a more significant capital, bringing in capitalist partners (*comanditarios*) who share in the profits risking only their contributed capital, being in return out of the company's ordinary management.

3.7 Capital and Working Partnership (*Sociedad de capital e industria*, Sections 141 Through 145, *LGS*)

There are capitalist partners (liable for partnership debts as if they were partners of a partnership) and working partners whose contribution is their own labor, and are liable only to the extent of the profits of the company. They all have management powers. This type is not much used, because usually capital-labor relationships between a capitalist partner and a labor-contributing one are informally materialized.

3.8 Limited Liability Company, (*Sociedad de responsabilidad limitada—SRL*, Sections 146 Through 162, *LGS*)

The SRL is an extensively used type of company in Argentina, its appeal lying in the fact that partners are only liable for company debts to the extent of the assets contributed by them, but not with the rest of their assets, not even subsidiarily. These companies may be made up of individuals or of stock companies, and cannot have more than fifty partners.

Partners' shareholding is expressed in quotas, as set in the partnership agreement (by-laws), because the identity of partners and the existence of *affectio societatis* among them are deemed relevant aspects of this company type. Consequently, the reassignment of quotas requires amendment of the partnership agreement (by-laws) and due registration thereof to be enforceable against third parties. Quotas transfer may be limited by the partnership agreement, but it cannot be forbidden.

The management of a SRL is carried out by one or more managers appointed for a limited or unlimited period of time, who may or may not be partners, according to the by-laws. A SRL may or may not have an oversight or audit commission, which becomes mandatory when capital exceeds a certain cap.

Major decisions are taken at partners' meetings by the majorities set forth under the partnership agreement, within certain limits prescribed by law.

3.9 Stock Company (*Sociedad Anónima—S.A.*, Sections 163 Through 307, *LGS*)

The stock company is the most extensively used type of company in Argentina. Although in theory it has been conceived for businesses requiring a significant capital and a large number of partners whose personal conditions are irrelevant, mattering only their capital contribution, reality shows that alongside a relatively small amount of large stock companies, there are plenty of small and middle-sized companies of a few partners, often members of a same family, who turn to this company form.

Capital is represented by shares, and partners limit their liability to payment of subscribed shares (Section 163, LGS). The name *anónima* (anonymous) originally made reference to the fact that partners' identity could be unknown because shares were bearer security bonds, and thus partners would only identify themselves when attending a shareholders' meeting. However, since several years ago in Argentina, shares must mandatorily be registered, meaning that the company must keep a register where shareholders are recorded, except in the case of stock corporations quoting in the Stock Exchange (which are few) where share circulation and holders anonymity still prevails. If provided for in the by-laws, the company may have book-entry shares, i.e., lacking physical existence and merely existing in the company's accounting books.

Shares are freely transferable. The by-laws may restrict transferability (for instance, by granting other shareholders rights of first refusal), but they cannot ban it. Shares may be of different classes, entitling their owners to diverse rights, as set forth by the by-laws within certain limits prescribed by law.

A stock company must be created by a public instrument. Public subscription of capital is permitted, yet it is uncommon. More often, incorporation is a single event where all of the capital is subscribed and may be partially paid later on. At the incorporation of the company, its governing by-laws are approved, and must be registered. By-laws record the company's purpose, domicile (city and jurisdiction of the head office, which may not be set in the by-laws), name and further operational rules.

The highest-ranking body of stock companies is the General Meeting of shareholders, which may be ordinary or extraordinary according to its agenda. Law sets terms and formalities on notice, constitution and celebration of these meetings, and the shareholders' rights in them. Their management lies with a Board of Directors made up of one or more directors (according to the by-laws, except for companies listed in the stock exchange or whose capital stock renders a plural board of directors mandatory). Directors are elected by the meeting of shareholders for no more than three fiscal years (but then can be reelected) and may or may not be partners. The by-laws contain the rules governing the operation of the Board, and the meeting of shareholders fixes their pay. The Chairman represents the company. The Board of Directors may also appoint managers, whether or not they are directors, to discharge executive functions.

The company's oversight may be undertaken by a surveillance committee appointed by the meeting of shareholders (if prescribed by the by-laws), or by an individual or plural audit commission of accountants or lawyers (or a severally liable company exclusively made up of lawyers or accountants), or in the case of small stock companies not listed in the stock market, directly by the partners. Additionally, in all cases stock companies are overseen by the pertinent domicile authority, upon request from shareholders representing at least 10% of the capital, or when reasons of public interest call for such control.

Since 2015, the *CCC* permits sole-shareholder companies (*Sociedades Anónimas Unipersonales—SAU*) made up of a single partner who may be an individual or another entity. Also, a company initially made up of multiple partners may continue to exist with only one remaining partner, provided it adopts the SAU form by amending its original type if necessary. This type of companies, however, is subject to special and ongoing oversight by the state. An *SAU* must have a plural board of directors (at least three members), and an also plural audit or surveillance committee (at least three members and their substitutes). Moreover, an *SAU* cannot be the sole shareholder of another *SAU*.

The administrative complexity imposed on sole-shareholder companies turn them into a hardly feasible instrument for small companies and for persons seeking to limit their liability or risk when embarking on a business in order not to compromise all of their assets. Whenever there is a sole real owner, the most common practice is to incorporate an ordinary stock corporation with one or more partners who are mere men of straw holding a minimum share percentage (called shell companies or *sociedades de cómodo*).

3.10 Limited Partnership with a Share Capital, (*Sociedad en Comandita por Acciones*, Sections 315 Through 324, *LGS*)

This type of company (SCA) is similar to the limited partnership, the difference being that the equity of the silent partners (*socios comanditarios*) is represented in shares (similarly to stock companies). They were much used in the past, but now new companies of this type are rare, except for very specific purposes (activities regulated by the State requiring the use of this type of company, as is the case of pharmacies' management in certain provinces).

3.11 Irregular or Informal Companies (*Sociedades irregulares o informales*, Sections 21 Through 26, *LGS*)

Any company not strictly complying with the requisites of one of the types above, or which has incurred in nonfulfillment of any of the incorporation or registration formal requisites is an irregular company. However, as have been said, since the 2015 *LGS* amendment these companies may function as legal persons or legal entities under the terms of the partnership agreement, and are not subject to sanctions for having failed to fulfill formal requisites. This implies to acknowledge a wide scope for freedom of association, although its reverse side is an increase of partners' personal liability for the acts and dealings of the irregular company.

This chapter includes companies which for some reason have failed to complete the registration process, those having a defect in form, de facto companies which do not have any written agreement, and any other arrangement which is indeed a company (i.e., to say, where partners make contributions for a profitable common activity and results in a subject of law distinct form the individual partners, with its own equity), but which fail to comply with all the requisites of the aforementioned types.

The existence of the company may be shown by any means of evidence (Section 23, *LGS*), therefore this group includes de facto companies which do not have a written agreement.

Among the partners, relationships are ruled by the partnership agreement. As regards third parties, relations are governed by the agreement if it is evidenced that they were acquainted with it. Irregular companies, as legal persons, are expressly authorized to own registrable property (Section 23, *LGS*), like real estate or cars. All partners are subsidiarily liable before third parties, simply jointly (not severally) liable and for equal portions, except if provided otherwise (Section 24, *LGS*).

The irregularity may be rectified by the company fulfilling the requisites of any of the types provided by law (Section 25, *LGS*).

The *LGS* rules the way in which a company of a certain type may turn into one of another type (Sections 74 through 81), as well as company merger and split mechanisms (Sections 82 through 88).

Up to 2015, Argentina provided for what were known as "civil companies." They had a "civil" purpose, such as the practice of a profession like law or medicine, or an educational or any nonprofit goal which would entail the incorporation of a business company. With the enactment of the new CCC, this type no longer exists, and there is a strong debate about the rules applicable to preexisting civil companies. Part of the doctrine concludes that former civil companies are now included in what the authors have called "irregular companies" above, considered in Chapter IV, Section I, *LGS*.

3.12 Other Private Legal Persons

Further to the persons described so far, the *CCC* lists other private legal persons, namely:

(a) *Churches, communities, denominations and religious entities* (Article 148, Section e). It refers to those different from and that do not belong to the Catholic Church, which as have been said, is a public juridical person. They were included in the 2015 *CCC*, although with no specific legal framework.

General rules on private legal persons apply to them, construed in the light of the principle of religious freedom upheld in international human rights treaties. Such religious freedom calls for acknowledgement of broad autonomy for these persons, so that they may organize themselves after the requirements arising from their own doctrine and nature (for instance, when defining the conditions to become a member and the expulsion of members, the organization of their internal government, the selection, training, appointment and removal of worship ministers, and so on). This is an open type admitting diverse organizational forms, some associational or assembly-like and others of a nondemocratic hierarchical constitution. Law 21.745, enacted by the last Argentine military dictatorship but still in force, requires that religious organizations other than the Roman Catholic Church register themselves with the National Registry or Religious bodies (*Registro Nacional de Cultos*) of the Ministry of Foreign Affairs and Religious Affairs. Such registration, however, does not grant legal personality, and in the absence of a body of rules designed for them, churches and religious communities, usually adopt the civil association form.

(b) *Mutual Associations* (*mutuales,* Article 148, Section f, *CCC*). They are ruled by Law 20.321, which defines them as "non-profit associations, freely incorporated by persons inspired in solidarity, with the purpose of providing assistance for eventual risks or wellbeing and spiritual help, through periodic contributions." Unlike civil associations, subject to the control of provincial authorities, mutual associations (as do cooperatives below) are overseen by the federal state (National Institute of Associative and Social Economy, *INAES,* after its acronym in Spanish).

(c) *Cooperatives* (*asociaciones cooperativas,* Article 148, Section g, *CCC*). They are ruled by Law 20.337, which defines them as "entities founded in self-help and mutual help to organize and render services." They have a variable capital and unlimited duration, with at least ten partners and no limit to the maximum number of associates, all of whom have one right to vote each, and render services to their associates (and eventually to nonassociates). Cooperatives may be for consumption, credit (authorized financial entities may be cooperatives) and services, especially in towns and small cities. They require authorization from the national authorities to function, issued through the *INAES*. The cooperative movement is very important in Argentina, mostly in towns and small cities, where cooperatives render multiple services to their associates. In the last years, Argentina has witnessed the spread of work cooperatives, which bring in individuals who have no access to the formal labor market and receive subsidies from the state through cooperatives that not always comply with the standard formalities of this corporate type.

(d) *Commonhold Associations* (*consorcios de propiedad horizontal,* Article 148, Section h, *CCC*), made up of the coowners of buildings split into commonhold units or of other real estate premises governed by the rules applicable to that special right in rem, such as condominiums, industrial parks and private graveyards. The *CCC* provides for their functioning (Articles 2044, 2056 through 2069, and concurring ones). The 2015 *CCC* has defined commonhold as an autonomous right in rem with rules of its own further applicable to the said special ownership forms with the necessary adjustments (rather than being a single building, it is a wider land subdivided into plots, each having its own building). The commonhold association is domiciled in the building for which it has been created, its highest governing body is the owners' assembly, it may have an administrative council and must have an administrator (either an individual or an entity) representing the commonhold before third parties.

Finally, there are several other types of private legal persons provided for under special laws, not nominally mentioned in the *CCC*. Usually, they are special forms of civil associations or stock companies, but with their own rules. For instance:

(a) *State Companies* (Law 20.705), business companies wherein the State is the sole shareholder, or whose shareholders are diverse state public legal persons, engaged in a commercial or industrial activity within the frame of the private law.
(b) *Reciprocal Guaranty Companies* (*Sociedades de Garantía Recíproca, SGR*, Law 24.467), with two categories of partners: on the one side, protecting partners provide the participating partners access to credit by contributions to the *SGR* used to guarantee the credits taken by the latter, and on the other hand, participating partners are the beneficiaries of the guarantees offered by the SGR. The condition of protecting partner of an *SGR* entails tax advantages, which renders them popular among large companies that profit from these advantages while allowing their clients access to credit, thus strengthening their own businesses.
(c) *Volunteer Firemen Associations* (Law 25.054), civil associations created for the specific purpose of building volunteer firemen corps, who for this altruistic task receive a series of labor and social security benefits.
(d) *Student Centers* (Law 26.877), which function within publicly and privately run schools, high-schools and colleges, and are made up of students.
(e) *Local and town clubs* (Law 27.098), for a sporting or cultural purpose, or both. These civil associations receive special support from the state owing to their activity, materialized in tax benefits and access to own the necessary property to perform their task.

It is worth noticing that the last three types are special forms of civil associations.

4 FOREIGN LEGAL PERSONS IN ARGENTINA

As regards legal persons incorporated outside the Argentine Republic, but intending to transact business in the country, the *CCC* makes a clear distinction.

On the one hand, "foreign states, organizations to which public international law acknowledges legal personality and any other juridical person incorporated abroad whose public character arises from the law applicable thereto" (Article 146, Section b), "are governed by the laws and provisions of their incorporation insofar as their recognition, beginning, capacity, operation, organization and expiry are concerned" (Article 147). Foreign public legal persons, therefore, are governed by their own laws and are acknowledged as such by Argentina.

On the other hand, for private legal persons, the *CCC* incorporates Article 150, which reads that "private legal persons incorporated abroad are ruled by the provisions of the General Companies Act (LGS)." In turn, The *CCC* title dealing with Private International Law has omitted a rule on legal persons, except for a generic rulemaking applicable "to legal persons incorporated, authorized or registered pursuant to the laws of a foreign state" the equal treatment rule as regards the national ones (Section 2610).

Indeed, the companies act provides for foreign companies, but it would appear to be much more reasonable to hold that foreign legal persons are ruled by the law of their place of incorporation and, on a supplementary basis, by the Argentine rules applicable to the Argentine type closest to them—provisions applicable to companies, but also to cooperatives, mutual associations, civil associations or foundations, as the case may be.

The rule of application to foreign legal persons of the national rules written for the "companies, associations and foundations of equal type" also arises from the Convention Concerning the Recognition of the Juridical Personality Of Foreign Companies, Associations and Institutions adopted by The Hague Conference of Private International Law on June 1, 1956, and approved in Argentina by Law 24.409 of 1994, currently in force.

The provisions of the companies act on foreign companies (applicable to all private legal persons according to the *CCC*) set forth that as to their existence and incorporation, legal persons created abroad are governed by the laws of their place of incorporation (Section 118, *LGS*).

If these persons intend to act in Argentina, the law distinguishes between their intending to perform an "isolated act" in Argentina, or their pursuing to carry on permanent business or establish a branch or share in an Argentine company.

Foreign legal persons can perform isolated acts in Argentina, or be on trial, without having to fulfill any prior enrollment or registration requirement.

Instead, if they want to establish a branch or act on a regular basis, they must register themselves in Argentina, submit records of their governing rules and set a domicile. They must keep separate accounting books reflecting their transactions in Argentina and subject themselves to oversight according to the pertinent juridical person type (Section 120, *LGS*). The same applies if they seek to share in an Argentine company or juridical entity (Section 123, *LGS*).

If the juridical person has been incorporated overseas, but has its head office in Argentina or its primary purpose or activity is fulfilled in Argentina, the law deems that it is actually a local company or juridical person, therefore bound to discharge all incorporation and registration formalities for Argentine legal persons (Section 124, *LGS*). In these cases, overseas incorporation is deemed fraud against the Argentine law, which cannot be admitted.

Further Reading

Boretto, Mauricio, *La persona juridica,* Educa, Buenos Aires, 2015.

Rivera, Julio César & Crovi, Daniel, *Derecho Civil. Parte General,* Buenos Aires, Abeledo Perrot, 2016.

Lorenzetti, Ricardo (Director), *Código Civil y Comercial Comentado* [Civil and Commercial Code Commented], Rubinzal-Culzoni Editores, Santa Fe, 2014, Volume 1.

Tobìas, Josè W., in Alterini, Jorge H. *Còdigo Civil y Comercial. Tratado Exegètico,* Buenos Aires, La Ley, 2016*2da. Ed.* Volumes 1 and 2.

CHAPTER 6

Family Law

Ursula Basset

1 SOURCES

Family law is dealt with in Argentine's Civil and Commercial Code (hereinafter, CCC). However, there is separate legislation concerning family violence and violence against women (Ley Nacional de Violencia Familiar Nro. 24.417 (1994) and Ley Nacional de Protección Integral para prevenir, sancionar y erradicar la violencia contra las mujeres en los ámbitos en que desarrollen sus relaciones interpersonales, Nro. 26.485 (2009)) and the various children protections acts (the national one is the Ley Nacional de Protección Integral de los Derechos de las Niñas, Niños y Adolescentes Nro. 26.061 (2005)), to be found, both, at a national and local level. Since the Constitution is directly applicable, the International treaties concerning family law may be invoked by the judges as a direct source to ground their decisions, especially the International Convention on the Rights of the Child.

The contents of family law are divided in two spheres: the regulation of marriage and de facto cohabitations, on the one hand, and the regulation of kinship, filiation and parental responsibility on the other. All of these subjects are competence of national law (the provinces may not legislate on these matters). The book of family relations (*Libro de relaciones de familia*) constitutes the second book of the CCC.

This chapter will follow the order of the CCC, that is: Section 2, marriage, Section 3, Matrimonial property regimes, Section 4, Civil Unions, Section 5, Rules of kinship, Section 6, Filiation, Section 7, Adoption, Section 8, Parental responsibility, and Section 9, Procedural laws. At the end of the chapter, main bibliography will be provided.

2 MARRIAGE

Argentina enacted in 2010 a same sex marriage act, thus being the first country in Latin America to do so. Ever since marriage is conceived as a neutral sexual relationship, where sex and sexual orientation do not have a bearing. Legal impediments to marriage are: (a) forbidden degrees of kinship (ascendants with their descendants, brothers and sisters, in-laws in the first degree, e.g., father-in-law with daughter-in-law); (b) previous marriage not dissolved; (c) lack of age or discernment.[1] Adolescents may marry if they obtain the contentment of their parents (after 16) or the authorization of the judge (if parental consent is denied and always before 16). In case of lack of discernment, a judge may authorize the wedding after a hearing of the parties and their caretakers.[2]

Spouses may enter prenuptial agreements before marriage. These are valid only upon the condition that marriage is celebrated, are to be celebrated before a notary and are restricted to an inventory of assets and debts or the choice of the matrimonial property regime (*see* below).

The duties of marriage are stated in Article 431 CCC, and they are the "moral" duty of fidelity, cohabitation, the project of a life in common, mutual aid and cooperation and alimony. Marriage has several effects upon spouses: (a) it creates a legal status; (b) one spouse may choose to add the last name of other; (c) they enter a special regime concerning their patrimony; (d) a legal presumption of paternity is ascribed to one of the spouses in the case of pregnancy of the other.

De facto separation of the spouses has also some legal effects: (a) it suspends the application of the legal presumption of paternity; (b) spouses are expected to provide alimony; (c) the right to inherit the other spouse, ceases; (d) the dissolution of the regime of community of assets (*see* below) may be backdated to the day the spouses separated.

Divorce is an uncomplicated procedure,[3] which must be ruled in any case, by a judge. Any party may ask for divorce without any waiting period after marriage. Divorce relies upon the mere will of the parties (one of the spouses or both together) to dissolve marriage. The sole legal requirement is to add to the application a proposal of agreement *(propuesta de convenio regulador*) on the distribution of matrimonial property, alimony, compensations, attribution of the matrimonial home and dispositions concerning parental responsibility.[4] If the application was presented by one party, the other party must be notified and has an opportunity to expound objections and proposals. The judge must call for a hearing. If a settling is unattainable, the judge must declare the divorce without delay. The issues on which the parties did not arrive to an agreement are settled separately afterwards.

One spouse may claim alimony from the other if it has a serious condition acquired before marriage that impedes its ability to work and provide for itself. The

1. Article 403, Civil and Commercial Code.
2. Articles 404–5, Civil and Commercial Code.
3. Articles 436 and ff. Civil and Commercial Code.
4. Articles 438 and ff. Civil and Commercial Code.

obligation is transmissible to the heirs of the liable spouse. Provided that one of the spouses is not able to attain sufficient means in order to provide for himself, exceptionally and for a limited period of time the other spouse may provide alimony. The interpretation of the criteria to admit alimony are restricted.

Spouses may claim a compensation. This may occur if one of the spouses suffers a financial imbalance caused because of the way spouses lived during marriage and because of the consequences of divorce.[5] Alimony can be granted after divorce, but it is uncommon and exceptional.[6] If the claimant has asked for alimony it may not obtain the legal compensation as well. Legal compensation prescribes after six months of the divorce ruling.

As to the attribution of the family home, it depends on several factors: the caretaking of the children of both, a disadvantageous economic standing or inability to provide a home after divorce, health issues and age or "the interest of other members of the family group."[7]

3 MATRIMONIAL PROPERTY REGIMES

Since August 2015, Argentina accepts matrimonial agreements in order to rule over matrimonial property regimes. However, taking into account that it was one of the sole countries in the world to disregard them (Argentina had a mandatory regime of common property limited to the earnings during marriage), spouses have heavily restrictions on the contents of those matrimonial agreements. First, concerning the content of them: spouses may inventory their assets and debts, detail the gifts they received before marriage or chose a matrimonial property regimen.

Matrimonial agreements can be celebrated before and after marriage.[8] If celebrated before, they enter in force upon the celebration of marriage. Spouses may not allege their matrimonial property regimes against third parties unless it was previously registered in a marginal note to the marriage entry of the National Registry for births, marriages and deaths (*Registro Civil y de Capacidad de las Personas*). Matrimonial agreements may only be celebrated in a public instrument; they are otherwise subject to annulment since the formal requirement is a condition of its validity.

Once celebrated, the choice of the property regime can be changed upon a waiting period of one year. Again, they cannot be alleged against third parties before they are entered into the National Registry.

Argentina limits the choices of matrimonial property regimes to two: partial community of assets (*comunidad*) and separation of assets (*separación de bienes*). Both property regimes are submitted to a primary regime (*regimen primario*), containing mandatory regulations for the safeguarding of the patrimony of each of the spouses,

5. Article 441 Civil and Commercial Code.
6. Article 434 Civil and Commercial Code.
7. Article 443 Civil and Commercial Code. The clause concerning the interest of "other members of the family group" has not been applied yet. It is an open clause that might well be applied to take into account elderly people (grandfathers, grandmothers) or disabled members of the family who had been taken into the care of one of the spouses.
8. Articles 446 and ff. Civil and Commercial Code.

the administration of those goods essential to family life and responsibility for debts contracted in order to support family life. Whichever matrimonial property regime is chosen; spouses have to comply with mandatory rules stemming out of the primary regime.[9]

3.1 Mandatory Regime to Protect the Spouses

In either regime one spouse is due to express its consent if the other wants to sell the matrimonial home and the goods necessary to lead a life in common (i.e., bed, table, chairs, fridge, etc.).

This institution works in order to avoid the proprietary of the matrimonial home to dispose of it without the agreement of the other. It is therefore aimed at those goods that are essential to the development of family life, such as the matrimonial home and those household equipment and furniture deemed indispensable.

Consent can be previous to the legally binding act of disposition, simultaneous or posterior. If posterior, it will work as a confirmation. Matrimonial consent can be bestowed by an attorney. However, it is forbidden to extend a power of attorney to consent to the nonconsenting spouse. As to the requirements of the content of that

The formalities required to such consent are those required for the legal act of disposition of those goods. For example, to sell the hose a public deed is needed, therefore, in order to express consent to that sale the spouse will have to subject it to the same formalities (public deed).

As to the contents, the consent has to be detailed. It must include the essential elements of the legally binding act so that by the means of the enunciation of them, the object of consent can be isolated. The aim of it is to avoid consents of a general nature, for the may dilute the protective purpose of it. The spouse should know exactly which good is going to be sold and to what prize. Therefore, if the main elements of the legally binding act are not detailed in the act of consent, that consent maybe declared void.

Should the spouse deny unreasonably the consent to sell one of the items referred to above, the proprietary may sue him to obtain an authorization to sell by the judge. If the consenting spouse is absent or unable to consent, the other may also require the authorization from the judge.

If one of the goods protected by the regime of consent was to be sold without it, the other spouse may claim the annulment of the act up to six months after he or she knew about its existence.

3.2 Administration of Matrimonial Property

There is a general principle, applicable to both property regimes, that every spouse is entitled to manage their own property as they deem appropriate, without having to account to the other. The sole exception to the general principle are the mandatory

9. Articles 454 and ff. Civil and Commercial Code.

regulations to protect spouses concerning the matrimonial home and the essential household equipment and furniture (*see* above).

3.3 Responsibility for the Costs of Family Life

Both spouses are equally responsible for the expenses of family life. Per Article 461, both spouses should support each other, for the costs of maintenance of the matrimonial home, provide for the children they have in common or the minor children of one of them that lives with them in the family home. Children of one of the spouses, who has reached the age of majority and still lives in the family home is a responsibility of both spouses, but only if he has a mental or physical disability or is mentally impaired.

Responsibility of the spouses is double folded:

- Liability between spouses: spouses are expected to contribute to the mutual support, to the maintenance of the matrimonial home and the children as above. As a consequence, one may claim from the other, even during marriage, the due contribution to the household, mutual support or the support of children.
- Joint liability of the spouses before third parties: Because of the common nature of certain obligations contracted by the spouses (the support of the household and of common children or minor children from one of them that lives with the couple), both spouses are jointly liable before third parties for the debts they contracted with third parties, when these debts attain the maintenance of children (as above) or the expenses deemed necessary for the household.

3.4 Control and Powers of Attorney

In Argentine law, since each of the spouses is granted a separate administration and disposition of their goods, even under common property regimes, some structures of control had to be devised to ensure the basics of family life. Article 456 mandates that if a spouse who has the ownership of the family home or of the furniture cannot dispose of its rights or move the furniture without the assent of the other under penalty of nullity. If one of the spouses denies its assent or is not able to give it, the other may obtain a judicial order authorizing the disposition of its own property. Furniture or personal or professional items of one of the spouses, owned by the other, are subject to the same regime.

Law provides not only for distrust, but also for trust between spouses. Therefore, one of the spouses may constitute the other his or her attorney in fact to control and dispose of his or her property. This appointment may be tacit, and it is understood that unless otherwise specified, they do not have to account for their agency. Any of the spouses can revoke the appointment at any time. However, the law prohibits to appoint the other spouse as attorney to assent to the disposition of the rights on the family home or its furniture.

3.5 Community Regime

There are two regimes regulated by statute that may be chosen by the spouses: separation of goods and partial community of goods. Community of goods acts as a default regime: if spouses did not make a contract, the community of property applies.[10]

The partial community of property regime (*regimen de comunidad*) implies the virtual existence of two categories of assets: common and personal property (*bienes gananciales* and *bienes propios*). Common property is basically composed by those goods acquired by the spouses during marriage, plus the earnings they had because of their personal assets or employment. Personal property is composed by those goods the spouses inherited or received by donation.

Spouses may freely dispose or administer those assets owned by them, whether they are common or personal. However, if they wish to dispose the rights on the family home or its furniture, or if they wish to dispose registered common assets, they need the assent of the other spouse, under the penalty of nullity.

In community of property regimes joint liability of the spouses extends further than under the rules of the mandatory regime valid for both property regimes. The spouse that did not contract the debt is liable with the whole of the common assets under his ownership for the expenses made to preserve and repair common property.

The community regime ceases by decision of the spouses (because they agree to a separation of property regime under a new convention), judicial separation of property, death or dissolution of marriage. The cessation of the community regimes occurs upon the new convention, the sentence of judicial separation of property, death or divorce decree. However, the dissolution of the community might be backdated.[11] If divorce was preceded by de facto separation, it can be backdated to the date the spouses began living apart. Even more, the judge could go further back or forward if he found that there was a fraud or abuse of rights that benefitted one of the spouses.

From the moment upon which the dissolution of the matrimonial property regime occurs to liquidation and final distribution of common marital property, there is a period called "indivision" (joint possession and ownership while the division of property has not yet occurred).[12] During this period, there are different rules that apply depending upon if the dissolution occurred because of the death of a spouse or because of marriage annulment or divorce. If the dissolution occurred because of death, the case is deferred to be ruled by the law of successions. If the dissolution occurs because of an annulment, a divorce or a separation of goods, the rules that apply are the ones described next. Concerning the administration of goods, each spouse may dispose and

10. Article 463 Civil and Commercial Code.
11. Article 480 Civil and Commercial Code.
12. Articles 481 and ff. Civil and Commercial Code.

administer as during the community regime, however, it must inform sufficiently in advance to the other spouse, so that he may oppose. Each of the spouses may use common property. However, if there is a disagreement, a judge should decide. If one of them opposes to the exclusive use of common property his right is only valid from the moment in which he claims opposition. Each spouse may claim for precautionary measures such as the authorization to dispose of common property or the appointment of a third party to administer common property.

Liquidation of common property is quite a complex procedure. First, the amount of the common assets must be established. To do so, the debts between spouses must be paid. Spouses might have spent common assets to pay for personal debts or they might have paid with personal assets for common debts. They might also have failed to comply with the obligation to support their children or household debts. All these debts must be collected to establish the net assets of the community and the credits of each spouse. Once the net assets of the community property are established, division of property may proceed.

As for the distribution of property, once the regime is dissolved, in principle common property is to be distributed equally between spouses.[13] Each of the spouses has a right to claim the division and distribution of property any time. Nonetheless, spouses can settle an agreement on how they wish their common property to be distributed. The agreement is valid if both spouses are in full capacity to act.

There are, nevertheless, some exceptions to equal distribution. One of the spouses might claim a preferential right to be awarded an item of their common property. If this item was part of its intellectual or artistic property, or is related to his profession or employment, or it is a commercial or business establishment or it is the household he lived in upon dissolution of marriage, he may claim his or her right to it. If this item exceeds his or her part in the distribution of goods, he or she must pay the difference to the other spouse or its heirs.[14]

3.6 Separation of Property Regime

The separation of property regime can be entered by an agreement or by a judicial decision via a separation of common property regime.

In appearance, separation of property regimes are rather simple. It is family realities that add to its complexity: spouses live together, and it is rather difficult to keep their economies neatly separated when their lives are enmeshed.

The administration and disposition of their assets is separate. Each of them, exception made for the rules of the mandatory regime (view above), is liable for their own debts. The property of the ownership of each asset is to be proofed by any mean available. If exclusive property cannot be demonstrated, it is understood that the asset is owned by both spouses in halves. The regime ceases with the end of marriage or with a new marital agreement.

13. Article 496 Civil and Commercial Code.
14. Article 499 Civil and Commercial Code.

4 CIVIL UNIONS

The new CCC comes with an innovation. For the first time in Argentinean legal history conjugality other than marriage is formally recognized. Argentina's first Civil Code did not recognize any form of conjugality apart from marriage. Several laws recognized partial effects on de facto cohabitations, mostly referred to social security. There was also some local legislation that created civil unions in order to provide some form of legal recognition to same sex partners. Surprisingly, Argentina had a same sex marriage law before providing for any integral recognition to *de facto* cohabitations. Only in 2015, and for the first time in Argentinian history, the CCC granted legal recognition at a national level to a sole form of cohabitations: the *uniones convivenciales* which is a neologism created by the legislator. The word "convivenciales" does not exist so far in Spanish language.

The legal recognition provided for cohabitations, is, however, restricted. There are certain requirements to be met for the couple to access the benefits of the institution: (a) it is gender neutral union (couples can be from same or different sexes) but both members must be of legal age; (b) both members are not to be related in a family tie; (c) they should not have any ongoing registered partnership or marriage; (d) they should live together in an exclusive, stable and uninterrupted and continuous relationship sharing a living project.[15]

The benefits of entering such a partnership are rather limited. Cohabitants are due to assist each other during their partnership (provide alimony, assist in sickness and in health). They are obliged to provide for any household expense to the same extent as husband and wife. They are jointly liable for the same items as husband and wife are (*see* above).

Probably, the most important device provided by the regulation of the *uniones convivenciales* is the protection of the family home. If the civil partnership has been registered (which is usually done before the local civil registry) each cohabitant needs the assent of the other to dispose the rights or the furniture of the family home. A judge can waive the lack of assent if the interest of the whole family would not be compromised in doing so. The other spouse can claim the nullity of the act of disposition if it was done without its assent. An eviction or auction order cannot be carried out against a family home after the registration of the civil partnership, unless the debt has been contracted by both members of the civil union. The regulations stated above are mandatory and cannot be bypassed by any private agreement of the cohabitants.

Beyond those mandatory regulations, cohabitants are free to make any private agreement they wish. To be valid, those agreements should be done in writing, they cannot be contrary to public order, they should respect the equality principle and they may not be contrary to the fundamental rights of each of the cohabitants. They can be modified at any time during the cohabitation.

15. *See* Arts. 509, 510, Civil and Commercial Code.

The third-party effects is presided by the principle of publicity: if agreements or their termination are registered before the civil registry, they produce effects, if not, they do not. The dissolution of the cohabitation terminates automatically any valid agreement. Agreements between partners produce an effect vis-à-vis third parties if they are registered in the same document as the civil partnerships before the civil registry. They cease to produce such effects as soon as the termination of the civil partnership is also registered before the civil registry.

The dissolution of a civil partnership may have several grounds: (a) by death of one of the cohabitants; (b) by marriage or a new civil union by one of the partners; (c) by agreement; (d) by the decision of any of the cohabitants, if he or she has given notice to the other one; (e) if partners begin living apart by the decision of one or both.

There are some effects ascribed to the dissolution of a civil partnership. Partners can claim for a compensatory allowance and for the allocation of the family home. A compensatory allowance is owed when the cohabitation comes to an end, if one of the cohabitants suffers an imbalance due to the separation and the way of life both partners led during their life in common. It may be paid as a lump sum, in periodical payments or in property or the right of usufruct. If it is paid in periodical payments, those payments may not exceed the duration of the civil partnership. To grant the compensatory allowance the judge must take into account: (a) the patrimony of each of the cohabitants; (b) the dedication to household or children during the civil partnership each of them had; (c) the age and health of each and of their children; (d) the professional training of each of the spouses; (e) the contribution made to the business activities or property of the other; (f) to whom the family home has been allocated. The claim prescribes six months after the end of the civil partnership.

Civil partners can also claim for the allocation of the family home. The use of the house in which the family dwelled during their life in common may be allocated to one of the cohabitants if he is the primary caretaker of their minor children, or of a son or a daughter with mental or physical impairments. The judge must establish the period of this allocation, which may not be indefinite: it may not exceed two years to be counted from the moment of the dissolution of the civil partnership. The other party may claim a compensatory allowance for the use of the house. The interested party may also claim that the house is not sold without the agreement of both parties whilst the duration of its allocation, or that, if it is in condominium that it should not be liquidated. Should the judge grant any of these claims, they produce effects vis-à-vis third parties from the moment of its registration in the property registry. Partners also have the right to continue the tenancy of the other.

In the case of death (and this is the only right partners have in the case of dissolution by death), the surviving partner has the right to claim for the allocation of the house in which both partners dwelled at the time of death. This allocation cannot last more than two years. However, contrary to the allocation in case of separation of the partners, the surviving partner may claim for a free property right to use or habitation of the family home. Creditors of the cujus may not be affected by this allocation. This allocation ends if the surviving partner enters a new civil partnership or a new marriage. The redaction of the clause is obviously very confusing. To enter a new civil partnership two years of cohabitation are need, by which time the right to occupation of the house will be concluded.

5 KINSHIP

Argentinean law has always comprised a specific regulation of kinship. In Argentinean law kinship bears the obligation to provide alimony. Family relatives are due to alimony in a certain order of persons: (a) first, children and grandparents, second, grandchildren and grand, grandparents, third, grand grandchildren and other ancestors; (b) first, brothers, second half-brothers. This order of persons is obligatory, and in case a person of a certain degree does not have the ability to pay the alimony, the latter is owed. If there are several persons of a certain degree of kinship, the alimony is owed by them according to their capabilities.

In-laws owe alimony only if they are related in the first degree to the person who needs them.

Parents are obliged to pay child support, but the parent-child obligation is regulated separately under the title of parental responsibility.

The content of alimony owed between relatives includes everything necessary to personal subsistence: a place to live, adequate clothing, medical assistance, according to the condition of the person who receives them and the capabilities of the person obliged to pay them. If the person who receives alimony is a minor, they should include everything necessary to their education.

Usually alimony should be paid monthly, but it may be paid otherwise if the person obliged to pay them, can justify the reasons. The judge may also fix shorter periods if it is deemed convenient or necessary.

Once there is a judicial order to pay alimony, if this order is to be executed against a company in which the person who owes them works, if the company does not release the funds, it becomes jointly liable for the payment.

The obligation of alimony ceases: (a) if the person who needs the alimony incurs in a ground of unworthiness to succeed;[16] (b) if the person who needs alimony or the person obliged to pay them die; (c) if there is no longer ground for asking them (e.g., there is no further need of them).

16. Indignity is an institution by which a person is not able to succeed another upon his death (Art. 2281 Civil and Commercial Code). This may occur if: (a) the potential heir was condemned for the homicide of the deceased; (b) when there is an omission to denounce the violent death of the deceased; (c) those who have denounced the deceased for a crime punished with prison, unless it is the victim of the crime, its spouse or cohabitant, his child, grandchild, grandparent or brother; (d) those who have gravely dishonored or mistreated the deceased even after his death; (e) the relatives or the spouse that has paid alimony when the deceased needed them, or did not hospitalize him in case of need; (f) the parent out of wedlock that has denied his paternity during the minor age of the deceased; (g) the father or mother of the deceased who has been deprived of parental authority during its minor age; (h) those who have induced or restricted the liberty to testate of the deceased; (i) those who have incurred in the grounds to revoke donations (there are mostly similar to the grounds above).

6 FILIATION

The chapter of filiation is the part that arouse the most bitter discussions. The new CCC proposes three types of filiation: (a) filiation "by nature" (*por naturaleza*); (b) by artificial reproductive techniques (ART) (*técnicas de reproducciòn humana asistida*); and (c) by adoption. According to Article 558, all three types should have the same effects. It is also established that no one may have more than two parents, whatever their sex.

As it happened in other legal systems, in vitro fertilization techniques caused a revision of previously accepted rules. Filiation may now be a choice of the parents to be, even if they are not related to the child in any of the senses previously known: parents by intention express their consent in a form not before a public authority and without any certainty of their qualifications to exert the caretaking of the children. If compared with adoption, where parents are not genetically related and are therefore submitted to countless controls, and are expected to live with the child for a time before the adoption decree is pronounced, so as to make sure that there is a compatibility between them and the child, children by assisted procreation, are not deemed to deserve such a protection of the State.

On the other hand, whereas children born from their biological parents in a natural way have the right to investigate and contest the paternity of their legal parents, children born by in vitro fertilization do not have that right.

Moreover, compared to natural and adoptive filiation, children born by in vitro fertilization techniques have a limited access to their personal identity and to their ancestors.

When the regulation of filiation is viewed as a whole, there is a certain doubt whether the general principle of nondiscrimination and equality established by Article 2 of the Convention of the Child is complied with.

6.1 Filiation by ART

One of the first surprises to be found in the new CCC, is that in vitro fertilization is regulated before any other form of filiation. Usually, in most compared legal systems, in vitro fertilization is regulated after the still paradigmatic biological filiation. In Argentina, this order is inverted. The chapter of filiation starts with ART.

The filiation through ART is established via a consent given by the parents to be before the laboratory in which the technique is to be performed. Filiation by ART is therefore issued not from nature, not from a complex intervention of the State with several controls on the parents to see if they are fit to take care of the child, but by a contract between two private parties. The dignity of the child is naturally in questions: he becomes the object of a contract, which up to now was completely unconceivable.

There are no obligations toward the laboratory nor the parents to be. The parents to be can revoke the consent at any point before the implantation of the selected embryos, yet they have to renew the consent each time that the embryos or the gametes are made use of.[17]

The consent has to be expressed in a notarial document, properly registered or before a health authority. The child will be son or daughter to the mother who gave birth and gave its consent, and to the other person who gave the consent. This means that no tie is needed between both parents to be. They may be just two persons who agreed to have a child. It also means that for Argentinean law, mother is she who gave birth, which has obvious implications concerning surrogate motherhood. However, even if such a clause, introduced later on in the parliamentary discussion of the definitive text of the CCC, would appear to exclude such practice, in fact, some judgements declared that mother is she who expressed her consent and not the one who gave birth.

Children born by heterologous ART should have access to the genetic and health information of their donors. Information concerning the donor should be kept in a dossier by the laboratory, but there are no sanctions if obligation is not fulfilled. Children may also have access to the identity of the donor through a petition before a judge who may evaluate the reasons to claim access to his or her identity.

Filiation by ART is further regulated in the chapter dealing with filiation "by nature." Matrimonial filiation by ART stems both form the consent and from the presumptions of paternity (*see* below). Furthermore, children conceived by ART are forbidden to contest their paternity in any case.

In every case, children born by ART are to be registered before the Civil Registry with a birth certificate and the informed consent the parents gave before the laboratory.

6.2 Filiation "by Nature"

Filiation "by nature" (*por naturaleza*) resends to the traditional filiation, in which the child is conceived by both their parents without the intervention of a third party. However, in the new Argentine Civil Code this is not so. Since same sex marriage is admitted, filiation by nature includes not only filiation out of wedlock, in which mother is she who gives birth, and father he who is genetically and biologically related to the child, but also matrimonial filiation, in which mother is she who gave birth but the other parent may well be another woman, who did not conceive (in the biological sense) the child.

Argentina has a longstanding history of fighting to favor the right of the children to their true identity. Therefore, the legal presumption of parenthood in same sex marriage is controversial. It sanctions a denial of the true genetic identity of the child by law. However, contrary to the establishment of parenthood by ART, the presumption might be contested by the child or by any interested party in the case of a disagreement between biological and legal identity. In that case (again, contrary to

17. Article 560, Civil and Commercial Code.

filiation per ART), biological and genetic filiation will prevail over the will of the parents and over the legal presumption. The legal presumption starts with the celebration of marriage and ends 300 days after its dissolution. In the case of de facto separation, the presumption ceases, but the child might be registered as a matrimonial child as long as both parents agree to it.

Legal filiation must be registered before the Civil Registry with the birth certificate and the documents that identify the parents.

Out of wedlock paternity is established by recognition of the child by his father. Recognition is a voluntary legal act by a notarial document, by testament, before a proper authority or simply by a written document.[18] The recognition must be notified by the Civil Registry to the mother and to the child or its legal attorney. Recognition of a child is irrevocable and may not be subject to any condition. It does not require the consent of the child. The recognition of a deceased child does not attribute any rights in his succession unless there has been a *possession d'état* (a public treatment of the child as a son or a daughter) previous to that act.

A child might be recognized before his or her birth.[19] This is because Argentinian law has a strong culture of recognizing the existence of the child and even parental authority from the moment of conception. A child is a human person from the moment in which he or she is conceived, which is a contradiction with the ART legislation, that presupposes normally embryo selection. The recognition acquires full validity upon live birth.

6.3 Actions to Establish and Dispute Parentage

As in many legal systems, Argentina recognizes a right to a "real" parenthood. This means that the child has a right to have his legal parentage coincide with his biological one.

Parentage is far more than just biology or genetics; therefore, there are certain limits to exert such actions. Usually, limits are imposed to parents and not to children. For some reason, legislators seem to think that there is a greater urge for children to establish a parentage in accord to their real origins that for parents to do so.

The table below indicates the actions available to determine and contest parentage in Argentinian CCC:

Actions to determine legal parentage ("*Acciones de reclamación de la filiación*"):

- Action to determine legal parentage (Arts. 582–587)

Actions to dispute matrimonial filiation:

- Action to dispute maternity (Art. 589–590, "*Impugnación de la filiación presumida por la ley*")
- Action to disavow a legal presumption of filiation (Art. 591, "*Acción de negación de la filiación presumida por la ley*")

18. Article 571, Civil and Commercial Code.
19. Article 574, Civil and Commercial Code.

- Action to disavow preventively a legal presumption of filiation (Art. 592, "*Impugnación preventive de la filiación presumida por la ley*")

Actions to dispute out of wedlock filiation:

- Action to disavow a legal acknowledgement of paternity (Art. 593, "*Impugnación del reconocimiento*").

Let us begin with the actions to determine legal parentage. As seen above, legal maternity is determined by birth, so usually the problem will be to determine who the legal father is. Since there is the principle of "double parentage" a child cannot have more than to parents (whatever their sex). However, if the two rules are combined, and if it is understood that actions to establish or dispute parenthood rely on the coincidence between legal status and biological reality, in principle (not in practice) there could be only the following combinations: two mothers or a father and a mother. Mother would be only she who gave birth. The other mother or the father could be determined by a legal presumption, thus then disputed or disavowed by the child.

Yet, since none of this actions can be undertaken when a child is born by ART, it could be possible that a child has no action left in a couple of two mothers or even of a mother and a father. Its filiation will be determined, fixed, by the intention of their parents as long as it is done before a laboratory and not privately.

Even if surrogate motherhood was deliberately excluded from the CCC, there have been several judgements in which, once the child was already born, it has been registered as a child of both parents by intention. Furthermore, in one case, during pregnancy of the surrogate mother, the judge accepted that it should be registered as a child to the parents by intention. The two parents rule also had its exception. A couple of two women managed to obtain a permit to register a child with three parents (the two mothers and the donor). So, the fresh rules of the new CCC are already subject to several exceptions.

A child can claim its filiation against their parents. If they are married, he has to sue both of them. If he or she was born out of wedlock, he can sue whoever he or she thinks are their parents. If they have died he may sue his heirs. For the child this actions do not prescribe. If the child dies, his or her heirs can continue the legal action initiated by him or initiate the action if he or she was a minor, or before a year of the coming of age or the discovery of the evidence.

When the filiation of the child has only its motherhood established, special rules apply. The new CCC takes a strong position against mothers who hide the identity of the fathers. This is odd, if compared with the regulation of matrimonial filiation and filiation by ART in which the anonymity of the biological parent is the rule or might be hidden by a legal presumption. The Civil Registry has to communicate to the Public Ministry the fact that a mother has registered a child without a father, and the Public Ministry will act like a public prosecutor trying to determine the paternity or the acknowledgement of the child by its father. It is interesting to note, that this is the only time in which the CCC talks of "fathers" instead of choosing the gender-neutral language. Since the establishment of fatherhood will be made by genetic testing, and mother is she who gave birth, it has to be a man.

The Civil Registry urges the mother to give the name of the person believed to be the parent or any information she has that would allow to determine who he is. The mother should be made aware of the consequences of lying or denying the child its identity. Later on the chief of the Civil Registry has to summon the mother to inform her the rights of the child and her duties towards him or her (Article 583).

There are certain facts that help to presume parenthood. First, if there is a possession of status, this possession will count as if it were an acknowledgement of paternity, save if it is stroked by genetic testing. Second, if the person believed to be the father lived with the mother at the time of conception, it is presumed that he is the father.

The mother might claim for alimony during the trial. The father who refused to acknowledge the child might be liable for compensations for damages.

As for the actions to contest parentage, there are several. First, the action to contest maternity. The filiation might be disputed by the woman believed to be the mother, by the child, by the biological mother or by a third party with a legitimate interest. The right to perform such action expires a year from the moment the facts were known to the party or a year after the registration of that filiation.

Second, matrimonial filiation can be contested by the child, the legal parents, or any third party with a legitimate interest. For the child, the action does not expire, for the rest of them the action expires a year from the moment the facts were known to the party or a year after the registration of the child. In the case of death of any of the parties with a right to sue, the action may be performed by their heirs, and it expires as if the party with a right to sue had been alive (they have the same expiring period as the living party would have had).

Third, matrimonial filiation can be contested by a disavowal of the legal presumption.

Since the legal presumption of filiation starts with marriage, a mother that was pregnant before marriage may not bear the child of her husband. Therefore, the husband (or the wife) has the right to disavow the legal presumption of filiation of a child born within the first 180 days of marriage, claiming that he or she did not know about the pregnancy and that there was not possession of status by the child. The expiring time is a year since the registration of the child or since the legal parent knew that the child could not be his/hers. Of course, when the marriage is between two women the other woman must have known ever since that the child was not hers. This is why the gender neutral legislation for this issues is not always well suited.

In the fourth place, a parent might dispute preventively the application of the legal presumption during pregnancy. No conditions apply to this actions, that might be performed by the mother, the spouse or any third party with a legitimate interest.

Finally, the acknowledgement of the child born out of wedlock might be disputed by the child himself or by any third party with legitimate interest. For the child, there is no expiring date, for the adult parties there is always the expiring date of one year to be counted from the date of the voluntary acknowledgement act or since evidence was discovered that it was not the father's child.

As it can be noted, expiring dates are the same in every action. And almost anyone has sufficient standing for a claim: third parties with legitimate interest, legal parents, children. This shows the open mindedness of the legal system when it comes to establish a filiation that coincides with the biological origins. Once again, this is at odds with the principles to determine filiation to be found in the regulation of ART and legal presumptions in same sex marriages.

7 ADOPTION

For some reason, even if adoption is considered to be a third form of filiation, it has a chapter of its own. The aim of adoption in Argentinian legal system is to fulfill the right to family life for those children who have been abandoned or abused by their parents. The approach to adoption is a child-centered one, and it does not focus on the rights of adults to form a family and have children, not even on infertility, just on alternative care for children in need.

7.1 Cultural Framework

Argentina has several historical fears concerning adoption. One of them has to do with denial: during the last dictatorship, some children of rebel parties were separated from their biological parents and raised as biological children by third parties. Their biological identity was denied. Ever since, Argentina has always had a strong position concerning the right to know and the ties between the family of origin and the adoptees.

Second, Argentina has a long history of selling and buying children, that has been denounced by the Inter-American Court of Human Rights. In many other countries, there are private agencies that deal with adoption. In Argentina this is unthinkable. Adoption is dealt with a great intervention of the State, and therefore, at some point, with bureaucracy. Everything goes through a Registry and under the control of a judge.

Third, Argentina has a deep division when it comes to adoption. On the one hand, there are those who favor easy adoptions, where a mother can even choose to which adoptive parents she wants to give her child. On the other hand, there are those who distrust this approach. Some think that adoption is a way by which rich adoptive parents get hold of the children of those parents who are poor. And so they think the State should encourage poor people to stick to their children with the help of public services and assistance.

Finally, Argentina is against international adoption. Argentina receives children from abroad, but does not "export" Argentinian children. This is so, probably out of fear of its previous experiences with the selling of children and to preserve the right of the child to preserve its ties with its family of origin.

Most of these positions might be seen as odd by other cultures. And yet they have to do with a country's history, with its fears and hopes.

7.2 General Principles

There are some general principles who should guide the judge in the application of the rules.

These are: (a) the "superior" interest of the child; (b) the respect for the child's identity; (c) the exhaustion of all the means trying to reestablish family life with the family of origin; (d) the preservation of the ties with the brothers and sisters; (e) the right to have access to its origins; (f) the right of the child to be heard during the procedures.[20]

The right to have access to its origins is granted throughout the CCC. First, by a specific device that should enable the child to have access to every information concerning its adoption. The adoptee with sufficient age and maturity has the right to know and have access to the file of its adoption. If it is a minor, he can be assisted by an interdisciplinary team. The adoptive parents may ask for assistance as well.

Second, the adoptive parents have commit to tell the adoptive child about its origins.

Third, even in a plenary adoption, the judge might rule a visitation right for the members of the biological family of the child or even preserve the legal kinship to some of them (a child might have more than one father or mother in this case, or the ties to its brothers or sisters might be preserved).

Finally, whenever possible the child should be adopted with their brothers and sisters.

Only minors might be adopted, if they are declared as adoptable (*declaradas en situación de adoptabilidad*). Adult children might only be adopted if it is the son or daughter of a spouse (*adopción de integración, see* below) or if there was a possession of status of the child before he came of age.

Adoptive parents should be registered before the National or local registry of adoptive parents. The adoption is void if they are not registered. They should be at least 16 years older than the child to be adopted and be at least 25 years old. A child can be adopted jointly by a married couple or by a couple who entered a *union convivencial* (*see* above). Adoptive parents have to reside permanently in Argentina for at least five years before asking for ab adoption, unless they are Argentinians. A grandfather may not adopt its grandchildren. A brother may not adopt his brother or sister. Adoption is an institution that can only proceed between strangers that are not related.

7.3 The Adoption Procedure

As explained above, a child may only be adopted, if he has been declared adoptable (*declaración de adoptabilidad*). The declaration of adoptability of a child is a procedure of its own. A child can only be declared adoptable: (a) if his or her parents have died and the search for relatives has been exhausted; this search may last 30 days extendable to another 30 days; (b) if his or her parents have decided freely that the

20. Article 595.

child should be adopted (this decision can be made only 45 days after birth); (c) if the exceptional measures taken to prevent the separation of the child from its family have been unsuccessful for a period of 180 days. However brief this terms might appear to be, they are undermined by the fact that no decree of adoptability can be pronounced as long as there is a member of the family of the child or a meaningful person to the child (*referente afectivo*) is willing to take care of the child. This means that each time that someone (a meaningful person or a relative) expresses its willfulness to take care of the child, it prevents the child from being adopted.

The child itself, its parents, the child's office (an administrative entity who represents the child) and the public ministry have to take part in the procedures to declare the adoptability of the child. The judge may hold a hearing with other members of the family or meaningful persons.

The procedure takes place before the judge who heard the case for the exceptional measures, or else, before a judge in family affairs. The judge must hear the child and its parents. The decree with the declaration of adoptability must include an order in which the National Registry of Adoptive Parents should send to the Tribunal a file with proposed adoptive parents for that child.

The second step in the procedure towards adoption is the pre-adoption fostering (*guarda preadoptiva*) of the child, which is also decided by a judge. The CCC establishes a special procedure in order to decide who is to foster the child in order to become, if everything turns out right, its adoptive parent.

The pre-adoption fostering is an institution meant to be a test: adoptive parents and adoptive child or children experience how their relation works out. The (theoretical) maximal duration of pre-adoptive fostering is of six months. The procedure of pre-adoptive fostering takes place before the judge of family affaires.

First of all, it is strictly forbidden for the parents to give their child to the adoptive parents without the intervention of the National Registry and the judge. This is such a strong prohibition, that the judge may separate the child from its prospective adoptive parents if they have dealt with the biological mother or parents directly. The time the child spent with its prospective adoptive parents by irregular means cannot be counted in order to achieve adoption.

The procedure of pre-adoptive fostering starts with the selection of the prospective adoptive parents. The judge should take into account personal traits of character, age, conditions and suitability to care for the child of the prospective parents, their motivations and expectations concerning adoption and their willfulness to respect the right to the child's identity.

During the procedure, the judge must hear the opinion of the child and take it into account according to their age and maturity.

The procedure ends with the decree that grants the pre-adoptive fostering to the selected adoptive parents, that from then on have six months to test if the relationship between them and the child will work out.

The third step is the procedure of adoption. The judge competent to rule the adoption is the one who ruled the pre-adoptive fostering or the one of the habitual residence of the child. Once the six months of the pre-adoption fostering have concluded, the judge, the adoptive parents or the administrative body may seize the court to proceed to adoption.

Parties to the adoption procedure are the prospective adoptive parents, the child if he/she has sufficient maturity and age, the judge must hear the child and the Public Ministry and the administrative body that intervened before are also expected to take part during adoption procedures. If the adoptive child elder than 10 years, he or she can consent or refuse the adoption.

The decree of adoption will be backdated to the day in which pre-adoptive fostering started.

7.4 Types of Adoption

Argentina recognizes three types of adoption: (a) plenary adoption (*adopción plena*); (b) simple adoption *(adopción simple*); (c) adoption by the partner or spouse (*adopción de integración*). The enunciation is faulty. As a matter of fact, there are only two types of adoption (simple and plenary), and the adoption by the spouse may be either plenary or simple, it just differs from the usual adoption because it is a sort of status for stepparents.

In principle, plenary adoption gives the child the same standing as a biological child: it severs any tie with the biological parents and it may not be revoked. In principle, simple adoption creates a tie restricted to the adoptive parents and the child, preserves some legal ties between the biological parents and the child, and may be revoked. Only in principle, because in the new CCC grants the judge the faculty to determine the extent of the kinship of the adoptive child. It may preserve biological ties in a plenary adoption or extend the adoptive ties to adoptive grandparents in simple adoption.[21] This implies that the two-parent rule, in this cases, will be inevitably broken: A child might have four parents (two adoptive, two biological parents). A judge may also transform a simple adoption into a plenary adoption. It is for the judge to decide which type of adoption is granted.

Plenary adoption is an irrevocable and in principle, as above, creates for the child the same status as a biological child. However, the child may promote an action to determine its filiation to ask for alimony or have succession rights toward its biological parent. Here again, a child may end having more than two parents.

Adoption may be plenary only if the child has been declared as adoptable, when its parents have been deprived from parental responsibility, when the child's parents died, or when the child's parents have given their "informed consent" so that their child may be adopted before a judge. Here again, a contradiction arises: a parent may consent to give their child in adoption, yet they may not decide which adoptive parents will take care of that child.

Simple adoption produces quite different effects. The rule is that the ties between biological parents and the child are not extinguished with simple adoption, however

21. Article 621.

the parental responsibility is given to the adoptive parents. In that light, simple adoption looks more like an institution of care than a form of filiation. The biological family has still the right of visitation and contact with the adopted child except if it is contrary to the child's interests. The adoptive child may claim alimony from the biological parents and they are still obliged to provide them, which raises the issue of the position of poor biological parents, who give their child to adoption, because they feel unable to provide for him, and later on, having given the child, are nevertheless obliged to provide alimony. If the adoptee has sufficient age and maturity they may ask that they surname of origin is preserved. As in plenary adoption, a child might be acknowledge by its biological father or may exert an action of determination of paternity towards its biological parents. Whatever the results of these actions, they may not compromise simple adoption and its effects.

Simple adoption is revocable if the child or the adoptive parents have incurred in a form of indignity, if there is a justified claim to revoke it from the adoptive child when he comes of age, if there is an agreement between an adoptive child (of age) and its adoptive parents before a court. Revocation extinguishes adoption to all effects but only to the future.

Finally, the adoption by the spouse or the partner. In this kind of adoption, the child keeps all of his or her biological ties and all the effects of both biological and adoptive parenthood. Once again, the multiple parenthood scenario is there. This is especially concerning in those cases in which a mother wishes to break the relationship of the child with its biological father after divorce. Creating a new parent is a way to sever the biological tie.

Of course, to make from step-parenthood a real parenthood is maybe a step to far. Step-parents are usually parents by-proxy, because of their relationship with the mother or the father of those children. Family law has strived to preserve biological ties beyond divorce. Now it may have to deal either with multiparentality or the replacement of a father by a stepfather. In any case, the advantage of this kind of adoption is that it depends on the free will of the partner of spouse of the parent, contrary to the stepparent statute included in the CCC, which is imposed upon stepparents without any choice or respect to their private family life.

Adoption by the spouse or the partner may take the form of a plenary adoption or a simple adoption. However, since this kind of adoption is a by proxy parenthood, it has rules of its own: (a) biological parents must be heard for the proceeding; (b) the adoptive parents needs not to be registered in the national registry for adoptive parents; (c) there is no need of a judicial declaration of adoptability; (d) there is no need of a pre-adoption fostering; (e) there is no need to proof that the family of origin is unable to provide for the child.

Regardless of the kind of adoption granted to the spouse (plenary or simple) may always be revoked. It is the first time plenary adoption may be revoked in Argentinian law, and it makes sense, because, as explained before, this is a sort of by proxy adoption that relies heavily on the conjugal relationship of the biological parent and the stepparent. It may be revoked invoking the same grounds as simple adoption.

7.5 Nullity and Registration

Finally, the CCC deals with the grounds of invalidity of an adoption and its registration.

The grounds of absolute invalidity are: (a) the age of adoptive parents; (b) the lack of sufficient difference of age between adoptive parent and adoptive child; (c) if adoption presupposed an unlawful act; (d) if it is a joint adoption, except for spouses or partners of a civil union; (e) the adoption of grandchildren or grand grandchildren; (f) the adoption between brothers or sisters; (g) the lack of the decree of adoptability; (h) the lack of registration of the adoptive parents in the national registry of adoptive parents; (i) the lack of consent of a child of more than 10 years of age.

There is also a relative invalidity if the adoptive parent had not the minimum age, if there are vices to the consent given by the parents or the children, if the right of the child to be heard was not respected.

Adoption must be registered in the National Civil Registry.

8 PARENTAL RESPONSIBILITY

Parental responsibility (*responsabilidad parental*) is defined in the new CCC as a set of rights and duties attributed to the parents over the person and the patrimony of the child, for this protection and full for as long as he is under age.[22]

As with adoption, parental responsibility starts with a number of principles meant to guide the judges in the application of the law. These are: (a) the superior interest of the child; (b) the respect for the progressive autonomy of the child with consideration to their own personality; and (c) the right of the child to be heard according to his age and maturity.

The Argentinian CCC introduces three institutions: the hold of parental responsibility (*titularidad de la responsabilidad parental*), the care of the child (*cuidado parental*) and the guard of the child (*guarda*). No definitions are provided. Authors hesitate if they are equivalents to former institutions in the Civil Code of Vélez Sársfield. To simplify, the hold of parental responsibility deals with who is entitled to it. The right to care of the child is an emanation of parental responsibility, and may be distributed or joined between the parents. Whereas the guardianship of the child refers to the fact of providing daily care by third parties.

8.1 Exercise of Parental Responsibility

In principle, both parents exert jointly parental responsibility, whether they are married or not, whether they cohabit or not. There is a legal presumption that the acts of one of them has the consent of the other, whether it is spouses, partners, whether they are divorced or separated. In this cases, if it would be more convenient, certain areas of the care of the child may be distributed between former spouses or cohabitants

22. Article 638.

(e.g., the father undertakes sports, the mother undertakes language formation, or just medical care). Of course, the presumption may fall, if one of the parents disputes before the court the actions of the other.

This presumption of consent is not valid for certain acts the law deems to be crucial for the life of the child. These are: (a) consent to marriage when they the child is under age; (b) consent for the child to enter religious communities (as joining them); (c) authorize the child to reside permanently abroad or just to travel abroad; (d) authorize the child to participate in a trial, safe from the cases in which he is already authorized; (e) administer the patrimony of the child, safe if it was delegated to one of the spouses or third parties. In all of these cases, if the other spouse does not approve or is incapable of rendering its consent a judge might replace the lack of consent with a court order if it is in interest of the family. If the child is elder than 13, his own consent is needed as well (which, authors say, might be difficult to handle when it is a simple decision as traveling abroad).

If a child was born out of wedlock, and paternity was established after judicial decision, the father has not the right to exert parental responsibility. However, if mother and father agree, they may decide otherwise: to jointly exercise parental authority or to distribute the tasks and competences with regard to the child. To do so, they need a joint declaration before the court.

The parents may decide to delegate parental authority.[23] This may occur only in interest of the child and by reasonable grounds. They may agree to delegate the exercise of parental responsibility to a relative or to the stepparent.[24] The agreement of delegation of parental responsibility must be presented before the judge who will revise it and approve it. It may not last more than a year, but it may be extended to another year if there are reasonable grounds to it. Parents retain the right to supervise the exercise of parental authority.

If parents are adolescents (more than 13 years old), whether they are married or not, they have the right to exercise parental responsibility concerning the child's care, health and education. However, the parents of the adolescent may oppose to the acts that can result in prejudice of the child. Grave decisions, such as the decision to give the child in adoption or medical treatments that may endanger the child's life, require a double consent: the consent of the adolescent parent plus the consent of any of their parents. If those who are in charge of the adolescent parent and the adolescent parent do not agree, a judge on family affairs decides for them.

Parental Care (*cuidado personal*) might be exercised jointly or exclusively by one parent. When the parents live together there is no question: they exercise it jointly. When parents are divorced or do not live together the joint exercise of parental care is preferred, it could however happen that parents decide or the judge orders an exclusive exercise of parental care. If parents choose in an agreement or the judge decides by a court order to grant joint care, they may choose between two options: (a) an "alternate" care (*cuidado compartido alternado*) in which the child spends equal time with each of the parents; (b) an "undifferentiated" care (*cuidado compartido*

23. Article 643.
24. Article 674.

indiferenciado) in which the child spends more time with a parent than with the other. In this alternative a child would have a main residence with one of the two parents. This second option should be preferred in case the judges had to decide over a couple. In any case both parents must ensure adequate access to the other.

In case the parties or a judge decide for exclusive care there is a duty of collaboration of the noncohabiting parent towards the cohabiting one. In order to take this decision the judge must consider which of the two parents prioritizes fluid access to the other parent, the age of the child, its opinion, and the preservation of the main residence of the child, in which his friends and school take place. The parent that exercises the exclusive care has a duty to properly inform the other about the decisions he takes concerning the child.

Parents may present before the court a parental agreement in which they decide about the time the child will spend with each of the, about how they will spend holidays, vacations, among other things.

Guardianship may also be given to a third party (always a relative) by decision of the court for a maximum period of a year, renewable to another year. Guardianship is sometimes a way to avoid adoption. Among the poorest people in Argentina, there are usual irregular situations in which a child is taken care of by another family member, such as grandparents or uncles. This institution offers a way out, without separating the child from the family. However, the limited period of one or two years is very short.

8.2 Rights and Duties for Parents and Children

The rights and duties for parents and children are spread along the chapter of parental responsibility.

The duties of the parents are to care for the child, to live together with him or her, to provide alimony and to educate him. He is also obliged to consider the special needs of the child according to its own personality. He should respect the child's right to be heard and to "participate in its education" as in any matter concerning his most intimate rights, he should guide the child, so that he or her may "fully exercise their rights," and, finally, the parent should also respect the right of the child to have access to grandparents, other family members or any person with whom the child has "a relationship of affection." As in many other legal regimes, the legislator spells out rights and duties that exceed any possible control of the judge. It might be noted that some of those duties are noteworthy: the parent are expected to ensure the full exercise of the rights of the child or any relationship of affection, leaving a small margin for the parents to exercise a fuller role of guidance and education of its children, as it is expected from him according to the International Convention on the Rights of the Child.

Any form of child maltreatment is forbidden. Parents may ask for the help of parental orientation services instead.

Both parents are also obliged to pay alimony to the child until he or her reaches the age of 21. Alimony comprises education, leisure activities, clothing, habitation and medical care. Basically everything a child needs to his full development. They may be paid in monthly installments or in species, and should keep a double proportionality:

to the incomes of both parents and to the needs of the child. The tasks undertaken by one of the parents in the daily care of the child count as a payment in species. If parental care is shared equally in a joint manner, and both parents have a similar income, they should maintain the child whilst he or she resides with each parent. If incomes are not equal, even if parents have joint parental care, the parent who has a better standing should pay for alimony so that the child has a similar way of life in both homes. Common expenses should be, in principle, split in halves.

Any of the parents may be sued if he does not comply with alimony by the other parent, by the child, by a public prosecutor or by any other relative. If the child has come of age, the parent whom which he lives can sue for alimony in his representation. This strange decision was taken to avoid a difficult confrontation between a child and his parents, when it comes to alimony.

If the son or daughter between 21 and 25 endeavors a career or any sort of professional studies, parents are obliged to provide alimony in case his studies do not allow enough time in order to provide for him or herself.

Other peculiarities of Argentinian law are the right of alimony of a child towards the person who is deemed to be its parent before parenthood was established and the right to alimony for the pregnant woman. According to Article 664, a child may claim alimony from a person who has not acknowledge paternity as a preventive measure before establishing paternity. Article 665 establishes the duty to provide alimony for the pregnant woman from the alleged father, as long as the woman may proof that there is a high possibility that he is the father for the child.

Grandparents may be sued for alimony in the same procedure as its son or daughter (the parent of the child). However, their obligation only exists, if the parent of the child is proven unable to provide for its child.

Argentinian CCC also rules about the duties of children towards their parents. These are: (a) a duty of respect; (b) a duty to comply with the decision of their parents "that are not contrary to their superior interest" (the child should decide what is contrary and what not?); (c) collaborate with their parents or grandparents in the tasks they can afford to do.

8.3 The Status of the Stepparent

Argentine CCC creates a new status for the stepparent (*progenitor afín*). Stepparent is he who lives with or is married to the parent of the child.[25] This means that a person who lives with or marries another, if there are children, becomes automatically, whether he agrees or not, into a stepparent, with the duties and rights as below.

Stepparents have duties: they have to cooperate with the education of the child, help out in everyday tasks and take decisions in case of an urgency. Any decision taken by a stepparent should be made in respect of the will of the parents of the child. They also are subsidiary liable to provide alimony for the child. The duty to provide alimony

25. Article 672.

ceases in case of breakup. However, it might continue after breakup if the cessation of alimony might cause a grave prejudice to the child. In that case, the stepparent is obliged to a reduced provision of alimony.

Children, on the other hand, cannot choose either. The status is imposed on them, without even hearing them to see if they agree or not. Children have a duty to respect stepparents.

Stepparents, from the fact of that status, apart from the mandatory obligations stemming from the status, have several frameworks they can choose in order to structure their relationships with the child. First, parental responsibility might be delegated to them in case that both parents agree to it. Second, if one of the parent dies, he might sign an agreement with the other in order to exercise parental authority jointly. Finally, the stepparent might adopt the child (as seen above).

8.4 Expiration of Parental Authority

Parental responsibility ceases in the case of death of the parent, if the parent enters a religion community in which he pronounces permanent vows (a reminiscence of Catholicism, which used to be very strong in Argentina), if the child comes of age, if he is emancipated.

Parents are deprived of parental responsibility if they are condemned for a crime against the child, if they abandon the child or if the endanger the safety or the health of the child or if the child is declared adoptable.

The deprivation of parental authority may be revised if it is in benefit of the child's interest.

Parental authority might also be suspended. This happens when a parent is absent and its death is presumed, while he is in prison, if he does not have the capacity to perform his or her duties towards the child because of its mental health, or if a child lives with a third party because of a court order.

If only one of the two parents is deprived of its parental responsibility or if its parental responsibility is suspended, the other has the full exercise of parental responsibility.

Parents are still obliged to pay for alimony, whatever form of suspension or deprivation of parental responsibility they undergo.

9 FAMILY PROCEDURES

The Argentine CCC has deemed it necessary to make some provisions as to family procedures, even if, in principle, procedure matters are a competence of each Province of Argentina, according to the National Constitution (*see* chapter "Constitutional Law"). The legislators thought, however, that some aspects of family procedures are intimately related to the regulation of the institutions contained by the CCC and provided therefore a frame with certain principles and rules, as it can be read below.

Please note that measures to protect abandoned children or children at risk *(medidas de protección de la niñez)* and family violence is dealt with provincial regulations (they should be looked up according the jurisdiction of the case). Also note that, in general, family procedure is a matter of provincial legislation (*see* chapter of Procedure Law). That is why specific procedure law may be applicable according to the jurisdiction in which the case falls and maybe found in a Civil and Commercial Procedure Code of each Province or in a special Family procedure code (some provinces have special procedure codes for family law).

9.1 Principles in Family Procedures

Family procedures should respect the principles of good faith, secrecy, orality, right to effective judicial protection, right of access to justice, immediacy of proceedings, promptness and transparency.

Judges must specialize in family law and have a multidisciplinary team to deal with family matters. Any decision taken in which children are involved should take into account their best interest.

Children or persons with disabilities have the right to be heard in any procedure that affects them. His opinion must be considered according to its ability to understand the issues under debate.

The judge has a main role in family procedures. Judges are expected to begin and promote at its own initiative all the proceedings, except from those cases that have to do with patrimonial aspects of the family.

Witnesses in family procedures may be related to the parties (which is an exception to the general principles).

9.2 Actions to Determine the Family Status

The right to determine the status of a person is inalienable. It does not ever prescribe. They may only be exercised by their holders, it is a nontransferable right.

9.3 Rules of Competency

In the cases concerning minors, the habitual residence of the minor determines the competency of the judge. If the action to determine or exclude parenthood takes place when the son or daughter is already an adult, the judge of the residence of the person who is sued is competent.

In the cases of divorce and nullity of marriage, the judge of the last joint residence of the parties is competence, or of the person who is sued, or of any of the spouses. For civil unions, the judge of the last common residence or of the person who is sued. The person who sues, has the choice.

Alimony and compensations are dealt with before the judge chosen by the person who sues. She or he may choose between of the last common residence or of the beneficiary or of the person sued, or were the obligation has to be paid.

As for the dissolution of matrimonial property regimes, the same rules apply. However, if there is a bankruptcy procedure, the judge of the bankruptcy proceedings is competent.

Further Reading

Basset, Ursula C. (Dir. and Author), in Alterini, Jorge H., *Código Civil y Comercial, Tratado Exegético, T. III,* Buenos Aires, Thomson Reuters, 2017.

Belluscio, Augusto, *Derecho de Familia,* Buenos Aires, Thomson Reuters, 2016.

Kemelmajer, Aída R. (Dir), *Tratado de Derecho de Familia,* 4 volumes, Santa Fe, Rubinzal Culzoni, 2015.

Krasnow, Adriana N. (Dir), *Tratado de Derecho de Familia,* 3 volumes, Buenos Aires, Thomson Reuters, 2015.

Medina, Graciela & Roveda, Eduardo, *Manual de derecho de Familia,* Buenos Aires, Thomson Reuters, 2017.

Perrino, Jorge O. & Basset, Ursula C. (Act)., *Tratado de Derecho de Familia,* 3 volumes, Buenos Aires, Thomson Reuters, 2017.

CHAPTER 7

Law of Obligations: Contract Law and Tort Law

Alejandro Borda & Ursula Basset

1 GENERAL OVERVIEW

The Civil and Commercial Code (CCC) has tried to give an equal standing, to the liabilities stemming out of an infringement of a contract or those stemming out of the unlawfulness of an action, thus erasing, in principle, the difference between the effects of contractual and not contractual torts. This chapter deals first with the law of contracts (Alejandro Borda) and second, with the law of torts (Ursula Basset).

2 GENERAL PRINCIPLES ON CONTRACTS LAW

Contract law in Argentina is divided in two parts: a general part, describing general principles on contract law, and a second part in which each contract and its special statutes are expounded.

2.1 Definition

The contract is defined by Article 957 of the CCC as a legal act by which two or more parties give their consent to create, regulate, amend, or terminate legal and financial relationships.

The Argentine legislation supports the broader sense of contracts. This means that a contract exists not only when a legal relationship is created (i.e., the restricted sense of contract) but also when it is modified, transferred or terminated. However, an agreement may be considered a contract only if it has a pecuniary content and purpose.

In Argentina, the most general principle in contract law is that of freedom of agreement, only limited by public order, morals and good customs (Article 958, CCC). A validly celebrated contract binds the parties to the agreed terms and creates a liability between them in case of a breach (Article 959, CCC). Judges may not alter the contents of a contract, except when the public order is affected, or the law expressly authorizes their intervention (Article 960, CCC). Contracts are presumed to be celebrated in good faith, must be interpreted and executed in good faith (Article 961, CCC). They oblige beyond the content of the contract to the extent of a peculiar legal standard stated by the law: every contract party is obliged to act as a "farsighted and careful" party (Article 961, CCC). The rights emerging from a contract constitute a patrimonial right to each of the contract parties (Article 965, CCC).

2.2 Types of Contracts

Following a classic criterion, Argentine legislation classifies contracts as follows.

(a) *Bilateral or unilateral*, depending on whether (i) both parties mutually bind themselves, or (ii) only one of the parties binds itself to a second one, without the latter being bound (Article 966, CCC). This article expressly provides that the rules of bilateral contracts are applied on a subsidiary basis to multilateral contracts.

(b) *Gratuitous and nongratuitous*, depending on whether (i) either of the parties receives an advantage, independently of any consideration, or (ii) the parties obtain advantages through reciprocal consideration (Article 967, CCC).

(c) *Commutative and aleatory*, depending on whether (i) the benefits obtained by all the parties concerned are certain, or (ii) the benefits or losses, for one of them or for all, depend on the occurrence of an uncertain event (Article 968, CCC).

(d) *Nominate and innominate*, depending on whether the law especially regulates them or not (Article 970, CCC).

(e) *Formal and informal*, depending on whether the law requires a certain formality or not. In the former case, in formal contracts the following types may be distinguished: a *mandatory formality*, when the absence of the form set by law implies that the contract is void; a *nonmandatory formality*, when, in spite of the infringement of the form required by law, the contract is valid as a contract in which the parties agree to fulfill such formality; and an *evidentiary formality* when the form required by law or that agreed by the parties only serves as evidence to prove the making of the contract (Article 969, CCC).

The CCC, in force since August 1, 2015, contains some innovations with respect to the former code. The first one is that "real" contracts, that used to require the delivery of something of value for the existence of the contract, have disappeared. The second change is the incorporation of long term contracts, with the primary purpose of obliging the parties to exercise their rights pursuant to a duty to collaborate, respecting the contracts' reciprocity of obligations, and of considering the total term of duration of the contract, so that the party that decides to terminate the contract is obliged to give the other party a reasonable possibility of renegotiating in good faith, for the purpose of not falling into abusive rights (Article 1011, CCC). The last novelty is the introduction of related contracts, i.e., those related to each other by a previously established common economic purpose, so that one of them has been decisive for the other one for the fulfillment of the purpose sought, and as a consequence thereof, both must be interpreted together, giving them the appropriate sense that arises from the group of contracts, their economic function and the purpose sought (Articles 1073 and 1074, CCC).

2.3 New Trends

The CCC, as a general rule, regulates those contracts made by two parties with a similar negotiation power (*contratos paritarios*). However, it has incorporated, as a form of consent, the contract of adhesion to general clauses provided beforehand.

Indeed, the contract of adhesion is more than a simple form of consent. In fact, the Code itself defines it as the contract by means of which one of the contracting parties adheres to general terms unilaterally provided for by the other party or by a third party, without the adherent having participated in the drafting thereof (Article 984, CCC).

Besides, specific rules of interpretation are established: ambiguous clauses provided for by one of the parties shall be interpreted against the providing party (Article 987, CCC); abusive clauses are penalized and considered not written down (Article 988, CCC) and judicial control of ambiguous clauses is accepted, even if they have been approved by the administrative authority (Article 989, CCC).

Another new trend of the CCC is the incorporation of a title referring to consumer contracts (Articles 1092–1122), in which relationships of consumption are regulated, together with abusive practices, information and advertising aimed at consumers, certain special modalities in consumer contracts and abusive clauses. The problem posed by this regulation is that, parallel to the Code, there is a law for the protection of consumers (Law 24.240) that governs the same situations and does not always agree, a situation that will inevitably cause problems.

2.4 Formation of Consent. Offer and Acceptance. Requirements for Validity

Consent, purpose and cause are considered essential elements of the contract, i.e., if one of them is absent, there is no contract.

Consent implies the agreement of the parties concerned, materialized through offer and acceptance.

The offer is the expression directed at a person specified or to be specified, made with the intention to be binding once accepted by the person to whom it is addressed, containing the necessary details to establish the effects to be produced if accepted

(Article 972, CCC). There are therefore three requirements for an offer to be valid: (i) that it is addressed to a person specified or to be specified; (ii) that there is intention to be bound; and (iii) that the effects produced by the acceptance are defined.

Generally speaking, the offer addressed to an indefinite person is considered an invitation to make offers; however, such offer is binding if, according to its terms or to the circumstances originating it, the offeror shows his intention to contract (Article 973, CCC). A clear example of a valid offer addressed to an indefinite person and that binds the offeror during its duration is the one directed at prospective customers who, if the case may be, shall give origin to a contract of consumption (Article 7, Law 24.240).

Acceptance is also an expression of will, given by the persons who receive the offer, where they express their full consent to the offer received. As a rule, if the recipient of the offer introduces changes, there will be no contract, since the offer received has not been fully accepted. There will be in that case a counteroffer (Article 978, CCC).

2.5 Contract Formation. Withdrawal and Expiration

The contract is made when the offeror receives the acceptance of the offer (without it being necessary for the offeror to actually know about it), or else, when the parties' conduct sufficiently shows that there is agreement (Article 971, CCC). This latter statement is clear, there is no need for me to explain it in more detail; however, the former may give rise to some doubt as regards withdrawal of the offer or acceptance and death of the parties.

The offer may be withdrawn provided its recipient receives the withdrawal before the offer or together with it. The acceptance may be withdrawn if the communication is received by the offeror before the offer or together with it. The offer expires if the offeror or the offeree die or are disabled before they receive the acceptance (Articles 975, 981 and 976, CCC). In the first case, once the offer is accepted, it may not be withdrawn; however, it shall lose its validity if the term set for the expression of the acceptance expires, or if no term has been set and a reasonable period of time elapses without an answer (Article 974, CCC). In the rest of the cases, it is the receipt of the acceptance that is relevant: if the parties die or are disabled before reception or if the recipient of the offer changes his mind as to the acceptance, before he receives it or simultaneously with reception, the acceptance shall have no legal effects.

2.6 Partial Agreements

As stated above, in order for there to be a contract, the acceptance must express full consent with the offer.

However, Article 982 of the CCC provides for the possibility of considering partial agreements to be reached by the parties as a valid contract, provided there is consent on the essential and specific elements of the contract involved. In this case, it is clear that it will be necessary to supplement the contract, for which purpose it will be necessary to resort to: (i) nonnegotiable rules; (ii) default rules of the contract involved; and (iii) the usage and practices of the place where the contract is made, if they are applicable because they are well known and regularly observed in the place the contract is made, and with the exception that the contract is unreasonable (Article 963, CCC).

All in all, the delicate solution provided for by Article 982 should be applied restrictively. There are two reasons for this. The first one, because, as has already been mentioned, the rule states that in order for there to be a contract, acceptance must express full consent to the offer, and one of the conditions of the latter, if accepted, is that it should contain all the necessary precisions in order to cause the expected effects. The second one is that Article 982 itself provides that, in case of doubt, the contract is considered not concluded; and it adds that the minutes or a draft related to one or all of the elements shall not serve as a valid agreement.

2.7 Contractual Negotiations

The CCC establishes the principle of freedom of negotiation. The parties are free to enter into a contract and determine its content, provided this occurs within the framework of the law, public order, morale and proper conduct (Article 958 Civil and Com. C). In other words, within those limits, the parties are free to: (i) enter or not into a contract; (ii) choose who to enter into a contract with; and (iii) decide the content of the contract.

Under the same guidelines, as a general rule, it is considered that the parties are free to promote negotiations directed at the making of the contract and also free to abandon them whenever they please (Article 990, Civ. and Com, C). However, the behavior of those making the contract must not be arbitrary. In fact, while the preliminary negotiations are taking place, and even though an offer is not made, they must act in good faith so as not to frustrate them unreasonably. Breach of good faith results in the obligation to pay damages to the affected party for having trusted that the contract would be made, without responsibility of his part (Article 991, CCC).

2.8 Capacity to Enter a Contract

Full legal capacity is acquired when a person is eighteen years old (Article 25, CCC). Notwithstanding this, *minors*, besides being able to exercise their rights through their legal representatives, have the right, if they are of age and mature enough, to exercise by themselves those acts that are permitted by law (Article 26, CCC). Clearly they may enter into the so-called small contracts, like the purchase and sale of things of low value.

Minors who have obtained a degree to perform a profession may do so on their own, without previous authorization of their parents or legal representatives; they can also administer and decide what to do with the assets they acquire as a result of their profession (Article 30, CCC), which reveals a broad capacity to make contracts. This broad capacity to celebrate contracts, it must be said, is partially restricted by the international regulations of ILO concerning the limitations for paid work for children. Further on, the Civil Code establishes under the title of Parental Responsibility (Family Law) other restrictions and authorizations needed for a child to work.

Those who are *emancipated* are also entitled to exercise their rights on their own, with some limitations set by the Code. Emancipation is acquired by getting married before coming off age (Article 27, CCC).

Someone who has been declared a *prodigal*, i.e., those who in managing their property expose their spouse, partner, underage or disabled children to lose their property, shall have a limited capacity, once their disability is declared. When this happens, they shall be appointed a "helper" (*apoyo, see* chapter on the Law of Persons), who shall help them grant acts of disposition of property *inter vivos* and in those other acts the judge may determine in his judgment (Articles 48 and 49, CCC). The prodigal shall have full capacity to enter into the legal contracts permitted by the judge.

Likewise, the judge may *restrict the capacity* for certain acts of a person over thirteen who has an addiction or a permanent or prolonged mental alteration, serious enough, provided he considers that as a consequence of the performance of his full capacity he may damage himself or his property. In this sense, the judge must appoint the helper/s (whose goal is to help the person in need take decisions to direct his person, administer his property and make legal acts in general), specifying his functions, considering the person's needs and circumstances. Only by exception, when the person is absolutely incapable of interacting with his environment and of expressing his will in any adequate way, means or format and the help is insufficient, will the judge declare the *incapacity* and appoint a trustee.

2.9 Legal Capacity to Enter a Contract

The CCC prohibits those who have no legal capacity to enter into contracts, in their own interest or that of others, pursuant to special provisions. Moreover, those contracts prohibited to certain persons may not be made by intermediaries either (Article 1001).

Besides the general principle above, there are certain special prohibitions for specific persons from entering into contracts in their own interests (Article 1002, CCC). They are:

(a) *Public officials*, over property whose administration or sale is or was commissioned.
(b) *Judges, officers or assistants of justice, referees or mediators and their assistants*, over property related to the processes in which they take or took part.
(c) *Lawyers and prosecutors*, over contentious property in processes in which they intervene or have intervened.

(d) *Spouses*, under the joint marital property system. However, in the alternative system of separation of property established by the Code itself, spouses are fully entitled to make contracts with each other. All in all, the prohibition mentioned should be interpreted with care. There are contracts expressly recognized by law (such as the partnership contract, of any kind, Article 27, Law 19.550) and others that show no problem at all, such as the contract for the provision of professional services or the collateral loan agreement.

(e) Finally, *executors* that are not heirs may not enter into purchase and sales contracts on the property of the estates under their charge.

2.10 Effects of Consent and of the Legal Act

The CCC in its Title IV of Book One, that regulates legal acts and matters, refers to defects of consent (error, fraud and violence) in Chapters 2, 3 and 4 and in Chapter 6, to defects of legal acts (lesion, simulation, fraud).

2.11 Nullity of Consent

In order to cause the nullity of a legal act, error must be a mistake of fact, essential and recognizable by the addressee if it is a bilateral act or a unilateral act that takes effect on receipt (Article 265, CCC). Therefore, the mistake of law, accidental and that could not be recognized by the recipient, does not invalidate an act.

The mistake of fact is considered to be essential, if it relates to: (i) the nature of the act; (ii) an asset or act, quality or extension different from that appointed; (iii) the substantial quality of the asset that was determinant of the legal will pursuant to common belief or to the circumstances of the case; (iv) personal relevant reasons that were expressly or tacitly incorporated; and (v) the person with which the contract was made or the person implied in the act if that person was decisive for its making (Article 267, CCC).

The error is considered to be recognizable by the recipient when the recipient may have learnt about it due to the nature of the act or the circumstances of person, time and place (Article 268, CCC).

Although the Code in force does not mention the necessary excusability of the error (which was in fact provided for by Article 929 of the derogated Civil Code), it is inevitable. The thing is that for error to result in the invalidation of the legal act, there needs to be a reason for erring. If, on the other hand, error is the result of active negligence of the one making the statement, it is clear that the error is inexcusable and prevents the act from being declared null.

Fraud is any false representation or misleading of the truth, any deceit, cunning or trickery, reluctance or concealment used to enter into the contract (Article 271, CCC).

But not any deceit will result in the invalidation of the legal act. Fraud must be serious, essential, determinant of the will, resulting in serious damage and there must not be fraud by both parties (Article 272, CCC). The author of fraud may be one of the parties or even a third party (Article 273, CCC).

Irresistible force and threats that result in fear of suffering a serious and imminent harm that cannot be prevented or counteracted, in the person or property of the party or of a third party, make the act null (Article 276, CCC). In other words, both physical violence and intimidation or moral violence, originated in one of the parties or in a third party, make the legal act null (Article 278, CCC).

If one of the parties, abusing of the necessity, psychological weakness or inexperience of the other party, obtains a clear disproportionate economic benefit and this is without justification, the other party may sue to invalidate the legal act or to claim a fair readjustment of what was agreed (Article 332, CCC). The same rule expressly adds that this abuse is presumed to exist when there is a significant disproportion of services rendered, unless there is evidence to the contrary. The calculations must be done pursuant to values at the time the act was entered into and the disproportion must subsist when making the claim (Article 332, CCC).

Simulation takes place when the legal nature of an act is disguised under the appearance of another, or when it contains clauses that are not sincere or dates that are not exact, or when as a result of it, rights are constituted or transmitted to intermediaries who in fact are not the beneficiaries (Article 333, CCC).

Simulation may be legal or illegal. The former has no legal consequences; the latter, i.e., the act addressed at violating the law or damaging a third party, results in the invalidation of the act. If the simulated act disguises another real act, the latter is fully valid if the requirements typical of its category are met and it is not illegal, nor does it damage a third party (Article 334, CCC).

Those who make an illegal simulated act may not proceed against each other on the simulation, except if they cannot obtain any benefit as a result of the simulation (Article 335, CCC). On the other hand, third parties whose rights or legitimate interests have been affected by the simulated act may claim its nullity and use any kind of evidence (Article 336, CCC).

Any creditor may request the unenforceability of the acts entered into by his debtor in fraud of his rights, and of resigning to the exercise of rights or powers by which he could have improved or prevented his condition (Article 338, CCC).

Therefore, it is necessary that (i) the loan must be previous to the act contested, except if the debtor has acted with the intention of deceiving his future creditors; (ii) the act has caused or worsened the debtor's insolvency; and (iii) the person who entered into a contract with the debtor for consideration had known or should have known that the act would result in or worsen the insolvency (Article 339, CCC).

2.12 Cause

The cause is the immediate goal authorized by law, determinant of will. Cause also comprises reasons when they are legal and have been incorporated expressly in the act, or impliedly if they are essential to both parties (Article 281, CCC).

Cause has been described before as one of the essential elements of a contract (together with consent and purpose). Therefore, the cause must exist when the contract is formed and thereafter. And not only then, it must subsist for the term of its duration (Article 1013, CCC).

Although the parties many times do not express the cause that moved them to make the contract, it is always supposed, except evidence to the contrary. Moreover, the contract shall be valid although the cause expressed is false, provided the contract is based on another valid cause (Article 282, CCC). But if in fact there is no cause at all, it may result in invalidation, modification, or termination of the contract.

Finally, if the cause is contrary to morale, public order or proper conduct, or if both parties have entered into the contract with an illegal or immoral intention, the contract shall be null and void. On the other hand, if only one of the parties has had an illegal or immoral reason, that party will not have the right to claim the contract before the other party, but the latter may claim what it has given, without obligation to comply with its offer (Article 1014, CCC).

2.13 Purpose

The purpose is the third essential element of the contract and is the promised consideration (the act or the asset). This results from Articles 279 and 1004 of the CCC, that establish that the purpose shall not be a fact that is impossible or contrary to morals, good customs or public order, forbidden by law or affecting the dignity of the person, or damaging third party's rights. It is added that the purpose of a contract shall not be an asset that is forbidden by any special reason to be so.

The purpose of the contract must then be legal and possible. But it must also be determined or determinable, capable of being economically assessed and it must be in the interest of both parties, even if it is not related to proprietary interests (Article 1003, CCC). The proprietary nature of the purpose is what distinguishes the contract form other legal acts.

The purpose is determined when the parties establish the fact or the asset they want with precision. It is also considered that the purpose is determined when the type or nature of an asset, although its quantity is not established but can be determined (Article 1005, CCC).

The purpose, on the other hand, is determinable: (i) when sufficient criteria are established to identify the asset (Article 1005, CCC); (ii) when the parties agree that the determination of the purpose is affected by a third person. If the third person does not choose, they may resort to a legal determination (Article 1006, CCC).

Both current and future assets may be the purpose of a contract (Article 1007, CCC). Third persons' assets may also be the purpose of contracts, the responsibility of the transmitter varies, depending if he has guaranteed the success of the promise (Article 1008, CCC). Even contentious, encumbered assets or those subject to precautionary measures may be the purpose of contracts, safeguarding of course third persons' rights (Article 1009, CCC).

Although the CCC keeps the traditional rule that the future inheritance may not be the purpose of a contract, the possibility of making agreements that may include provisions related to future inheritance rights is excepted, if they refer to a productive activity or to shareholder interest of any kind, with the purpose of keeping the business asset or preventing or solving conflicts. These agreements (in which the future decedent may not necessarily be a part) are valid, if they do not affect the forced heirship, the spouse's rights or third persons' rights (Article 1010, CCC).

2.14 Form of Contracts

As have already been said that contracts may be classified into *formal and informal*, depending on whether the law requires a certain formality or not. I added that formal contracts could, in turn, be classified into those of *mandatory formality, nonmandatory formality and evidentiary formality*.

It is necessary to point out that, besides this classification, the rule is freedom of forms, since the law requires a certain form only for formal contracts (Article 1015, CCC). Of course, if the contract requires a certain formality, modifications that are later introduced shall have identical form, unless these are only accessory or secondary provisions, or there is a legal provision on the contrary (Article 1016, CCC).

Among public instruments, the most important one is the deed, which has been defined as a matrix instrument issued by notary publics or by another authorized officer exercising the same functions, containing one or more legal acts (Article 299, CCC). But the main feature of this deed is that it bears witness of the acts made before a notary public; therefore, the contract made by public deed and according to formal requirements imposed by law, is authentic, i.e., evidence its contents on its own and does not need previous acknowledgement by the party concerned, until it is declared false.

The Argentine law requires the following instruments to be made by public deed (i) those contracts whose purpose is the acquisition, modification or extinction of property rights; (ii) contracts whose purpose is rights on real property that are dubious or contentious; (iii) acts that are accessory to others made by public deed; and (iv) all other contracts that, by agreement of the parties or the operation of law, must be made by public deed (Article 1017, CCC).

However, unless the contract requires the making it by public deed as a mandatory formality, in which case the violation of this requirement results in the invalidation of the act, as happens with donations of real property, entering into a contract in a private instrument is a valid contract in which the parties have assumed the obligation of making a public deed. Even if one of the parties is slow at making the deed, the judge shall do so on his behalf, provided consideration has been fulfilled, or its performance has been ensured (Article 1018, CCC). In this sense, it is common practice that the real property purchase and sales contract is made by private instrument ("called sales agreement"); if either party refuses to make the public deed required by Article 1017, paragraph a, CCC., the other party may claim to do so and if be the case, the judge shall be entitled to make the deed on behalf of the reluctant party.

2.15 Proof of Contracts

Contracts as a rule may be proved by all means available to reach a reasonable conviction pursuant to the rules of healthy criticism and to the laws of procedure. But it is forbidden to prove exclusively by witnesses those contracts that are usually instrumented (Article 1019, CCC.), i.e., that must be made by public instrument, private instrument or not signed instrument, and that must comprise electronic documents.

When the formality is required for evidentiary purposes (i.e., when it is not mandatory or not mandatory formality), it may be approved by other means, including witnesses, if it is impossible to obtain the evidence of the formality having been accomplished or if there is instrumental evidence, or the contract has started to be implemented (Article 1020, CCC). Instrumental evidence is understood to be any instrument that is issued by the other party, his heirs or a party concerned, which makes the contract credible.

Besides the wording of the rules not being able to obtain the evidence of having accomplished the formality it is not enough to prove the contract only by witnesses. If it were so, it would be very easy to bypass the evidentiary form required. Therefore, it is absolutely necessary to add to the impossibility a principle of instrumental evidence or the starting of implementation of the contract.

2.16 Interpretation of Contracts

The CCC has established different rules that shall be applied when interpreting a contract.

The first of them and no doubt the most important is the one that provides that the contract must be interpreted according to the *principle of good faith* (Article 1061, CCC). This has been highlighted in several parts of the code and not only in the chapter referred to contract interpretation.

Already in the Preliminary Title, Article 10 provides that rights should be exercised in good faith. It later establishes that contracts must be made, interpreted and performed in good faith. And explaining the idea of good faith, to this is added that contracts bind not only what is formally expressed but all the consequences that may be considered comprised by them, with the scope a careful and prudent contractor may have reasonably made (Article 961, CCC).

The second rule is that which provides that the contract should be interpreted according to a *common intention* of the parties (Article 1061, CCC). What is important is the common intention and not the intention each party had when entering the contract.

The third rule when interpreting a contract is to understand the words used in it according to the sense given by general use, unless such words have a specific meaning given by law, the parties' agreement or the usage and practice of the place it was entered into (Article 1063, CCC). This being said, it should be pointed out that if the law or the parties' will have expressly stated a restrictive construction, when expressing their will, the parties must stick to the literal words. This latter rule, however, is not applicable to the duties of the stipulator and the provider in contracts of adhesion and in those of consumption, respectively (Article 1062, CCC).

The fourth rule is the so-called *contextual interpretation*; i.e., the clauses of the contract are interpreted through each other and should be given the appropriate sense of the whole act (Article 1064, CCC). This is a clear derivation of the principle of good faith, since whoever seeks to be favored with an isolated interpretation of a given clause, ignoring the rest of the contract that might modify its sense, is acting in bad faith.

The fifth rule of interpretation is the *principle of conservation*, by which if there is doubt as to the efficacy of the contract or any of its clauses, it must be interpreted so as to give them effect (Article 1066, CCC). It would be meaningless to think that the parties have decided to make a null contract.

However, if the meaning of the words, interpreted in context, is not enough to interpret the contract, resort should be had to the other rules (Article 1065, CCC). These are:

(i) The *circumstances in which it was made*, including preliminary negotiations. It is clear that the circumstances that surrounded the making of the contract are important to determine what the parties wanted. On the other hand, the reference made to preliminary negotiations is not so clear. These negotiations are relevant to fill in gaps that might have been left when making the contract; but if there is a contradiction between such negotiations and the final contract, it is clear that the parties have modified such original opinion.

(ii) The *parties' conduct*, even that subsequent to the making of the contract. This rule causes certain surprise. It is clear that what is truly relevant is the behavior of the parties after making the contract. Such behavior strongly reveals their will. On the other hand, the behavior prior to making the contract is only important to fill in contract gaps, since as has been said in the previous paragraph, if there is inconsistency between the previous and what had been agreed upon, the agreed terms shall be valid.

(iii) The *nature and goal* of the contract. It is essential when interpreting the contract to discover its legal nature. In other words, the classification or name the parties may have given the contract is not important, what counts is what was actually contracted. On the other hand, the goal set by the parties clearly reveals why they made this agreement. It is only a chapter of the cause.

Finally, if although having applied the rules contained in the provisions above there are still doubts, it will be necessary to distinguish the gratuitous from the nongratuitous contract. In the former, the interpretation should be done in the less burdensome sense for the party obliged; in the latter, in the sense that may result in an equitable adjustment of interests for both parties (Article 1065, CCC).

The CCC comprises the so-called *theory of own acts* (in Spanish *Teoría de los actos propios*[1]) as a rule of contractual interpretation. This theory states that the interpretation must protect the parties' mutual trust and loyalty, and any contradiction with a legally relevant conduct, previous or subsequent and pertaining to the same subject shall be inadmissible (Article 1067. CCC). This statement does not seem very reasonable. First, because the "theory of own acts" has a residual application; in second place because it applies to contracts and other legal situations; and lastly because the central aspect of the theory has been omitted: the binding conduct must not only be legally relevant but effective.

Even though the law does not expressly mention them, there are other rules that should also be taken into account when interpreting a contract. *Equity and analogy* are some of them.

2.17 Termination

If the parties agree, they may terminate the contract. This is called bilateral termination. Bilateral termination may not affect rights of third parties, unless provided for to the contrary, it only has future consequences (Article 1076, CCC).

Likewise, the contract may be totally or partially terminated by the statement of one of the parties, when the contract or the law should have entitled them to do so. This is the case of unilateral rescission, revocation or discharge for breach of contract (Article 1077, CCC). Except for legal provision to the contrary, unilateral rescission and revocation only have future consequences, on the other hand, discharge for breach of contract has retroactive effects between the parties, but does not affect the right acquired for good and valuable consideration by third persons in good faith (Article 1079, CCC).

If the contract is totally or partially terminated by unilateral rescission, revocation or discharge for breach of contract, the parties must restore, refund or repay, as appropriate, what they received due to the contract, or its value, pursuant to the laws of give for restitution (Article 1080, CCC).

Besides, if the case is the termination of a bilateral contract; (i) restitution must be reciprocal and simultaneous; (ii) performances fulfilled shall be valid and shall produce their effects inasmuch as they are equivalent, divisible and have been received without reserve as to the obligation's cancellation effect; and (iii) to estimate the value of creditor's restitutions, advantages that may arise if the performance had not been fulfilled are taken into account, their frustrated profits and, if it be the case, other damages (Article 1081, CCC).

The parties may expressly agree that unilateral termination occurs in case of duly identified generic or specific breaches. This is called *express cancellation clause*. In this case, termination takes place when the party concerned formally communicates the

1. The Theory of Own Acts has many aspects in common with the Theory of Estoppel but is not exactly identical. Among other differences, it should be pointed out that the latter is a kind of defense that can only be applied at the request of one party, while the former may be applied as a defense and as grounds to take action, at the request of a party or of the judge.

nonperforming party his will to terminate (Article 1086, CCC). But in bilateral contracts this cancellation clause is implied, i.e., even though nothing is agreed, breach by one of the parties entitles the other one to claim the termination of the contract (Article 1087, CCC).

In this latter case, certain conditions are necessary. These are: (i) that breach is essential; (ii) that debtor is delinquent; and (iii) that creditor summons debtor, under express penalty of contract termination, to fulfill his promise, within the term of at least fifteen days, except if owing to usage or to the nature of the performance, a shorter term should be set. Cancellation occurs by law upon the expiration of this term (Article 1088, CCC).

This requirement is not necessary if the essential term for fulfillment has elapsed, if the nonperforming party has expressed his decision of not fulfilling his duty or if the accomplishment should be impossible, and also if the law entitles the party to unilaterally declare the termination of the contract (Articles 1088 and 1089, CCC).

The final frustration of the goal of the contract entitles the damaged party to declare its termination, if its cause is an extraordinary alteration of the circumstances existing when the contract was made, beyond the parties' responsibility and that surpasses the risk assumed by the damaged party. However, if the frustration is temporary, the contract may only be terminated by duly avoiding the duty whose performance term is essential (Article 1088, CCC).

On the other hand, if in a commutative contract of deferred or permanent performance the obligation by one of the parties is excessively burdensome, due to an extraordinary alteration of the circumstances existing at the time the contract was made, occurred due to reasons beyond the parties responsibility and beyond the risk assumed by the affected party, this party shall be entitled to claim extra-judicially, to ask the judge, by action or defense, the full or partial termination of the contract, or its amendment. This is the "unforeseeability doctrine" (*doctrina de la imprevisión*) also called "the excessive subsequent burden" (*teoría de la excesiva onerasidad sobreveniente*). This power is extended to third parties who have been assigned rights or duties resulting from the contract; and is extended to the aleatory contract if the performance becomes excessively burdensome for reasons beyond their own *alea* (Article 1088, CCC).

3 LAW OF OBLIGATIONS, LAW OF TORTS, GENERAL OVERVIEW[2]

Tort Law in Argentina is regulated in the CCC, in the last part of the law of obligations, under the title "Other sources of obligations." Law of obligations is regulated mostly under the Book 3 (Personal rights). The below discussion first focuses on the general overview on the law of obligations, and second, on the general outline of the law of torts.

2. A special thanks to Marìa Zúñiga for her collaboration in the section of Tort Law.

4 LAW OF OBLIGATIONS

Law of obligations is now regulated mostly in the Third book of the CCC from Argentina. The approach is new, since it regulates civil and commercial obligations (a unified perspective). However, the outline of contents of the new CCC concerning the law of obligations are scattered within the CCC, as follows:

- Book 3. Title I. Obligations in General
    - o Chapter 1. General Dispositions
    - o Chapter 2. Legal actions and guarantees
    - o Chapter 3. Classes of obligations
    - o Chapter 4. Payment
    - o Chapter 5. Other forms of extinction
- Title V. Other Sources of Obligations
    - o Chapter 1. Civil Liability
    - o Chapter 2. Agency
    - o Chapter 4. Unjust enrichment
    - o Chapter 5. Unilateral declaration of will
- Book 6 (Common Disposition to Personal Rights and Rights in Rem). Title I. Prescription and limitation periods.
- Title III. Lien of property.

4.1 General Dispositions on Obligations

The new CCC has chosen to define what an obligation is. According to Article 724 an obligation is defined as a juridical relationship in which the creditor has a right to demand from the debtor a performance or a rendering to satisfied a legitimate interest. It includes the cause of the obligation according to this the sense of a source. Moral obligations are considered unenforceable, and what is more, the new CCC understands they are not juridical in any sense.

4.2 Legal Actions and Guarantees

Concerning legal actions, the new CCC introduces a direct action. A direct action is the action a creditor has, to perceive directly what a third party owes to his debtor, up to the amount of his debt in in his exclusive benefit. It has an exceptional character, and it can only proceed when: (a) there is an enforceable credit against the debtor; (b) a correlative debt is enforceable between the debtor and the third party; (c) there is an homogeneity between both credits; (d) none of the credits has been seized before the filing of the direct action; (e) the debtor has been sued.

The new CCC also includes subrogation action and the list of those goods that might be seized and those which are excluded from the power of the creditors. Concerning the latter, Article 743 states that the creditor may demand the judicial sale of the goods of the debtor only up to the debt. There are certain goods that are exempted from a judicial sale: the goods a debtor needs to work, the personal goods, the goods of a church or a religion that has been recognized by the state, such as the right of use of a property or the right to alimony, for instance (Articles 743–744). The first creditor to seize goods have a privilege on them.

4.3 Privileges

In Book VI Title 2 the new CCC deals with privileges. General privileges shall be invoked only in universal proceedings (probate proceedings, bankruptcy proceedings, Article 2580). Privileges are acquired only by law. They are transmissible but they may be transmitted only undividedly.

Special privileges are the expenses for building or preservation of things, to those things, credits for wages for workers, taxes have a privileges to the things they apply to, credits with a right in rem guarantee, and the privileges established in the Navigation Act and Aeronautical Act, Financial Entities Act, etc.

4.4 Lien of Property

Every creditor of a determined and enforceable obligation has a right of lien of property (Articles 2587–2593). The creditor has the right to exert all the actions in order to preserve and perceive their credit, perceive a payment for the deposit, perceive the fruits or rents of the goods he retains.

4.5 Classification of Obligations

The obligations covered in the CCC are the obligations to give (if they are to transfer of property, tradition and title are required), obligations to do or not to do, alternative obligations, optional obligations, divisible and indivisible obligations, obligations with a plural subject, concurrent obligations, disjunctive obligations, principal obligations and accessory obligations, and obligations with a penal clause or comminatory sanctions.

As implied before, natural obligations are suppressed from the new regulation. Conversely it introduces the obligations "of value," concurrent and disjunctive obligations. An obligation of value, is an obligation that might be expressed in terms of money, but that expresses a value. The value of the obligation does not change across time, the way it is coined may vary (Article 722).

Concurrent obligations (Article 850) are those in which several debtors owe the same object. In this case, the creditor has a right to demand the payment from any creditor or for a group or all of them, simultaneously or successively. The payment made by one of the debtors extinguishes the obligation of the others.

Disjunctive obligations are obligations that must be satisfied by one of several subject. Except otherwise agreed, the creditor decides whom of the debtors will satisfy the obligation. He who pays, has no right to demand the payment of the others (Articles 853 and ff).

5 TORT LAW

Tort is defined by the CCC in Article 1737 to be the impairment of a right or interest not disapproved by law. The broadness of this definition is then conditioned by the requisites needed for a tort to cause compensation. These are:

(1) Illegality/ Unlawfulness. The term illegality is not only considered to be that which is against law, but any act that causes harm to another person,[3] except in some cases in which no compensation is originated such as when the illegal act is caused by legitimate self-defense, state of need, or regular exercise of the right.[4]

The expression used by the Code (any act that causes harm) has a constitutional source. In its Article 19, the Argentine Constitution,[5] demarcates the actions that interest law of those which are private, setting the limit in the harm to third parties.

(2) A relationship between the author of the damage and the tort. This means there must be a way to attribute the tort to the conduct of the author of the damage. However, the Code indicates this attribution may be by subjective as well by objective factors.[6]

Subjective factors are fault and negligence.[7] While fault finds its defining core in the intention or will to cause a harm, negligence finds it in the carelessness towards the effects of one's own actions. The Code measures the severity of this carelessness according to an assessment of the author of the damage's conduct, taking into consideration the existence of a duty to act with due care and prudence, and the existence of a special confidence.[8]

Objective factors of attribution revolve mainly around risk and guarantee (these cases would include the liability for the acts of others[9]). Tort must be compensated in all cases in which the tort is a consequence of the introduction of the risk by someone, or if someone takes advantage of the activity which results in a risk. Such cases include, for example, the liability of the

3. Article 1717, Civil and Commercial Code (CCC).
4. Article 1718, CCC.
5. This was said by our Supreme Court. Corte Suprema de Justicia de la Nación, 21/09/2004, Recurso de hecho deducido por la demandada en la causa Aquino, Isacio c. Cargo Servicios Industriales S.A.
6. Article 1721, CCC.
7. Article 1724, CCC.
8. Article 1725, CCC.
9. Articles 1753–1756, CCC.

owners of risky objects or machines.[10] In these cases, the Code says, the fault or negligence is indifferent for the attribution of the obligation to compensate.[11]

(3) Causal connection between the author of the damage's action and the tort.[12] In order to establish a relation between these two, the Argentine Code, adopts the adequate causation theory. The Codes expresses that torts are only compensated when they can be derived of the author of the damage's acts according to what usually happens in natural courses of events. However, when tort can only result of the author of the damage's actions by a connection to a certain fact, it is also compensated.[13]

Existence of tort. Tort has multiplied in its types, inspired by the Italian Code, and has included in its articles the nonpecuniary harm and spiritual harm,[14] the harm to one's life project,[15] among others.

5.1 Tort Law and Civil Liability and Its New Functions

The new CCC has expanded the functions of Civil liability. The new functions of Civil liability are:

- Prevention function first, then reparation. The first article referring to tort law[16] in our CCC intentionally places first the duty of prevention and then the duty to repair the consequences of harmful actions. This duty to prevent is demanded to all citizens in general,[17] and a special legal action is given to stop an action that may potentially generate tort.[18] Prevention expands to environmental damage, consumer damage, damage to personal rights, etc.
- Full reparation.[19] This idea was already perceived as present in the normative system through the interpretation of Articles 14, 17, 19, 33, 42, 75. 22 of our Constitution. It was also considered this way by our Supreme Court of Justice.[20] The objective, although impossible in realistic terms, tends to search for the best way to achieve a reversal of the damage inflicted.[21] This directly relates to the multiplied types of tort, in fact this are recognized to be concrete

10. Articles 1757–1759, CCC.
11. Article 1722, CCC.
12. Article 1726, CCC.
13. Article 1727, CCC.
14. Articles 1741 and 1738, CCC.
15. Article 1738, CCC.
16. Article 1708, CCC.
17. Article 1710, CCC.
18. Article 1711, CCC.
19. Article 1740, CCC.
20. Santa Coloma c. Ferrocarriles Argentinos, 05/08/1986 & Ruiz c. Estado Nacional, 24/05/1993.
21. Article 1740, CCC.

applications of this principle.[22] Since by offering the victim of the damage many torts to claim for and seek legal compensation, the law seeks to offer a fulfillment of the reparation. The reparatory function regulates in a unified manner contractual and noncontractual tort.

5.2 The Unification of Contractual and Noncontractual Relations When Considering Tort

The CCC establishes little or no difference between the tort which is originated as a breach of contract, from the one originating from noncontractual relationships. A clear differentiated regime of the previous Civil Code, has now turned into a set of rules that apply for both. The unification reflects the comprehension of tort as any kind of act that causes harm to another person,[23] even if slight differences persists, they are reduced to its minimum.

The unified regime applies to the definition of unlawfulness, factors for assigning responsibility, the estimation of damages, age of discernment and fortuitous events. In all of these respects, the same rules apply for contractual and tort law.

By this approach, any action that causes harm to another person must be prevented and repaired, except—of course—in the cases of self-defense, state of need, among others.

5.3 Special Liabilities

The Civil and Commercial Code distinguishes between several types of responsibility according to the position of he who the law considers to be the one to be held responsible of the damages. If the author of the damage is he who the law considers to be responsible, the CCCs calls it "direct liability" (responsabilidad directa). If, the material author of the damages is not held accountable for the law, then the juridical relation between the victim and the person who the law holds as responsible is indirect, thus, the responsibility is an "indirect liability." The CCC also calls the different types of "indirect liability" a "liability for the acts of a third party."

The direct liability is the one stemming from a direct infringement of an obligation that causes a damage by action or omission.[24] He who causes a damage by an involuntary act, may be held accountable by the application of the principle of equity. The judge may lessen the responsibility in consideration of the patrimony of the person who caused the damage, personal situation of the victim, the facts surrounding the damage.[25] If a person causes a damage because he himself suffered an irresistible

22. Meza, Jorge Alfredo and Boragina, Juan Carlos, El daño extrapatrimonial en el Código Civil y Comercial, La Ley.
23. Gagliardo, Mariano, "Enfoques legales de la responsabilidad civil", La Ley.
24. Article 1749, CCC.
25. Article 1742, CCC.

force, the author of the damage is not to be held responsible, notwithstanding the liability of the person who caused the irresistible force.

If there are several liable persons they are held jointly liable for the tort. If the liability stems of different causes, the liability maybe concurrent.

The CCC, as in many comparative legal systems, also divides the responsibility in two types according to the degree of fault. The traditional responsibility is called "subjective liability" (*responsabilidad subjetiva*) because it takes the subject and its fault into account. New forms of responsibility move away from personal and subjective examination of fault, and attribute liability by objective grounds, such as duties to prevent the damage or the use of a risky object. This second kind of responsibility is called "objective liability" (*responsabilidad objetiva*) because it disregards the examination of the fault. Sometimes, objective liability is based on an implicit presumption of a duty to veil on a subject dependent on a principal, thus indirect liability would coincide with objective liability On the other hand, a presumption of responsibility provokes an objective liability when a person uses risky objects.

Liability for the acts of the principal for the acts of the agents is attributed objectively to the principal. That is, the fault or negligence of the principal is indifferent to law. Article 1753 defines acts of agents as those of which the principal takes advantage to fulfill his obligations. When the harm occurs because of these acts, the principal must compensate. However, the agent will compensate concurrently.

Liability of the parents for the acts of their children is regulated in Articles 1754–1756. Article 1754 indicates the requisites for this liability are parental responsibility and for the children to live with their parents (however, if the child doesn't live with his/her parents due to fault of the parents, they will still be liable[26]). Parents will answer jointly, directly for their own responsibility and concurrently with the eventual liability of their child.

Article 1755 establishes cases of exemption in two cases. First, when the child has been put in the care of another person (except in the cases of delegation of the exercise parental responsibility, in which the parents keep the entitlement to parental responsibility and are then, still liable). Second, if the harm is a consequence of the child´s profession or of an activity commissioned by a third party.

Regarding children, the Code establishes the liability of the delegates in the exercise of parental responsibility, tutors and guardians for the children in their care. Nevertheless, their liability is not as objective as that of the parents, given they can be exempted if they can prove they could not have prevented the damage. Establishments where persons are being held (e.g., hospital, boarding schools, nursing homes), are also liable for the negligence in the care given to persons entrusted to their care.[27]

The use of risky things and the endangerment caused by certain activities create a presumption of liability of an objective nature.[28] The author may not invoke the exception of an administrative authorization for the use of risky things or for the deeds that caused the damage, for the responsibility is of an objective nature. The owner and

26. Article 1755.
27. Article 1756.
28. Article 1757.

the guardian of the risky things are liable in a concurrent manner, except if they manage to proof that the thing was used against their will. He who executes or takes profit from a risky deed is deemed to be liable for it. As for the damage caused by animals, it is dealt with as the damaged caused by risky things.

There is a special form of objective liability dealt with in the CCC: the anonymous liability. The Code deems to be jointly liable to the owners and inhabitants of a building from which a part is thrown or falls. He who can proof he could not have provoked the damage, may obtain an exemption.[29] If the damage comes from an unidentified member of a group of persons, the whole group is deemed liable, unless he may proof he has not produced the damage. Finally, if a group executes a dangerous deed, and they cause a damage they are all held jointly responsible. However, the member who can proof that he was not the author of the damage may exempt himself. In all of these forms, the objective liability presented by the code is different from the other forms of objective responsibility seen above. The group of so-called collective and anonymous liabilities are based on presumptions, but these presumptions are always rebuttable. Legal doctrine has not yet called this a *tertium genus* as in other legal systems, but it is foreseeable that the legal doctrine will move toward that language.

There are other special forms of liability. Juridical persons are liable for damaged caused by their employees while performing their tasks.[30] Schools and educational establishments are liable for the damaged caused or suffered by their students if minors. The sole defense they may argue is unforeseen circumstances. Educational establishments are obliged to have a civil liability insurance. Liberal professions are also liable, but under subjective liability, except if they have promised a certain result.

The new CCC makes a special provision for unjust enrichment.[31] It is a novelty. The actual regulation relegates the institution of unjust enrichment to a subsidiary place. Article 1794, CCC states that "Every person that without a lawful cause enriches himself at the expense of another, is obliged to compensate the loss of the victim taking into account his enrichment." If the enrichment consists in the incorporation to the patrimony of a certain property or asset, he must restitute it if it is still available. However, Article 1795 establishes that the legal action to claim the compensation may only proceed if there is no other action available for the victim in order to obtain compensation. The legislator has regarded the institution of unjust enrichment with a certain mistrust. Even though, within the figure of unjust enrichment the civil code regulates the unjust payment.

Further Reading

Aicega, Valentina, Gomez Leo, Osvaldo R., Leiva Fernàndez, Luis F. P., in Alterini, Jorge H. *Còdigo Civil y Comercial Comentado, Tratado Exegètico,* Volumes V and VI, Buenos Aires, La Ley, 2016.

29. Article 1760, CCC.
30. Article 1763, CCC.
31. Article 1794, CCC.

Alferillo, Pascual, Santarelli, Fulvio, Gomez Leo, Osvaldo in Alterini, Jorge H. *Còdigo Civil y Comercial Comentado, Tratado Exegètico,* Volumes VII, Buenos Aires, La Ley, 2016.

Gagliardo Mariano, "Enfoques legales de la responsabilidad civil", La Ley, Revista del Codigo Civil y Comercial, n° of August of 2015, p. 194.

Medina, Graciela, "Daños en el derecho de familia en el Codigo Civil y Comercial", La Ley, Revista de Responsabilidad Civil y Seguros, n° 4 of 2015, p. 287.

Meza, Jorge Alfredo & Boragina, Juan Carlos, "El daño extrapatrimonial en el Código Civil y Comercial", La Ley, Revista de Responsabilidad Civil y Seguros, n° 4 of 2015, p. 104.

Picasso, Sebastian, "Las funciones del derecho de daños en el Codigo Civil y Comercial de la Nación", La Ley, Revista de Responsabilidad Civil y Seguros, n° 4 of 2015, p. 5.

Quadri, Mariano, "Incidencia del Codigo Civil y Comercial en materia probatoria", La Ley, Revista del Codigo Civil y Comercial, n° of August of 2015, p. 38.

Ubirìa, Fernando, *Derecho de Daños en el Còdigo Civil y Comercial de la Naciòn,* Buenos Aires, Abeledo Perrot, 2016.

Vàzquez Ferreyra, Roberto A., "La antijuridicidad en el Codigo Civil y Comercial", La Ley, Revista de Responsabilidad Civil y Seguros, n° 4 of 2015, p. 38.

CHAPTER 8
Law of Property

Ignacio Ezequiel Alterini

Property, in the civil law tradition is mostly built upon the historical and intellectual foundations provided by Roman law, as it has developed throughout centuries in the Western world. According to this tradition, the founding idea is that of a direct relationship between a person and a tangible thing (right in rem). The common law tradition relies instead on a structure of property law that does not reflect this Roman sense of a direct relation: the idea of property relations among individuals is far more relevant. Actually, the idea of property relations is not absent of Civil law systems, however its foundations are preponderantly on the idea of the rights in rem. Further on, property law has evolved following the traditions of each domestic law and has been influenced by transnational sources and rapid economic developments. Argentina follows the Civil law model, with a stark influence of its own legal traditions, as it will be outlined below.

1 DEFINITION OF RIGHTS IN REM

Section 1882 of the Civil and Commercial Code defines rights in rem as "… the legal power, of a legal structure, that is directly and autonomously exercised over its object, which confers to its holder the powers to claim and of preference, and the other powers established in this Code."

1.1 Legal Power

Based on their essence, subjective rights may be considered as legal relations or legal powers. Rights in rem—unlike creditor's rights, which entail an inter-subjective relation between creditor and debtor—are legal powers, given that they consist in the dominion of a person's will over an object.[1]

The modern conception of rights in rem, without setting aside the "internal aspect" of the law, focused on the legal power enjoyed by the holder over the object, also stresses on an "external aspect" consisting in the duty to respect each and all of the members of the community, which translates into the Roman *neminem laedere*, that is, the duty not to harm others.

The "external aspect" of rights in rem enables capturing the legal relation in a *broad sense*, but the legal relation in a *strict sense* will only arise upon third parties' infringement of their legal duty to abide by this right, and shall be composed of the infringing party and the damaged holder of the right in rem.[2]

1.2 Direct Exercise over the Object

The idea that rights in rem are "directly [...] exercised over an object" points to the fact that the holder does not require any other person to obtain the advantages inherent to the object, as in the case of rights in personam. That is, in the case of rights in rem there are no determined passive subjects.

It shall be noted that in the framework of creditor's rights, the active subject (creditor) needs the cooperation of the passive subject (debtor) in order to satisfy its interest. This cooperation translates into the relevant duty (object), which could entail giving, doing or refraining.

According to the Argentine legal system, the holder of a right in rem has a direct relationship with the thing to which the right refers. For the right in rem to exist, there is not a requisite to relate this right to any other person in order. The right exists by a direct, nonmediated relationship between the holder and the thing he owns. By way of example, the holder of a right in rem of ownership may use, enjoy and dispose of the thing materially and legally, authoritatively, and subject to no other limits than those established by law.

1.3 Powers to Claim and of Preference

A typical feature of rights in rem is that they adhere to the object, so that it is affirmed that they are "inherent" to the object. These features give rise to the two typical advantages of rights in rem: the powers to claim and of preference.

The power to "claim" means that the holder of the right in rem is empowered to claim for the object and to recover it regardless of its location and of the person holding

1. According to Gatti, a legal power is "... a subjective right, whose 'essence' consists in a dominion of will, over persons or things, exercised authoritatively, '*autonomously*', and independently from any other will; through whose action it is possible to obtain the proposed effect not withholding the existence of any contrary will, even through private justice"—emphasis ours—(Gatti, Edmundo, *Derechos subjetivos y relaciones jurídicas*, Abeledo-Perrot, Buenos Aires, 1992, p. 155).
2. *See* Alterini, Jorge H. & Alterini, Ignacio E., *Código Civil y Comercial Comentado. Tratado exegético*, La Ley, Buenos Aires, 2015, Vol. IX, p. 20.

it; thus, the holder of a right in rem is protected by actions in rem.[3] The power of "preference" translates into the Roman maxim *prior in tempore potior in iure* (prior in time, stronger in law); hence, if several people acquire the same right in rem over the same object at different times, the right of the prior acquirer is preferred by law.[4]

After making reference to the powers to claim and of preference, Section 1882 sets forth that rights in rem also confer to their holders "the other powers established in this Code." This is due to the fact that the various types of rights in rem have different contents in terms of the powers conferred to their holders,[5] but they all share the powers to claim and of preference.

2 OBJECT

The object of rights in rem are chiefly things, that is, material objects of an economic value (Section 15, Civil and Commercial Code). Rights in rem can be exercised over the thing in whole, in part, or over a material part.

The Civil and Commercial Code brings in an innovation in this respect—following Section 1816 of the 1998 Draft—and sets forth that rights can also be the object of rights in rem where expressly established by law[6] (Section 1883, Civil and Commercial Code).

3 STRUCTURE

3.1 Impact of Public Order

Given their political, social and economic importance, the regulation of rights in rem is imbued with the notion of public order.

It is frequently stated that rules related to rights in rem are substantially rules of public order,[7] but this does not mean that all such rules are of this nature. It is explained that: "Public order has a prevailing role in rights in rem—but it is not exclusive. We understand that only the rules that lie at the core of rights in rem are rules of public order, and we shall call them 'statutory' (...). Mere regulations related to rights in rem are not rules of public order."[8]

"Statutory rules" are the rules that refer to the structure of rights in rem, that is, "their elements, content, acquisition, creation, modification, transfer, duration and

3. *See* s. 9 *infra*.
4. *See* s. 5.3 *infra*.
5. *See* s. 8 *infra*.
6. Thus, a right in rem to a security interest may be levied on third-party rights in rem (Section 2140, in relation to surface rights) or on third-party creditor's rights (e.g., Sections 2232 et seq. in relation to pledges on credit).
7. *Conf.* Allende, Guillermo L., *Panorama de los derechos reales*, La Ley, Buenos Aires, 1965, pp. 19, 69 et seq.
8. Gatti, Edmundo & Alterini, Jorge H., *El derecho real*, Abeledo Perrot, Buenos Aires, 1974, p. 74.

termination" (Section 1884, Civil and Commercial Code). The legal mandate is crystal-clear: individuals cannot modify the structure of rights in rem, since this "is only determined by law."

However, individuals can apply variations to the provisions of "mere regulations," since these are centered on the notion of autonomy of will. Hence, for instance, the holder of a right in rem of pledge cannot use the pledged thing, unless the holder of the object has given consent (Section 2226, Civil and Commercial Code).[9]

The rule is that in the realm of rights in rem, anything that is not expressly allowed by legal order is banned.

3.2 Configuration of Rights In Rem. Closed Number

As mentioned in the preceding paragraph, rights in rem can only be configured by law,[10] so that individuals shall adjust their endeavors to the rights expressly provided by law. This legal statement implies the adoption of the system of *numerus clausus* ("closed number"), as against the system of *numerus apertus* ("open number"), as established in Spanish law.[11]

The closed number system is aimed at preventing individuals from hindering, and even hurdling, the circulation of wealth through their will for configuration. There is a belief that allowing multiple rights in rem over a single object could constitute an important source for litigation among the various holders.[12]

In addition to establishing that rights in rem shall be configured by law, the closed number system points towards a narrow array of rights being allowed.[13] In this respect, lawmakers shall only regulate such rights in rem as are indispensable to cover the economic and social needs.

Section 1887 of the Civil and Commercial Code sets forth that: "In this Code, rights in rem are: a) ownership, b) tenancy in common, c) condominium, d) real estate

9. Other mere regulations are those included in Sections 2120, 2122, 2126, 2145, 2154, 2165, 2216, 2225, 2229 and 2236 of the Civil and Commercial Code.
10. The abrogated Civil Code stated that rights in rem "may only be created by law." In line with the 1998 Draft, the Civil and Commercial Code substitutes the idea of "creation" by that of "configuration," since creating is of a divine nature, and human persons may only act in the human sphere (Alterini, Jorge H. & Alterini, Ignacio E., *supra.*, p. 39).
11. *See* Castán Tobeñas, José, *Derecho civil español, común y foral,* revised and updated by García Cantero Gabriel, 14th edition, Reus, Madrid, 1992, No. II, Vol. 1°, p. 79; Puig Brutau, José, *Fundamentos del derecho civil,* 4th edition, Bosch, Barcelona, 1994, No. III, Vol. 1°, p. 34.
12. In the note to Section 2502 of the abrogated Civil Code, Vélez Sarsfield explained: "Multiple rights in rem over the same goods make up a wide source for litigation and complications, and may extensively undermine the exploitation of such goods and the free circulation of property, perpetually disturbed, where based on the laws of succession these rights are divided among many heirs but the thing subject to such rights cannot be divided among them too. Properties degrade and litigation arises where rights in rem are applied to a material part of the thing that constitutes a property that is detached and different from the thing itself; and where it does not constitute a tenancy in common that can give place to division among tenants in common or to tenders."
13. *Cfr.* Alterini, Jorge H., *"Previsiones normativas contenidas en el proyecto de unificación del año 1998. Proyecto de urbanizaciones especiales"*, Revista del Notariado No. 903, pp. 197 et seq.

developments, e) interval ownership, f) private cemeteries, g) surface rights, h) usufruct, i) use, j) habitation, k) easement, i) mortgage, m) antichresis, n) pledge."

The inclusion of the rights in rem of "real estate developments," "interval ownership" and "private cemeteries" may be subject to challenge, since these are potential objects over which rights in rem may fall, but by pointing to the object it was discarded that the listing, and subsequent regulating, are to focus on the rights and not on their seat.[14]

3.3 Consequences of the Intended Configuration of Other Rights In Rem or the Modification of Those Established

The configuration of a right in rem that is not allowed by law, or the modification of the structure of one allowed, are not subject to any reparation whatsoever, since they are null and void by reason of endangering public order (Section 387, Civil and Commercial Code).[15]

4 CLASSIFICATION

The various criteria for classification are outlined below, except for criteria used merely in books of authority.

4.1 Classification Based on the Holder of the Object

Rights in rem may fall on an object that belongs to the same holder of the right in rem or to a third party. Section 1888 of the Civil and Commercial Code establishes that the following types of rights in rem fall on objects that belong to the same holder of the right:[16] "ownership, tenancy in common, condominium, real estate developments, interval ownership, private cemeteries and surface rights, if there is surface property. The remaining rights in rem fall on an object that belongs to a third party [i.e., a foreign object]," that is, surface rights if there is no surface property, usufruct, use, habitation, easement, mortgage, antichresis and pledge.

Seen from the viewpoint of the passive party, rights in rem over objects belonging to third parties are "burdens in rem" or "encumbrances in rem" (*cargas reales or gravámenes reales*) that determine holdings that are detached from powers.

By introducing an important hermeneutic norm, Section 1888 *in fine* provides that objects "are presumed unencumbered, except as otherwise evidenced. Any doubt on the existence of an encumbrance in rem, its scope or exercise, shall be construed in

14. *Cfr.* Alterini, Jorge H., *"Primeras consideraciones sobre los Derechos reales en el Proyecto de Código"*, Acad. Nac. de Derecho 2012 (September)—LA LEY 2012-E, 898.
15. Alterini, Jorge H. & Alterini, Ignacio E., *supra.*, pp. 43/44.
16. Section 1888 of the Civil and Commercial Code states that rights in rem "may fall on an object that belongs to the same holder of the right in rem or to a third party," disregarding that rights in rem may also fall on goods other than things, that is, on other rights. *See* s. 2 *supra*.

favor of the holder of the encumbered good," that is, in principle, there is freedom to constitute the object of encumbrances in rem by the parties.

4.2 Classification Based on Dependence on Creditor's Rights

Rights in rem are principal rights, except for those that depend on creditor's rights. Mortgages, antichresis and pledges are accessory based on the security interest (Section 1889, Civil and Commercial Code).

The scope of accessory rights is established in Section 2186 of the Civil and Commercial Code: "Security interests are accessory to the credit they secure, they cannot be transferred without the credit and they terminate with the principal right, except as otherwise provided by law. The termination of a security interest on any grounds, including waiver, does not affect the existence of the credit."

It is worth adding that only principal rights in rem that are exercised through possession may be acquired by way of adverse possession.[17]

4.3 Classification Based on Exercise

Section 1891 of the Civil and Commercial Code sets forth that: "Any and all rights in rem regulated herein are exercised through possession, except for easement and mortgage. Affirmative easements are exercised by way of specific and determined acts of possession without their holder being in possession."

As shall be seen, possession is always exercised through acts of possession, so that it is inappropriate for the legal rule to point out a distinction between exercise through possession and exercise through acts of possession, since if acts of possession are conducted, there is—in fact—possession.[18]

5 REAL-LEGAL MODIFICATIONS

5.1 Acquisition

It shall first be noted that acquisition may be original or derived. Original acquisition occurs where the right is acquired independently from another person's rights on that object and free from any limitation. The forms of original acquisition are: adverse possession (Sections 1897 et seq., Civil and Commercial Code), appropriation (Sections 1947 et seq., Civil and Commercial Code), transformation and accession of personal property (Sections 1957 and 1958, Civil and Commercial Code), accession of real property (Sections 1959 et seq., Civil and Commercial Code), and acquisition by operation of law (Sections 1894 and 1895, Civil and Commercial Code).

Instead, derived acquisition occurs where a person transfers a certain right and another receives it with all limitations and burdens in rem related to such right.

17. *See* s. 5.1 *infra.*
18. *Cfr.* Alterini, Jorge H., *"Primeras..." supra* and *infra. See* s. 6.6 *infra.*

Derived acquisition may occur *inter vivos* or *mortis causa.* In the case of acquisition *mortis causa,* the successor takes the place of the decedent (Section 2277, Civil and Commercial Code).

Derived acquisitions inter vivos require, as a rule, the concurrence of sufficient means and title (Section 1892).

"Sufficient title" consists in the legal act that observes the legal formalities and whose purpose is to transfer the right in rem from a capable and legally qualified transferor (Section 1892, Civil and Commercial Code).

Above all, since it is a legal act, it is a "lawful and voluntary act whose immediate purpose is the acquisition (...) of legal relations or situations" (Section 259, Civil and Commercial Code).

The requirement for this legal act to "observe[s] the legal formalities" shall be correlated to Section 1017 (a) of the Civil and Commercial Code, which provides that "contracts for the acquisition, modification or termination of rights in rem over real property shall be executed in the form of a public deed" (Section 1017, Civil and Commercial Code).

The end of the sufficient title is the transfer of the right in rem. Purchase and sale, barter and gift agreements are aimed at a transfer.

As in any legal act, transferors shall be fully capable, that is, they must be fit to hold the rights (Section 22, Civil and Commercial Code) and legally authorized to exercise such rights (Section 23, Civil and Commercial Code). As a rule, full capacity is acquired with legal age, that is, at eighteen years of age (Section 25, Civil and Commercial Code). For further precisions on legal capacity to acquire rights see the Chapter of Law of Persons and Law of Contracts, respectively.

The Civil and Commercial Code adheres to the Roman maxim *nemo plus iuris,* according to which "no one can transfer a right to another which he has not himself" (Section 399, Civil and Commercial Code). This is the basis for the requirement that transferors in a legal act be legally qualified. Then: When is a person legally qualified to transfer a right? When the person is the holder of the rights whose transfer is intended.

If the formal requirements for the legal act intended for the transfer were fulfilled, but the capacity or the legal qualification of the transferors failed, the result would be a legitimate title.[19]

Of course, if someone transfers a right in rem which he has not himself and subsequently acquires such right, the transfer becomes perfected through validation (Section 1885, Civil and Commercial Code).

For the real-legal modification to operate, sufficient title shall be accompanied by a "sufficient means" to make effective the transfer of the right in rem.

Conveyance is—as a rule—the sufficient means to transfer rights in rem exercised by way of possession. Conveyance makes the possession of the thing possible. Conveyance is a bilateral legal act of an economic content, observing legal formalities, intended to transfer a right in rem and to terminate an obligation[20]

19. *See* s. 5.1 *infra.*
20. Alterini, Jorge H. & Alterini, Ignacio E., *supra.*, p. 268.

The Civil and Commercial Code does not classify legal acts as unilateral and bilateral, unlike Section 946 of the abrogated Civil Code. Nonetheless, this nuance underlies its regime and, hence, there is no doubt that conveyance it—at its essence—a bilateral legal act, since for conveyance to take place it is necessary that two wills converge: *tradens* and *accipiens* (Section 1924, Civil and Commercial Code).

Within the sphere of bilateral legal acts, conveyance falls under the wide scope of "contracts"—included under Section 957 of the Civil and Commercial Code—which is so broad that it also covers conveyance.[21]

Pursuant to Section 260 of the Civil and Commercial Code, a voluntary legal act is that which is "expressed by an external event." Such expression of will may be expressed "through the execution of a material act" (*por la ejecución de un hecho material,* Section 262, Civil and Commercial Code). This means that a voluntary legal act may be performed by several means, that must be always apparent (external) to be perceived by the law: by oral or written expression of will, by unequivocal signs or just by a fact that exteriorizes the will of the party. In relation to form, Section 284 entails that an act is formal when law "specifies a certain form for the expression of will."

In the case of conveyance, the external event or execution of a material event "shall consist in the performance of material acts by—at least—one of the parties" (Section 1924, Civil and Commercial Code), and such material acts shall make it possible to transfer the possession of the thing.

If will shall be expressed in a "certain form" (Section 284, Civil and Commercial Code) which, thus, cannot be replaced by another—since conveyance "shall consist in the performance of material acts by—at least—one of the parties"—such material events denote the requirement of an absolute solemn form. Section 969 of the Civil and Commercial Code sets forth that: "Contracts for which the law requires certain form for validity are null and void where such form has not been observed."

The unarguable end of conveyance for the transfer of a right in rem is precisely the transfer of such right in rem and, in the same breadth, the termination of an obligation by reason of compliance thereof, that is, payment. In view that that the preceding statements hold true, it shall be concluded that conveyance for the transfer of a right in rem is a prototype of a bipolar legal act, both in rem and in personam.

Conveyance of the thing becomes unnecessary where the mere holder becomes the possessor,[22] or where the mere holder has the thing on behalf of the possessor and comes to hold it on behalf of another possessor[23] (*traditio brevi manu*).

Conveyance is not necessary either where the prior possessor transfers the thing, but reserves actual possession[24] (*constituto posesorio*).

Insofar as positive easements are concerned, sufficient means shall consist in the first use.

21. Section 957 establishes that: "A contract is the legal act through which two or more parties express their consent to create, regulate, modify, transfer or terminate economic legal relations."
22. For instance, the mere holder under a lease agreement acquires the thing based on a purchase and sale and becomes the possessor.
23. Another example would be that of a mere holder under a lease agreement who becomes to represent the possession of another based on a transfer of the right in rem.
24. For instance, the owner of a thing could sell it, but keep it under a lease agreement.

Furthermore, in some cases sufficient means shall consist in registration. This is the case of certain personal property, such as motor vehicles (Section 1, Decree-Law No. 6582/1958), purebred racehorses (Section 2, Law No. 20.378), and carrier pigeons (Section 6, Executive Order No. 17,160/1943, ratified by Law No. 12.913).

Despite of the silence in the Civil and Commercial Code, the right in rem of mortgage is transferred with sufficient title alone,[25] since exercise through possession is rare.

Adverse possession is a form of original acquisition of principal rights in rem that are exercised by means of possession (Sections 1891, 1897 and 2565, Civil and Commercial Code).

Possession in good faith based on legitimate title during the statutory term results in the acquisition of the right in rem concerned.

A "legitimate title" is aimed at the transfer of a right in rem and observes the formalities required for validity, but—unlike sufficient title—its transferor is incapable or not legally qualified to that effect (Section 1902, Civil and Commercial Code). For example, a real-estate purchase and sale executed in a pubic deed, but where the seller was not the owner of the thing.

The possessor's good faith consists in not having known and not having been able to know of the lack of entitlement. Nonetheless, if the thing whose transfer is intended is subject to registration (e.g., real property), good faith also requires that a civil-law notary analyze the titles and that the registration certificates be reviewed.

The term for possession varies depending on the object subject to adverse possession. Ten years are required in the case of real property; while only two years are required in the case of personal property that was previously subject to loss or larceny.

In the absence of legitimate title or good faith by possessor, the law requires twenty years of possession to acquire the right in rem through adverse possession, with no distinction based on the object (Section 1899, Civil and Commercial Code).

The effects of a judgment declaring the operation of short-term adverse possession go back to the time when the possession started. Instead, the effects of a judgment declaring the operation of long-term adverse possession do not go back to the time when the possession started; but rather, it is considered that title to the right in rem is acquired after the lapse of the twenty-year term.

What are the consequences of this difference?

In the case of a possessor in bad faith, as it is frequently the case in the event of long-term adverse possession, the possessor should revert the proceeds perceived and such proceeds as were not perceived on account of the possessor (Section 1935, Civil and Commercial Code).

The author of this chapter objects to this legal solution, since the duty to revert the proceeds imposed on the adverse possessor in bad faith could amount to such a value that it could equal or even exceed the value of the thing acquired.[26]

25. The 1998 Draft proposed the following rule: "Section 1825.- Sufficient title. Special case. Derived acquisition *inter vivos* of rights in rem that are not exercised through possession only requires sufficient title."

26. *Cfr.* Alterini, Jorge H., *"Primeras..." supra* and *infra*.

5.2 Transfer

The transfer of rights in rem is related to their structure and thus its regulation "is only determined by law" (Section 1884, Civil and Commercial Code), and the rule is that "all rights in rem are transferable, except as otherwise provided by law" (Section 1906, Civil and Commercial Code).

This is to say that unless the law allows individuals to ban the transfer of rights in rem, such as Section 1972 of the Civil and Commercial Code, which authorizes nontransferability clauses,[27] contractual clauses or testamentary provisions including such prohibition shall be rendered null and void (Section 387, Civil and Commercial Code).[28]

Besides, there are certain exceptions to the rule on transferability made by the law itself: the right in rem of habitation is always nontransferable (Section 2160, Civil and Commercial Code), and the rights in rem of usufruct, use and personal easement are transferable *inter vivos,* but not *mortis causa* (Sections 2140, 2142, 2155 and 2172, Civil and Commercial Code).

5.3 Enforceability Against Third Parties

Within the classification of subjective rights, rights in rem are absolute because they are enforceable *erga omnes,* unlike creditor's rights, which are only effective between the parties.

Thus, rights in rem are not enforceable against interested partied in good faith unless they were sufficiently made public. This disclosure may be accomplished through registration (publicity through registration) or by exercising possession (publicity through possession).

Of course, persons who participated in the relevant acts or who should have known of the existence of a title to a right in rem (Section 1893, Civil and Commercial Code) may not claim lack of publicity, since this would entail bad faith.

27. Section 1972: "In acts for valuable consideration, clauses banning the transfer of ownership of a certain thing to any person or banning the creation of other rights in rem over such thing shall be null and void. These non transferability clauses shall be held valid if they refer to a certain person or persons. In acts for no consideration, all the clauses mentioned in the first paragraph shall be deemed valid as long as their term is not in excess of ten years. If the covenant does not establish a term, establishes an uncertain term, or a term over ten years, it shall be deemed made for such term. The covenant may be expressly extended for a period of no more than ten years counted as from the time it was established. In acts *mortis causa,* clauses affecting forced heir's portion of the estate or implying the substitution of a trust beneficiary shall be deemed null and void."
28. *See* Alterini, Ignacio E., *"Límites de la transmisión del derecho real de usufructo"* (Limitations on the Transfer of the Right in Rem of Usufruct), presentation made in the 25th. National Civil Law Convention held in 2015 in Bahía Blanca. http://jndcbahiablanca2015.com/wp-content/uploads/2015/10/Alterini_Limites-transmision.pdf (last visited on October 5, 2015).

What would occur in the event of disagreement between publicity through registration and through possession? What kind of publicity would prevail? As a corollary to the right of preference, the kind of publicity that occurred first would prevail, provided it was in good faith.[29]

5.4 Termination

Section 1907 of the Civil and Commercial Code sets forth that: "Without prejudice to the means of termination of all economic rights and special means of termination of rights in rem, the latter are terminated by the total loss of the thing if the law does not authorize its reconstruction, by abandonment and by the consolidation of rights in rem over a foreign thing."

A particular means of termination that is common to economic rights and rights in rem is the expropriation of property for public utility, which shall be mandated by law and previously compensated (Article 17, Argentine Constitution, Law No. 21.499).

Total loss of the thing terminates rights in rem, because they are left with no object. As an exception, rights survive when the law envisages the reconstruction of the thing, as in the case of the right in rem of condominium (Section 2055, Civil and Commercial Code) and surface rights (Section 2122, Civil and Commercial Code).

Rights in rem are also terminated by abandonment of the thing; this is the manner in which the holder of a right in rem may waive it.

Finally, all rights in rem on a foreign object are terminated by consolidation, that is, the matching of the titles to a right in rem over a foreign object and to a right in rem over an own object that split upon the creation of such right.

Division of the thing terminates condominium (Sections 1996–1998, Civil and Commercial Code).

Interval ownership is terminated by the expiration of the term and if no disposals were made or if all contracts are terminated (Section 2099, Civil and Commercial Code).

Surface rights are terminated by express waiver; expiration of the term for which they were established; occurrence of a condition subsequent; and lack of use for ten years, in the case of the right to build, and for five years, in the case of the right to plant or forest (Section 2124, Civil and Commercial Code).

The right of usufruct, and hence the rights of use and habitation, are terminated by expiration of the term or occurrence of a condition subsequent; the death of the usufructuary; the dissolution of the legal entity; the lack of use for ten years; abusive use; and alteration of the substance evidenced in court (Section 2152, Civil and Commercial Code).

29. Section 1843 *in fine* of the 1998 Draft expressly proposed: "In the event of disagreement between the enforceability against third parties based on publicity through registration and that based on possession, the first in time shall prevail, provided that it was in good faith. Nonetheless, publicity through possession is not enforceable against holders whose right in rem or other registered legal situation is not exercised by possession, except that an adverse possession whose term has lapsed is materialized."

Easement is terminated by the disappearance of any and all uses for the dominant real property; lack of use for ten years; expiration of the term; or occurrence of a condition subsequent (Section 2182, Civil and Commercial Code).

Rights in rem to a security interest are terminated with the credit they secure (Section 2186, Civil and Commercial Code). These also terminate upon the public auction of the levied good (Section 2203, Civil and Commercial Code).

6 RELATIONS IN REM

6.1 Concept and Terminology

These are relations in fact that might exist between a person and a thing, as against relations stemming from a right in rem (ownership, usufruct, etc.) or a right in personam (lease, loan for use, etc.).

The Civil and Commercial Code governs this topic under the misnomer of "relations of power." Section 1908 of the Civil and Commercial Code sets forth that: "The relations of power between a person and a thing are possession and actual possession."

First, this rule fails to clarify to what kind of powers it refers, whether powers in fact, or powers in law, to which rights in rem belong.

Second, the term "power" means "to have expeditious authority or ability to do something;" and the term "expeditious" means that something is "unhampered, free from all hindrance." Thus, it excludes the idea of subordination. As shall be examined, the idea of power does not apply to all relations in rem.

It is also inaccurate for the Code to limit relations between a person and a thing to possession and actual possession, since it later regulates the figure of the servant in possession.

6.2 Forms of Regulated Relations In Rem

"Possession" occurs where a person exercises a power in fact over a thing, behaving as the holder of a right in rem, whether this person is the holder or not (Section 1909, Civil and Commercial Code); instead, "actual possession" occurs where the person exercising power in fact over a thing "behaves as an agent of the possessor" (Section 1910, Civil and Commercial Code).

In sum, possession consists of two elements: *corpus* and *animus domini,* while actual possession consists in only one element: *corpus.*

Corpus, or the body of possession and actual possession, is the physical power of the holder of the relation in rem over the thing, which may be expressed "by means of contact with the thing, the physical possibility to establish it, or when the thing becomes under the scope of the custody of the acquirer" (Section 1922 (b), Civil and Commercial Code). This power requires will in order to produce legal effects: it shall be acquired "by a capable person, except for minors, for whom it shall suffice to be ten years of age" (Section 1922 (a), Civil and Commercial Code).

Animus domini, or the will to own, implies behaving like the owner would. Of course, this behavior does not refer to the inner will of the possessor, but rather to intention materialized in external facts. Although it is usual for this intention to translate into acts of possession, it may also be reflected into acts that do not reveal physical contact with the thing; such as paying taxes, rates and contributions.

These relations in rem also include persons who "use a thing under a relationship of employment, service, accommodation or hospitality ..." (Section 1911 *in fine*, Civil and Commercial Code), that is, the "servant in possession."

6.3 Classification

Relations in rem are lawful where they entail the exercising of a right in rem (possession) or in personam (actual possession); while they are unlawful where they do not concern the exercising of these rights, for example, a possessor who acquired the thing by way of violence (Section 1916, Civil and Commercial Code).

In turn, relations in rem may be in good faith or in bad faith. Relations in rem are in good faith if the holder did not know and could not have known that he lacks of any right; that is, where he was certain of legal qualification based on an excusable and material error in fact. If the holder of a relation in rem knew, or could have known, of the lack of legal qualification for the relation, the holder would be in bad faith (Section 1918, Civil and Commercial Code).

There is an additional, ephemeral and futile[30] category of flawed possession,[31] like a sort of qualified possession in bad faith, with a sole distinctive effect: the flawed possessor is liable for the destruction of the thing, even if it would have occurred anyway in the hands of the person really entitled to possession (Section 1936 *in fine*, Civil and Commercial Code). This is to say that a flawed possessor bears liability for events of force majeure or acts of God, which implies a questionable exception to the rule of causation captured in the Code (Section 1726, Civil and Commercial Code).

6.4 Assumptions

The Code establishes various assumptions *iuris tantum*, which are rebuttable through contrary evidence, with the purpose of facilitating the proof of the states of fact that relations in rem entail.

Thus, it is assumed that he who maintains a relation in fact with a thing is the possessor (Section 1911); that relations in rem begin and continue pursuant to the title that originated them (Section 1916); that they are lawful, that is, that they entail the

30. *Cfr.* Alterini, Jorge H., *"Inconsistencia y esterilidad de la categoría de la posesión viciosa"*, Acad.Nac. de Derecho 2004 (March).
31. Section 1921 of the Civil and Commercial Code sets forth that: "Possession in bad faith is flawed when it has been acquired through larceny, fraud or breach of trust, in the case of personal property; and through violence, clandestineness or breach of trust, in the case of real property. Flaws in possession are relative in respect of him against whom they are exercised. In any case, whether it is the same person causing the flaw or his agents, or whether against the possessor or his representatives."

exercising of a right in personam or right in rem (Section 1916); that their holders are in good faith (Section 1919[32]); and that the current holders evidencing prior exercise have maintained them during the time in between (Section 1930).

6.5 Means of Acquisition. Immutability of Cause

Relations in rem are acquired by way of conveyance, that is, the delivery of a thing from a person to another. Possession may also be acquired unilaterally: taking of the thing (Section 1923, Civil and Commercial Code).

The Civil and Commercial Code empowers he who is entitled to require the relation in rem over the thing to bring legal action (Section 2239, Civil and Commercial Code).

Regarding conveyance, *see* section 5.1.

Where the object of a relation in rem is a universe in fact—that is, a set of things that the legal order treats as one, such as a library—the relation in rem shall be acquired over each of the things that make up that universe, and global acquisition does not suffice (Section 1927, Civil and Commercial Code). However, the regulation of actions for dispossession (Section 2241, Civil and Commercial Code) and for recovery (Section 2252, Civil and Commercial Code), which imply the reacquisition of the relation in rem, admits that this relation be acquired globally over the set of things.

6.6 Exercising of Possession

Possession is exercised through acts of possession. The following are acts of possession over the thing: farming, perceiving proceeds, marking boundaries or printing material signs, making improvements, excluding third parties and, in general, taking the thing by any means (Section 1928, Civil and Commercial Code).

In other words, possession is materialized through the exercising of acts of possession.

6.7 Conservation

A relation in rem subsists as long as it is physically possible to establish contact with the thing, for instance, a summer house that is only occupied during the season. The relation also subsists as long as the thing remains under the sphere of control of the holder of the relation in rem.

Therefore, *corpus* remains unaffected where exercising the relation in rem is "temporarily hindered" (Section 1929, Civil and Commercial Code), since

32. Bad faith is assumed at certain occasions. Thus, Section 1919 of the Civil and Commercial Code sets forth that: "... Bad faith is assumed where: a) the title is manifestly null; b) possession is acquired from a person who does not usually convey that kind of thing and lacks the means to acquire them; c) it falls on marked or branded cattle, if the design was registered by another person."

temporariness discards "lasting physical impossibility" (Section 1931 (c), Civil and Commercial Code), which is in effect grounds for termination of relations in rem.

In short, relations in rem are conserved with *corpus* alone, and terminated once this is lost.

6.8 Termination

Relations in rem are terminated where: "a) the thing is terminated; b) another deprives the person of the thing; c) the person is in lasting physical impossibility to exercise possession or actual possession; d) there is no reasonable likelihood of finding the lost thing; e) the person expressly and willfully abandons the thing" (Section 1931, Civil and Commercial Code).

To summarize, relations in rem are terminated where there is a lasting or definitive absence of *corpus*.

7 DEFENSES FOR RELATIONS IN REM

7.1 Rationale

Defenses for relations in rem are warranted by the basis of the Rule of Law, which discards someone outside such Rule from exercising force. The State has the monopoly of force and shall exercise it pursuant to the Law.

This rationale demands that the protection of relations in rem be articulated through the judiciary, and that its safeguard be broad and effective.[33]

7.2 Out-of-Court Defense

As an exception, the legal order allows holders of relations in rem to raise a defense that does not call for the involvement of the State. Holders of relations in rem may bring an out-of-court defense, "... where an assault must be repelled and repulsed through the use of sufficient force in cases where the assistance of the police or legal authorities would be too late. The affected party shall recover [the relation in rem] without an interruption in time and without surpassing the limits of self defense" (Section 2240, Civil and Commercial Code).

7.3 In-Court Defenses

In-court defenses are aimed at maintaining or recovering the object over which a relation in rem is exercised, and they are conferred against material acts which have

33. *See* Alterini, Jorge H., *"Protección posesoria"*, in *Cuestiones esenciales en Derechos Reales*, Abeledo-Perrot, Buenos Aires, 2002, pp. 9 et seq.

been produced or of imminent production that express the intention to acquire possession of the object against the will of the holder of the relation in rem (Section 2238, Civil and Commercial Code).

Should the acts imply disappropriation—that is, should they result in the absolute exclusion of the holder of the relation in rem—, the damaged party could claim for the restitution of the objection through the "action for dispossession" (Section 2241, Civil and Commercial Code).

Instead, if the acts conducted did not result in the absolute exclusion of the holder of the relation, but rather in a disturbance intended to divest the holder of the relation in rem, he could raise an "action for preservation" for the Court to order the ceasing of the disturbance and to adopt the relevant measures (Section 2242, Civil Code).

8 DESCRIPTION OF RIGHTS IN REM ENVISAGED BY THE CIVIL AND COMMERCIAL CODE

8.1 Ownership

Ownership is the right in rem that confers all powers to use, enjoy and dispose of a thing within the limits prescribed by law (Section 1941, Civil and Commercial Code).

It is the broadest right in rem, since it gathers the largest amount of powers.

8.2 Tenancy in Common

Tenancy in common is the right in rem that confers each of its holders the prerogative power to dispose of its portion, and to use and enjoy the thing in common in concurrence with the other holders.[34]

This right in rem is the communion or community of the right in rem of ownership.[35]

8.3 Condominium

Condominium is the right in rem over real property that confers the powers to use, enjoy and dispose of pursuant to the Civil and Commercial Code and the relevant condominium rules (Section 2037, Civil and Commercial Code).

The right of condominium is determined in the functional unit, which consists in floors, apartments, stores or other spaces that can be independently exploited based on their nature or purpose, which are functionally independent and communicated to public roadways directly or through a common passage way.

34. The proposed description is contained in Section 1923 of the 1998 Draft. Section 1983 of the Civil and Commercial Code defines tenancy in common inaccurately, as "... the right in rem of ownership of a thing that is owned in common by various persons and of which an indivisible portion corresponds to each person."
35. *Cfr.* Gatti & Alterini, *supra.*, p. 101.

The ownership of the functional unit comprises the portion of land, of the things and portions of common use in the real property or that are indispensable to maintain security, and may cover on or more complementary units intended to serve the functional unit (Section 2039, Civil and Commercial Code).

8.4 Special Ownership: Real-Estate Developments, Interval Ownership and Private Cemeteries

The Civil and Commercial Code regulates these special forms of ownership as rights in rem.

"Real-estate developments" are constructions for urbanization regardless of their purpose as a permanent or temporary residence, work, commercial or business building (Section 2073, Civil and Commercial Code). Although they are apparently regulated as autonomous rights in rem (Section 1887, Civil and Commercial Code), they are in fact rights in rem of condominium on special objects (Sections 2075, 2076, 2078, 2080, 2081, 2085 and 2086, Civil and Commercial Code).

The right in rem of "interval ownership" exists where "... one or more properties are subject to periodical use in turns for accommodation, hospitality, trade, tourism, industry or other ends ..." (Section 2087, Civil and Commercial Code).

Pursuant to Section 2103 of the Civil and Commercial Code, "private cemeteries" are "... privately owned real property for the burial of human corpses" (Section 2103, Civil and Commercial Code).

It is worth noting that the Code regulates potential objects of other rights (constructions for urbanization; properties for periodical use in turns; real property for the burial of human corpses) as autonomous rights in rem, without referring to the titles or powers conferred by these rights in rem.[36]

8.5 Surface Rights

Surface rights are the rights in rem to plant, forest or build on a third-party real property and to take what has been included as their holder's own or to acquire what has been planted, forested or built separately from the real property where it is located, for a certain term of not more than fifty years in the case of plantations and forestations, and of not more than seventy years for buildings (Sections 2114, 2115 and 2117, Civil and Commercial Code).

8.6 Usufruct, Use and Habitation

Usufruct is the right in rem that confers the powers to use and enjoy a third-party property without altering its substance, and to legally dispose of the right. In the case

36. *See* s. 3.2 *supra*.

of things, there is alteration of substance when their matter, form or purpose are modified; and in the case of rights, when they are undermined (Section 2129, Civil and Commercial Code).

Use is the right in rem that confers the powers to use and enjoy a foreign thing, a material part or portion thereof, insofar as established in the title, without altering its substance. If the title does not establish the scope or use and enjoyment, it is understood that it confers usufruct. It can only be constituted in favor of a natural person (Section 2154, Civil and Commercial Code).

Habitation is the right in rem that consists in living in a third party's real property or in a material part thereof, without altering its substance. It can only be constituted in favor of a natural person (Section 2158, Civil and Commercial Code).

8.7 Easement

Easement is the right in rem established between two real properties that confers the holder of the dominant real property certain use over the other third party's real property. This use may be that of mere recreation (Section 2162, Civil and Commercial Code).

8.8 Rights In Rem to Security Interests: Mortgage, Antichresis and Pledge

Section 2088 of the 1998 Draft proposed the following global definition: "Rights in rem to security interests may only be created through a formal contract to secure credits, and in addition to the powers common to rights in rem, they confer the power to realize assets and perceive the credits over their proceeds."

A mortgage is the right in rem to a security interest over an identified real property that remains in the power of its owner; a mortgage can only be granted by public deed (Section 2205, Civil and Commercial Code).

An antichresis is the right in rem to a security interest over an identified thing subject to registration whose possession is delivered to the creditor or to a third-party designated by the parties, authorized to perceive the proceeds to charge them against a debt (Section 2212, Civil and Commercial Code).

A pledge is the right in rem to a security interest over personal property that is no subject to registration or over evidenced credits. A pledge is granted by the owner or by all the tenants in common, by means of a contract executed in a private or public instrument and through conveyance to the pledgee or to a third party designated by the parties (Section 2219, Civil and Commercial Code).

9 DEFENSES FOR RIGHTS IN REM

9.1 Actions In Rem

The protection of rights in rem is enforced through actions in rem, which are the means to defend at trial the existence, completeness, freedom and scope of rights in rem against violations preventing their exercising.

An "action for recovery" is intended to defend the existence of a right in rem exercised through possession, and takes place before acts that produce disappropriation.

An "action to quiet title" is intended to defend the freedom of a right in rem exercised through possession, and takes place before acts that constitute a disturbance, in particular due to the undue conferring of an easement or of another right inherent to possession.

An "action for recognition and enforcement" is intended to defend the completeness of a right in rem, and takes place before acts that prevent the exercising of an easement or of another right inherent to possession.

An "action to settle boundaries" is intended to defend the scope of the right in rem falling over plots of land—even if they contain buildings—, for the purposes of researching on uncertain boundaries and measuring and marking the boundaries of the plot.

9.2 Options Available upon Damage of a Right In Rem

The holder of a damaged right in rem may choose to reestablish such right in rem through actions in rem, or may claim for compensation for the damage sustained. Section 2250 of the Civil and Commercial Code sets forth that: "If he chooses to reestablish the right, he may claim for complementary compensation for the damage sustained. If he chooses to claim for compensation for the damage sustained, he forfeits the right to bring an action in rem."

Further Reading

Cossari, Nelson G.A., in Alterini, Jorge H., *Còdigo Civil y Comercial Comentado. Tratado Exegètico,* Volumes IX and X, Buenos Aires, La Ley, 2016.

Kiper, Claudio, *Manual de Derechos Reales,* Rubinzal Culzoni, Santa Fe, 2017.

CHAPTER 9
Inheritance Law

Ursula Basset

1 INHERITANCE LAW IN ARGENTINA: MAIN FEATURES

Inheritance law covers testate and intestate successions. A succession could be partly testate, partly intestate. However, testamentary successions tend to be rare, and the estate of the deceased is mostly passed by an intestate succession.

Argentinian Succession law is based upon the obligations towards family, and imposes therefore strict limitations on individual's freedom of testation. Freedom of testation is strongly curtailed, arguably, to protect family members. Argentina has, like France and Spain, a "réserve" (*legítima hereditaria*, legal portion), this is a portion of the estate of the deceased cannot be disposed of by a will. To protect the legal portion even the gifts advanced to the legal heirs while the defunct was alive must be brought to the inheritance to ensure an equal share of the heirs. Even if in the new Civil and Commercial Code (2015, from now on CCC) has lowered the legal portion for family members, they are still high compared to other similar legal systems. Further, the new CCC, has removed the right of the testator to disinherit their heirs.

Ever since, Argentine inheritance law has adhered to the Roman system, according to which *hereditas personae vicem sustinet.* The inheritance represents the *persona* of the defunct, even if, in a mitigated way. The choice for the "in persona" system implies a distinct set of rules. First, inheritance passes to the heirs at the very instant in which death occurs. It is, undoubtedly, a legal fiction. However, in Argentine inheritance law, this fiction is so powerful as to cause a vast number of consequences: (a) first, the heirs will occupy the place of the defunct from the very moment of his death for all legal purposes, whether they know of his death or not; (b) second, only those who exist at the moment of the death are capable of receiving the inheritance; (c) third, partition (the division and attribution of the estate to the heirs) will have retroactive effects: for all purposes, heirs will be deemed owners of the part of the estate that is allocated to them from the very moment of the death of the deceased; (d) the applicable law to the procedure is the *lex domicilii* at the time of death.

Argentine inheritance law is still attached to ancient traditions, even if the new CCC has tried to modernize it introducing institutions like an agreement *inter vivos* to organize the transmission of a family company (*pacto de herencia futura*), or a special system of protection in case of death for disabled family members, basically, it is still the same system designed by Argentina's first Civil Code in 1869.[1]

To see the applicable law to probate proceedings see the chapter of international private law.

2 ORGANIZATION OF CONTENTS

Inheritance law is regulated in the fifth book of the new CCC of 2015 (*Transmisión de Derechos por Causa de Muerte*). This book has eleven subdivisions, as follows:

Title 1. Successions
Title 2. Acceptance and renounce
Title 3. Contract of cession of inheritance
Title 4. Petition of inheritance
Title 5. Liability of heirs and legatees
Title 6. Community of heirs
Title 7. Inheritance proceedings
Title 8. Partition
Title 9. Intestate succession
Title 10. Legal reserve ("*legítima hereditaria*", "réserve héréditaire")
Title 11. Testate successions

3 THE OPENING OF THE SUCCESSION

Since Argentina adopted the Roman legal system by which heirs take the place of the defunct, the opening of the succession occurs at the exact moment in which the death of the deceased takes place. The estate, by the means of this legal fiction, will have always an owner: before his death, it will be owned by the deceased; after his death, immediately, it is owned by his heirs (automatically, directly, without the mediation of the State, there is not an instant in which the inheritance has not an owner).

Therefore, determining the time of death becomes a key issue. Time of death will determine who is capable of receiving the inheritance, since the heir must survive the deceased and exist at the time of death. Inheritance can only be accepted or renounced after death, and it is from then on that the closing period to accept is counted. Debts acquired before death (*deudas*) have to be paid in a different way then debts contracted

1. For the same reason (the attachment to ancient tradition), inheritance law in Argentina has a vocabulary of its own. Here and there the author will be obliged to refer to Spanish terms and try to define them and translate them into English. Common Spanish words may have a specific meaning when applied to inheritance law.

after death (*cargas*). The first (*deudas*) have a privilege over the second (*cargas*). Death creates *ipso iure* a form of joint property between the heirs (*comunidad hereditaria*). The retroactive effects of partition of this community of heirs will go back to the time of death.

When the CCC refers to the "opening of the succession" (*apertura de la sucesión*) it should be distinguished from the opening of the inheritance proceedings. The opening of the succession refers always to the time of death.

4 THE MAIN SUBJECTS: HEIR AND LEGATEE

Argentine inheritance law distinguishes between heirs and legatees. A heir is, generally speaking, a person who has a calling (*vocación hereditaria*) by a testament or by the law, to occupy and represent the deceased partly or totally. The CCC describes two sorts of heirs: (a) the heir; (b) the heir of a quota.

Heir, in principle, is he who was called to inherit by the law or by a will without any restriction. His call is to the whole of the estate, that he may have to share, eventually, with other heirs. However, the new CCC included a second category of heirs called heir of a quota (*heredero de cuota*). The heir of a quota receives a universality, but restricted to the part that was allocated to him by a will. The differences between the simple universal heir and the heir of quota are mainly that the first has no limit to his rights and may expand them if other heirs fall out, whilst the second has a limited heirship, restricted to the quota fixed by the testator in the will.[2]

Heirs can become their heirship by a testament or by law. As for those who become their heirship by law, two types of heirship should be distinguished: a mandatory heirship and a subsidiary heirship: the *herederos forzosos* (lit. "compulsory heirs" or "forced heirs," a metaphor, since they can always renounce the inheritance) and the *herederos legítimos* ("legal heirs"). The former are mandatory heirs, in the sense that any testament that had excluded them would be invalid as to the exclusion of them (it will be further explained below). The latter are subsidiary heirs, in the sense that if they had been excluded by a will, that will would be perfectly valid.

First, the *herederos forzosos,* also called *herederos legitimarios.* These are the descendants and ascendants of the defunct and the surviving spouse. Law has a special interest in these three orders of successors, since it is understood they are the closest persons to the defunct, and the law presumes that he would not want to disinherit them. As said before, not even the written will of the deceased has the power of cutting them out of the inheritance. Only the other heirs or legatees could claim that they are not worthy to receive the estate if they have committed an offense against the deceased or his close relatives (*see* below *indignidad*).[3] So, whenever there are a surviving spouse, ascendants or descendants (*herederos forzosos*), there will be a "reserve," a legal portion, that will be protected by several legal means (collation, petition of the

2. Medina, Graciela, Miguez de Bruno, María Soledad, "Principios generales sucesorios y los principios generales de la sucesión intentada en particular", DFuP, p. 109.
3. Rolleri, Gabriel, "La exclusión hereditaria en el nuevo Código Civil: Fortalecimiento de la indignidad y supresión de la desheredación", DFyP 2015, p. 105.

inheritance, etc.). A testator cannot skip a legal heir by a will. If a will should omit a legal heir or curtail his rights, the legal heir might be entitled to his rights irrespectively of the contents of the will.

On the other hand, there are the *herederos legítimos* (simple legal heirs). In Argentinian law, these are brothers and sisters, uncles, aunts, and nephews. This second category of legal heirs has a subsidiary legal calling to receive the inheritance. This means that if the testator should make a will and exclude them, they would have no claim. The law protects simple legal heirs in a weaker way than the closer family members (*herederos forzosos*).

Finally, there are the legatees. A legatee does not represent the deceased. He receives because of a disposition in a will, something left by the deceased for him.

The main differences between a heir and a legatee are as follows:

- In principle, the heir has to pay the debts of the deceased, while the legatee is exempted (unless it is a legacy of a universality or he had it imposed as a condition to the will).
- The heir obtains its heirship without any intervention of any judge, and even if he is not aware that he is an heir (because of the system of succession *in persona*). The legatee has to claim for his bequeath.

5 WHO CAN SUCCEED THE DEFUNCT

In Argentina, only those persons who exist at the time of the death may succeed the defunct (Article 2279 CCC). As in many other compared legal systems, the word "persons" is used in an analogic manner to refer human persons as well as legal persons. Both of them are able to succeed. There are some peculiarities to be attended to. Concerning human persons, Argentinian law is one of those rare systems in which the existence of a human person begins with conception. This means that once a human person is conceived (within the womb of a mother, or by artificial reproductive techniques—ART), it will be granted all legal rights with the same extent as any person already born. So, persons who have been conceived by the time of death, are considered heirs to the defunct. However, their heirship depends on the fact that they are later born alive. If they do not, another legal fiction takes place: it is as if they never existed. Applying the same principle (human life begins with conception within or outside the womb of the mother), there is a second rule, that may sound surprising: those persons conceived by ART, born after the death of the defunct, if legal procedure for ART has been followed, will be their rightful heirs. This article was supposed to deal with post-mortem ART techniques, that were later on excluded from the final text of the CCC. However, the legislator apparently forgot to exclude this reference to the children so conceived. Right now, a literal interpretation of that article could imply that every embryo that is cryopreserved, should he be implanted and later born alive, would be an heir to the defunct.

There are also some particularities to be noted concerning legal persons. Legal persons can be heirs if they exist at the time of death. However, there is one exception.

The testator could create a foundation by a will. Only in this case, a nonexistent person at the time of death, would, nonetheless, be an heir to the deceased. The defunct would have the power, by law, to engender a legal person after death, and still make it its heir. A beautiful legal fiction, to protect the charitable ends of foundations.

6 ACCEPT OR REFUSE AN HEIRSHIP

An heir (even a "forced heir") is free to accept or renounce their heirship (Article 2287 CCC). This right (to accept or refuse) is called *derecho de opción* (lit. right to opt). The right to decide is transmissible to the heirs of the heirs if it has not been exerted (e.g., if the heir dies before having had the chance to pronounce himself on the matter). Acceptance or refusal are always of the inheritance as a whole. An heir may not accept a part of the estate and refuse another. The act of acceptance or refusal is, therefore, indivisible.

An heirship can be accepted or refused only once it is opened (after the death of the deceased). Heirs have ten years, counted from the moment of death, to accept or refuse the inheritance. If the heir does not exert his right during this period, it will be understood that he refused the inheritance (Article 2288).

The acceptance of a will can be made expressly or implicitly. An express acceptation has no formal requirements, except that it should be written. It is implicit when the heir performs certain acts revealing that he perceives himself as an heir to that estate (e.g., if he sells a good pertaining to the estate, if he transfers his share to the inheritance by a cession).

In Argentina, the acceptance implies always a separation between the estate of the heir and the estate of the defunct. Contrary to what would have naturally followed the succession *in persona* system (acceptance would have implied a confusion of estates), Argentina has had a longstanding tradition to maintain both estates separate.[4] Creditors to the defunct will have no claim on the estate of their heirs. Unless, there is what is called "forced acceptance."

Aceptación forzada (forced acceptance) occurs as penalty to an heir who behaves dishonestly or fraudulently towards the estate of the defunct. He who hides or robs goods from the estate will turned his acceptance into an unlimited acceptance. Thus, his estate will be confused with that of the defunct, and the creditors of the defunct will have a claim on the whole of the estate of the heir. This fraudulent heir will have no share in the goods he tried to hide or rob.

Finally, the refusal or renouncement of the heirship takes more than the acceptance. There are special formal requirements to refuse: it has to be done by a notarial deed or by a document during the proceedings of the succession. If an heir renounces to the inheritance, it will be understood as if he never existed as heir,[5] in a very peculiar wording (if thought in terms of its deep meaning in family relations).

4. After a legal reform that took place in 1968 (Law 17.711).
5. Lit. "como si nunca hubiera sido llamado a la herencia."

7 ADMINISTRATION OF THE ESTATE

Once the death of person occurs, its estate passes immediately (according to the succession *in persona* system) to his heirs. However, by the means of this legal fiction, the estate previously owned by one person (the defunct) will now be owned probably by a plurality of heirs. Heirs will have, from then on and until partition, a sort of coownership of the estate (Article 2323 CCC).

This coownership is called *indivisión hereditaria* (lit. refers to the period of time in which the inheritance remains undivided) or also *comunidad hereditaria* (community of heirs, to imply the legal community created by the group of heirs who have ownership rights towards the inheritance) and during the period in which the estate is undivided, heirs, creditors and legatees have a number of rights and obligations to protect their interests.

In the meantime, the estate needs an administrator. The Argentine CCC makes provision for two kinds of administrators: (a) those who administrate beyond the legal procedure; (b) those who are appointed by a legal procedure of succession.

At all events, the faculties of the administrator are fairly limited to take reasonable measures to preserve the estate until partition (Article 2324 CCC). Any ordinary or extraordinary acts of administration (such as renting a building, making an investment) would need a special authorization from the community of heirs or a special mandate (conferred by a power of attorney) expressly including those faculties, the unanimous approval of the community of heirs, or, if the latter could not be obtained, the authorization of a judge (Article 2325 CCC).

It sometimes happens that before the legal procedure of succession begins or that, spontaneously, one or several heirs take upon themselves the administration of the estate. The CCC has now special rules for this "extrajudicial administration." The extrajudicial administration may have three legal sources: (a) a power of attorney (mandate) given by the community of heirs; (b) a legal provision; (c) de facto legal administration.

Even if it is uncommon, sometimes the heirs may celebrate a contract to provide for the administration of a complex estate. They may designate a legal person (e.g., a company with an expertise in operating a farm enterprise), an heir or one or several third parties to administrate the estate.

Extrajudicial administrators are hinted by the law in the case of "forced undivided wealth or goods" (*indivisiones forzosas*, Articles 2330 and ff. CCC, *see below*). In the case that the surviving spouse should or an heir should obtain that a family company or shares remain undivided, he who opposes the division of those goods have a claim to administer the company or decide upon the shares (to see how this works, *see* below).

Otherwise, an extrajudicial administration is the outcome of a spontaneous decision or the dynamics of certain families in which one of their members is more suited or usually takes it upon himself to administer the wealth of the family. If the other heirs do not oppose to this de facto administration, general rules will apply to it as to any other administration of the estate.

A judicial administrator maybe a legal or human person, or even several legal or human persons. A legal person needs a special administrative authorization to act as administrator of the inheritance.

There are some rules to appoint a judicial administrator. First of all, the testator may designate them and even plan how they will be substituted. If there were no administrator appointed by the will, the majority of heirs may appoint an administrator and devise rules to substitute him. If the majority of heirs do not reach an agreement, a Judge may appoint him. A judge should appoint preferably the surviving spouse. If the spouse should be found unsuited to perform the administration of the estate, the judge should appoint preferably another heir, unless there are reasons that make it best to appoint a third party.[6]

8 RIGHTS OF THE CREDITORS

To understand the position of creditors towards the succession, some prior clarifications should be made.

As it was explained above, once the death occurs, the estate of the defunct forms an undivided totality. This undivided totality is conceived as a separate patrimony (as a sort of patrimony of affectation or as an insolvency estate): it will evolve, grow or decrease, as any other estate would.

As explained before, except for those cases in which the heir is punished with a "forced acceptance" of the inheritance (*see* above), which would therefore mean a confusion between his own estate and the estate of the defunct, under normal circumstances, the estate of the heirs is separated from the undivided totality (*indivisión hereditaria*) that began at the time of death.

With this prior clarification, it should be possible to identify several classes of creditors:

- Creditors to the defunct (before his death).
- Creditors to the mass (*indivisión hereditaria,* the undivided estate created because of the death with the estate of the defunct). Creditors to the mass are those who claim for expenditures made by the administrator in order to pay for the conservation of goods, inheritance proceedings or any other expense derived from the mass or the administration of it.
- Creditors to each heir.
- Creditors to the legatees.

Each of these creditors have a different standing and differentiated rights towards the mass.

First, it should be stated that there is an order of preference between them, as follows:

- First, creditors to the mass.

6. Article 2347.

- Second, creditors to the defunct.

Now, once the passive of the estate has been settled, heirs and legatees have to be paid. To this end, it should be established if heirs are forced heirs or simple legal or testamentary heirs:

- If they are forced heirs, they have a right to their legal portion. In that case, the legal portion has to be established, and once it is, legatees and other heirs may be paid from the disposable portion (the remaining of the estate, once the legal portion has been established).[7] If legacies and other bequest exceed the disposable portions, they must be reduced to the disposable portion in a very specific order.[8]
- If there are no forced heirs, legatees are paid, and the remaining estate is split pro rata between the heirs.

In turn, creditors must file the evidence of their credits into the probate proceedings.

Creditors to the heirs and creditors to the legatees will have to wait until heirs and legatees receive their shares, to be paid. This does not mean that they may not seize the presumable rights of the debtor (heir or legatee), or that they may not surrogate themselves to their rights, However, since the rights of heirs and legatees are not certain until they are allocated to them, which will not occur until the division of the inheritance, they may not be paid until then.[9]

To grant their credits, obligees are provided with a number of rights: (a) they may summon the heirs to accept or refuse the heirship (Article 2288 CCC), if the heir does not pronounce himself within three month, he will be held as acceptant; (b) He may also initiate probate proceedings (after he summoned the heirs to accept or refuse, and a waiting period established by local civil procedures codes has passed); (c) they may obtain a declaration of *legítimo abono* (rightful payment, Article 2357 CCC), by which their credits are recognized by the heirs; (d) they may claim the payment of their debts against directly against the heirs (Articles 2277, 2280 CCC); (e) they may seize the goods of the inheritance, even those forcedly undivided (Article 2330/2333 CCC); (f) they may claim that before partition, a share of the good is set apart in order to settle their credits; (g) they may request the bankruptcy of the inheritance (Article 2360, Articles 80 and 83, Law 24.522); (h) they may request the administrator to provide an accounting; (i) they may request the administrator to provide adequate assurances or even to demand the removal of the administrator (Articles 2350, 2351 CCC); (j) undertake administration and liquidation of the inheritance in case that the heirs abandon or repudiate the inheritance.[10]

7. First, according to the will of the defunct if he has established an order of payment in his will. Subsidiarily according to the Art. 2358 CCC.
8. Cfr. Art. 2452 CCC.
9. Ferrer, Francisco A.M., *Comunidad hereditaria e indivisión postganancial*, Santa Fe, Rubinzal Culzoni, 2017, pp. 350-351.
10. Ferrer, Francisco A.M., *Comunidad hereditaria e indivisión postganancial*, Santa Fe, Rubinzal Culzoni, 2017, p. 376.

9 HEREDITARY PARTITION

The distribution of the estate of the defunct is called partition (*partición*).[11] Partition provides an end to the hereditary mass (*indivisión hereditaria*). Partition may be requested by heirs, assignees, creditors and legatees or bequeaths. It can be requested at any time. Nonetheless, any rightsholder who has a share in the hereditary mass may ask to postpone partition, in case it would turn out to be inconvenient at that time.

Partition can be partial or total (of all the goods, or some goods). It may also be provisional or final. It is provisional if only the right of use has been divided, but the ownership remains undivided (Article 2370). Partition may be made by fathers and mothers and other ascendants, as they may make a distribution of their property among their children and legitimate descendants, either by the designation of the quantum of the parts which they assign to each of them, or in designating the property that shall compose their respective lots. These partitions may be made inter vivos or by testament, if they respect the legal portion of each heir (Articles 2411 and ff).

It is private when it is reached by an agreement of all parties. However, if there are minors or persons with disabilities, or if creditors do not approve of the agreement of the parties, then the partition will have to be made within the probate proceedings.

If a partition takes place within probate proceedings, the judge will have to appoint an expert or several experts to divide the inheritance (Article 2373). Coowners may appoint him by a unanimous agreement. Otherwise, he will be appointed by the Judge.

There are two general principles governing partition: partition should be made preferably in kind and even if the property could be divided, it should not be done if this division is uneconomic.

The estate to be divided is composed by the property that the defunct had at the time of death, the property that substituted the property of the defunct during proceedings, and any rents that may have come from them. To this mass, heirs are obliged to collate the value of the property they received during the life of the deceased (Article 2385 CCC). Once that the debts are settled, and legacies are paid, the expert in partition will divide the lots allocating them to the heirs according to their share.

The Argentine CCC has devised several legal instruments so that the heirs may be allocated a specific piece of property of the estate of the defunct:

(a) Call for bids ("licitación"): any of the joint owners of the hereditary mass may call for bids for any property he is interested in. (*See* Article 2372).
(b) Preferential allocation for the surviving spouse (*atribución preferencial*): the surviving spouse may ask to be allocated the agricultural, commercial, or any other enterprise forming an economic unit, if he helped to build it up (Article 2380). The same applies to the shares of the defunct in such enterprises. If the allocation would exceed his share in the inheritance, he must pay the remainder in cash. The surviving spouse may also ask for the

11. Article 2363 CCC and ff.

right to continue the lease, or be allocated the property of the place where spouses resided together before death. He may also ask for the allocation of the place the surviving spouse uses to develop their professional activities or just the sum of movable property that the surviving spouse might need to exploit the rural property.

(c) Preferential allocation by coowners of the hereditary mass: Any coowner, or several coowners may ask to be allocated a specific property of the inheritance (Article 2382).

Partition has a retroactive effect to the time of death. It means that the heir will substitute the defunct only to the extent of the property he receives upon partition. This means that for the law it will be as from the very moment of the death of the defunct, the heir were the owner of each piece of property he received upon partition.

10 RIGHT TO IMPOSE THAT THE WHOLE ESTATE OR SOME GOODS REMAIN TEMPORARILY UNDIVIDED

The *indivisión forzosa* (forced undivided wealth or goods) is an institution ruled in Argentine CCC (Articles 2330 and ff), By the means of a forced imposition, some of the goods or even the whole estate may remain undivided for a period of time that may go from ten years to even the death of some rightsholders. They are usually devised to protect a source of income of one or several heirs, their housing or even the continuity of a commercial company (and thus protect the source of income of the workers of such company). Such imposition implies indeed a grievance for the other heirs or creditors. In order to mitigate this grievance, the legislation provides safeguards for creditors and other heirs, as shown below.

To begin with, the cases in which this imposition may proceed is listed as follows:

(a) The testator has a right to decide upon the living, that the whole of the estate or certain goods will or all goods[12] are not to be divided by a certain period of time.[13]

(b) The surviving spouse has the right:
    (i) to impose on other heirs the house in which both spouses had their habitual residence before the death[14] remain undivided until his own death;

12. Article 2330 stipulates precisely which goods may remain undivided: (a) a specific good; (b) a commercial, industrial, agricultural or mining enterprise that constitutes "an economical unit"; (c) shares in a society in which the testator was a main shareholder.
13. A maximum of ten years, which could be extended to the coming off age of minor heirs if there were such (Art. 2330).
14. Only if it was build or bought with common funds under the community of property regime, and unless it cannot be allocated to his share in the inheritance by the time of partition. Movables within the house are included. If the spouse has means to provide himself housing, the other heirs may demand the partition, since there is no longer ground for sustaining it (Art. 2332).

(ii) or to demand that the enterprise or shares of a society remain undivided if he had partly bought or formed, or from which he has his incomes, and unless they can be allocated to his share for a period of ten years to be counted after the death of the deceased or, if he claims for it, until his own death.

(c) The heirs may:
   (i) Celebrate a pact of "indivisión" (Article 2331). The heirs may celebrate a pact to impose on themselves that the whole estate or a part of the estate remain undivided for ten years, which may be extended for another ten years.
   (ii) Any of the heirs may oppose the division of the estate in the same circumstances as the surviving spouse (*see supra*).[15]

The heirs who suffer a grievance by these impositions, may claim its total or partial termination, if they can proof "grave circumstances or reasons of evident utility;"[16] or, in the case of the pact between heirs, just "justified causes."[17] In the case of the house for the surviving spouse, if the other heirs may proof that the spouse has enough means to provide himself housing (in which case, the special protection for housing loses its meaning).

The legislator has provided some safeguards for the creditors. First of all, an imposition not to divide a registrable immovable to be effective against third parties should be registered at the Property Register. Else, there is a double regime, according if the creditor is creditor to the heir or creditor to the defunct. Creditors to the heirs may not execute the goods subject to these impositions, but they may collect credits from the earnings these goods produce (e.g., from a rental income). Unlike the latter, creditors to the defunct have full access to undivided goods: they may collect their debts even from such goods.[18] They may as well seize or foreclose them.

11 INTESTATE SUCCESSION

In Argentina, the most common way to pass the wealth in the case of death are intestate successions. It is a cultural matter. An intestate succession may coexist with a testamentary one.

Before entering into the main principles of intestate succession, there is a matter of language that should be clarified to understand mandatory and nonmandatory heirship. Argentine CCC refers to *órdenes (de preferencia)* (lit. order of preference), and *grados (de parentesco)* (lit. degree of kinship).

An order is a class of heirs used by the legislator to establish a hierarchy. There are four orders of heirs: the descendants, the ascendants, the surviving spouse, and relatives in collateral line. The law establishes a hierarchy between these orders,

15. Article 2333.
16. Articles 2330, 2332.
17. Article 2331.
18. Article 2334.

according to the value allocated to each family relation. Descendants are overall preferred. They constitute the first order. Next, ascendants. The surviving spouse comes third, has nevertheless a greater share in the wealth of his deceased spouse. Collateral relations are not mandatory heirs, as seen before, but they are still legal heirs (subsidiary).

Within the orders, preference is established according the degree of kinship. The closest degree has preference over the more remote family relations.

There is still a third rule to learn (beside those of order and degree). Orders may concur between them or displace each other. Two orders may coincide when they share a part (equal or unequal) in the wealth of the defunct. An order displaces another: if there are members of the family of a privileged order, the members of a less important order lose their ability to inherit. As follows:

(a) If there are descendants (daughters, sons, grandchildren, etc), they will exclude any ascendant (grandparents) of the estate of the defunct. Ascendants have no right to succeed if the concur with descendants. That is how Argentinian law privileges the place of the offspring.
(b) If there are descendants and they concur with the surviving spouse, the law will place the surviving spouse in equal standing as the offspring. Each of the children will have an equal share with the spouse. For example, if there are three children and a spouse, each will receive ¼ of the inheritance.
(c) If there are ascendants and a spouse, the spouse will receive half of the inheritance. The other half will be split amongst ascendants.
(d) Collaterals are excluded by any of the former. They inherit only if there are no descendants, ascendants, or spouse.

12 THE SPECIAL POSITION OF THE SURVIVING SPOUSE IN ARGENTINIAN CCC

The rights of the surviving spouse strike as a surprise, if compared with other legal systems. Ever since the first Civil Code, the surviving spouse has received a special consideration from the legislator, who felt (probably inspired by an indissoluble marriage) that after having shared a long life together, the grieved surviving spouse should deserve at least a number of safeguards. Even if the legislator did not refer to wives, protection of female widows might have been a significant driving force.

As it is, Argentinian CCC gives the surviving spouse the following advantages:

- If he lived under the common property matrimonial regime, he or she will be able to receive his share (not by right of inheritance, but as spouse). The division of common property occurs before the partition of the estate of the deceased.
- The surviving spouse is heir to the deceased spouse, and he will inherit no matter what other orders of heirs will eventually share the inheritance with

him or her. If there are children, his share will equal that of the children (plus what he received as a spouse if he lived under common property regime during marriage). If there are ascendants, he will receive a half of the inheritance (plus what he received as a spouse, if they lived under common property regime), and the other half will be split between the ascendants.
- The surviving spouse has a "réserve" of his own: he is entitled to a half of the estate (*see* below).
- The surviving spouse has a right (in rem) of habitation in the house in which both spouses live together. The surviving spouse does not need to claim for this right, he is automatically entitled to dwell in the house, even if it were exclusive property of the defunct. This right is for life and free of any dues.
- The surviving spouse may oppose to the division of the common house in which he spent the live in common with the spouse of the deceased, or the division of the company both spouses founded together or ran together, or similar venture.
- The surviving spouse may claim that the house in which both spouses lived in common be allocated to him at the time of partition.
- The surviving spouse has a privilege right to be appointed by the judge as administrator to the estate, in case that the heirs did not agree on any other appointment.

To counterbalance, such privileged position is only attained in case that, at the time of death, spouses lived together, shared their residency, and their marriage was not broken. The mere separation at the time of death, even if it is because a judicial measure, even if it is for the protection of the surviving spouse from his maybe aggressive other spouse, will terminate his heirship. A spouse is only an heir if his marriage is at its peak at the time of death.

13 THE LEGAL PORTION (LEGÍTIMA)

As explained above, Argentina strongly protects family relations from the individual and autonomous decisions that could be reached by the deceased. One of these strong safeguards is the "réserve" (*legítima hereditaria,* legal portion). The legal portion is a portion or share of the estate of the deceased that cannot be disposed by a will. The legal portion varies according to the intensity of the protection allocated by the legislator to family members: the weaker the position is judged by the legislator, the higher the legal portion. The amounts of the legal portion in the new CCC are as follows:

- Descendants: $2/3$.
- Ascendants: $1/2$.
- Surviving spouse: $1/2$.

The legislator has provided heirs with several devices to protect the legal portion from testamentary dispositions eventually made by the deceased.

First, if a testator should infringe the legal portion, this clause of the testament would produce no effect, it will be as if he had not written it. The testator has the right to request that the legal portion to which he is entitled, is accorded to him (Article 2450, *acción de entrega de la legítima*).

Second, the heirs have a claim to ask the reduction of heirships of share (herederos de cuota) or legacies made in his testament if they exceed the disposable portion (Article 2452, *acción de reducción*). The same would apply to gifts *inter vivos* that would exceed the disposable portion (Article 2453).

Third, heirs have a claim to supplement their portion (Article 2451, *acción de complemento*), in case it is less than the "reserve" they have a right to receive.

14 A SPECIAL PROVISION FOR HANDICAPPED HEIRS

Article 2448 allows a person to use a portion otherwise reserved to family members to improve the situation of a handicapped ascendants or descendants. The spouse has been sadly excluded from this benefit. The defunct might also establish a trust, but according to actual regulation of trusts, the amount that can be passed by the trust is very restricted (the rules of the "réserve" apply, and according to the new wording, only the disposable portion could be passed by a trust).

15 RIGHT OF REPRESENTATION

Heirship might come by own right of the heir or by representation (Articles 2426 and ff.). Heirship by representation takes place when the descendants of an heir who is unworthy or renounces to the heirship, inherit taking his place in the inheritance (per stirpes). Descendants that have equal standing inherit by number of people. For example if a father of three children, son the defunct would die before the defunct or repudiate the inheritance, their three children would inherit the share that the father would have received in the succession of their grandfather.

The right of representation only works within intestate succession.

16 TESTAMENTARY SUCCESSION

A person may decide to pass with wealth to the living by making a will. Since this testament will become effective only upon death, when the testator will no longer there to explain himself, as it usually happens in comparative legal systems, a will must be clothed in certain solemnities, and will be interpreted under strict rules. Because it is a will, freedom and full capacity of the testator are required. Since it is the last will the law is interested in, wills may be revoked any time before death.

In Argentina, the right to dispose of wealth by a testament is restricted to the disposable portion. To grant free will, joint reciprocal testaments are forbidden.

Testaments must be written, solemn (according to the formalities determined by the law, Articles 2477, 2479, defects will imply the nullity of the testament), it is revocable, it is a personal an individual act, and it the document in which it is written is autosufficient (it may not be completed with external documents or proof).[19]

A testament may not only contain the disposal of the wealth, it may also contain a clause of recognition of a child or other dispositions of spiritual, personal or medical nature, such as decisions on how the testator wants to be buried, if he wants to be an organ donor, he may appoint an executor to the will, or revoke a previous will.

Interpretation of wills will be based on the determination of the real will of the testator. Words will be understood preferably in their current use, unless the testator had a special qualification. The rules or interpretation of contracts apply subsidiarily.

Any person can make a will, if they have come off age and they are mentally able. A person is not able to testate if he is unable to communicate his will or express it in any way. This is the case of a person who cannot communicate themselves in oral or written manner.

A testament is a juridical act. So, if it was made without willfulness, because of an error, fraud or deceit or violence. It is also void if it does not have the required formalities.

There are two kinds of testaments are admitted. The holographic will and will by a public deed. Holographic testament is the testament that has been entirely written, dated and signed by the testator. A testament by a notary act is a testament made before a notary and two witnesses (Article 2479).

Testaments may be revoked at any time. A revocation of a testament maybe express or implicit. If the testator marries after the testament, it is understood that the former testament is no longer valid, unless he appointed as universal inheritor the person he later married.

17 PROBATE PROCEEDINGS

Probate proceedings are meant to identify successors, to determine the contents of the heirship, settle the debts and pay legacies and bequeaths.

The jurisdiction is determined according to the last domicile of the defunct. The same judge has jurisdiction on the petition of the inheritance, administration, partition, administration, etc.

When filing the proceeding, the plaintiff has to state the name of the defunct, with the death record, the last domicile of the defunct (which will establish the jurisdiction), indicate who the presumptive heirs are, with their domicile if possible, and whatever other circumstance relevant to the case.

The judge will usually request to service the process to the other heirs. It will usually ask for a service of process by publication of one or two days in a newspaper. A judicial request will be made to the registry of testaments to find out if the defunct had left any wills. Another judicial request will be made to the registry of universal proceedings, to find out if any other probate proceeding concerning the same party is going in another jurisdiction. Once all these tasks are completed, and if there are no

19. Medina, Graciela, Rolleri, Gabriel, *Derecho de sucesiones*, Buenos Aires, La Ley, 2017.

other heirs, the judge will dictate the "declaration of heirship." From then on the proceedings in order to achieve partition will start.

If there were a will, the judge will have to open the testament, if it were a holographic testament and see that the writing corresponds to that of the testator. A list of assets and an appraisal of those assets takes place. The heirs or the judge appoint an administrator of the inheritance. In turn, an expert will be appointed to perform the division of the heirship.

Further Reading

Cordoba, Marcos M., Ferrer, Francisco M., *Manual de Sucesiones,* Buenos Aires, Eudeba, 2016.

Cordoba, Marcos M., Ferrer, Francisco M., *Práctica de derecho sucesorio,* Buenos Aires, Astrea, 2016.

Medina, Graciela M., Rolleri, Gabriel, *Derecho sucesorio,* Buenos Aires, Abeledo Perrot, 2017.

Ferrer, Francisco M. In Alterini, Jorge H., *Código Civil y Comercial Comentado. Tratado Exegético. Volume XI.* Buenos Aires, La Ley, 2016.

CHAPTER 10
Criminal Law

Juan Manuel Sarrabayrouse & Facundo Sarrabayrouse

1 CRIMINAL LAW IN THE ARGENTINE CONSTITUTION

Criminal Law in Argentina is limited by a series of principles that derive from the National Constitution. At the same time, these principles legitimate the criminal system as a whole, as it is the most intense tool bestowed upon the State to face crime. These principles, as the rest of the rights included in the Constitution, are superior and preeminent to any law of Congress and, therefore, no law can be opposed to them. If in any specific case, it is understood that an article in the Penal Code or a supplementary law opposes to any Constitutional clause, its unconstitutionality must be declared.

The Argentine Republic is a federal country that is subdivided into twenty-three provinces and the Autonomous City of Buenos Aires, which has a similar status to a province and it is the federal capital of the nation (*See* chapter on Constitutional law). The word "federal" when applied to law or a body rule in the whole country. The rights codified in the National Constitution are applicable all around the country, both in the federal and the provinces justice system. Notwithstanding, most of these rights are also established in the Constitutions of the local states.

In Argentina any Judge of the Nation, both of the federal or local justice system, can declare that a law is unconstitutional. In a similar way to the United States judicial review system, the Constitution does not expressly provide that the judicial power has this power but the Supreme Court has implied it from other constitutional clauses since the end of the Nineteenth century.[1] Although any judge can review the constitutionality of a law, the Supreme Court has said that this is an act of serious institutional

1. *D. Eduardo Sojo, por recurso de Habeas Corpus, contra una resolución de la H. Cámara de Diputados de la Nación*, CVIII., CSJN 32:120 (1887) and *La Municipalidad de la Capital c. D. Isabel A. De Elortondo, sobre expropiación; por inconstitucionalidad de la ley de 31 de Octubre de 1881*, XL., CSJN 33:162 (1888).

relevance and, therefore, must be the last resort of the Judiciary (it can only happen when there is no other possible interpretation that can preserve the validity of the law) and *ad casum* (i.e., it has effects only in the concrete case and does not imply the overruling of the law).

The most relevant constitutional rights and principles in Argentine Criminal Law are the legality, culpability, proportionality and privacy principles.

1.1 Principle of Legality

Principle of Legality has a fundamental relevance in Criminal Law as it establishes that no person can be punished as a criminal offender unless his conduct is defined as a crime (a felony or a misdemeanor) by a statute issued by the National or Federal Congress. Article 75 (12) of the National Constitution rule that only the National Congress can issue statutes regarding Criminal Law and responsibility. On this matter, local governments can only issue statutes regarding Criminal Procedure. Therefore, Provinces and the City of Buenos Aires cannot create, modify or in any way regulate criminal offenses.

This principle is derived from Articles 18 and 19 of the National Constitution.

Article 18 is one of the constitutional clauses with the most profuse Criminal Law content, states that "No habitant of the Nation can be punished without a previous trial founded in a statute issued before the facts of the process… ."

On the other hand, Article 19 states in its final sentence that "No habitant of the Nation will be obliged to do what law does not requires nor deprived of whatever it is not through it forbidden."

From both constitutional clauses, in addition to the cited Article 75 (12) of the Constitution (that states that the Federal Congress, i.e., the Legislative Power, is the only one in charge of regulating the Penal Code), it has been interpreted by case law and doctrine that criminal offenses and punishment not only have to be regulated by Congress Law, but—to be constitutional under the scope of the Principle of Legality—this law must be written, previous to the conduct, strictly interpreted, and certain (*nullum crimen nulla poena sine lege scripta, praevia, stricta et certa*).[2]

The consequence of the written requirement is the exclusion of the existence of criminal offenses created by custom or habit. Under this scope, habits or customs cannot create or modify Criminal Law. The philosophical reason is that, as Criminal Law is the most extreme and serious means that a State has to react against harmful individual conducts, a citizen should have the possibility to effectively know which are the prohibited or banned actions and which conducts are permitted. This does not normally happen when a criminal offense can be created by custom or habit.

Additionally, the statute that creates the criminal offense must be *previous* to the accused action. This means that an offense cannot be prosecuted under the scope of a law that is subsequent to it. This principle has also been called of nonretroactivity of

2. Cf. Guillermo J. Yacobucci, *El sentido de los principios penales. Su naturaleza y funciones en la argumentación penal*, 261–291 (1st ed., Editorial Ábaco de Rodolfo Depalma, Buenos Aires 2002).

criminal law. The only exception to this rule is when the subsequent law is more benign to the defendant´s interests (i.e., if a criminal offense is overruled by a new statute, then the defendant that committed such action prior to the modification should be acquitted).

This principle of *irretroactivity* is regulated by Article 2 of the Penal Code, which states:

> If the applicable law at the time of commission of the crime was different to the one existing at the verdict time or any moment in between, the applicable law will be the one that is more beneficial to the defendant interests. If during the sentence a more beneficial law is passed, actual punishment will be limited to the amount established by that new law… .

The Principle of Legality also demands the criminal law or statute to be strictly interpreted, which means that analogy is forbidden as a valid method of interpretation. Analogy is a mechanism that assigns the same legal consequence to similar factual situations not expressly provided by the statute. If analogy was allowed in criminal law interpretation, it could imply the sentencing of defendants to sanctions for conducts that were not initially provided by the statute. The only exception to this rule is when analogy is used *in bonam partem*, this means, when it benefits the defendant´s position in some way. For this reason, if the statute is deemed obscure or incomplete the court could appeal to analogical reasoning either as a base for an acquittal or a not guilty verdict or as a way to give the defendant a more lenient treatment.

Finally, the Principle of Legality requires the law or statute to be certain, this is, that the statute should narrowly tailor the definition of criminal offenses. As a consequence, the Constitution prohibits ambiguous or excessively open statutory definition of criminal offenses. The reason that supports this rule is that an ambiguous or unclear law may allow an unreasonably amount of plausible interpretations, becoming very difficult for individuals to understand the limits of their actions (which, in consequence, will not be able to motivate its conduct properly).

1.2 Principle of Culpability

The Principle of Culpability it is implicitly derived from Articles 18 and 19 of de Constitution.

In addition to the past transcriptions of those clauses, and independently of the fact that it deals with an implicitly derived principle, Article 18 states the following:

> All prisons of the Nation shall be healthy and clean, for security and not for the punishment of the prisoners, and any judge that authorizes a measure that inflicts an excessive mortification under the pretext of precaution will be held liable.

As a foundation of punishment, this principle requires the criminal offense to be attributed both objectively and subjectively to its author.[3] First, this means that a

3. *Parafina del Plata S.A.C.I. s/ recurso de apelación—impuesto a los réditos (multa)*, CSJN 271:97 (1968).

person shall only be criminally liable and punished for a personal conduct of his own, not being possible to attribute him conducts carried out by third parties (personality principle).

As it was said, culpability principle demands the criminal offense to be attributed to the defendant both objectively and subjectively. The objective attribution of an offense in Argentine law has a similar content to the *actus reus* concept on common law and it demands the prosecutor to prove that the defendant's voluntary act complies with the legal description of a criminal offense and that it has caused the harm stated by the law.

Finally, the exigency of a subjective attribution has some parallel with the common law concept of *mens rea* and requires the criminal act to be done with the particular mental state provided for in the statutory definition of the offense. In Argentine Criminal Law, statutes provide for two main types of criminal mental states: intent or negligence. In this sense, strict liability offenses are unconstitutional and criminal responsibility can only be subsequent to a knowing and willful conduct or to a reckless or negligent action.

1.3 Principle of Proportionality

The Principle of Proportionality has been implicitly derived by case law from Articles 18 and 28 of the Constitution. Article 28 states that "The principles, guarantees and rights recognized by the previous articles, shall not be altered by the laws that regulate its exercise." Although the clause makes no reference to criminal punishment, it establishes a general standard of adequacy for every law regarding the constitutional human rights. Extrapolated to Criminal Law standards, this principle requires the punishment to be appropriated or adequate to the harm caused by the criminal conduct.

In this sense, the Constitution establishes a threshold on the amount of punishment that should be inflicted as a consequence to a conviction. With some exceptions (i.e., life imprisonment), the Argentine Penal Code provides the court with the option of sentencing the defendant to different punishments (prison, economic fine or disqualification) between a statutory maximum and minimum. The proportionality principle mandates that at sentencing, courts shall not determine a punishment which is disproportional to the seriousness of the offense committed and the defendant's moral blameworthiness.

As it was already mentioned *supra*, Article 18 of the Constitution states:

> All prisons of the Nation shall be healthy and clean, for security and not for the punishment of the prisoners, and any judge that authorizes a measure that inflicts an excessive mortification under the pretext of precaution will be held liable.

Additionally, that same clause establishes that "death penalty for political causes shall be abolished forever, as well as all means of torment and physical punishments." Therefore, it can be concluded that the purpose of punishment in Argentinean legal system is the rehabilitation of the convicted criminal. For this reason, while sentencing courts shall to promote the rehabilitation of the offender. Any excess in relation to that measurement, must be considered unconstitutional on the grounds of the principle of proportionality.

1.4 Right to Privacy

Criminal Law cannot punish any conduct or human action. One of the thresholds of criminal penalties is given by the right to privacy.

Regarding this issue, Article 19 of the Constitution provides that:

> The private actions of men, that in no way offend order and public morals, nor produce harm on a third party, are only reserved to God's judgement, and exempted from the Courts authority.

From this scope, Criminal Law cannot impose any punishment for actions that do not produce harm to the rights or interests of others than the offender. In continental legal systems, it has been interpreted that to be defined as a criminal offenses, a conduct has to produce harm to or endanger what has been called legal interests or goods. These are individual or social interests fundamental for the life in community and that have a certain value to society. Therefore, it is not possible to consider a conduct as a criminal offense when it does not affect or alter those third party interests and it only and exclusively affect the interests of the offender itself. These kind of actions are considered "self-referred" conducts and are excluded from Criminal Law regulations. As a consequence, if a law defines self-referred conduct as a criminal offense, it must be considered unconstitutional. From this perspective, Criminal Law would not be able to punish conducts such as sleeping in a public park, drinking an excessive amount of coffee, smoking tobacco cigarettes, or eating foods with high sodium content. They are all conducts that, in the worst case, only affect the health or other interests exclusively of whom it performs them.

The most recently discussed example is the drug possession offense, when the amount indicates an exclusive personal use. Article 14 of Law No. 23.737 states:

> He who has drugs in its possession shall be imprisoned from one to six years and fine.... The penalty will be from one month to two years when, considering its scarce quantity and other circumstances, possession undoubtedly corresponds to personal use.

Recently, the Supreme Court has ruled that the possession of drugs for personal use cannot be punished as a criminal offense as long as these conducts do not transcend the personal privacy sphere.[4]

4. *Arriola, Sebastián y otros s/causa n° 9080*, A. 891. XLV., CSJN 332:1963 (2009).

2 SOURCES OF CRIMINAL LAW: PRINCIPLE OF LEGALITY, THE PENAL CODE AND SUPPLEMENTARY LEGISLATION

As stated before, one of the consequences derived from the Principle of Legality is that judicial precedents have no binding effects on the definition of a criminal offense. Although they do have interpretative relevance, they cannot be considered as binding to inferior courts as the *stare decisis* doctrine is not applicable in Argentine case law. Therefore, the only source of Criminal Law is a statute issued by the Federal Congress.

The only partial exception to this principle is the Supreme Court precedents, which have been said to be morally binding to inferior courts,[5] and the plenary decisions. These plenary decisions are provided by federal and some local procedure statutes and normally take place when the different Courts of Appeal of the same jurisdiction have different or contradictory precedents regarding equivalent cases. The plenary decisions involve a deliberation between all the specific Court of Appeal's justices, who finally issue the plenary decision which is resolved by the simple majority and whose interpretation shall be binding to inferior courts of the same jurisdiction from that case onward, t. On the Federal Procedure, this binding effect was stated by Article 303 of the National Civil and Commercial Procedure Code. Notwithstanding that, the binding effect of plenary decision is highly controversial and has been ruled unconstitutional by some Courts under the Principle of Legality. On 2013, Law No. 26.853 abrogated Articles 294–299 and 303 of the National Civil and Commercial Procedure Code so, although on local jurisdictions there are still discussions over the binding effect of plenary cases, on the federal system this constitutional problem has been solved.

Taking into account the previous considerations, judicial precedents generally only preserve an interpretative value and are only considered a source of knowledge, but not a binding source of law.

On the other hand, as in most of continental legal systems, doctrine and legal expert opinion's have no authority at all. It is simply a source of knowledge and can only be useful as a means of interpretation of the law, but in no way it can create it or modify it.

According to the previously stated considerations, only the following statutes are the source of Argentine Criminal Law.

2.1 The Argentine Penal Code

The most important Criminal Law source is the Argentine Penal Code, which is divided in two books. In the scope of Article 75 (12) of the Constitution, only the National Congress can legislate on criminal matters and can issue, overrule or amend the Penal Code.

5. *Pastorino, Bernardo capitán de la barca "Nuovo Principio" v. Ronillon Marini y Cía.*, LXVII., CSIN 25.364 (1883).

The First Book establishes the general rules applicable to Criminal Law as a whole and to the attribution of the criminal offenses described in the Penal Code and the supplementary or special criminal legislation. In the case of supplementary or special criminal legislation, the general rules provided at the Penal Code are applicable as long as there is no other contradictory rule in the corresponding special law.

In this sense, Article 4 of the Penal code states, "The general rules of this code will be applicable to all criminal offenses established by special laws, as long as these do not specify the contrary."

Among the rules included in the First Book of the Penal Code, there are the "Criminal Law Application" (Title, Articles 1–4), "The Penalties" (Title II, Articles 5–25), "Conditional Conviction" similar to common law Probation (Title III, Articles 26–29), "Reparation of Damages" (Title III, Articles 30–33), "Attribution of Criminal Responsibility" (Title IV, Articles 34–41), "Attempt" (Title V, Articles 42–44), "Main Offender and Accomplice Liability" (Title VII, Articles 45–49), "Recidivism" (Title VII, Articles 50–53), "Rules for the Treatment of Multiplicity of Criminal Offenses" (Title IX, Articles 54–58), "Extinction of Criminal Action and Penalties" (Title X, Articles 59–70), "The Exercise of Criminal Action" (Title XI, Articles 71–76), "Suspension of Trial on Probation" (Title XII, Articles 76*bis*–76*quater*), "Meaning of Terms Used in the Penal Code" (Title XIII, Articles 77–78).

On the other hand, the Second Book of the Penal Code establishes a catalogue of common (nonfederal) offenses and its extenuating and aggravating circumstances which are organized according to the legal interests affected by each of them, beginning with individual interests through general, social or community interests. In this way, this Book first describe the "Offenses that affect Life and Physical Integrity" (Title I, Articles 79–108), "Offenses that affect against Private Honor or Reputation" (Title II, Articles 109–117*bis*), "Sexual Offenses" (Title III, Articles 118–133), "Offenses against Civil Status" (Title IV, Articles 134–*139bis*), "Offenses that affect Individual Liberty" (Title V, Articles 140–161), "Property Offenses" (Title VI, Articles 162–185), "Public Security Offenses" (Title VII, Articles 186–208), "Offenses that affect Public Order" (Title VIII, Articles 209–213bis), "Offenses that affect National Security" (Title IX, Articles 214–225), "Offenses against the Constitutional Order" (Title X, Articles 226–236), "Public Administration and Corruption Offenses" (Title XI, Articles 237–281*bis*), "Offenses that affect Public Faith" (Title XII, Articles 282–302), and "Economic and Financial Order Offenses" (Title XIII, Articles 303–313).

The structure of the crimes established in the Second Book is built with a factual description of the criminal conduct and the specification of the legal consequence or penalty for it. For example, the Article 79 of the Penal Code states the homicide felony: "He who kills another person shall be secluded or imprisoned from eight to twenty-five years, unless this code does establishes another penalty for this action." The kinds of penalties or sanctions that can be imposed as a consequence of a criminal offense are defined by Article 5 of the Penal Code: "The penalties that can be imposed under this Code are the following: seclusion, prison, fine, and disqualification."

Originally, seclusion and imprisonment penalties were sought to be served in different establishments (and the former included the imposition of forced labor and physical punishments) and had a number of practical differences (feasibility of domiciliary detention—Article 10—, terms to be eligible for parole—Article 13—, how the preventive imprisonment or detention is counted at sentencing—Article 24—, feasibility of conditional conviction—Article 26—, a more severe mandatory minimum and maximum for an attempted offense that when fully committed is sanctioned with life seclusion—Article 44—and for a secondary accomplice—Article 46—of an offense sanctioned with life seclusion. Nevertheless, the Supreme Court recently ruled that, in the scope of Law No. 24.660 of Penitentiary Regime, any difference in the execution of both types of imprisonment have been abrogated.[6]

Prison, fine and disqualification penalties are often divisible and, as such, established between a mandatory minimum and a maximum stated for each specific criminal offense and the Court is in charge of determining the applicable term of imprisonment at sentencing, under the objective and subjective circumstances enumerated in Articles 40 and 41 of the Penal Code. The former states:

> When a penalty is divisible in terms of time or quantity, Courts will establish a sentence according to particular extenuating or aggravating circumstances of each case and according to the rules of the following article.

Coherently, Article 41 states:

> To the effects of the previous article, it will be considered: (1) The nature of the conduct and of the means used to execute it and the extent of the damage and the danger caused; (2) The age, education, customs, and precedent conduct of the individual, the quality of the motives that determined him to commit the crime, especially the misery or the difficulty to earn its own living or their relatives, the degree of involvement in the criminal action, the recidivism in which he would have incurred, and the rest of his background and personal conditions, as well as its personal bonds, the quality of people and circumstances of time, place, manner and occasion that exhibit his dangerousness … .

2.2 Supplementary Legislation

The most important supplementary legislation of the Penal Code are the International Human Rights Treaties with Constitutional Hierarchy. Article 75 (22), second paragraph, of the Constitution, gives a catalogue of Human Rights International Treaties to which assigns constitutional hierarchy. The clause, however, specifies those treaties:

> have constitutional hierarchy, do not abrogate any article from the first part of this constitution [the one that specifies the principles, rights and guarantees of the individuals], and must be considered supplementary to the rights and guarantees recognized by it.

Most of the treaties mentioned in that clause (e.g., the American Declaration of Rights and Duties of the Man, the Universal Declaration of Human Rights, the American Convention of Human Rights, and the International Pact of Civil and Political

6. *Méndez, Nancy Noemí s/homicidio atenuado -causa n° 862-*, M. 447. XXXIX., CSJN 328:137 (2005).

Rights) contemplate and establish Criminal Law principles and rights, such as due process, legality, reasonable duration of criminal process, culpability, proportionality, and privacy, along with many other.

The first paragraph of Article 75 (22), states that any other treaty (many of those which have relevant Criminal Law clauses) signed with another nation and with international organizations, does not have constitutional hierarchy but are superior to Congress Law. In this way, both kinds of treaties are of superior hierarchy than the Penal Code.

Additionally, the Criminal Law system is also integrated by a very vast number of special criminal laws and criminal law clauses included in common Congress Law, which may describe other criminal offenses or provide rules that are related to the prosecution of criminal conducts. These laws also regulate criminal matter and are supplementary to the Penal Code. Examples of special criminal laws are Law No. 19.359 of Foreign Exchange Criminal Regime (which provides the regulation of foreign exchange regime crimes and its special judiciary system), Law No. 24.769 of Tax Evasion and Fiscal Fraud Regime (that provides the regulation to that kind of federal offenses), and Law No. 23.737 of Drug Traffic and Possession. On the other hand, some examples of criminal law clauses included in common Congress Law are Articles 860–891 of the Law No. 22.415 of Customs Law Code (which provides the regulations related to the contraband offense) and the Articles 71–78 of the Law No. 11.723 of Intellectual Property.

2.3 Crime and Criminal Liability in the Penal Code. The Tripartite Structure of Theory of Crime in Argentina. Crime as a Typical, Unlawful, and Blameworthy Conduct

Although not specifically or literally stated in the Penal Code, it has been considered by judicial precedents and doctrine that a criminal offense is defined as a conduct or human act legally described as an offense by the law, which is unlawful or opposed to the legal system and whose offender is blameworthy or culpable). This tripartite structure of a criminal offense is the consequence of the evolution of the continental Theory of Crime. Only a human act consisting in all four characteristics can be considered as a criminal offense and, accordingly, only in those cases a conviction and a punishment can be imposed to the offender. If any of those qualities is missing in the human act, it is not possible to conclude that a crime was committed, and therefore a conviction and the imposition of a penalty are forbidden.

2.3.1 Criminal Conduct: Act and Omission

In Criminal Law, a conduct is considered as a human positive act or an omission (i.e., excluding thoughts or mere intentions), which are voluntary and conscious. These requirements are similar to common law *actus reus* requirement. Although the punished conduct can be either a human act a simple omission, the Principle of Legality demands either one of them to be expressly descripted as such in the criminal statute.

In proportion, omission crimes are significantly reduced in relation to active conduct crimes. The philosophical foundation of this is that on any liberal political system, omission offenses can invade or affect individual liberty in a more intense way than active conduct offenses; therefore, they must be exceptional. This is why the general rule is that a regular person has no criminal obligation to prevent crime.

An example of an active conduct crime is Article 172 of the Penal Code (Embezzlement), which states:

> He who economically deceives another person through the use of a false name, a simulated quality, false titles, false influence, abuse of trust or by faking goods possession, credit, commission, enterprise or negotiation, or any other scheme or ruse will be punished with imprisonment from one month to six years.

Opposed to the prior, an example of an omission offense can be found in Article 108 of the Penal Code (Omission of Assistance), which states:

> He who, having found a minor under ten years old or a wounded or disabled person or one threatened by whatever danger who is lost or helpless and omits to give him the necessary assistance when he could do so without personal risk, or does not give immediate call to authority shall be punished with a fine from seven hundred and fifty to twelve thousand five hundred ARS.

Another exception to the general rule occurs when the person is legally or contractually obliged to prevent it (i.e., a mother has to feed her newborn child and purposely failing to do so could be considered as homicide; a life guard must help a person drowning in a pool and intentional omission of aiding and the subsequent death of the swimmer could also be considered as homicide). This kind of cases are the only ones in which an active conduct offense can be charged to someone that omitted a conduct.

Notwithstanding the above mentioned, the Penal Code excludes from the concept of conduct certain forms of human acts that are not considered as such, like acts affected by complete unconsciousness or irresistible force, and reflex acts.

Article 34 (1), first paragraph, states that it is not punishable:

> He who could not, at the moment of the event... because of his state of unconsciousness... not attributed to his fault, understand the criminality of his acts or direct his actions.

This clause excludes from the concept of conduct and, accordingly, reliefs from criminal consequences, those human acts that happen under an unconscious state (e.g., sleep-walking, complete intoxication by drugs or alcohol, and reflex acts) and that cannot be attributed to the person's will.

Additionally, Article 34 (2) of the Penal Code states it is also not punishable:

> He who acted moved by irresistible physical force ... .

This clause excludes the concept of conduct and, accordingly, exempts from criminal consequences, to the human acts that are a direct consequence of inevitable physical forces, for example, the pushing of a person by a crowd or any natural force that, as a result, forces that person to cause harm.

As a summary, a conduct includes a voluntary, conscious and positive act or omission that it is not excluded by any of the causes mentioned above.

2.3.2 Legal Description of the Criminal Offense (Hereinafter Named as "Tipicity")

For a conduct to be deemed as a criminal offense it should be legally described as such by the Penal Code or supplementary legislation. The concept of *"Tipicity"* is derived, first, from the German sociologist Max Webber who, in the late nineteenth century, defined *tipus* as a conceptual criteria to place certain social events in causal sociological processes. That concept was then collected by Ernst Beling, a German jurist who, in the early 1930s elaborated the analogue concept of *Tatbestand* (or *Deliktstypus*) that served as the objective factual platform to consider a certain conduct as a crime. For that reason, there is no identical term for Tipicity in common law, which analyses many of its elements when discussing the occurrence of *actus reus* and *mens rea*. Notwithstanding that, this concept must be understood as the legal description of the objective and subjective elements of the criminal offense.

Accordingly, to fulfill with the Tipicity objective and subjective requirements the conduct must be provided exactly and strictly in the criminal legal description and, on the other hand, the particular state of mind provided in the definition of the offense (intent or negligence) must be fulfilled.

From the objective point of view, Tipicity has a strict relationship with the Principle of Legality, as it requires the conduct to be able to be subsumed as strictly as possible in the criminal legal description. In this way, each and every relevant characteristic of the conduct must be included in the description, whereas—if not—that conduct must be judged atypical and therefore not a criminal offense.

From the subjective perspective, once that a conduct can be objectively subsumed upon the terms provided by the legal description of the offense, the statutory mental state must be verified, this is, the human act must respond to either intent or negligence. Although it is not specifically stated by the Penal Code, as a direct consequence of the Principle of Legality, Argentine Criminal Law is ruled by the *numerus clausus* principle, which means that the general rule is that criminal offenses descripted in the law are to be considered exclusively as intentional offenses. As an exception, the legislator can describe negligent offenses but these are only considered as such when formally described as such by the criminal statute. In this way, negligent offenses are normally drafted including the following wording.

As an example of a negligent offense, negligent homicide is provided by Article 84 of the Penal Code, which states:

> He who causes the death of another person as a result of imprudence, a negligence act, unskillfulness in its art or profession or a breach of regulations or duties at his charge shall be punished with imprisonment from six months to five years and special disqualification, if corresponds, from five to ten years.

On the other hand, an example of an intentional offense, assault is described by the Article 89, which states:

> He who causes harm to another person's body or health shall be punished with imprisonment from a month to a year, unless it is not punished by another clause of this code.

Another form of conduct that might be considered negligent is the result produced by a factual error or mistake of fact. In this way, Article 34 (1), first paragraph, states it is not punishable, "He who could not, at the moment of the event... because of... error... not attributed to his fault, understand the criminality of his acts ... ."

A Tipicity error or mistake (similar to common law mistake of fact) is considered by doctrine and judicial precedents as the one that relies on any of the objective elements of the legal description of the criminal offense. Accordingly, if the knowledge regarding those elements by the offender is mistaken, his actions cannot be considered intentional. For example, if a hunter believes he is shooting a deer but by mistake he shoots another hunter who is hidden in the bushes, his knowledge of the factual element "another person" in the scope of the homicide description (Article 79 of the Penal Code) is under error and, therefore, his conduct cannot be judged as intentional.

In the case that the error is evitable or unreasonable, under common prudence standards, his conduct could be considered as a negligent one in the scope of Article 84 of the Penal Code, described *supra*.

On the other hand, in the case the error is considered inevitable or reasonable, his conduct cannot be judged as intentional nor negligent, thus, it is not criminal.

It may also happen that the error is considered evitable, therefore his conduct might be negligent, but the action is not described in a negligent way in any Criminal Law clause. In that case, the conduct is considered atypical and, thus, not criminal. An example of this can be found with the crime of vandalism, which is only described as an intentional offense by Article 184 of the Penal Code, which states:

> He who destroys, renders useless, makes disappear, or in any way damages another person's movable property or real estate or an animal shall be punished with imprisonment from fifteen days to a year ... .

As this crime has not an equivalent negligent offense, in the case (e.g.,) that a person damages something that believes to be abandoned and, therefore, that is not property of another person, if it results that the item was effectively property of someone else, then his conduct is atypical and not criminal, even though his error was evitable.

If it is concluded that the conduct is described objectively as a felony in Criminal Law and that it responds to one of the both subjective standards (intention or negligence), the conduct is considered typical and, therefore, it can be analyzed in the next level of the Theory of Crime.

2.3.3 Unlawfulness or Opposition to the Rest of the Legal System

A conduct that is typical can, yet, be considered legal as it might be authorized by a justification defense. Some of the provisions that might permit a typical conduct are present in the Penal Code, but it can also be found others in the rest of the Legal System. The philosophical foundation for this requirement (the opposition to the rest of the legal system) is that a conduct cannot be considered a crime if, although being described as it in Criminal Law, is on the other hand admitted by the legal system in the scope of another provision. As Criminal Law has no higher hierarchy than any other Congress Law, a permit or a right regulated by another section (civil, administrative, etc.) of Law prevents the conduct of being considered a crime.

As an example of a right in the Legal System, outside the Penal Code, that prevents a conduct to be considered a Crime, it can be mentioned the retention right, that authorizes, in the scope of Article 2587 of the Civil and Commercial Code, any creditor of a certain and executable obligation to "retain in its possession the thing that must return to the debtor, until the payment of what it is owed in reason of that thing." The most common example to this case is the one of a mechanic, that retains in his possession the car that was delivered to him for fixing, as long as the debtor pays the fee he owes. Abstractly, retention of that sort would be typical in the scope of Article 173 (2) of the Penal Code, that states that it is punishable with prison:

> He who, in damage of another person, denies restitution or does not restitutes in due time, money, goods or any other movable property that has been given as a deposit, commission, administration or other title that produces the obligation of giving or returning.

Notwithstanding that Criminal Law clause, and although the conduct of the mechanic is described accurately by the Article 173 (2) of the Penal Code, it is not opposed to the rest of the legal system as it is specifically allowed or permitted by the Article 2587 of the Civil and Commercial Code. Consequently, it cannot be considered a crime.

The causes of unopposed to the legal system typical conducts that, on the other hand, are provided in the Penal Code are: the abiding of a duty, the exercise of a right, authority or charge, the due obedience, justified necessity state, and self-defense.

Article 34 (4) states it is not punishable "The one who acts in the abiding of a duty, or in the legitimate exercise of a right, authority or charge," and Article 34 (5), gives the same solution to "The one that acted in the scope of due obedience." All of those situations exclude the opposition to the legal system and, as they accordingly direct the interpretation to other legal clauses, their function is rather similar to the situation mentioned *supra* (the exercise of a right provided in the noncriminal legal system).

Justified necessity state is regulated by Article 34 (3), which states that it is not punishable "The one that causes harm with the intent of avoiding a major one, which is imminent and not created by him." In this case, the different in importance of the harm caused in relation to the one avoided is crucial, as this ponderation is the one that supports the justification of the conduct. If the harm provoked is higher or equally relevant to the one avoided, the conduct is not justified and, therefore, it is effectively opposed to the legal system. In the scope of that clause it is also relevant that the harm avoided is imminent (i.e., it must be just about to occur or already happening), and must not be caused by the same person who is avoiding it because, in that case, his conduct is not justified or permitted.

Lastly, self-defense is regulated in Article 34 (6) and 34 (7) (the latter establishes the defense ability of the rights or interests of a third party), as the former states it is not punishable:

> He who acts in self-defense or of his rights, as long as concur all the following circumstances:
>
> a) Illegitimate aggression;
> b) Rational necessity of the means used to prevent or repel it;
> c) Lack of sufficient provocation from the one who defends itself.

In the scope of this rule, it is required that one is suffering at the moment an aggression (because one can only "repel" an actual offense) or an imminent one (because only such conduct can be "prevent[ed]"), that has to be illegal, although not necessarily considered a crime (e.g., an invasion of privacy, which is not provided as a crime in the Penal Code, is still an illegitimate aggression according to Civil Law).

On the other hand, the means used to react to the aggression have to be rationally necessary, in the sense that it has to be proportionate; and the aggression should not have been provoked by the person who is defending himself, because, if that is so, the aggression is not illegitimate, but—precisely—a prior self-defense.

Once that the conduct is judged objectively and subjectively typical and the illegality of such conduct is not excluded by one of the causes of justification described *supra*, then the conduct is considered in opposition to the rest of the legal system and, although, and although the presence of a crime may not yet be established, it can be analyzed in the next level of *the Theory of Crime*.

2.3.4 Culpability or Blameworthiness

Culpability or blameworthiness is the recrimination or reproach judgment that the legal system exerts to a person who commits a criminal act as it is legally defined and he is morally accountable for it. In a comparison with common law, culpability takes place when both *actus reus* and *mens rea* occur and the offender has no legal excuse for his act. It was explained that on the prior level of the *Theory of Crime* (unlawfulness), certain conducts that are legally descripted as crimes are nonetheless permitted or authorized by the law (enabling a justification defense). Therefore, although objectively defined as a crime and *mens rea* occurs, the justified conduct is deemed as socially acceptable or even positively valued by society. On the other side, in the level of culpability or blameworthiness, the scope of analysis is not one of permission, authorization or justification, but one of tolerance or excuse. Under these circumstances, a person can carry out a conduct that could be legally defined as a crime with the statutory state of mind (*mens rea*) and no justification but yet his action could be tolerated or excused by the law because an exceptional factual situation made him unaccountable for his action.

The main practical difference between these two level of analysis (unlawfulness and blameworthiness/culpability or justification and excuse defenses) on Argentine Law is that a justified conduct excludes the defendant´s civil liability and an unlawful (but excused) act is considered as tortious and will result in civil liability and the burden to compensate for the damages. This is because lack of culpability or blameworthiness can make a conduct tolerable but in no way can exclude civil responsibility for the harm done.

The first excuse defense established by the Argentine Penal Code is the lack of capability of culpability. In some cases the law presumes the absence of this capacity, for example in the case of minors that commit an unlawful act. Law No. 22.278 rules the Juvenile Criminal Regime and on Article 1 defines that any minor under sixteen years old lacks of capacity of culpability for any crime, both misdemeanor or felony. The same clause says that minors between sixteen and eighteen years old lacks of blameworthiness for any misdemeanor punished with an economic fine, a disqualification or prison that doesn't exceeds of two years or any privately prosecutable offense.[7] The Juvenile Criminal Regime sets up the consequences applicable to any minor that lacks of blameworthiness (i.e., awarding a tutor, impose behavior rules, or any other security measures useful for the reeducation or rehabilitation of the minor).

The second excuse defense on the Penal Code is the insanity defense. On the Argentine legal system insanity by itself is not enough to prove the lack of culpability. Instead, this excuse legislated on Article 34 (1) of the Penal Code requires that the insane or mentally ill or perturbed person could not understand the criminal nature of its conduct or could not decide the curse of its actions, any of them required to take place at the same time the action was carried out. If the defendant proves the legal extents of the insanity excuse, the court must acquit him but it could order any security measure or reclusion necessary to neutralize the risk of harming itself or others. A person who suffers an alteration of its mental faculties because of intoxication can also fence the insanity excuse, although jurisprudence did not accept the defense when the defendant purposely intoxicated himself to expedite its action.

A third excuse defense is the mistake of law. Although as a general principle the rule is *ignorantia legis neminem excusat*, or ignorance of law excuse no one, Argentine case law has accepted some situations in which a mistake of law excuses an unlawful action. First of all, ignorance or error could involve the knowledge that a conduct constitutes an offense (direct mistake of law) or the knowledge about the existence of a justification or permit situation (indirect mistake of law, i.e., if the defendant wrongfully thought a self-defense situation occurred). Most Argentine courts have

7. These are a set of offenses that the Penal Code orders to be prosecuted only by the victim and no public prosecutor is involved. According to Art. 73 of the Penal Code, these are the libel or slander offenses (Arts. 109 and 110 of the Penal Code); disclosure of classified information offenses (Arts. 153 to 157*bis* of the Penal Code, except Arts. 154 and 157); unfair or unlawful competition (Art. 159) and breach of alimony burden, when the spouse is the victim.

ruled that such mistakes eliminate culpability when inevitable or reasonable, that is, when the defendant had no acceptable available means to correct the mistake. On the other hand, when the defendant had reasonable means to avoid it, the mistake can only reduce the degree of punishment as a mitigating factor.

Finally, Article 34 (2) establishes the lack of blameworthiness when the defendant acted forced by a menace of a serious and imminent harm. This happens when the defendant is under duress or necessity but, differently with the justification defense, the choice is between evils that affect interests of similar hierarchy (i.e., on a shipwreck, a person fights and drown another survivor for the only life-saving floatable jacket). In these cases, courts have accepted the exclusion of culpability (not unlawfulness) on the grounds that on extreme cases it may not be acceptable to demand heroism or sacrifice from someone who suffers a situation of grave danger. For as to this defense to be effective, the defendant must prove that he is not responsible for the risk that occurred (on the past example, that he did not provoke the shipwreck) or that he is not legally obliged to tolerate that risk (if the defendant was part of the crew).

Further Reading

Baigun, David & Zaffaroni, Eugenio (Directores), Terragni, Marco (coordinador), "Código Penal y normas complementarias". Editorial Hammurabi-José Luis Depalma-, 2da edición, Buenos Aires, mayo 2007.

Borinsky, Mariano Hernán, "Derecho Penal Económico y de la Empresa", Buenos Aires, Ad-Hoc, 2004.

Creus, Carlos, Derecho Penal, Parte especial, t.1 y 2, 3ra edición actualizada, Buenos Aires, Astrea 1990.

D'alessio, Andrés José (director) y DIVITO, Mauro(coordinador), "Código Penal de la Nación. Comentado y Anotado", 2da edición actualizada y ampliada, Editorial LL, Buenos Aires, 2009 (3 tomos).

Donna, Edgardo Alberto, Derecho Penal. Parte Especial, Tomo II-B, Santa Fe, Rubinzal, Culzoni, 2001.

Fontán Balestra, Tratado de Derecho Penal- Parte General, Bs. As., Abeledo Perrot, 1980.

Soler, Sebastián, Derecho Penal Argentino, tomos III, IV y V, Bs. As., Tea, 1978.

CHAPTER 11

Law of Procedure, Mediation and Arbitration

Andrea Mariel Brunetti, Ursula Basset & Eliana M. González

1 GENERAL OVERVIEW ON PROCEDURAL LAW IN ARGENTINA

The *legal process* is the "guarantee of the guarantees," according to Argentine legal doctrine. Indeed, in a Constitutional Rule of Law the judge stands as the main guarantor of the Human Rights and "necessarily in a very concrete way: through the process,"[1] because the ideal tool for the realization of all Human Rights is precisely the judicial process.[2] Nowadays, there is a consensus in the mainstream doctrine in Argentina, that procedural law has to follow the constitutional principles and rules in order to protect the fundamental rights of the persons. In other words, a process is a mean to grant access to the fundamental rights of the citizens under the Rule of Law, and it must therefore be adapted to the constitutional guidelines established for these purposes. States have signed supralegal international treaties and conventions that refer to the minimum or standard jurisdictional guarantees, which also constitute the guarantee of the due legal process, which it cannot be avoided by the infraconstitutional norms, constituting the frame of interpretation of the judicial decisions.[3]

Following this line of reasoning: (a) Argentina has signed a number of Human Rights International Treaties were incorporated in 1994, that was called "the federal

1. Moción de Valencia. Spain, 2006. http://www.academiadederecho.org/.
2. Brunetti, Andrea M.; "La Humanización del Derecho, la tutela judicial efectiva y el debido proceso judicial" Ponencia 1er. Premio: "Cortes del Litoral" XXVI CONGRESO NACIONAL DE DERECHO PROCESAL, Santa Fe, june 2011, Comission of Family Law; www.ar.microjuris.com cite: MJD5398.
3. Gozaini, Osvaldo A. El debidoprocesoconstitucional. Reglas para el control de lospoderesdesde laMagistraturaConstitucional. In Cuestiones Constitucionales No. 7 July—December 2002. http://www.journals.unam.mx/index.php/cuc/article/view/2061.

block of constitutionality" by the authors, or in the terminology of Hart,[4] "the rule of constitutional recognition"; (b) the Supreme Court has already stated, that the treaties must be applied as they were signed, without the possibility of changing or reinterpreting them,[5] therefore, the judges must apply the law according to these fundamental, universal and inalienable principles, and in this way the democracy is assured;[6] (c) this new paradigm applies to procedural law, and is contained in Articles 1 and 2 of the Civil and Commercial Code (CCC), that state the imperative to apply and interpret law according to the National Constitution and the Treaties signed by the Republic of Argentina.

Procedural Law is the branch of the legal science that studies the nature, the development and the effectiveness of all the legal relationships of the legal phenomenon *process*.[7] In the Argemtinian legal system, procedural law is divided by its specialty and by its jurisidiction. This means that: (a) as in other compared legal systems, is at the same time general and specific; (b) Procedure Law is a local matter, and thus each of the twenty-three provinces of Argentina has the competence to issue its own local Procedure Law (the status and competence of the district of Buenos Aires is disputed).

In other words, concerning a), Procedure Law is basically contained in the Civil and Commercial Procedure Law Codes, where the main concepts and foundations of Procedure Law are to be found. However, since some matters, due to the principle of specialty are too peculiar, they have special procedure acts or codes dealing in order to adjust to the specialty of the matter of the substantive law (e.g., Administrative procedure, criminal procedure code, family procedure rules, constitutional procedure, *see* below). On the other hand, for (b), even if Argentina has a National CCC, this code only applies in federal jurisdictions. Each province will issue a local CCC, and special procedure acts according to the specialty principle whenever needed.

4. Hart, Herbert L.A. (1998). El concepto de Derecho. Bs. As., This author says that the law is a complex system of rules, which is composed by imperative or primary rules and by secondary rules: (1) rules of decission; (2) rules of modification; (3) rules of recognition: these establish the guidelines of validity that must be complied by a rule that pretends to be part of the legal system. Meanwhile, Dworkin criticizes the positivism of Hart because it is very narrow. He points out that the legal system is also composed by principles, which incorporation to it is not determined by the way that these are created (i.e., to say, by its "pedigree"), but by the adecuation of its content to the moral *See*: Dworkin, Ronald: Los derechos en serio, Ariel, Barcelona, 1995.
5. "Giroldi" Case; SCJN; 7/4/1995; L.L., 1995-D, 462. *See also*: "Bramajo" Case, CSJN, 12/9/1996; L.L., 1996-E, 409, entre otros. Before the constitutional reform, Argentine Supreme Court supported the superior herarchy of the international treaties in the leading case Ekmedjian (CSJN, 7-7-92; LL, 1992-C-543). After that, it has existed a deep evolution regarding to several important and interesting paradigmatic pronouncements which treatment exceeds the frame of this article. (véase entre otros: CSJN, "Méndez Valles Fernando c/ .A..M. Pescio SCA s/ Ejecución de alquileres" (ED Boletín N° 8976 del 09/04/96), La Corte Suprema en abril de 1998, dentro de los autos "Petric Domagoj c/ Diario Pagina 12" (L.L. 1998—C, 284).
6. According to the concept of the substantial democracy that was expressed by Ferrajoli, which consists on the substantial norms of validity, linksthe protection, the respect to the fundamental rights and the other axiologic principles that are established in them. En Derecho y Razón, *supra*, p. 864.
7. Couture, Eduardo J. Obras, 5ª; Fundamentos del Derecho Procesal Civil. ed., Bs.As., La Ley, 2010, p. 1.

1.1 Procedure Law and Specialty Principle

First, as it happens in other legal systems, procedural law, when applied to certain branches of law acquires a peculiar nature, and is therefore dealt with as a part of each of these branches of law or in a special act or code. Administrativists have their own Administrative Procedure (*see* Chapter 3), family lawyers have a set with their own special procedure rules to be found in the CCC (*see* Chapter 6), there is a code of criminal procedure in Argentina (*see* Chapter 10), there are rules set by the Supreme Court of Justice, partially by the Constitution and by CCCs and special acts, which are usually called "constitutional procedure,"[8] etc.

Basically, it is understood that the essential concepts of the Procedural Law are unique for all the disciplines, and yet, whenever a certain area of law is too specific it might need its own set of rules adapted to its specialty. The basic concepts and foundations of Procedure Law are to be found in the Civil and Commercial Procedure Code and are shared by all of the specific branches. These main concepts are *action, jurisdiction, competence, instance and exception* and they are shared for all the disciplines. The diverse areas of procedural law are understood as "manifestations that develop certain specialties about the matter of the conflict [...] but that reconcile to a unique senior foundation that it is brought to each of these exposures."[9]

1.2 Procedure Law as a Competence of Each Province

Argentina is a federal government. One of the competences of the provinces is to have their own Procedure Law (Constitution, Article 75 inc. 12 and Article 121). Because of this reason, there are as many procedural codes as provinces.[10]

2 PROCEDURAL PRINCIPLES

It is generally agreed that there are several principles governing the procedure in Argentinian law. The dispositive principle (principio dispositivo) means that each party is, in general, responsible for the advancement of the trial (however, *see* discussion below, Section 6). The principle of contradiction (principio de

8. *See* for instance Sagüés, Néstor P., *Derecho Procesal Constitucional*, Buenos Aires, Astrea, 2013, 4 volumes. Basically, the sources of constitutional Procedure Law are the Constitution, the decisions of the Supreme Court, the Civil and Commercial Procedure Codes, the Law 16.986, called "de amparo" (urgent measures) and the "habeas corpus" order, Law 23.098.
9. This author points out: "... There is the General Theory of the Process, and also the study of the jurisdiction and the action, and all these design the general theory of the Procedural Law." Gozaíni, Osvaldo A. "Tratado de Derecho Procesal Civil", 1ª. Ed. Bs.s., La Ley, T. I, p. 50.
10. Nevertheless, the new Civil and Comercial Code of the Nation includes numerous procedural rules—in fact, the Code regulates the "Process of the Family" in the Title VIII of the Book II, from Art. 705 to Art. 711-, and a prestigious majority part of the processalist doctrine supports that this can affect the autonomy of the Procedural Law, stopping its evolution and affecting the judicial management. At the same time, this phenomenon "undermines the federal system and the provincial autonomy." Falcón, Enrique M.; "El Derecho Procesal en el Código Civil y Comercial de la Nación" 1st Ed. Santa Fe; Rubinzal-Culzoni, 2014, pp. 10, 145 and ff.

contradicción) implies that each trial should be whenever possible bilateral and that the right of defense should be accorded to each party. Procedures are usually written in Argentina. The trial should be open to the public, even if some of the trials because of their special nature are to be kept secret (family trials, for instance). The principle of preclusion (principio de preclusión), as seen in comparative legal systems, implies that the trial has an order that develops within a certain period of time. Once the time is over, there are no longer place for any procedural acts. The principle of procedure economy means that whenever possible procedures have to be abbreviated or simplified.

3 THE CIVIL AND COMMERCIAL PROCEDURE CODE AND OTHER SOURCES OF PROCEDURE LAW

As explained before, Argentina has as many procedure codes and instruments as provinces and special matters dealt with all along the country. However, since a vast part of trials takes place in the city of Buenos Aires, and since the National Civil and Commercial Procedure Code (hereinafter, CPCCN) usually serves as a model for provincial codes, it is worth saying a few words about its structure.

First of all, the sources of Argentine Procedure Law are not only the CPCCN, but, as stated above, Argentine Constitution and special laws and complementary regulations. To that, one should add the special rules of each jurisdiction sometimes issued by the Judiciary. However, the CPCCN remains the main source of Procedure Law. It was passed by law 17.454 in 1968, which several modifications introduced later on the original text.[11] It is composed by seven books: Book 1 deals with general dispositions (parties, judiciary, procedural acts, etc.), Book 2 with trials, Book 3 with enforcement of sentences or judgements, Book 4 with a number of special procedures (rights in rem procedures, trials concerning capacity, alimony, accountability procedures, forced eviction), Book 5 with the process concerning succession, Book 6 with arbitration and Book 7 with voluntary processes (like authorization to marry, guardianship, authorization to take part of a trial, right to examine the books kept by a society).

Argentina does not have a system of precedents. Case law is not mandatory for lower courts, with maybe the exception of what is called "plenary doctrine" of the Courts of Appeal at the national level in the city of Buenos Aires. Plenary doctrine means that all the chambers of the Court of Appeal decided on a controversial matter, and set a doctrine applicable to lower courts, yet only, in their jurisdiction.

As said before, the sources in Argentina are complex. The judgments of the Inter-American Court of Human Rights are directly applicable. The norms of Argentine Constitution as well. Procedure Laws are disseminated. And, to add up, each judiciary may issue its own local rules. A lawyer might find advice on the local sources asking in each local bar (colegio de abogados), who are usually the best informed as to the steps to follow and the sources to look up in each jurisdiction.

11. In this link which depends on the Presidency of Argentina, the reader will find the latest version available of the CPCCN, and in general, of every law: http://servicios.infoleg.gob.ar/infoleg Internet/anexos/15000-19999/16547/texact.htm (last seen April 16, 2017).

4 COURT STRUCTURE

The Courts in Argentina are divided by jurisdiction and by matter. Argentina, according to the republican principle of division of powers, states in Article 108 of Argentine National Constitution (hereinafter, CN) that the Judiciary will be exerted by the Supreme Court of Justice and all the inferior tribunals.

4.1 Division According to Jurisdictions

Argentina has a national and a local jurisdiction. National judges are competent to decide on federal matters, according to Article 116 CN. National courts have to decide in all issues concerning the National Constitution and national laws except for the competences given to the provinces (Article 75, inc. 12), in all issues concerning treaties with other nations, ambassadors, public ministers or foreign consuls, maritime jurisdiction, issues in which the National Government is part, in the cases between two provinces, between a private subject of a province and Province (as a legal person), or between a Province and a foreign citizen or State.

There are certain courts that have a federal competence because of their matter. For instance, the Court of Electoral matters (Cámara Nacional Electoral), since it deals with the elections, which are basic to grant democracy has a federal competence.[12] The National Criminal Cassation Court has also a national competence.[13] It has thirteen members divided in four chambers. The Federal Court of Social Security (Cámara Federal de Seguridad Social) is another example: it is composed by nine judges split in three chambers.[14]

Meanwhile, the Provinces have jurisdiction on all other issues, according to Articles 121 and 75, inc. 12 CN.

4.2 Division According to Matter

According the principle of specialty, many local and national jurisdiction may have special jurisdictions according to the matter of the issue. At a national level, there are administrative courts, labor courts, two sorts of criminal courts, family courts, civil courts, commercial courts, etc. Depending on the local authority and its resources, it may split a certain competence in two or three special courts. For instance, in the Province of Salta, there are family courts, courts for children and adolescents and family violence courts. In the city of Buenos Aires, criminal courts are divided between economic criminal offenses (Penal Económico) and other criminal offenses. However, there is one high court for criminal matters (*see* below, Corte de Casación Penal), which

12. Laws 19.108 and 19.277.
13. Laws 24.050, 26.371, 24.121.
14. Law 23.473.

deals with the legality of lower court decisions. There is no such thing when it comes to civil matters. Other jurisdiction with less resources may deal jointly with several matters, creating for instance a "Peace Court" (Juzgado de Paz). It is hard to state general rules, because depending on the jurisdiction and the matter, there may be a special competence to deal with the issue. It is safe to check on each jurisdiction before starting a trial. The creation of special competences and jurisdictions is a shifting issue, and may change from year to year.

4.3 Structure and Hierarchy

The last resort on all matters (even Criminal matters) is the Supreme Court of Justice (Corte Suprema de Justicia de la Nación). Below it, there are local Supremes Courts of Justice in each Province (e.g., Suprema Corte de la Provincia de Buenos Aires, Tribunal Superior de Justicia de la Ciudad Autónoma de Buenos Aires, Superior Tribunal de Justicia del Chacho, Tribunal de Justicia de Santa Cruz, and so on). Each local jurisdiction has then a second instance or Court of Appeal, and below, courts of first instance. However, it would not be right to assert that Argentina has four instances, since the access to the national court is restricted.

The Supreme Court of Justice (hereinafter, CSJN, according to its acronym in Spanish) is composed currently by five judges. There is also an Attorney general (Procurador General de la Nación), public defenders (Defensores Oficiales), and public prosecutors (Procurador Fiscal).[15] The CSJN has its siege at the City of Buenos Aires. It has its own rules of procedure.[16]

Lower Courts are usually composed by one or several judges, depending on the local or national regulations. For instance, the national Courts of Appeal in civil matters are composed of three judges, but first instance courts in civil matters at a national level are composed by one judge. Formerly, family courts in the province of Buenos Aires were and currently in the Province of Santa Fe still are composed by three judges.

The judge must conduct and decide a trial. Depending on the matter, and on the specific Procedure Law, he may have less or more initiative. The judges in Argentina have a permanent position. They are chosen by the president with the accord of the Senate, and they are not to be removed unless they are removed by a jury. So, even if not elected, the position of the judge depends a great deal on politics. Judges must graduate in a law school. They have competence in their own jurisdiction.

In Argentina there is an organ called Public Ministry, which is charged with the defense of those interests essential to the public order.[17] It is autonomous and it is basically composed by three organs: (a) the defendants of the interests of children and people without de due legal capacity (Defensor de Menores e Incapaces); (b) the public prosecutors (Ministerio Público Fiscal) who veil for the principle of legality; (c) and defendant of poor and absent people (Defensor de Pobres y Ausentes) who veil for the

15. Laws 24.946 and 26.183.
16. Decreto 1285/58, cfr. Art. 113 CN.
17. Article 120 CN.

interest of those who cannot pay an attorney or are absent, and cannot defend their interests. The participation of the defendant of the minors is mandatory in all processes concerning children or persons without the due legal capacity.

5 THE PARTIES AND THEIR LAWYERS

Aside from the judge and the public ministry, the trial needs the parties and their lawyers.

5.1 The Parties

Actions may be brought only by and against persons capable of being a party to a lawsuit. In Argentina a party is he who can bring a lawsuit by himself in his own interest.

In Argentina a party needs a lawyer to act in court. The juridical relationship he establishes with his attorney (abogado) may be a mandate (mandato) or a simple representation (patrocinio). A lawyer with a mandate can act in place of the party. A lawyer with a simple representation will need the signature of the party at almost every step of the procedure (remember: it is usually a written procedure).

To become a party to a trial there are two requisites: to have legal capacity to become a party (to have a legitimate interest recognized by the law), and to have procedural capacity to act (to have the legal age or the capacity to represent the parties own interests, view Chapter 4).

Parties should act on two leading principles: (a) the respect for the court; (b) they should act in loyalty and good faith. Judges may sanction the parties or the lawyers if they infringe those principles.[18]

A process in Argentina flows like a dialogue between parties before the judge. Therefore it is necessarily composed by bilateral instances because the starting point is the procedural action, and this is precisely what distinguishes the process to any other instance.[19]

In accordance with the ideas before, the process is a "logical and consequential serie of bilateral instances interconnected by the authority," who can be the judge or the arbitrator.[20]

Such logical order—which is unalterable, even on behalf of the procedural celerity—is necessarily constituted by four steps: the affirmation, the negation, the

18. Article 34, Codigo Procesal Civil y Comercial de la Nación.
19. Alvarado Velloso teaches: "The consequential serie is constituted by the instances of the parties in litigation: the action of the claimant and the reaction of the defendant, with an own peculiarity that is generated from the concept of the procedural action: each instance (action and reaction) must be necessarily bilateral, so it must be known by the party that did not exercise it, with the purpose of affirming,denying orconfirming whatever regarding to it." (*supra*, p. 236)
20. Cfr. Alvarado Velloso, *supra*, p. 234.

confirmation and the allegation,[21] and all of them tend to achieve the pronouncement of the judge regarding to the litigation which has been presented to him.[22]

An indigent plaintiff or defendant has a statutory right to free litigation. If he cannot afford a lawyer, he will be provided with a Public defendant. If he is not able to pay for the costs of the trial, he may pursue it with an exemption to pay (beneficio de litigar sin gastos).

5.2 The Lawyers

Lawyers act within their own jurisdiction. They have to join a bar (colegio de abogados) in most of the Provinces, for which they need no exam in order to be admitted. They just need to sign in. Once they are admitted in the bar, they may act within the jurisdiction of each bar. They are usually subject to a Code of Ethics, or rules for the exercise of the legal profession and they might have be sanctioned or even respond for damages for their legal acts.

6 THE TRIAL

The so-called due process is the process itself[23] and the real jurisdictional protection is only possible through the *due legal process*. The due legal process is understood "as a method which allows the man to keep the social peace, as it is the ideal instrument to

21. "It is not possible to start a process without the exercise of an action—procedural—and the stage of negation that allows the defendant to oppose to the pretension of the claimant. Therefore, it is not possible to avoid the stage of confirmation, because an affirmation that was denied, is a simple expression of the volition of the claimant. It is logically impossible to sever the stage of evaluation because in this step the party that confirmed its affirmation try to show to the judge how the party achieved it. To consider the process as such, it must be always inexorably constituted by the total of the elements that we mentioned before, and they must be always incorporated in the logical order that we have pointed out before: affirmation, denied, confirmation and evaluation."
22. Cfr. Teoría General del Proceso,of the outstanding Mexican processalist author Humberto Briseño Sierra. Derecho Procesal, Vol. I, México 1969, www.academiadederecho.org.
23. It is important to remark that the process was originated before the existance of the Constitutions of the states, so the adjective "due" does not appear in them, even when the inviolability of the judicial defense and the exigence of a rational and fair procedure are ensured in these Constitutions. This is the case of the Argentine Constitution. Alvarado Velloso points out: "... It is generally accepted that the origin of the adjective 'due' was in the Fifth Amendment of the Constitution of the United States of America. This mandate also appears in the Fourteenth Amendment (as a restriction to the power of the States). As the Constitutions of other countries, the Argentine Constitution does not mention the adjective 'due', so it has generated the idea that the due process is an innominate guarantee. Perhaps for this reason or for the terminological vagueness that is generally used by the authors who study the topic, the legal doctrine does not define in a positive form the due process. The authors only define it in a negative form: for example, they say that the due legal process is the one that does not restrict the right of defense for any reason." Alvarado Velloso, A.; "El debido proceso de la garantía constitucional"; Zeus, Rosario, 2003; p. 292.

enforce its freedom and to make effective its rights against any limitation, infringement, impediment or interference from other persons—whatever of their nature- even the State."[24]

In fact, the legal process in Argentina may present two opposite systems: the dispositive system—or accusatory system—and the inquisitorial system.[25] The dispositive system is based on the principles of parties equality, the impartiality of the judge and the congruity between the petition and the resolution of the claim. The impulse of the procedure depends upon the responsability of the parties, which also determine the *thema decidendum*. This system requires the rules of orality and inmediacy. On the other hand, the inquisitorial system is essentially based on the leading role of the judge, who has broad powers, including to the faculty to investigate, to prove and to decide. In charging the judge with the impulse of the procedure, the equality of the parties becomes less relevant, the impartiality of the judge becomes of the utmost importance and the principle of congruence is attenuated. The legal doctrine makes reference to the existence of a mixed system that is regulated by some legislations of South America as a consequence of the Spanish domination.[26] In Argentina mixed systems are to be found in the provinces, which are usually discribed as "predominantly dispositive with inquisitorial features".

Undoubtedly, Argentine constituents have devised a dispositive process according to an accusatory system, that is why they have incorporated the jury, the equality under the law, the inviolability of the judicial defense, the natural judge guarantee, the ban of sentence without previous trial and the principle of legality. At the same time, the procedural codes have continued adopting the Spanish model of prosecution (the inquisitory model) that was inherited because of the dominance of Spain over the territory of the Rio de la Plata in the colony times.

The new National Civil and Comercial Codeestablishes many procedural norms and it sometimes invades the provincial autonomy. More precisely, the Code regulates the Process of Family through principles and precepts that respond to an inquisitorial process, which is characterized by the officious procedural impulse, the extensive judicial powers regarding to the officious evidence, the dinamic burden of proof and the advance tutelages.[27]These are tendencies that are transforming the civil process in general through principles such as: the effective judicial protection, the immediacy, the orality, the best interest of the child, the freedom, the expanse and the flexibility of the evidence, the dinamic probative evidences, etc.

In Argentina there is a growing tendency to avoid the judicialisation of the conflicts through the admission of alternative methods of conflict resolution. Thus, several provinces have incorporated mediation, which sometimes is pre-judiciary and mandatory, as the case of the Province of Santa Fe. And so, the proocedural rules that

24. Calvinho, Gustavo. "La contribución del derechoprocesal al sistema democrático", presented at the X Congreso Nacional de Derecho Procesal Garantista. Azul, November 12th, 13th and 14th, 2008. http://www.academiadederecho.org/.
25. Alsina, Hugo; "Tratado teórico práctico de Derecho Procesal Civil y Comercial". 2ª Ed.; T. I Parte General; Ediar S.A. Editores, Buenos Aires, 1956, p. 98.
26. *See* Alvarado Velloso, A., "Sistemas Procesales," www.academiaderecho.org.
27. *See* Falcón E. "El Derecho Procesal en el....", *supra*, pp. 145 and ff.

should be established exclusively by the Provinces because of the rules of the federal system (see constitutional law) are being slowly absorbed by the national sphreres of regulation.

Another feature to take into acount is that in Argentina—as in other Latin American countries—the judicial activism, which is also called judicial decisionism, is gainning ground in different provincial legislations. Thus, every lawyer should be aware of a certain degree of legal uncertainty. It is always safe to check the latest case law on each matter.

6.1 The Commencing of a Trial

Apart from those issues in which mediation is mandatory (*see* below, always depending on the jurisdiction), a judicial action starts with a lawsuit. The Article 330 CPCCN states that a lawsuit has to be written, and it will contain the name of the parties, their domicile, the name and domicile of the defendant, the object claimed by the plaintiff, the facts in which it is founded, the evidence it will provide and the means by which this evidence will be provided. The petition should be clear. Concerning the means of proof, the proof of witnesses should be proposed indicating the name, profession and domicile of the witnesses, and the questions to be asked to them should be attached to the lawsuit. If the means of proof include documents, the plaintiff shall indicate where they are to be found. Otherwise those means of proof will be declared unadmissible.[28] The court cannot take facts into consideration if they were not allegued by the party before giving notice to the defendant. The petition is filed at the courts, which will assign it to a court.

Once the lawsuit is received by the court, the judge will order to give notice to the defendant (traslado de la demanda), with a copy of the petition. Mostly, the courts try to issue such notices via e-mail. However, the process to implement notification by email is still ongoing in most jurisdictions. The defendant will have a more extended deadline to submit his response if he leaves in another province or abroad.[29]

The defendant has to respond to the lawsuit. He may argue one of the following legal defenses: that there is another petition peding, that the plaintif has whether the legal nor the procecedure capacity to act, that the object has already been provided, that there has been a previous transaction, concitiation or that the legal action has been previously waive the right to claim, that there is a connection with a pending case, or legal defect.[30] Legal defenses must be raised immediately, when responding to the lawsuit. A defendant could also become a plaintiff, if, when responding, he acuses the other party (reconvención, a sort of counterclaim).[31] If the clairmant does not have domcile nor immovable property in Argentina, the defendant may claim the exception of "arraigo," which means that the plaintiff may not litigate in Argentina.

28. Articles 370, 371 CPCNN.
29. Article 339 and ff. CPCCN.
30. Article 347 CPCCN.
31. Article 346 CPCCN.

If, in the response of the lawsuit by the defendant, new facts are alleagued, the plaintiff has a chance to respond to those new facts and offer new evidence to proof their claim.[32]

Lack of jurisdiction or questioning the intervention of the appointed judge (recusación) may only occur at the beginning of the trial.

In its response, the defendant should dispute each or the main facts presented by the plaintiff or the applicable law. The response should provide for evidence to found their assertions.

Apart from mediation, pretrial practices are not usual, even if convenient.

6.2 Hearing

Once the lawsuit has been responded and the judge has decided upon the evenutal defenses argued by the defendant, the judge will call for a hearing to decide on the means of proof. This hearing is called "preliminar hearing" (audiencia preliminar).[33] During the hearing, the judge will call the parties for an amicable solution. He may even asked the parties to start a mediation process (*see* below). If there is an opposition of one of the parties to start the period in which the parties produce their proof, the judge will decide upon that opposition. The judge will hear the "confession" of the parties in this very hearing and he will decide upon the usefulness of the other means of proof provided by the parties. If both parties agreed the means of proof are no longer necessary to decide the lawsuit, the Judge will take this into account and render his final judgement on the matter. The resolution issued by the judge on the means of proof may not be appealed. The parties can further waive the means of proof they consider to be unnecessary if during the production of the proof they find that the proofs already provided are enough to demonstrate their assertions.[34]

The burden of proof applies onto he who allegates a fact. Foreign law must be proofed. However, if the party does not provide the proof, the judge may look for the laww for himself.[35]

If a party fails to produce the means of proof it offered in the period of time stated for each of them, the other party may demand that he is declared "negligent" (negligente), which means that he will loose the right to produce that proof and will have to pay the costs of the incident.

Witnesses are third parties to the trial that may proof because of their direct experience of them, some of the facts alleged by the parties. The events the witnesses learned from others are of no value to the trial. The witnesses[36] should be heard by the judge, who sometime delegates this faculty upon a member of the court. A withness must be older than 14 years. Members of the close family may not be witnesses to the trial. Each party can offer up to eight witnesses. A judge might only call those witnesses

32. Article 335 CPCCN.
33. Articles 360 and ff. CPCCN.
34. Article 373, CPCCN.
35. Article 377 CPCCN.
36. Articles 426 and ff. CPCCN.

proposed by the parties as mean of proof, except when third parties are mentioned in the lawsuit or its respond.[37] A witness is given notice by the interested party. Before the testimony, the witness will be asked for their personal data, and if he is related to the parties by kinship or friendship, if he is enemy to the party or if he has any interest in the lawsuit, if he is creditor or debitor to the party or if he has any relation to the party. After testifying the record of his deposition is read to him, so that he might be able to review it and sign it. Once called by a party to be a witness is an obligation for each citizen. If, without justified reasons a witness refuses to testify he might be taken to the court by police officers.

Expert witnesses[38] (peritos) may also be offered as a mean of proof.[39] They may be proposed by the party, and in that case, they will be called as normal witnesses or provide a written report. Both parties may also agree on an expert witness, which will then be designated by the judge. However, the judge may designate an expert witness from a catalogue provided by the court. In that case, the expert witness shall render his report to the court in time, and this report might be objected by each of the parties. Each party can propose the issues on which the expert witness shall pronounce his testimony in the lawsuit or its response.[40] Each party can provide their own expert witness to be present along the research or investigation done by the expert witness designated by the court. The expert witness of the parties will then render a parallel report to that of the expert witness designated by the court having had access to the same information that he had.

The lawyers who have a simple mandate to act (patrocinantes) and naturally those who act on mandate can petition the production of reports and documents by themselves. They do not need the signature of their client.

The proofs will be appreciated acoording to the common sense, in order to determine if they did proof or not the allegations of the party who produced it.

6.3 Rendition of the Final Judgement

Once all the proof is produced, the judge will close the period of proof. The parties may present their case in a written document called "alegatos" (pleadings). The pleadings are summary of the proof produced and how that proof demonstrates the party was right. Once the pleadings are presented, the lawsuit is called for its final judgement. After the final judgement is rendered, the parties may appeal. If they do not appeal in time, the judge becomes res iudicata, this is, final and absolute. He who loses the trial will have to pay for the costs unless stated otherwise in the final judgement.

37. Article 452 CPCCN.
38. Articles 457 and ff. CPCCN.
39. Articles 457 and ff. CPCCN.
40. Article 460 CPCCN.

6.4 Appeal

Under certain circumstances a party is allowed to appeal from a court decision of a lower instance to the court of the next instance. Once an appeal remedy is presented, the appealed judgement is not final and absolute, and the appeal usually has a suspensory effect on it (there are exceptions). There are several kinds of appeal remedies in Argentina.

The revision[41] (reposición) is a remedy in order to review those judgements that are not final so that the judges reviews his own decision and decides otherwise instead. The party has three days after having been noticed fo the judgement. It does not proceed against final judgements. The judge will order to give notice to the other party and hearing both parties it will afterwards decide.

If the revision fails, the party can always appeal.[42] The remedy of appeal proceed only against final judgements, partial judgements or simple judgements (but only when they cause an "irreparable damage" if not revised). The judgements that decide about low money cases may not be appealed (currently, the equivalent of approximately USD 6,000). However, this rule does not apply to alimony and eviction cases. The appeal can be granted in a free or restricted way, and with or without suspensory effect. In order that the appeal is declared admissible, the appelant party must state clearly its legimate interest and its grounds. While the revision aims at the reversal of a judgement by the same instance that rendered it, the appeal aims at the revision of the judgement by higher instance. The appeal might be filed orally or in a written document. It might be filed orally in midst of a hearing. Whatever means used to file the appeal, the appelant has five days to found it once the appeal was granted to be counted from the day he was given notice by the lower instance or the other party. The parties have three days to object the way the appeal was granted (with or without suspensory effect, free or restricted). A free appeal (aplación libre) is an appeal in which the parties may offer means of proof. A restricted appeal (efecto restringido) comprises only the points of law objected by the appelant. Finally, the appeal might be filed in a subsidiary way: e.g., the party files a remedy of revision, and in subsidiary way, an appeal.

The parties may also file for the nullity of the judgement, when there is a legal defect for the judgements.

6.5 Foreign Judgements (Exequatur)

Between several special procedures provided for by the Civil and Commercial Procedure Code, there is one worth taking a look at: the enforcement of foreign judgements. The judgements rendered by foreign courts will be enforced according to the terms of the country of origin.[43] If there are bilateral or multilateral treaties governing the relation between Argentina and the country of origin, those treaties apply. If not, there is a special procedure to be followed. The final judgment has to be issued by a

41. Articles 238 and ff. CPCCN.
42. Articles 242 and ff.
43. Article 517 CPCCN.

competent court according to Argentinian rules of international jurisdiction, the defendant against who the judgement is enforced must be given proper notice, the judgement has all the features it needs to have to be valid in the country of origin, it does not affect the international ordre public from Argentina, that it is not incompatible with another judgement on the same issue rendered in Argentina.[44]

The enforcement of the foreign judgement must be presented before the judge of first instance with its testimony legalized and translated by a registered translator. The compliance with the requisites above enounced must be detailed in the written lawsuit presented by the plaintiff.

The judge will analyze if the judgement can be enforced or not.

The same proceedings apply to the recognition and enforcement of arbitral awards.[45] The issues of the arbitral award must be contained in the agreement reached by the parties.

7 MEDIATION IN ARGENTINA

Because of its importance in legal culture as in legal practice, it appears convenient to add some paragraphs concerning mediation in Argentina.

7.1 Introduction

Mediation and Arbitration are two alternative dispute resolution methods (ADR).

In Arbitration, the dispute is submitted, by agreement of the parties, to an arbitrator: an independent and impartial third party who makes a binding decision on the dispute. The Code of Civil and Commercial Procedures sets out the rules regarding Arbitration (Articles 736 a 765).[46]

On the other hand, in mediation, an independent and impartial third party (the mediator) helps the parties to communicate and, eventually, reach an agreement.

7.2 About Mandatory Mediation in Argentina

In Argentina, Mediation is governed by Law 26.589 and Decree 1467/11,[47] which establish mandatory mediation prior to any judicial process.[48] By promoting a lawsuit, the report signed by the intervening mediator must be accompanied as a condition of admissibility.

44. Article 517 CPCCN.
45. Articles 519 and ff. CPCCN.
46. Rivera, Julio, "El arbitraje en Argentina" Revista de Derecho Comparado, N° 11, Santa Fe: RubinzalCulzoni, 2005, p. 157.
47. Antecedentes. Secretaria de Justicia, Ministerio de Justicia de la Nación, "Mediación. Proyecto Piloto. Implementación, desarrollo, evaluación." (1996).
48. Aiello de Almeida, María A. & Almeida, Mario, "Mediación y conciliación. Comentario exegético de la ley 26.589 y su reglamentación", Editorial Astrea (2012), Somer, Marcela Patricia, "La nueva ley de mediación: Aspectos procesales", LA LEY2010-C, 1298 (2010).

Even though liberty and voluntary are basic principles of mediation, mediation under Law 26.598 is mandatory to promote the culture of nonadversarial dispute resolution in Argentina.[49] Anyway, when attending, the parties are allowed to express their refusal to participate and the mediation process will be closed without any consequences for the parties. So, attending is mandatory; staying, not.

Law 26.589 surpasses the previous one (Law 24.573). First of all, because of its innovations (e.g., regulating family mediation[50]). Moreover, because it fills important gaps that have generated uncertainty under the previous law.[51]

Some cases are excluded from mediation (Law 26.589, Articles 5 and 6):

(a) Criminal proceedings (Although there are local regulations for Criminal Mediation in some Provinces).
(b) Divorce, annulment of marriage, filiation, custody and adoption, with the exception of patrimonial issues related to them.
(c) Cases in which the National Government, Provinces, Municipalities or the Autonomous city of Buenos Aires and its decentralized entities are party.
(d) Processes of disqualification, declaration of disability and rehabilitation.
(e) Constitutional protection (Amparo), habeas corpus, habeas data and interdicts.
(f) Precautionary measures.
(g) Preliminary proceedings and anticipated evidence.
(h) Inheritance proceedings.
(i) Reorganization and Bankruptcy.
(j) Call a meeting of coowners under Article 10 of Law 13.512.
(k) Conflicts of jurisdiction of the Labor Courts.
(l) Voluntary procedures.
(m) Conflicts in consumer relations.

In cases of execution and eviction mediation procedure will be optional for the claimant.

7.3 Principles of Mediation in Mandatory Mediation

At the first hearing, the mediator has to explain what a mediation is and how parties can make it work to settle disputes. Also, he must inform the parties on the principles of mandatory mediation (Law 26.589, Articles 7–9).

(a) Impartiality.

49. Jaef, Victor Jorge. Ley 24.573. Mediación y conciliación civil y comercial. Análisis exegético, Editorial Juris (1997), p. 1.
50. Auhad Calvelo & M. Estefanía, "Mediación familiar. Una solución favorable para las familias en crisis", Cuaderno Jurídico Familia, Editorial El Derecho, Número 29 (2012).
51. Roberts, Juan E. & Sapia, Eduardo C., "Nueva ley de mediación prejudicial obligatoria", Cuaderno Jurídico Familia, Editorial El Derecho, Número 29 (2012), p. 19.

The mediator is an outsider of the conflict. Mediators cannot give legal advice to the parties, that is why they have to attend with a lawyer.

(b) Liberty and voluntary.

Although mediation under Law 26.589 is mandatory, parties can leave at any time. They cannot be pressured into making an agreement.

(c) Equality.

The parties have equal rights; each one has equal opportunity to participate, to declare their will or to offer conclusion of settlement.

(d) Special consideration of the interests of children, disabled and elderly dependent people.

The mediation must comply with international human rights treaties such as Convention on the Rights of the Child, Convention on the Rights of Persons with Disabilities, International Covenant on Civil and Political Rights, International Covenant on Economic, Social and Cultural Rights, etc.

(e) Confidentiality.

Everyone must sign a confidential agreement before the beginning of the procedure to ensure that what is said or written during the mediation cannot be used later in a court proceeding. However, the duty of confidentiality ceases: (a) with the express waiver by all parties that intervened; or (b) To prevent the commission of a crime or if it is being committed, to prevent that it continues being committed.

(f) Promoting direct communication between the parties.

(g) Celerity.

Mediation should have a reasonable duration (time-efficiency).

(h) Consent of the parties to the presence of outsiders.

7.4 The Procedure

The mediators are enrolled in the National Registry of Mediation. The appointment of the mediator is made (Law 26.589, Articles 11-17):

(a) By agreement of the parties.
(b) By a random procedure.
(c) By proposal of the applicant.
(d) During the judicial process, the presiding judge may refer the case to mediation. In this case, the appointment is made by a random procedure (except in case of an agreement of the parties on the election of the mediator).

The mediator must recuse himself in the same cases provided for disqualification of judges (conflict of interests). Moreover, the mediator must excuse himself during the course of mediation, when notice the existence of causes that may affect his impartiality. When the mediator had been proposed by the applicant, he will be replaced by whoever follows him in the order of the proposal.

If the mediator does not recuse himself, the parties may file a motion for substitution under the same circumstances, within five days the designation is known. When the mediator had been drawn by a random procedure, a new one will be done immediately; when the mediator had been proposed by the applicant, he will be replaced by whoever follows him in the order of the proposal.

The mediator cannot advise or sponsor any of the parties to the preliminary mandatory mediation procedures in which he had intervened, until after one year of leaving the National Registry of Mediation. The prohibition is absolute in relation to the conflict in which he has intervened as a mediator.

Moreover, mediators may act, with the consent of all the parties, in cooperation with professionals trained in disciplines related to the conflict that is the subject of mediation (Law 26.589, Article 10).

The parties must attend personally, though legal counsel is mandatory[52](Law 26.589, Articles 19–22). They are the main actors[53] of the process and cannot do it by proxy, with the exception of legal entities and parties domiciled more than 150 kilometers away from the city where the hearings are held. The proxy must have power to make transactions.

Legal counsel is mandatory. The party attending hearings without legal counsel will be considered absent unless the parties agree to determine a new date.

Celerity is one of the most important principles regarding mediation. The mediation will proceed for a maximum of sixty days calendar days from the last notice. In the case provided for in Article 6, the term is thirty days. In both cases the term might be extended by agreement.

The parties will be able to contact the appointed mediator prior to the hearing, in order to make known their claims. When the mediator notices that the intervention of a third party is necessary, he can send him a notice (ex officio, at the request of either of the parties, or at the request of the third party); always with the consent of the parties.

The mediator will schedule the first hearing within fifteen days of being notified of his appointment (Law 26.589, Articles 23–25).

The mediator shall notify the hearing personally or by a reliable means. The notice must be received by the parties at least three business days before the hearing. If a party is domiciled in a foreign jurisdiction, the diligence will be conducted by the counsel of the requesting party. If the opposing party is domiciled in another country, extended periods are deemed during the term of the notification procedure.

If the opposing party is domiciled in another country, the deadlines are extended for the duration of the notification procedure. The mediator may request the

52. Alvarez Trongé, Manuel, "Técnicas de negociación para abogados", Editorial Abeledo Perrot (1996), Caram, María E., Eilbaum, Diana T. & Risolía, Matilde, "Mediación. Diseño de una práctica", Editorial Astrea, (2014).
53. Highton, Elena I. & Alvarez, Gladys, "Mediación para resolver conflictos", Editorial Ad-Hoc (1995), p.183.

cooperation of the judge appointed, to issue a rogatory letter or to use a medium that is considered reliable at the place where the party is domiciled.

If any of the parties does not attend the first hearing with a good cause, the mediator will set a new hearing. If the opposing party failed to appear without a good cause, the requesting party may choose to conclude the process of mediation or call new hearing. If the requesting party fails to appear without a good cause, he must restart the mediation procedure.

The mediation may end with or without an agreement. When the parties reach an agreement, the written report shall contain such terms. This is the last stage in mediation). It will be signed by the mediator, the parties, third parties (if any) and their attorneys. When the interests of a person under a disability are involved, the agreement requires court approval.

The agreement contained in the report will be executable by the process of execution of sentences. If the mediation process ends without agreement of the parties, the report including the results of the process will also be signed by the mediator, the parties involved and their attorneys. The requesting party is entitled to promote the lawsuit, accompanying a copy of the report (Law 26.589, Articles 26–30).

Methods of alternative conflict resolution have several advantages over litigation, especially: celerity, flexibility, confidentiality and lower costs. In Argentina, mandatory mediation is helping to promote the culture of nonadversarial dispute resolution.

8 ARBITRATION

Arbitration[54] is not widely used by Argentina's contract law but it is slowly spreading. They are mostly common in international contracts. The new CCC of Argentina contains a chapter concerning the arbitration agreement, with provisions concerning the definition, content and effects of the arbitration agreement, types of disputes that may not be subjected to arbitration, the form of appointment of arbitrators and the way to challenge the appointment as well as for the duties of arbitrators. These provisions are complemented by local regulations of each province or jurisdiction in which the application will take place.

According to the CCC the arbitral tribunal must be composed of one or more arbitrators always in odd numbers (Article 1659, CCC). It is forbidden to grant a privilege to one of the parties to appoint the arbitrator (Article 1661, CCC). Arbitrators must guarantee equal treatment and equal opportunity to present its case and defend its rights (Article 1662, CCC) and parties may not waive the option to seek annulment or to request clarification of the award (Article 760 Civil and Commercial Procedural Code).

There are certain matters that may not be subjected to arbitration, such as criminal matters, legal capacity of a human person, family matters, contracts of

54. Rivera, Julio C. & Julio C. Rivera Jr. "Arbitration and Practice in Argentina: Overview", https://uk.practicallaw.thomsonreuters.com/2-541-3886?transitionType=Default&contextData=(sc.Default)&firstPage=true&bhcp=1.

adhesion, consumer disputes and labor disputes (Article 1651 CCC). Evidently, public order may not be compromised by the object of the arbitration.

The validity requirements of arbitration agreements are as follows: they must be redacted in writing, in private or public instruments (Article 1650, CCC). The validity of an agreement is naturally subjected to the conditions of validity of any legal act and is subjected to nullity of voideness if it does not fulfill them (Article 979, CCC).

If a party starts courts proceedings in breach of an arbitration agreement, according to Article 1656 CCC, the Court is obliged to refuse the jurisdiction to the claimant. The defendant may use this action as a legal defense.

Arbitrators must be independent and impartial (Article 1663 CCC). The default number of arbitrators is three. Each party appoints one of them, and the third is appointed by the other two arbitrators. If there is a sole arbitrator, and the parties do not reach an agreement, he may be appointed by a competent domestic court or the entity administering the arbitration. Arbitrators may be removed according to Article 1663. The challenge to the appointment will be resolved by domestic courts.

Parties have the power to determine the procedural rules of the arbitration (Article 1658, CCC). The default rules are those of the domestic proceedings, unless the case is presided by the OAS-Inter-American Convention of 1975 (Panama Convention).

Parties may agree confidentiality on the arbitration by a confidentiality clause (Article 1658, CCC). Arbitrators are subjected to the confidentiality clause.

It is important to note that Argentina has not adopted the UNCITRAL model. However, the recognition and enforcement of foreign arbitral awards is ruled by: the UN Convention on the recognition and enforcement of Foreign Arbitral Awards of 1958 (New York Convention), the OAS Inter-American convention on International Commercial Arbitration of 1975 (Panama Convention) and the OAS Inter-American Convention on Extraterritorial Validity of Foreign Judgements and Arbitral Awards of 1979.

Further Reading

Quadri; Gabriel Hernán, *Derecho Procesal en el Código civil y comercial de la Nación*, Thomson Reuters, La Ley, 2017, 3 volumes.

Sagüés, Néstor P., *Derecho Procesal Constitucional*, Ed. Astrea, Buenos Aires, 2013.

Highton, Elena I. & Alvarez, Gladys, "Mediación para resolver conflictos", Editorial Ad-Hoc (1995).

Rivera, Julio C. & Julio C. Rivera Jr. "Arbitration and Practice in Argentina: Overview". https://uk.practicallaw.thomsonreuters.com/2-541-3886?transitionType=Default&contextData=(sc.Default)&firstPage=true&bhcp=1.

Chapter 12
Private International Law

Ursula Basset

Private International Law (PIL) in Argentina is since 2015 a Title in the new Civil and Commercial Code (CCC). Due to this, PIL has now a more systematic regulation.[1] This is an undeniable advance, that will, no doubt, facilitate the understanding of the Argentine PIL to foreigners and locals.[2]

Only thankfulness is to be conveyed to the renowned experts who worked on the matter of PIL. That said, the accomplishments of the CCC should be tempered: under the current regime it could neither be said that its compilation is complete nor that it accounts for the complexities that PIL faces in current times.

First of all, the option to include PIL within a Private Law Code was for some a lost opportunity to free it,[3] and give it the scientific autonomy contemporary PIL needs under the new landscape of international relations.[4] Not that the experts who worked on the draft preferred the "privatization" of PIL, it was probably just that it was the option available at the time.[5] On the other hand, even if the systematic regulations included in the CCC would create the impression of a complete PIL system, this is only a mirage. On a close look, only a small part of PIL has been compiled. Actually, the Argentinian CCC is in itself a visual illusion on this respect: it would seem to be a

1. Dreyzin de Klor, Adriana, "Las disposiciones generales del Derecho Internacional Privado en el Còdigo Civil y Comercial", RCCyC 2017 (Septiembre), p. 3.
2. Fernandez Arroyo, Diego P. "Main Characteristics of the New Private International Law of the Argentinian Republic", *RabelsZeitschrift, 80,* pp. 130–150 (2016).
3. Most of all, in times in which the private/public law division blurs. Muir Watt, Horatia, Fernandez Arroyo, Diego, *Private International Law and Global Governance,* OUP, 2014e, p. 2. *See also*: Mills, Alex, *The Confluence of Public and Private International Law,* Cambridge University Press, 2009.
4. *Ibid.* p. 133.
5. This is what seems implied in *ibid.* p. 134. *See also* Uzal, María Elsa (member of the drafting commission of the CCC), "Lineamientos de la reforma del Derecho Internacional privado en el Código Civil y Comercial de la Nación", Sup. Esp. Nuevo Código Civil y Comercial 2014 (November), p. 247.

recodification, a reaction against the centrifugal movement of de-codification undergone by many compared legal systems. If it intended to stop the leak, it failed to fulfill its promises. It is a CCC that has not legislated upon commercial companies, insolvency, intellectual property, checks, jurisdictional immunity of foreign states or even children's law. For an effort of reunification of Private law, it was a quite unsuccessful one. Finally, PIL did not include provisions on the recognition and enforcement of foreign decisions in the new CCC, which is regrettable. It was included by the experts who drafted it (too conscious of the importance of interjurisdictional cooperation), but it was later excluded in further revisions.[6] It is, however, true, that the expert commission managed to surpass the tight constraints and political urges that surrounded the CCC, to issue, even in this context, valuable and modern provisions.

This chapter aims to provide a glance at the complex regulation of PIL in Argentina, with legal dispositions now easily found in the Argentinian CCC, but, considering that the CCC does not provide a full compilation of PIL, which is still scattered in several special acts and international treaties to which, maybe, if faced with an international case, a lawyer might have need to refer to.

1 THE SOURCES OF ARGENTINIAN PIL

Main sources of Argentinian PIL are now the CCC, supplementary Acts containing PIL provisions and multilateral or international treaties to which Argentina is signatory party.

1.1 A Brief Sketch of the Spirit and Contents of the PI Regulations in the Argentinian CCC

In this section dedicated to the sources of PIL in Argentina, the regulation of the CCC will be discussed only referring to the issue of the legal sources of PIL and a short sketch of its contents. In Section 2, and mostly in the following sections, the reader will be able to find a presentation of its main features.

Concerning the issue of the sources of PIL, it should be stated right from the start that the regulation the CCC considers itself to be subsidiary to other autonomous sources of PIL: Art. 2594 states that "applicable norms to cases with international dimensions will be determined by treaties, international conventions currently in force applicable to the case, subsequently to norms of international source, and, in the absence of those, norms of Argentina PIL of an internal source."[7] The stress on the international dimensions of Argentine "private" international law strikes right from the start. Another issue to be noted is the special importance according to international treaties, and especially those referring to human rights matters, with local doctrine has

6. *Ibid.* p. 134.
7. "Las normas jurídicas aplicables a situaciones vinculadas con varios ordenamientos jurídicos nacionales se determinan por los tratados y las convenciones internacionales vigentes de aplicación en el caso y, en defecto de normas de fuente internacional, se aplican las normas del derecho internacional privado argentino de fuente interna."

put right at the source of PIL, aligning with current trends on the matter.[8] This prevalence of international law over domestic law mirrors a constitutional approach to the hierarchy of norms (it might be thus said to be a cultural matter), and is replicated further in the norms concerning international jurisdiction (Article 2601), international cooperation (Articles 2611–2612), and specific cooperation in regard to international restitution of children (Articles 2614, 2642).[9] It is also in line with Articles 1 and 2 of the Argentine CCC, when disposing on the sources of law and of interpretation of law.

One of the main derives of this internationalist approach is the quest of what local doctrine has called simply "justice,"[10] a part of which could be coined also a realization of the quest of universal access to justice even in cases with international dimensions. The new Argentinian CCC includes the right of international jurisdiction of national judges, in case of absence of international treaties and agreements between the parties, which will apply according to vernacular laws (Article 2601). Moreover, Article 2602, to avoid any loophole includes a *forum necessitatis* provision, by which Argentinian judges will have international jurisdiction even without any norm according it to them in order to prevent the denial of justice. On the other hand, and again making use of the rhetorics of international human rights treaties, Article 2010 establishes a clause of "equal treatment:" "Citizens and those who reside permanently abroad have free access to the jurisdiction to defend their rights and interests in the same conditions as citizens and permanent residents in Argentina." This equal treatment clause applies to legal persons registered abroad. The concern seems to be to address a concrete and real access to justice in cases with international dimensions.

As to the contents, as said before, the Argentine CCC has included PIL in Title IV ("Dispositions of Private International Law") within Book VI ("Common Dispositions for Personal Rights and Rights in Rem"). Title IV is divided into three chapters:

(1) Chapter 1 deals with general provisions.
(2) Chapter 2 deals with international jurisdictions.
(3) Chapter 3, with special provisions.

The dispositions within the CCC are structured, notwithstanding the formal presentation in three chapters, in two domains: (a) a general part (including general regulations and international jurisdiction, criteria to apply PI norms, international civil procedure and international cooperation norms); and (b) a special part, with PI norms divided by matter.

8. The starting point is the new place made for "justice" in PIL, which naturally derives in considering Human Rights treaties as a direct or indirect source. *See*, Mills, *The Confluence...*, *supra*. Fawcett, James J. et al., *Human Rights and Private International Law*, OUP, 2016. In Argentina: Uzal, María Elsa, *Derecho Internacional Privado*, La Ley, 2016, Chapter 2.
9. Fernandez Arroyo, "Main Characteristics...", *supra* p. 136.
10. Uzal, *Derecho Internacional...*, Chapter 1.

1.2 Special Acts Containing PIL Rules

Nevertheless, amidst its inclusion in the CCC, several parts of PIL are still contained in other private law sources such as the Act for Commercial Societies, the Bankruptcy act, the Navigation Act, Trade-marks Act, the Insurance Act, and the Aeronautical Code. PIL is still scattered, even though the codification intent, compiled at least a significant part of it.

1.3 International or Multilateral PIL Treaties

This section started with the prevalence given to international sources over the "privatized" PIL in the CCC and special acts. Putting aside international treaties on specific matters, there are also the international or multilateral treaties containing different aspects of private international relations, to which Argentina is a signatory part. To hint only some of them:

- Athens Convention relation to the Carriage of Passengers and Luggage by Sea, 1974.
- Berne Convention for the Protection of Literary and Artistic Works, 1971.
- Convention of Geneva on International Recognition of Rights in Aircraft, 1948.
- Convention of Paris for the Protection of Industrial Property, 1883.
- Convention of Unification of Certain Rules of Law Respecting Assistance and Salvage at Sea, Brussels, 1910.
- Hague Convention for the Protection of Cultural Property in the Event of Armed Conflict.
- Hague Convention on the Civil Aspects of International Child Abduction, 1980.
- Hague Conventions of 1899 and 1907.
- Inter-American Convention on Conflict of Laws concerning Bills of Exchange, Promissory Notes and Invoices, 1975 (CIDIP-I).
- Inter-American Convention on Conflicts of Laws concerning Commercial Companies, 1979 (CIDIP-II).
- Inter-American Convention on the Law Applicable to International Contracts, 1994 (CIDIP-V).
- Inter-American Convention on General Rules of Private International Law, 1979.
- Inter-American Convention on Support Obligations, 1989.
- Inter-American Convention on the International Return of Children, 1989.
- Inter-American Convention on the Law Applicable to International Traffic in Minors, 1994 (CIDIP-V).
- New York Convention on the Limitation Period in the International Sale of Goods, 1974.

- Treaty of Montevideo of 1889 (between Argentina, Bolivia, Peru)[11] about Civil and Commercial Law, Criminal Law, Procedure Law, Literary and Artistic property rights, patents of invention, trademarks and liberal professions.
- Treaty of Montevideo of 1940 (between Argentina, Paraguay, Uruguay) about Civil and Commercial Law, Navigation and terrestrial circulation.
- UN Convention on Consent to Marriage Minimum Age for Marriage and Registration of Marriages, 1964.
- United Nations Sales Convention, 1985.
- Warsaw Convention for Unification of Certain Rules Relating International Carriage by Air, 1929.

According to Articles 1 and 2 of the CCC, the hierarchy of norms according to Argentine National Constitution, and, last but not least, Argentine legal culture, international treaties dealing with human rights and even sometimes soft law, such as recommendations of international organizations or committees, or case law from the Inter-American Court of Human Rights have an effective influence on the application of PIL, not only on contouring policy norms, but also the on choice of law and the application of material law.

2 OUTLINE OF THE PRIVATE INTERNATIONAL CONTENTS OF THE NEW CCC: THE GENERAL PROVISIONS

As anticipated above, general provision covers manifold subjects beyond the neat labels of "general provisions" and "international jurisdiction." The sharp spirit of the legislator has to provide a flexible and open regulation.[12] Overregulation might be counterproductive. In the next sections, a broad overview of the main features will be provided.

2.1 Prevalence of International Norms

According to the Vienna Convention on the Rights of Treaties (1986) and the Argentine National Constitution (1994) the hierarchy of sources is clearly detailed (Article 2594, *see* above).[13] Faced with a case with international dimensions, the first question an Argentinian judge would ask, is if this case is subject to an international treaty.[14]

11. Uzal, María Elsa, *Derecho Internacional Privado*, La Ley, Buenos Aires, 2016.
12. Uzal, "Lineamientos...", *supra*.
13. Feldstein de Cárdenas, Sara, "Prelación de fuentes del derecho internacional privado en el nuevo Código", La Ley-2015-846. Dreyzin de Klor, "Las disposiciones...", *supra*.
14. Dreyzin de Klor, "Las disposiciones...", *supra*.

2.2 Application of International Law

Article 2595 has a flexible approach on the application of international law.[15] As to the interpretation of international norms, the legislator follows the directives of the Inter-American Convention on General Norms on International Private Law (1979), in the understanding that the application of foreign law must be made as the judges of the country of origin would have applied it. Subsidiary, if the content of foreign law could not be established, Argentine law will be applicable (Article 2595, a). The Argentine legislator did not dare to empower the judge to apply directly international law, however, an Argentinian judge is entitled to do so, because of the Inter-American Convention cited above.[16]

If there were several international systems converging on the same international relationship, applicable law is determined by the rules in force within the State to which this law pertains, or by application of the law that is closest to the international relationship (Article 2595, b). The convergence will be solved by a dialogue between legal sources, that will establish a reasonable motive to apply the more coherent legal system.

Finally, if there is convergence of several applicable laws to different aspects of a juridical situation, the plurality of laws has to be harmonized by the judge, adapting each legal system according to the ends of each of them (Article 2595, c). Here, the legislator chose a flexible coordination of normative systems, with a finalist interpretation of the norms. Applicable law is constructed by a dialogue of legal sources.[17]

Autonomy makes its entrance to the stage, interacting with more traditional principles.

The rules for "renvoi" are as usual: if a foreign law applies, its PIL is applied. Therefore, if its PIL sends back to the first legal system, the latter will apply. Renvoi applies also to choose of law: if the parties choose a certain foreign law, it is understood that they chose the material laws of that State.

One of the most interesting features of current PIL is the "exception clause,"[18] worded by the Article 2597. According to this clause, a conflict rule shall not be applied, "when by the factual circumstances of the case," it is evident that the situation has little link with such law, and conversely, it presents close links with the law of other state, which application is foreseeable, and "under which rules the relationship has been validly established." The exception clause does not apply when parties chose

15. Feldstein de Cárdenas, Sara, "La aplicación del derecho extranjero en el Código Civil y Comercial. Una mirada crítica", La Ley, 31/03/2016, p. 1.
16. Feldstein, "La aplicación...", *supra* p. 14. The principle *iura novit curia* would apply, always under strict conditions.
17. Jayme, Erik, "Identité culturelle et intégration: le droit internactional privé postmoderne", *Course general de droit international privé,* Collected Courses of the Hageu Academy of International Law, Vol. 251, p. 60.
18. Article 2597. "Cláusula de excepción. Excepcionalmente, el derecho designado por una norma de conflicto no debe ser aplicado cuando, en razón del conjunto de las circunstancias de hecho del caso, resulta manifiesto que la situación tiene lazos poco relevantes con ese derecho y, en cambio, presenta vínculos muy estrechos con el derecho de otro Estado, cuya aplicación resulta previsible y bajo cuyas reglas la relación se ha establecido válidamente."

the applicable law for the case. Article 2653 provides for an exception clause applicable to contract law: exceptionally, and if the parties ask for it, taking into account objective and subjective elements of the contract, a judge may apply the closes legal system to the case, except when the parties chose the applicable law.

There are other provisions that establish a certain flexibility in terms of the application of law, but for other reasons than "closeness." When it comes to alimony, parental responsibility or rules concerning the challenge of paternity,[19] applicable law is decided to take into consideration higher interests, like the interests of the creditor or the interests of the child. The latter would be explained more on the account of the hierarchy of international treaties on human rights and material values that stem from them, than on any other theory within the field of PIL.

Private autonomy and choice of law are now further recognized in Argentinian CCC. This right does not apply equally to all matters.[20] The choice of jurisdiction and arbitration was already recognized since 1976 in Argentina, yet only to patrimonial and international matters. Nowadays, this forum choice is expressly recognized in Article 2605 ("agreement of choice of jurisdiction").

Article 2607 establishes that the choice of forum may be either explicit or tacit. A tacit choice of forum can be proven by any means of written proof. The choice is also proven when the plaintiff files in a certain jurisdiction, and also when the defendant responds without a plea. Choice of forum is possible only there, where it is not forbidden (Article 2605).

There is also a limited choice of applicable law recognized concerning maintenance agreements (Article 2630, second paragraph). Parties may choose the law of the habitual residence of any of the parties at the time of the celebration of the agreement. Matrimonial property agreements also offer the spouses a reduced choice of law: if they move to another country they might choose the application of Argentinian law in the foreign country of their new residence (Article 2625).

When it comes to contracts, parties have freedom of choice concerning applicable law. Choice must be express. Parties can change applicable law at any time, however, this modification may not affect the validity of the contract or the rights of third parties. The elected national law will be applied, except for the conflict of law rules. Parties may create material norms excluding the material laws from the legal system they chose. The choice of laws may not be applied in a way that they violate mandatory norms of the foreign law (case in which the choice of law would not be valid). The election of an international forum does not include the choice of applicable law of that legal system.

Choice of law is limited when there are interests of vulnerable parties at stake. This is the case for consumer law.

19. Articles 2629, 2632, 2639.
20. Fernandez Arroyo, "Main Characteristics...", p. 145.

2.3 Evasion of the Law (*fraude à la loi*)

The evasion of law occurs when a party applies foreign law in order to evade the application of the rightful principles of another State Party's law. This means a voluntary evasion or mandatory law, and the alteration of the norm of conflict.

According to Article 2598, in case of fraud, the applicable law will be determined irrespectively of the acts or facts instrumented in order to evade the rightful legal system. For example, if a party changed residence just to evade the applicable law, this fact will not be taken into account when determining the applicable law. Of course, there is a matter of proof: in some cases the intent to evade might be difficult to ascertain.

Fraud occurs only when mandatory clauses are concerned, and it is these mandatory clauses that the party wants to avoid.

2.4 Mandatory International Laws and Policy Norms

Mandatory international laws prevail over private autonomy of the parties and exclude the application of conflict laws or even the choice of law by the parties. This means that there are mandatory international norms or policy norms that apply disregarding the usual conflict laws.

Article 2599 establishes that in case there were Argentinian mandatory international norms, applicable to the case, they prevail over personal autonomy of the parties or the foreign law indicated by conflict rules. Conversely, when a foreign law is applicable, then also its mandatory laws are applicable to the case. Moreover, mandatory international laws of foreign State Parties may be applicable if they present a preponderant closeness to the case.

Two kinds of mandatory norms should be distinguished: on the one hand, mandatory norms within private law, that are nonetheless so relevant, so deeply rooted in the values of the State party, that even if there is no express indication that they should be internationally applicable, they end up being applied to international cases.

On the other hand, there are the policy norms. Those are the rules to which the legislator ascribes deliberately and expressly an international character, indicating that they are to be applied in international cases.

2.5 *Ordre Public* International

As in many compared legal systems, the law declared applicable may be refused application in the territory of a State Party that considers it manifestly contrary to the principles of its public policy. *Ordre public* acts, thus, as a clause of exception. A State Party that has the jurisdiction of the case by *lex fori*, may exclude the application of the law pointed at by the conflict rule because of this collision with their internal principles of public policy.

Normally, *ordre public* is far more important in those matters that have a clear slant on mandatory regulation: rights in *rem*, marriage, paternity, protection of children, etc. *Ordre public* produces a unification of an international case that might be fragmented in several State laws.

Ordre public applies not only as a strong criterion to apply or disregard international law, but also when it comes to recognize foreign court decisions.

A decision based on the *ordre public* in Argentinian PIL implies also an integration of international sources, especially international human right treaties, according to Article 2594 and Articles 1 and 2 CCC.

The new CCC includes *ordre public* clause in Article 2600, by which the rules of foreign law are excluded when they imply legal solutions contrary to "the fundamental principles of the *ordre public* that inspire the Argentine legal system."

The meaning of *ordre public* is not always clear or easy to determine.[21] Most of all, the exclusion of the applicable law calls for a methodological issue: some understand that the exclusion should occur *a priori*, in a dogmatical manner; others understand that it should be decided on a case by case basis, considering what would be the consequences of the application of foreign law in the concrete international case under analysis.[22] The exception of *ordre public* begs the question of ideologies and values concerning the function of the judiciary (between activism and conservatism), so it mostly depends on the attitudes of the Judge who has to decide on the matter.

2.6 Matters Expressly Subject to *Ordre Public* Clauses

Typical *ordre public* matters are the protection of concurrence law, transfer of technology contracts, and the regulation of markets and capitals.[23]

Rights in rem have a special rule by which the law of situation of the immovables determines the applicable right (Article 2667). The same applies to registrable movables (Article 2668). This article creates an exception on probate proceedings, that are usually connected to the law of the last domicile of the defunct. If that succession would include immovables in a country other than the one of the last domicile, probate proceedings should be opened in the country of situation of the immovables.

Article 2609 ensures the exclusive jurisdiction of Argentinian judges in rights in rem located in Argentina, in the matter of the validity or annulment of the registration of Argentine registries and on the matter of the registration of patents and trademarks, designs or industrial models in Argentine registries.

Concerning probate proceedings, Article 2644 establishes that the applicable law is the last domicile of the defunct, except in respect of the immovables located in

21. Basset, Ursula C., "Peculiaridades del orden público en el régimen argentino. Estudio comparativo de las fuentes francesas y de los matices singulares del orden público en el Código argentino", Revista de Derecho Privado y Comunitario, 2007, III, pp. 419–254.
22. Dreyzin de Klor, "Las disposiciones…", *supra*.
23. These are mostly in the following special Acts: Law 25.156 on the defense of concurrence, Law 22.426 on transference of technology, Law 21.526 on financial institutions (Arts. 9, 11, 14); Law 20.081 on insurance companies; Law 20.094 on Navigation (Art. 604), and Law on Commercial Companies, 19.550.

Argentina. However, the jurisdiction could be that of the last domicile or that of the situation of the immovables. A peculiar outcome might take place: a possible interpretation is that Article 2644 is a mandatory internal rule. The international judge by application of the law of the last domicile might choose not to apply it. However, in the proceedings in order to get Argentine courts to recognize the foreign decision in local registries, it might be rejected by invocation of the Argentine *ordre public.*

Other clear *ordre public* rules can be found in labor law, consumer law, social security law, etc.

2.7 International Jurisdiction

The sources of international jurisdiction stem from the agreement of the parties or from the provisions of the law. Article 2602 establishes a *forum necessitatis*, according to which Argentine judges may have international jurisdiction, exceptionally if it is not reasonable to demand from the plaintiff to file his claim abroad, provided that the international case has sufficient closeness with national law and that the right of defense during trial is ensured.

Argentine judges may issue provisional and injunctions if they are acting in the main proceedings, when the proceedings are about a decision of a foreign judge that will be executed in Argentina or on demand of a foreign judge.

International lis pendens covers a situation in which there are two pending judicial proceedings pending between the same parties with the same object and cause of action, one initiated in Argentina, and another previously initiated in a different state. In principle, each court will determine its jurisdiction according with conflict rules that may be dissimilar. In these circumstances, the new code provides that the Argentine judge shall suspend the local proceedings if it is foreseeable that a judgement is to be issued in the foreign previously initiate law suit and this law judgement may be recognized by an Argentine judge in the future.

A judge may resume the process if the foreign judge declines its jurisdiction, if the foreign process terminates without a decision on merits of the disputes or if the foreign judgement cannot be recognized in Argentina (Article 2604).

The new Code contains general principles relating to international cooperation and procedural assistance. Article 2611 creates a duty of international cooperation between Argentine judges and foreign judges, beyond international conventions. Article 2612 orders Argentine judges to comply with procedural and evidentiary measures by foreign judges. Such measures shall not be executed if they are contrary to the *ordre public.* Argentine judges may communicate directly with foreign judges in the state in which such practice is accepted, as long as due process rules are kept. Judges may communicate through rogatory letters.

3 THE SPECIAL PROVISIONS

The CCC has a section called "special provision". This section deals with the PIL rules to be applied to the specific legal institutions.

3.1 Law of Persons

Lex domicilii applies to legal capacity of human persons. Once legal capacity has been acquired it may not be lost (Article 2616). The lack of legal incapacity may not be invoked against a juridical act celebrated in a State for which the person had full legal capacity. It also applies to the name, at the time of its imposition. Because of the axiological closeness between *lex fori* and *lex causae*, connecting factors and choice of law coincide.[24] It is always a statute of a person at stake, and not a relational statute, that is why it is logical to fix it to the domicile. Because of this, the sole exception to the *lex domicilii* is the capacity to marry, which is regulated by the *lex locus celebrationis.*

The Argentine CCC introduces its own characterizations and definitions on these matters ("qualifications"). The domicile of a minor is that of those who have parental responsibility over them. If several persons have parental responsibility on the child and they live in different States, the domicile is there, where they have their habitual residence (Article 2614). The same rationale applies to persons without full legal capacity. Also the Treaty of Montevideo of 1889 and the Treaty of Montevideo of 1940 had included direct qualifications when it came to the determine the concept of domicile.

3.2 Law of Marriage

Once again, as in most matters concerning personal and family status, *lex fori* and *lex causae* coincide. And, as it happened with the domicile in the *status personae,* Argentina choices to qualify unilaterally the concept of conjugal home (the place of indisputable common residence of the spouses).

Lex fori and *lex causae* for annulment, dissolution of marriage, as for the effects of marriage is the last conjugal domicile or before the habitual residence of the respondent.

Jurisdiction and applicable law to decide the capacity to marry, the form of marriage, its existence, the proof of the existence of marriage, its validity is the law of the State where marriage was celebrated. However, for reasons of public order, marriage contracted in a foreign country in violation of the impediments of Argentinian law, will not be recognized in Argentinian law (Article 2622).[25]

Jurisdiction and applicable law to personal effects of marriage is the law of the conjugal home. Applicable law to patrimonial effects of marriage like prenuptial agreements is the law of the first conjugal home. To further marital agreements, *lex loci celebrationis* applies.

In case that spouses should change their domicile, they may opt to apply Argentine law to their new domicile (Article 2625).

Jurisdiction and applicable law to divorce and dissolution of marriage is the law of the last conjugal domicile.

24. Soto, Alfredo, *Código Civil y Comercial Comentado. Tratado Exegético.* La Ley, Buenos Aires, 2016, Commentary to Art. 2616.
25. Kinship, previous marriage, attempted crime against.

Argentina was one of the last countries in the world to have a matrimonial property regime based on the community of property. Until the last CCC, spouses could not choose their property regime by a marital agreement. Most countries in Latin America had ever since had a plurality of eligible matrimonial property regimes. The Treaty of Montevideo of 1889 established that marital agreements (autonomy) regulate patrimonial relationships between spouses. In the absence of marital agreements, they are covered by the law of the conjugal home they had decided in common before marriage. And if they had not decided their domicile before marriage, it will be regulated by the domicile of the husband by the time of the celebration of marriage. If there is a movable conflict, the change of jurisdiction does not alter the original connecting factor.

The Treaty of Montevideo of 1940 establishes that marital property agreements are regulated by the law of the first conjugal home, except for rights in rem. A change of domicile may not alter the applicable law.

Within the Mercosur (Common market of the South) the Agreement between the Members States of Mercosur about jurisdiction and competence (58/2012[26]) established the jurisdiction of the courts of the conjugal home or the courts of the domicile of the plaintiff or the respondent (Article 3). Article 9 establishes that personal relations between spouses are regulated by the law of the last conjugal home, and subsidiarily by the place of celebration of marriage. As for patrimonial effects of marriage, Article 10 establishes the principle of autonomy: they are regulated by marital agreements. In the absence of those, the law of the first domicile. As in the Treaty of Montevideo of 1940, rights in rem are regulated by their special rules, according to the *lex loci rei sitae*. The change of domicile does not change the applicable law. Article 11 regulates divorce aby the law of the last conjugal home, in the absence of this by the law of the last conjugal home if there is at least one spouse living in that State, and in the absence of the latter, the law of the plaintiff or the respondent (the competent judge decides).

Also within the Mercosur, there is a special provision concerning the recognition of same sex marriages. Article 7 of the said Agreement establishes that reasons of public policy may be applied to reject the recognition of same sex marriages contracted in a State party that recognizes them. Currently, only two countries recognize same sex marriage by law in Latin America: Argentina (2010) and Uruguay (2013). Brazil (2011) and Colombia (2016) have had rulings by their Supreme Court and Constitutional Court respectively. By 2013, the National Justice Council of Brazil decided to legalize same sex marriage.[27]

26. Acuerdo Entre Los Estados Partes Del Mercosur Y Asociados Sobre Jurisdicción Internacionalmente Competente, Ley Aplicable Y Cooperación Jurídica Internacional En Materia De Matrimonio, Relaciones Personales Entre Los Cónyuges, Régimen Matrimonial De Bienes, Divorcio, Separación Conyugal Y Unión No Matrimonial, 2012, *See*: http://www.loa.org.ar/legNormaDetalle.aspx?id=22432.
27. *See supra.*

3.3 "Uniones Convivenciales"

The "*uniones convivenciales*" are monogamous de facto cohabitations for more than two years. *Lex fori* is the law of the effective domicile of both cohabitants. Applicable law is the law of the State in which they are invoked.

Article 5 of the Agreement between the State parties to the Mercosur establishes that the connecting factor to extramarital unions are the courts of the State party in which they are invoked (same rule as the CCC).

3.4 Alimony

Lex fori for alimony suits is quite ample. The plaintiff can choose between the judges of their domicile, of their habitual residence, or that of the domicile of habitual residence of the respondent, or before the judge that has decided the dissolution of marriage. If it were reasonable according to the circumstances of the case, the suit could be filed in the courts where the defendant has goods to seize.

When alimony suits are between spouses or cohabitants, *lex fori* is determined by the last domicile or the habitual residence of the defendant or before the judge who decided the dissolution of marriage.

If the source of the obligation of alimony was an agreement, the suite might be filed before the judge in which the obligation must be paid or where the agreement was celebrated if it coincides with the residence of the respondent.

Applicable law is the law of the domicile of the creditor, of the debtor or the most convenient law in the interest of creditor according to the competent authority or court (Article 2630). Applicable law to agreements about alimony is the law of the domicile or habitual residence of each of the parties at the time of the celebration of the agreement. Otherwise, the law for alimony becomes applicable.

Alimony between spouses is governed by the law of the last conjugal home or last common residence or of the law of the State applicable to the dissolution of marriage.

The Inter-American Convention on Alimony (CIDIP IV) establishes that the creditor may choose the *lex fori* from: the domicile or the habitual residence of the creditor, the domicile or the habitual residence of the debtor, the courts of the country to which the debtor has personal ties such as the possession of goods, income or economic benefits (forum patrimonii). As to the amount of alimony, the qualities of creditor and debtor, the amount of the alimony, the terms and conditions required for the right of alimony are regulated by the law more favorable to the interest of the creditor. The competent court chooses between the law of the domicile or habitual residence of the creditor or of the debtor.

There was an interesting case decided in a matter of international abduction of a child who was brought to Argentina. The abductor suit a file for alimony against the parent that had, in turn, sued for restitution of the abducted minor, and that, therefore, did not consent to the Argentinian jurisdiction on alimony. The Argentinian judge, applying the new CCC decided that he was competent to decide on alimony, since alimony is not covered by the Hague convention, and its urgency plus the connecting factors allow the competence of the local judge.[28]

3.5 Filliation "by Nature" and by ART

The plaintiff may choose to file its suit to determine or contest filiation before the courts of the domicile of the plaintiff or the domicile of the respondent. In case of paternity proceedings concerning the recognition of a child competent courts are those of the domicile of the person who recognizes the child or those of the recognized child or those of the place of birth.

Applicable law to paternity proceedings is the law of the domicile of the child at the time of birth or the domicile of the parent or parent-to-be at the time of birth or the law of the State in which marriage was celebrated. The authority shall choose the law most satisfactory to the interest of the child. The law governing the recognition of the child is that of the domicile of the child at the time of birth or at the time of the act of recognition of the child or the domicile of the parent who recognized the child at the time of recognition. The legal capacity to recognize is governed by the *lex domicilii*. The solemnities required to recognize a child are governed by the law of the act or by the law of the substantive law that governs recognition.

As for the recognition of filiations established abroad, Argentinian law establishes that they must be recognized according to the principles of public order, especially those who impose the judge to prioritize the best interest of the child (Article 2634). Implicitly, this section hints on surrogate motherhoods and other controversial issues. The legislator wanted to make sure that the child will be protected whatever the decision about their parents-to-be. As a matter of fact, it is common understanding that whilst Argentinian *ordre public* might repeal surrogate motherhood, an Argentinian judge might have to enforce a foreign decision or public deed of filiation of the child to guarantee his right to the establishment of paternity.

The legislator wanted to make sure that rules about ART are above all other forms of filiation. So they made them part of public order (Article 2634). This unusual provision is attached to the peculiar nature of the regulation of ART in Argentina, in many respects, disadvantageous for children if compared with adoption a "filiation by nature" (biological filiation). The legislator states that nay decision taken on these matters should comply with the best interest of the child standard.[29]

As for the conventional source, the Treaties of Montevideo of 1889 and 1940 establish that the law presiding the celebration of marriage determines the in wedlock filiation. The questions derived from rights and obligation of an out-of-wedlock paternity are governed by the law of the State in which they have to be made effective.

28. Court of Appeal 1 for Mendoza, 19/8/2015 "F v. K."
29. A follow-up on case law criteria can be found in Scotti, Luciana B. "El interés superior del niño en la jurisprudencia argentina: una mirada desde el derecho internacional privado", DFyP, 2014 (Agosto), p. 26.

3.6 Adoption

Argentina has strong feelings about adoption, because of the harsh political times during military governments in which children of "disappeared" parents were registered as biological children to adoptive parents, thus suppressing a part of their identity and biography. Further, Argentina resents the fact that poorer families might not be able to raise their own children only because of economic problems. Argentina has also been accused of trafficking of children: selling children from poorer families to rich families, that later on register the children as their own or fake that parents gave up children to parents in a better position to raise them, when they are actually selling them.[30] Because of this peculiar cultural scenario, Argentina is strongly against international adoption of Argentine children, and this prohibition is included in Argentine Constitutional Law (it is that important[31]).

So, an international adoption settled abroad must be enforced in Argentina when it has been accorded by the judges of the domicile of the adopted child at the time of adoption. Adoptions conferred in the State of adoptive parents have to be enforced in case that the adoption could also be enforced in the country of the adoptee. To annul or revoke an adoption, competent courts are those of the domicile of the adoptee or of the place of the adoption. Argentina may invoke the *ordre public* to reject the recognition of an international adoption only if the interest of the child is compromised and the adoption has close ties to Argentina.

In general, connecting factors and applicable law to adoptions is the law of the domicile of the adoptee at the time of adoption. This law governs the requisites and defects of adoption. The annulment of an adoption is governed by the domicile at the adoption or the domicile of the adoptee. Conversion of an adoption *minus plena* into a full adoption is admitted in Argentina if the requisites of Argentine law are met and if adoptive parents and children give their consent. Because of the said cultural frame of adoption in Argentina, Argentina imposes that the judge appreciates on a case-by-case basis the convenience of an open adoption (to maintain the links with the biological family).

The Treaty of Montevideo of 1940, in which *lex causae* and *lex fori* are the domicile of adoptive parents and adoptive child if they are the same and they are expressed in a public instrument. For annulment or revocation, *lex locus celebrationis* or the domicile of the adoptive child.

Argentina has also signed to the UN Nations Convention on the Recovery Abroad of Maintenance (1956) and the Inter-American Convention on Support Obligations (1989). It never signed the Hague Convention of 2007 on the International Recovery of Child Support and Other Forms of Family Maintenance.

30. These are the allegations made by the Inter-American Court of Human Rights in the Case "Fornerón vs. Argentina", April 27, 2012.
31. It is coined as a reservation to Art. 24 of the International Convention on the Rights of the Child, and the ICRC is a part to Argentine Constitution (Art. 75.22).

3.7 Parental Responsibility

Everything concerning parental responsibility is logically covered by the law of the habitual residence of the child once the conflict arises. Once again superior principles interfere with strict PIL criteria. The principle *favor minoris* may be considered in order to decide the applicable law if the child has close tights with the law of another State. This once again an exemption clause, in order to protect higher values.

Tutorship and curatorship are centered on the domicile f minors or persons with restrictions to their legal capacity.

The competent authority in the case that urgent measures need to be taken, shall take them applying its own law, if they are to protect children or persons with restricted capacity (their persons or their patrimony) while they dwell in that country. Competent authorities of the domicile or nationality of the affected persons have to be given notice. If the urgent measures are for refugees, law for refugees apply.

The Treaties of Montevideo of 1889 and 1940 have a different approach. The 1940 Treaty regulates everything relating to parental responsibility according to the law of the domicile of he who has parental responsibility.

Argentina signed the 1996 Convention on Jurisdiction, Applicable Law, Recognition, Enforcement and Co-operation in Respect of Parental Responsibility and Measure for the Protection of Children (Law 27.237), yet Argentina did not ratify this Convention, it is not yet in vigor.

3.8 Return of Children

Argentina is signatory to the Inter-American Convention on the International Return of Children of 1989 (CIDIP IV), Inter-American Convention on International Traffic in Minors (Mexico, 1994) and The Hague Convention on the Civil Aspects of the International of International Abduction. It has also signed the bilateral Treaty between Argentina-Uruguay about international protection of minors.

The new CCC introduced Article 2642, under the title of "general principles and cooperation," according to which in the matter of displacement, retentions or abduction, of minors, that are followed by request of localization or international return, the conventions in vigor apply. In absence of them Argentine judges must try to adapt to the principles of such conventions, ensuring the best interest of the child.

The judge who is competent to decide the return of a child must supervise the secure return of the child, striving to convince the parties to comply voluntarily.

At the request of an interested party or the competent foreign authority, the Argentine judge may take preventative measures to ensure the protection of a child or the accompanying adult who are expected to enter the country.

Most part of children abductions are resolved applying The Hague Convention, and only some of them, by the Inter-American Convention.[32] The main problem seems

32. All, Paula & Rubaja, Nieve, "El protocolo de actuación para el funcionamiento de los convenios de sustracción internacional de menores" La Ley, 14/06/2017, p. 1.

to be, it still takes too much time until the return order is issued. This triggered a number of controversial cases, in which the length of the stay in Argentina implied that the return was sometimes contrary to the best interest of the child. The child had developed for certain years his life in Argentina (illegitimately, but the child would not understand such terms). By the time he would have to return, he would have to leave friends and family and a life he grew into. This is why Argentina, in collaboration with The Hague Convention Office in Latin America and Argentine authorities a protocol was issued by December 12, 2016.

The Protocol to apply the conventions on child abduction[33] applies to all abducted minors younger than 16. The interest of the child is paramount, and the child has a right to be heard and to take part in the procedures. He has a right to receive adequate information according to his age. Mediation should be promoted. The whole proceeding should be decided in six weeks.

The Central Authority in Argentina is the Office of International Juridical Assistance, from the Ministry of Justice of Argentina.[34] They provide assistance and help to any procedures.

3.9 Inheritance Law

Connecting factors and choice of law coincide: it is the last domicile of the defunct. There is, however, a concurrent jurisdiction: *lex rei sitae*, that applies to the immovables in the country in respect to them.

The solemnities of the testament issued abroad are regulated by the law of the place in which the testament was issued, the law of the domicile, of usual residence, or of the nationality of the testator at the time in which the testament was written or by Argentine law. The principle *favor testament* applies.

The legal capacity to testate is covered by the law of the domicile of the testator at the time of the writing to the testament (Article 2647).

The applicable law to a succession of a person who dies intestate without heirs in a foreign country, does not apply for the goods in Argentina which will pass to the Argentinian State, the City of Buenos Aires or the Province in which they are located.

The Treaties of Montevideo of 1889 and 1940 also choose the split jurisdiction (*lex domicilii, lex rei sitae*).

3.10 Solemnities of Juridical Acts

The solemnities are regulated by the *lex loci celebrationis*. This way form and substance of the act might be split.[35] Interestingly, powers of attorney are regulated by the Inter-American Convention on the Powers of Attorney to be used abroad (CIDIP-I, 1975).

33. Protocolo De Actuación Para El Funcionamiento De Los Convenios De Sustracción Internacional De Niños, available at: http://www.cnaj.gob.ar/cnaj/archivos/2017/ARC_675.pdf.
34. The site is available: http://www.menores.gob.ar/autoridades-centrales.
35. Soto, *Codigo Civil y Comercial...*, "Comentario al Art. 2649."

3.11 Contract Law

Contract law is regulated by the jurisdiction and choice of law of the parties. But if they did not choose, the plaintiff may decide between: (a) the judges of the domicile or habitual residence of the respondent. If there are several respondents, the domicile or habitual residence of any of them, the judge of the place of performance of the contractual obligation or the judge of any of the branches of the company of the respondent, as long as it was involved in the negotiation or celebration of the contract.

The choice of law is regulated by private autonomy. However:

(a) Choice must be express or result in a clear manner from the terms of contract or the circumstances of the case.
(b) At any time, parties may change their agreement on applicable law. However, this modification may not affect the validity of the contract or the rights of third parties.
(c) The elected national law will be applied, except for the conflict of law rules.
(d) Parties may create material norms excluding the material laws from the legal system they chose.
(e) The choice of laws may not be applied in a way that they violate mandatory norms of the foreign law (case in which the choice of law would not be valid).
(f) The election of an international forum does not include the choice of applicable law of that legal system.

Of course, consumer law is excluded since there are higher principles of equality to protect consumer.

If the parties did not select the applicable law, the contract is regulated by the laws or customs of the country of the place of performance of the obligation. If it is not designated, it is understood that the law of the domicile of the debtor of the most important performance of the contract. In the case that even this could not be determined, the contract will be regulated by the law and customs of the State of celebration of the contract. Contracts between absent parties is governed by the law of the State in which it was accepted.

There is also a clause of exception for contract law: Exceptionally and at the request of a party, and taking all objective and subjective elements into account, the judge may order the application of the law of the State with which the "juridical relation" presents the closest ties. The exception clause is also residual (it applies only if the parties did not choose otherwise).

3.12 Consumer Law

Argentinian CCC created a special section to deal with consumer contract. The Draft CCC included a similar section for labor contract: the similarity comes from a very peculiar relationship in which contracting parties have a very unequal standing. To protect the consumer, private autonomy is limited. Forum may not be chosen, nor may the applicable law.

There are a number of options as to the available forums in order to facilitate the access to justice. Conversely the suit against a consumer may only proceed against the judges of their domicile. As for the applicable law, once again PIL becomes protective of the place of the consumer.

No place for private autonomy. Applicable law is determined by the law of the domicile or habitual residence of the consumer in the following cases: if the celebration of the contract was anteceded by an offer or publicity or an activity in the State of the domicile of the consumer, and he has done all the acts to conclude the contract, if the supplier has received the order in the State of the domicile of the consumer, if the consumer was induced by his supplier to move to a foreign State in order to place his order or if the contracts to travel contract comprise transport and accommodation in the package. In absence of this elements the consumer contract is regulated by the law of the State of the performance. In case this could not be determined, the contract is regulated by the law of the country of the celebration.

3.13 Tort Law

On jurisdiction, the plaintiff may choose the *forae* of justified closeness with the facts surrounding the tort as the domicile of the respondent or the courts of the place in which the fact that cause the damage has occurred, or where the tort produced its direct damages. This covers a vast spectrum of possible damages.

As for the applicable law, Argentinian law has followed the criteria of comparative legal systems, that find the closes tie to the tort in the place in which it was produced it (*lex loci delicti comissi)*. It is the place in which the facts take place, and thus the only law in which the parties might have foreseen to be applicable. However, it is also admitted that if the person whose responsibility for the tort is alleged, and the victim are domiciled or have their habitual residence in the same State, *lex domicilii* is applied. If the circumstances of the case show that the tort has tight links with another law, of another State, this law might be invoked and applied.

3.14 Securities and Checks

The jurisdiction for securities is that of the place in which the obligation has to be performed or that of the domicile of the respondent. The plaintiff has the option. For checks it is the domicile of the drawee bank or of the respondent.

Applicable law relies on the autonomy principle that governs exchange obligations, by which each obligation is tied to the law of the State in whose territory the act takes place.

As for the checks, the law of the domicile of the drawee bank determines its nature, its effects, the term of presentation, the person to which it can be made out, and in general everything regarding checks (Article 2662).

3.15 Rights in Rem

Concerning rights in rem, Argentinian law qualifies unilaterally what a right in rem is.

The jurisdiction on an immovable relies on the State in which the immovable is located. If it is a registrable good, it is the courts of the State in which the good is registered. If it is actions in *rem* of no registrable goods, the judges of the domicile of the respondent or the place in which the goods are located.

The applicable law on rights in rem on an immovable are governed by the *lex loci rei sitae.*

The contract made in a foreign State to transfer rights in rem on an immovable located in Argentina, are to be recognized as long as they are made in public legalized instruments.

The rights in rem on movables that the owner takes with him are regulated by the law of the domicile of the owner. If the ownership is contested, the law of the situation of the goods will apply.

3.16 Company Law

Company law is a very complex matter, that still does not have a complete PIL regulation. There are some indications in the General Company Act (19.550). A general rule is that the place in which the society was constituted is a connecting factor (*lex fori*). There is also the State in which the society was registered (Article 7, 19.550). Article 124, from the Act 19.550 proposes also the place of the siege of the Company, which work as an exception applicable to formalities of constitution, reforms, etc. This exception explains itself considering that Argentina might want a policy norm.

3.17 Bankruptcy Law

Bankruptcy law of internal source is dealt with in the Act. 19.551, modified by the acts 22.917 and 24.522. According to Article 2, debtors with a domicile abroad may suit and have their debts recognized in Argentina in respect to the goods located in Argentina. For further information, it would be best to consult specific bibliography on these matters (*see* below).

3.18 Statutes of Limitations

Applicable law to prescription is the same law that applies to the substantive right.

Further Reading

Dreyzin de Klor, Adriana, *Private International Law,* Kluwer, 2016.

Fernandez Arroyo, Diego P. "Main Characteristics of the New Private International Law of the Argentinian Republic", *RabelsZeitschrift, 80,* pp. 130–150 (2016).

Soto, Alfredo, *Código Civil y Comercial Comentado. Tratado Exegético.* La Ley, Buenos Aires, 2016.
Uzal, María Elsa, *Derecho Internacional Privado,* La Ley, Buenos Aires, 2016.

Index

V

W